JONI MITCHELL
SHADOWS AND LIGHT

Karen O'Brien

Virgin
BOOKS

First published in Great Britain in 2001 by
Virgin Books Ltd
Thames Wharf Studios
Rainville Road
London W6 9HA

A catalogue record for the book is available from
the British Library.

ISBN 1 85227 976 1

Typeset by Phoenix Photosetting, Chatham, Kent
Printed and bound in Great Britain by
Mackays of Chatham

For S. R. B.

*It is important throughout your
life to proclaim your joy.*

Mark Eitzel, 'Proclaim Your Joy'

Contents

Acknowledgements

Eternal thanks to Sean Body, whose idea inspired this book and whose boundless encouragement, enthusiasm and support sustained it and me.

This is not an authorised biography but I am immensely grateful to Joni Mitchell for her kindness in allowing close friends and colleagues to talk to me.

Special thanks to the many people who spoke or corresponded with me, especially the following: Amy Adler; Joel Bernstein; Brian Blade; Patrick Close and CARFAC Saskatchewan Visual Arts; Shawn Colvin; Nicholas Jennings; Natalie Kallio at the Mendel Gallery, Saskatoon; Larry Klein; Lora McPhail at Los Angeles Contemporary Exhibitions (LACE); Graham Nash; Elliot Roberts; Spider Robinson; Tom Rush; Gene Shay; Jane Siberry; Greg Tate; Vicky Taylor; Richard Thompson; Suzanne Vega.

Also to Sam Feldman at S. L. Feldman and Associates; Lisa Arzt at AGF; BBC World Service; the British Library, London; Peter Doggett; Rob Haywood at hollies.co.uk; the Maidstone museum, Saskatchewan (for being so welcoming on Canada Day 2000); the Joni Mitchell Discussion List (www.jmdl.com), especially Les Irvin, Jim L'Hommedieu, Joe Farrell, Dave Foer, Mauro Rossi and Simon; the official Joni Mitchell website, jonimitchell.com, Jim Johansen and the late Wally Breese; Lacerba Records; Bonnie Levetin at Lookout Management; Nash Editions (www.nasheditions.com); Alan Jenkins and the Neil Young Appreciation Society (2A Llynfi St, Bridgend, CF31 1SY, Wales); David Sholemson at Ted Kurland Associates; Regina Public Library, Saskatchewan; Saskatoon Public Library and especially the staff in the Local History room, Saskatchewan; Paul Castle; Erik James at Warner Music UK.

And to my agent Rachel Calder and the Sayle Agency; Ian Gittins for encouragement, advice and for not denouncing my punk credentials even though I like the Clash *and* Joni Mitchell; James Bennett and Virgin Books; Jay Blakesberg for a superb cover photo and helpfulness; Mark Eitzel for kindness and 'Proclaim Your Joy'.

I'm very grateful to the directors of the Georgia O'Keeffe Foundation – particularly Judy Lopez and Juan Hamilton – for their assistance and kind permission to reproduce the correspondence between Georgia O'Keeffe and Joni Mitchell, and my thanks to the Beinecke Rare Books and Manuscripts Library at Yale University for locating this material in the Georgia O'Keeffe archive there.

My love and gratitude to friends and family, especially my mother and my brother, Stephen; Margaret, Jim and all the Bartles, la Pines and Bairds; Diana Quay and George Pensotti; Sally, Pete and Nick Fincher; Carol Brown and Ben Martin; Lorraine Gill; Morag Panther (Canadian women totally rule!); Sean, Mike and Tracy at Helter Skelter music bookshop, London; Michael O'Connell and yer man, W.B.Yeats ('Rave on, Mr Yeats!'); my home-boys, Roger Quail, Mick Fish, Dave Hallbery – the SAF Publishing/Lacerba massive and Noreen Hallbery; my home-girls, Lauris Lowe, Kris Smith and Jenny Tidswell (NZ women totally rule!); Sarah Litvinoff; Caroline Ross, Jim Brook, Delicate awol and day release records.

'If you want me, I'll be in the bar . . .'

Karen O'Brien
London
2001

We cannot all be expected to be scientists, but we are so constituted by nature that we can all be artists – not, indeed, artists of special kinds, such as painters, sculptors, musicians, poets etc, but artists of life. This profession, 'artist of life', may sound new and quite odd, but in point of fact we are all born artists of life and, not knowing it, most of us fail to be so and the result is that we make a mess of our lives, asking, 'What is the meaning of life?' – 'Are we facing blank nothingness?' – 'After living seventy-eight or ninety years, where do we go from? Nobody knows.' etc, etc. I am told that most modern men and women are neurotic on this account. But the Zen-man can tell them that they all have forgotten that they are born artists, creative artists of life, and that as soon as they realise this fact and truth they will be cured of neurosis or psychosis or whatever name they have for their trouble.

(D.T. Suzuki, *Studies in Zen*, 1960)

Introduction

I've been beat up, I've been thrown
Out but I'm not down, I'm not down
I've been shown up, but I've grown up
And I'm not down, I'm not down
          (The Clash, 'I'm Not Down')

Sometimes, as Tammy Wynette observed so sagely, it's hard to be a woman – especially if you are, as Joni Mitchell is, a woman in an industry where one's value is rated purely in sales and marketability. She has often lacked both. Renaissance woman, painter and poet, one of the great formative influences of contemporary popular music, Mitchell resembles no one else and has made all preconceived labels redundant over an artistic career spanning almost four decades. She was the first woman of her generation to show that a songwriter does not need to use or to be a male narrator to describe the world of emotions, experiences and events. She has never thrown in her lot with those who understand the rules of success in the music industry and play by them, who refuse to change a winning formula, who abhor self-analysis, who resist challenging the preconceptions of success, image and ageing, who refrain from airing their private lives in their public work, who reduce their ego to a Zen-like nothingness or cloak themselves in false humility.

I'm in no doubt that any musician who has, within the past three decades, picked up a guitar, called themselves a singer-songwriter and claimed Bob Dylan as a primary influence, has *also* been influenced by Joni Mitchell – whether or not they believe or acknowledge it. Dylan and few others rank with her as artists who can claim the over-hyped label 'legend' in contemporary music. Yet her influence has seldom been recognised as being as pivotal as Dylan's, for reasons that have little to do with artistic merit, vocal dexterity or creative innovation. Unlike Dylan, Mitchell has never set out to create myth and mystique; she has always been too open, too real, too much herself to need masks and mystery, too involved in creating art without resort to artifice. She is in the curious position of being both revered and at the same time undervalued, doomed forever, it seems, to be thought of as the upstart female Pretender to the Throne of Dylan.

Mitchell's appeal has more often been seen, inaccurately, as being directed at women or the terminally bleak and broken-hearted. The dissection of love relationships has been a strong element of her work, but by no means the only element, and labelling it thus many critics have therefore found it easy to take the work less seriously. The myth that relationships – and work that examines them – are women's territory is per-petuated. Other critics have been consistent in their refusal to listen without prejudice and their willingness to trot out the same clichés, frayed at the edges from years of over-use, the same old anecdotes and roll-call of names of supposed lovers, served up with the same dollop of fiction and (invariably male) fantasy masquerading as fact. Yet Mitchell's own writing has often fuelled the speculation, as she has persistently fol-lowed the exhortation of one of her philosophical mentors, Friedrich Nietzsche, to master the alchemist's trick of turning the mud of one's life into the gold of literature. And just as Nietzsche influenced W.B. Yeats, Rainer Maria Rilke, D. H. Lawrence, Thomas Mann, George Bernard Shaw and Bob Dylan (who credits him in the sleeve notes to *Highway 61 Revisited*), Joni too has been inspired by his broadsides against the nay-sayers who choose to remain only half-alive, and who resent those who try to make the most of the possibilities the world holds.

Mitchell has inspired the baby-boomers – the generation described by the British political commentator Peter Hitchens as the first to obtain both power and wealth without ever having to grow up – and their offspring alike. The first baby-boomer President of the United States, Bill Clinton, and his wife, Hillary, were so smitten with Mitchell's song 'Chelsea Morning' that it inspired the name they chose for their daughter. Mitchell created a soundtrack for the Woodstock generation – her song 'Woodstock' is inextricably linked with the great hippie happening, yet she never made it to the festival. But a younger generation of creative talents has seen in Mitchell something more than the ethereal blonde who trilled through the late 60s into the 70s until she was largely written off by the mainstream music industry and the critics and abandoned by some of her more fickle – or simply just puzzled – fans.

Joni Mitchell is credited – or blamed, depending on your musical viewpoint – for having influenced an entire generation of musicians and songwriters: women like Suzanne Vega, Rickie Lee Jones, Sheryl Crow, Tori Amos and Alanis Morissette, and male artists like Prince, Morrissey, Seal and Beck. Having admired Mitchell for many years, Prince recorded a song for her, a ballad with the curious title 'Emotional Pump'. Mitchell declined to use the song, considering it not in her style: 'I called him up and said, "I can't sing this." He's a strange little duck, but I like him.' In a 1985 interview with *Rolling Stone,* Prince said that Mitchell's 1975 album *The Hissing of Summer Lawns* was the last album he 'loved all the way through'. Trying to pinpoint Mitchell's musical influence on him, Prince said that he learned about 'the importance of silence' from her. She was acknowledged by a thanks to a 'certain Joni' on *Dirty Mind* and her name appeared on the sleeve of *Controversy;* Prince first performed Mitchell's 'A Case Of You' during a 1983 benefit concert; the title of his song 'Ice Cream Castle' came from a line in Mitchell's 'Both Sides, Now' and she was mentioned in the lyrics of 'The Ballad Of Dorothy Parker'.

The British indie miserabilist, Morrissey – forgetting temporarily his own cool, minor iconic status – gushed fan-like when he interviewed Mitchell for *Rolling Stone* in 1997, 'I must say that *The Hissing of Summer Lawns* was the first album that completely captivated me. I think you're the greatest lyricist that ever lived. I think you're very underrated.' He told her that in the annals of British pop and punk, the Sex Pistols were rumoured to have sacked their original bass player, Glen Matlock, because he listened to Mitchell's music. Matlock – like Mitchell, an only child and former art student – had been a quiet, well-mannered, creative, affable young man with an affection for melody and Mod pop like the Small Faces and the Kinks, and not inconsiderable musical talent. Then he joined the Sex Pistols. John Lydon, the erstwhile Johnny Rotten, would later accuse Matlock of – among other things – wanting the Pistols to be a camp version of the Bay City Rollers. (Matlock would later describe Lydon as a 'fucked-up Roman Catholic', among other things.) Mitchell told Morrissey that when she finally met John Lydon she liked him immediately. She said he reminded her of her younger self: 'he was a lot like I was in high school: fashion conscious . . . kind of pale and pimply and avoiding the sun. But *I'm* a punk. I've never really been in the mainstream.'

Mitchell's relationship to the women who have ploughed the singer-songwriter field has been complex. The media have often presented the issue as either a simplistic women musicians' family tree or a highly competitive race for market share and media attention. Goaded by journalists, Mitchell has often resisted pressure to identify with the women who have followed her path: 'People tend to lump me always with groups of women. I always thought, "They don't put Dylan with Men of Rock; why do they do that to me with women?"' And the women themselves have often fought back against such comparisons, wanting to be seen in their own light rather than the reflected images of another. Mitchell has dubbed it the 'kill Mommy' syndrome and beyond her own admitted influences of Edith Piaf and Laura Nyro she has often opted to ally herself with men. Yet her longevity and insistence on self-determination, her unwillingness to go against her internal grain, even when to do so would have made her personal life more tranquil and her commercial career more lucrative, made Joni Mitchell a role model for the New Feminism long before the term became fashionable in the 1990s. And she had long since shunned the Old Feminism: 'It was ineffective from the beginning. I remember when the word first came up. Warren Beatty and Jack Nicholson and I used to go out to dinner quite a bit, and they were amused that I'd never heard about the feminists.'

Music journalists are not alone in isolating the Joni Clone. Stylists and fashion directors have been doing it for years; she stepped out of her dressing room and into a Gap commercial, unretouched and un-airbrushed. The 70s blonde California-babe era Joni has been cited as a style influence on Gwyneth

Paltrow, Lisa Kudrow and Heather Graham, on Madonna and ubiquitous socialites like Meg Mathews, the ex-wife of Noel 'Oasis' Gallagher. Others believed that the Joni Clone style went below the surface as well. Writing in *Rolling Stone* in 1979, Cameron Crowe said, 'Ten years ago, [Mitchell] had begun to represent the Woodstock ethic. Someone could say "there is a Joni Mitchell type" and you would know exactly what he meant.' Similarly, in the introduction to his excellent book on the music industry, *The Mansion on the Hill*, Fred Goodman wrote about his *High Fidelity*-esque youth in the 1960s and 70s, when taste in music was a secret language. It was vitally important, such an indicator of compatibility that therein rested not only the future of friendships and romances, but the basis of an entire psychological profile:

> First you'd check to see if the basic language was there
> – the Beatles, the Stones, and the British Invasion
> bands; Motown and Stax; the San Francisco groups;
> Dylan. After that, you'd probe special interests for
> signs of sophistication or character flaws ... a girl
> who listened to a lot of Joni Mitchell could probably
> be talked into bed but you might regret it later ...

The inference is of course that a young woman who related to Mitchell's literate, intelligent style of music, who articulated feelings, asserted herself and questioned the nature of relationships, was going to be Trouble with a capital T. Mitchell herself is a complex and charismatic woman who was once described affectionately by her close friend and former beau, David Crosby, as being about as humble as Mussolini. In a good way. But even in jest, it could be read as a jibe against 'uppity' women, the opinionated ones who believe in the value of their work. It's this self-belief that has given Mitchell the will and the ability to survive in an industry which has, by turns, celebrated and denigrated her.

Joni Mitchell has defied musical fashion and genre, experimenting with samples and exploring world music before they were 'discovered' by the mainstream, and merged jazz, 50s scat, poetry and spoken-word at a time when it was painfully unhip to do so. Seemingly incapable of creative complacency,

she has disregarded the old rules of engagement and declared
that all is fair: she set to music a poem by Yeats, 'The Second
Coming', and adapted it – with the permission of the Yeats
estate – because she believed it needed to be 'corrected'.
Mitchell did the same with Biblical verses, adapting
Corinthians 1:13 as the song 'Love', devised first for a film
project (a ten-minute short as part of a series initiated by film
producer Barry Levinson), then later appearing on the album
Wild Things Run Fast. She outraged jazz purists and her
pop/rock fans with her idiosyncratic collaboration with jazz
bassist and composer Charles Mingus in the late 1970s. And
more recently, breaking all the rules of marketing, she agreed
to the release of a 'best of' greatest hits compilation, on the
condition that a 'Misses' collection was released as well.

Mitchell has become a post-modernist Muse, an unlikely
Zelig of popular culture who has permeated our consciousness. Her song lyrics have found their way into numerous film
and television soundtracks including *Almost Famous* (where in
one scene the character played by Patrick Fugit is shown in
1969 looking through a pile of records including Mitchell's
Blue – which was not released until 1971); *Grace of My Heart*
and *After Hours* and TV's intelligently cultish *Dawson's Creek*
and the anorexically acerbic *Ally McBeal*, in which Robert
Downey Jnr sang a version of Mitchell's song 'River'; major
poetry anthologies ('Woodstock' was included in *Scanning the
Century: The Penguin Book of the Twentieth Century in Poetry*);
college classes; crossword puzzles and television game shows;
children's playgrounds and common usage (viz. the conversa-
tional 'you don't know what you've got 'til it's gone'.) Academic
tomes have deconstructed her chord changes; popular novels
have name-checked her or her songs (including Ben Elton's
book *Inconceivable* and Nick Hornby's *High Fidelity* and *About
a Boy*).

Mitchell comes to represent a totem in *About a Boy*, an atlas
marker for a young teenager's rage against the world, his
mum, music and his hormones. Early in the book, the loath-
some chancer, Will, sees the opportunity to fulfil his mission
in life – to bed single mothers – by ingratiating himself with
their children and friends' children. He asks twelve-year-old
Marcus about his favourite music:

'OK. My favourite singer is Joni Mitchell.'

'Joni Mitchell? Don't you like MC Hammer? or Snoop Doggy Dogg? or Paul Weller?'

'No, don't like any of them.' Marcus looked Will up and down, taking in the trainers, the haircut and the sunglasses, and added, cruelly, 'Nobody does. Only old people.'

'What, everyone in your school listens to Joni Mitchell?'

'Most people.'

Will knew about hip hop and acid house and grunge and Madchester and indie; he read *Time Out* and *iD* and *The Face* and *Arena* and the *NME* still. But nobody had ever mentioned anything about a Joni Mitchell revival. He felt dispirited.

The bizarre post-modern nature of fame today has many forms. If imitation is the sincerest form of flattery then the current vogue in 'tribute' bands has not left Mitchell behind – the aptly named Foni Mitchell has performed at clubs and festivals in England. And Mitchell has inspired her own female impersonator: John Kelly, a fan, who devised his *Paved Paradise* show as a homage to her music. The show had its debut in 1984 at Wigstock, the legendary annual drag queen extravaganza in New York, but has gained a wider audience since then. Mitchell herself has seen his performance and declared herself delighted and touched by the poignancy of his act. Natalie Merchant was so taken with his show that she invited Kelly to perform as a support act at her own gigs. A multi-talented performance artist, John Kelly takes on the Mitchell persona, the long, flaxen wig, guitar and dulcimer, and extraordinary vocal similarities, without making mock. This despite the appearance of his backing band comprised appropriately enough of two Mitchellesque Muses in costume, 'Georgia O'Keeffe' on guitar and 'Vincent van Gogh' on keyboards.

Our culture's obsession with celebrity also has less endearing forms: Mitchell has had her share of stalker-like fans. Her music has found an unlikely fan in Mark Chapman, the imprisoned killer of John Lennon. In an interview with a British newspaper ahead of an unsuccessful parole board hearing in October 2000, Chapman spoke of finding solace in music and playing the guitar. 'I'm working on some Joni Mitchell stuff. I like what you call folk rock now: Joni Mitchell, America, Don McLean. I've mellowed. The music soothes me.'

Less creepy to behold are the hundreds of other cover versions of her songs – from heavy metallists Nazareth, to lounge lizard crooner Tony Bennett, British indie band Travis and born-again Christian popster Amy Grant. The proto-environmentalist 'Big Yellow Taxi' provided separate pop-star cover versions for Grant and Janet Jackson two decades after Mitchell released it. And she had a cameo role in Janet Jackson's video for the single 'Got 'Til It's Gone', which sampled heavily Mitchell's own version of 'Big Yellow Taxi'. Artists as diverse as Neil Young, Prince and Alanis Morissette have name-checked her in their songs.

Her social circle has included some of the great American artistic and cultural figures and music industry movers, shakers and creators of the past forty years – among them modernist pioneer artist Georgia O'Keeffe, artist Larry Rivers, pop culture chameleon Andy Warhol, entertainment industry mogul David Geffen and jazz great Charles Mingus, with whom she collaborated in the last years of his life, first discussing a tentative project based on T.S. Eliot's *Four Quartets*, and then on her own album, *Mingus*, which became a touching epitaph.

Her romantic relationships moved *Rolling Stone* in the early 70s to wallow in sexist hypocrisy and dub her dismissively as the Queen of El Lay and Old Lady of The Year, drawing a family tree of her alleged lovers – in large part a work of fiction, rumour and supposition. The inherent sexism of the times was often masked by a libertarian spirit, only to reappear at moments like that. It would of course have been unthinkable for *Rolling Stone* to compile a similar compendium highlighting the romantic escapades of Mitchell's male contemporaries like Bob Dylan. For all of its liberalism, *Rolling Stone* was happy to collude with the myth that there are few things more interesting about a woman than her lovers, real or imagined. It wasn't true then and it isn't true now.

For all of her celebrity, Joni Mitchell's life has mirrored that of many of her generation of baby-boomers, now into their fifties and sixties: the hippie promise and passion of the 1960s, soured and aged by the Vietnam war, the civil strife and the disco hedonism years of the 70s Me Decade, evaporated during the greed-is-good materialist arrogance of the 80s, and the *fin de siècle* weariness of the late 90s. Mother to a child whose existence she long evaded in media interviews but sought through her songs, Mitchell for years referred to her creative output as her equivalent of maternity. But then, in her early fifties, she set about trying to find the daughter she'd given up for adoption more than thirty years earlier. They were reunited through a combination of luck, coincidence, tabloid sensationalism and Internet technology. She has embraced her role as mother and grandmother.

In an industry where youth and malleability have an absurdly high value, the role models for older women are few: the ersatz, painstakingly tended youthfulness of Cher and Tina Turner sits uneasily alongside the more natural vigour of Mitchell and her contemporaries like Bonnie Raitt, Joan Baez and Marianne Faithfull. The mainstream music industry has a problem with grown-ups; not the ones they're selling to, but simply the ones they're selling. It's woefully neglectful in marketing any woman who falls outside the stereotypical nymphet, pop tart, diva and air-brushed glamour templates, let alone being able to find a niche for music that is equally resistant to the deeply shallow. Mainstream record company publicity machines have long since succumbed to the ease and superficiality of the vacuous and vain pop marketplace, and are now largely unwilling even to try to translate good musicianship and strong reviews into radio play or video promo exposure for artists who are not Top Ten chart material – artists like Mitchell, Bob Dylan, Neil Young and, to a lesser extent, Van Morrison. But these are artists who look at the Big Picture, who take the long view, who don't measure their career longevity in conformist terms. Their longevity can also be attributed to their inability to be slaves to musical fashion; they've never felt compelled to display the Madonna-like shape-shifting that so often smacks of desperation. It's little wonder that musicians like Aimee Mann, Ani DiFranco and Jane Siberry abandoned the mainstream industry to create their own record labels, websites and distribution.

Mitchell's first creative passion, and the one on which she now lavishes more time than her music, is visual art. Her paintings adorn almost all of her album covers and she has exhibited in Canada, England, Scotland, the United States and Japan. She takes pride in recounting a conversation with Georgia O'Keeffe: 'Georgia said to me, "Well, I would like to have been a painter and a musician, but you can't do both." I said, "Oh yes, you can!"'

And she has. Of her two great creative passions, she says simply, 'The difference is that I write my frustration and I paint my joy.'

Unlike Dylan, Mitchell's music and art have not been documented in a seemingly endless cycle of biographies, memoirs, deconstructionist tomes and fanzines. The *New York Times* critic Ann Power, who has edited anthologies about women musicians, says that male artists continue to hog the historical spotlight: 'Are there twenty biographies of Joni Mitchell, the way there are of Bob Dylan? I don't think so?' An entire industry has grown up around music biography, and within that, a sub-industry around a small coterie of stars. Just when you think the world's forested areas could not sustain one more tree-felling operation to provide the paper for yet another book about Bob Dylan or The Beatles, you become dimly aware of the far-off sound of the rural chainsaws segueing into the urban scratch of pen on paper as another advance cheque is signed, and the subsequent echo of the *kerr-ching* of the cash register. There's always room for one more.

But every time fiction is passed off as fact, or another 'someone said something about someone saying something about . . .' scenario unfolds, or a self-proclaimed member of the subject's intimate circle from decades ago offers to trade information for a 'premium price', it's hard not to feel some sympathy with a rueful Van Morrison when he sang in 'New Biography':

> See you've got the new biography
> Where did they get the info from
> Same as before, some so-called friends
> Who claim to have known me then
> How come they've got such good memories
> And I can't even remember last week
> Got to question where they're coming from

What knowledge of me is it that they speak . . .
Reinvented all the stories they know
Give them all a different slant
What is it that they're really looking for
Just a hobby on the Internet . . .

Roland Barthes called biography 'a novel that dare not speak its name'. In plot and outline, structure and characterisation, we're often drawn into the territory of 'once upon a time', of inquisitions and suppositions. Do we declare our allegiances, establish our neutrality or simply say, 'this is my Truth, tell me Yours'? There are no single truths, no totally definitive studies, no last-word analyses. We are all too infinitely complex, too insistent on being changeable and unpredictable and surprising; we are too opinionated, too much in the world and too vulnerable to being smacked around by experiences and emotions. There is too much to us to be contained in a single version of any story.

In *The Silent Woman*, Janet Malcolm's superb book about the biography industry surrounding Sylvia Plath and Ted Hughes, we are introduced to the biographer-as-burglar, metaphorically breaking into houses, rifling through drawers and bags and boxes until s/he then sneaks away with a sack full of treasures. Malcolm goes on to describe persuasively how:

> the voyeurism and busybodyism that impel writers and readers alike are obscured by an apparatus of scholarship designed to give the enterprise an appearance of banklike blandness and solidity. The biographer is portrayed almost as a kind of benefactor . . . sacrificing years of his life to his task, tirelessly sitting in archives and libraries and patiently conducting interviews with witnesses. There is no length he will not go to, and the more his book reflects his industry the more the reader believes he is having an elevating literary experience, rather than simply listening to backstairs gossip and reading other people's mail.

So however you approach it – as writer or reader – a biographical work can be a perplexing enterprise. In her book *Writing a*

Woman's Life, the academic Carolyn Heilbrun has highlighted the particular difficulties:

> Where should it begin? With her birth, and the disappointment, or reason for no disappointment, that she was not a boy? Do we then slide her into the Freudian family romance, the Oedipal configuration; if not, how do we view the childhood? . . . what in short is the subject's relation – inevitably complex – with her mother? The relation with the father will be less complex, clearer in its emotions and desires, partaking less of either terrible pity or binding love. How does the process of becoming, or failing to become a sex object operate in a woman's life; how does she cope with the fact that her value is determined by how attractive men find her? If she marries, why does the marriage fail, or succeed? . . . what of women friends, of middle age or of active old age (the years between sixty and seventy-five)?

That template would be a particularly apt one if I chose to apply it to Joni Mitchell's life, and simply fill in those gaps. But what of the woman's work? What of the creative process, the daily grind or jubilation, the disappointments and desires, the achievements and losses, the hits and misses?

Having lauded her from the time of her first album in the late 1960s through the chart successes of the mid-70s, the music industry then ignored much of her work for years, although the decade from 1970 to 1980 showed an extraordinary artistic evolutionary process and was her most creatively prolific – she released ten albums, including three double-albums, painted the artwork for several of them, took up photography, went on tour, took sabbaticals for writing, painting, travelling and escaping from the public gaze. The music and media industries woke up in a lather of uncharacteristic sincerity in the 1990s and Mitchell underwent a commercial renaissance, fuelled by winning Grammy awards for best pop album and album artwork for 1994's *Turbulent Indigo*. Other accolades rained down on her included *Billboard* magazine's Century Award, the National Academy of Songwriters'

Lifetime Achievement Award, the Canadian Governor-General's Performing Arts Award and the Swedish Polar Music Award. She was nominated again for two Grammys in 2001, and won the award for Best Traditional Pop Vocal for the lush, orchestral 'Both Sides, Now'. Mitchell was inducted into the Rock and Roll Hall of Fame in 1997, but was miffed at having to wait behind what she regarded as many lesser talents, thanks to the vagaries of the Hall of Fame selection panel. She accepted her induction but did not attend the ceremony in Cleveland, Ohio, and dismissed the award as a 'dubious honour, in that they held me out conspicuously for three years . . . they're putting everyone in, so the honour is dubious on that level'.

There is so much within us that needs to come to life. Music, art and literature can slap us into wakefulness, coax us from our dormant state, thaw out that frozen core inside. So can the everyday experiences of life. But at least with great music you get to dance as well. My eye is on the rare breed who try to combine all of the above. These Renaissance spirits may succeed gloriously or fail miserably but they'd agree with Kafka: the meaning of life is that it ends.

The Japanese have a tradition of according certain cultural figures with the status of Living Treasure, which has also been adopted by countries like New Zealand. Individuals are honoured and revered for what they have to teach society and the culture; one may love or loathe their work, but there is a consensus that what they do has real value. There is an active respect for them while they are still alive, which seems eminently sensible given that this is when they are still *creating*, still challenging, still with us. How painful to look back and lament – of anyone – you don't know who you've got 'til they've gone.

On a style point, the artist formerly known as Joan adopted the name 'Joni' when she was a teenager. In the text, I've used 'Joan' up until around that time. I've used 'Mitchell' from the time of her marriage to Chuck Mitchell. Her family and close friends call her Joan.

1 The birth of rock 'n' roll days . . .

Disease was the most basic ground
Of my creative urge and stress:
Creating, I could convalesce,
Creating, I again grew sound.
(Heinrich Heine, *Schopfungslieder*)

L ET'S TELL THE FUTURE. The Tea-Leaf Prophecy:
Make one pot of tea, with real tea leaves. Let it brew; pour into a white or pastel cup with a wide brim. Have your subject drink all but a tiny bit of liquid. Take the cup in your left hand and swirl it around clockwise three times. Cover the top of the cup with your right hand, making sure to swirl the leaves completely up and around the sides and rim of the cup. Look at what is left. The tea-leaf prophecy. Begin the interpretation with the simplest symbols first. Shapes, perhaps – a triangle signifies good karma; a square, the need for caution; a circle, great success. Letters may refer to the names of friends, relatives, a beloved. Numbers may indicate spans of time in months or years.

Myrtle 'Mickey' Marguerite McKee smiled; it was only meant to be a joke, a harmless bit of fun. She and her friend had gone for tea at the nicest hotel in Regina. There was the sense of a special occasion because the Lord alone knew there was little else to brighten the day during wartime in Canada. And what harm would it do to have the gypsy read the leaves after Myrtle had sipped the last from the near-transparent china cup? The gypsy woman looked down at the cup, then up at the beautiful craftwork of that face, the cheekbones, the eyes, the Celtic paleness reddening a little, as she pronounced, 'You will be married within the month, you will have a child within the year, and you will die a long, agonising death.' What did she see? Maybe a ring, for a forthcoming marriage; an oyster, for love, for an impending engagement; a forked line, a coming decision; a tree, for health.

Myrtle laughed. Oh, come on now! That's ridiculous. Look at this town, there's no one here to choose from. It was wartime; all the available men were away, only women and kids, old men and frail boys left. Love's young dream for me? I don't think so. She used to be a teacher but now she had her job at the bank, had her friends and her family. But a man? It was impossible of course. Except in the movies, maybe! A husband within the month? A baby within the year? And for all the joyful promise of this beckoning future, the finality of the end: a long, agonising death. Two out of three ain't bad.

Myrtle had been born on 24 May; a birthday shared decades earlier by Queen Victoria, decades later by Bob Dylan. Within two weeks of the reading, Myrtle met William Andrew Anderson; it was a blind date. Bill was a flight lieutenant in the Royal Canadian Air Force, on brief leave. They took the road out of Regina and headed west, stopping in Moose Jaw, where they married before he had to return to base at the end of his two weeks' leave. Where does it say you need years rather than days to know, to decide, be sure? The only rule of love is, there are no rules.

Let's tell the future.

Within a year of the marriage, the second part of the prediction came true. Myrtle gave birth to their only child, a daughter, Roberta Joan, on 7 November 1943, in a three-storey hospital with roof-top turrets and colonnaded verandas in the small town of Fort Macleod. Their daughter would later remark that they'd expected a boy and had planned to call him Robert John. Bill was a training instructor at Pearce Air Base, a few miles east of the town. They made their home in a humble apartment rented from their Cockney landlady, Mrs Crow, who – as the baby grew into a toddler – would teach the child sing-song rhymes.

By the time of their daughter's birth, Fort Macleod, on the Great Plains of north-western Canada, had barely emerged from the post-Depression era with the strength to face the war years. Money was spent on essentials, there was never anything left over for luxuries or indulgences. Gardens were non-existent, home decor was minimal. But people did what they could to bring a sense of beauty to their spartan surroundings. One of Joan's earliest memories was of the chicken feed and broken glass mixed in with the rough-cast stucco on the exterior of many homes in the small town. The glass shards glinted in the sun's rays. The young child was enchanted by the magical fragments that fell from the walls, rounded, smooth-edged glass that she'd stuff into her mouth, until the treasures were discovered by her horrified mother. Colours fascinated her; when still barely forming words, she'd found some oranges and placed them on a purple scarf, exclaiming to her bemused parents, 'Pretty!' Here too, the child's first experience of snow provided more stim-ulation for her senses; family photographs show an ecstatic tod-dler playing outside, shrouded under layers of woollens.

There are few glass-encrusted houses left to reflect the Fort Macleod sunshine now; one, just off Main Street, sits like a story-book gingerbread house preserved among the manicured newness of the well-tended homes on the rest of the street. There are surely volumes of building regulations that would prevent such humble adornments today. The town had begun life as an outpost for the North-West Mounted Police in 1874. The force had been sent out to establish a semblance of order in the Canadian West. After stopping briefly at the wonderfully named Fort Whoop-Up settlement in nearby Lethbridge, the men moved on to set up camp on an island on the Oldman River. The surgeon travelling with the force, Dr Richard Nevitt, described their final destination as 'a beau-tiful place in the valley of the rivers'. The fort and settlement estab-lished by the NWMP were named after the man who had led the three-month trek across the plains, Colonel James F. Macleod.

Today, with a population of about three thousand, and in the way of very small towns, it has the air of a plucky place trying hard to make a lot out of relatively little. It's one of the oldest commu-nities in southern Alberta and was declared the province's first his-toric area. Walking around the downtown area – in truth, the town's too small really to have an 'uptown' – brings reminders of the fron-tier past. There are more than thirty historic and architecturally significant buildings dating from the 1890s, among them the faded glory of the oldest court house in Alberta, the brown brick Territorial Court House/Palais de Justice. It's one of the few buildings sur-viving from the period of territorial administration in the prairies. But the centrepiece of the town's tourist attractions remains the small fort and the museum preserving its past. In July and August, visitors can see costumed 'Mounties' and their horses performing gently synchronised equine stunts in performances of the Musical Ride. It's a far cry from taming the Plains tribes and keeping order among the homesteaders, but the tourists seem to enjoy it.

On Main Street, the Empress Theatre, just the right side of grand-shabby, once boasted performances by vaudeville acts like Texas Tony and His Wonder Horse, Baby Doll. Both Tony and Baby Doll have gone to that great VIP backstage area in the sky, giving way to more contemporary Canadian acts like Sarah McLachlan and Blue Rodeo. For all the industry generated by tourism, some of the townspeople are still struggling in the way their grandparents would have done in the early 1940s. A sign in a shop window advertises the 'Sow-a-row' campaign, urging people to grow surplus vegetables in their gardens and donate them to the food bank set up for the poor of the area.

One of the area's best-known attractions is a few miles south of town: the Head-Smashed-In Buffalo Jump where for more than five-and-a-half thousand years, Indian or First Nations tribes killed buffalo en masse by stampeding them over sandstone cliffs. But it was not the dwindling herds of buffalo which inspired the name of the site. As local legend has it, a hapless young brave who wanted to get a ringside seat as the buffalo plummeted stood below a cliff ledge as the poor beasts fell to their deaths. But in what some may interpret as the buffaloes' revenge, he became trapped as the animal carcasses piled up, preventing his escape from under the ledge. When his tribespeople came to butcher the carcasses they found his body, with his head smashed in under the weight of the buffalo.

The area was designated a National Historic Site in 1968, and a UNESCO World Heritage Site in 1981, but when Joan and her parents lived nearby it was considered little more than a rocky outcrop overlooking the plains.

Life after wartime

Bill left the airforce for civvy street and he, Myrtle and young Joan moved first to Calgary, then prepared to return to Myrtle's home province of Saskatchewan. Myrtle and Joan stayed with Myrtle's mother near Regina while their new house in the village of Maidstone was being built. The family settled into their home at 214 Railway Avenue East; Bill put up a swing in the garden, but one of Joan's favourite pastimes required little more than a chair at the large window in the living-room, at the front of the house. The view across the road to the railway line was to give Joan a literal window on the world, a yearning for the wider universe beyond, symbolised by the rattle and hum of the daily steam train. The young child would perch at the window each day and wave to the driver as the train passed slowly. Years later, long after the family had left Maidstone, her parents met a man who once worked in the area for Canadian railways. When he found out where they'd lived, he recalled his only memory of the uneventful trip along the line through Maidstone – an exuberant tow-haired little girl who'd be waiting each day to exchange a wave.

Bill worked a couple of minutes' walk from the house; he'd taken over the management of a small grocery shop, part of the chain of OK Economy stores. Today, the groceries have long since disappeared from the shelves, giving way to a laundrette and flower shop; a video rental place is next door and the Co-op Food store, the electrolysis studio and the Seniors Recreation Centre are conveniently situated across the road. It's typical of villages and towns all over the province. Saskatchewan, noted the Canadian writer Guy Vanderhaeghe, has never climbed out of the Depression.

When the Andersons arrived in Maidstone, it was a hamlet with few amenities, not even running water. The family settled in and quickly became part of the close-knit community. Bill played trumpet in Cliff Milnes' dance orchestra; Joan befriended the other young children of the village and family photos show the children clowning around at Joan's third birthday party, or playing dress-up or gathering self-consciously on the Andersons' back steps to pose for the camera. Early childhood was marked by a succession of ordinary days and extraordinary moments, like the drama of a burst appendix when Joan was three, and the frantic dash to get her to hospital in time. The excitement of the royal wedding of Princess Elizabeth and Prince Philip in 1947 prompted Joan and her young friend, Sharon Bell, to turn up at the village's nearest equivalent – a wedding in the local United Church. Barely four years old, the pair were eventually found in a pew, enthralled as they watched the service unfold. Just such a moment was later recalled in 'Song for Sharon':

When we were kids in Maidstone, Sharon
I went to every wedding in that little town
To see the tears and the kisses
And the pretty lady in the white lace gown . . .

Maidstone is proud of its most famous former resident. There is a small display in a corner of the village museum devoted to her – a few clippings and posters and some photographs donated by Myrtle Anderson, detailing the family's years in the village. The museum is a lovingly tended piece of local history. It's in the old railway station and station house, which was moved to the site next to the Delfrari-Victoria Park in 1989. The exhibits trace the life of the community through memorabilia, wedding dresses, baby shoes, family photographs, personal treasures. There's a copy of a poster advertising a 'Public Sale of Negroes' including 'a valuable Negro woman, accustomed to all kinds of housework'. The story of Maidstone's black community is also told: Mattie Mayes, born into slavery, brought forty family members with her from Oklahoma in 1910 to make a new life in Canada. She lived to be a hundred years old.

Within a couple of years, the Andersons had moved again, on to the larger town of North Battleford, named unsurprisingly after a ford in the Battle River. Linked to its sister community, Battleford, by the longest bridge in the province, the area is steeped in the history of the tribal nations – Cree and Blackfoot – and of white settlement and law enforcement. Like Fort Macleod, Battleford was once an outpost of the North-West Mounted Police, and had been the original seat of government for the Northwest Territories.

The Battlefords, as they are known, had another thing going for them, beyond the history and their popularity as a holiday spot. Although in some ways the town was undeveloped – at Christmas, the mail still came on open wagons drawn by horses with sleigh-runners – the shopping area was larger than Maidstone's and opposite Bill Anderson's OK Economy grocery was a department store, with a listening booth for records. That proved a magnet for a young Joan developing a passion for music, the dominant form of culture in the local community. North Battleford was proud of its musical traditions – a superlative marching band and an annual two-week music festival that attracted all the local schools and church groups. Joan had young friends who were studying classical voice and piano and she'd go along to watch them perform; the event could bring either triumph or torture for the participants, as she recalled years later:

a lot of little pig-tailed girls standing up singing "hey nonny-nonny, on yonder hill, there stands a maiden ..." then a stout woman would come up in a grey suit, put her glasses on and tear the little performance apart or praise it. The game was to sit back there and decide what she was going to say, where they missed a note, and what was good and what was bad. Some Grade One student always peed their pants ... it was more of a spectacle. So in a way, this small town had pretensions to European classicism and so you were exposed to it.

But with the attachment to classicism came the expectation of conformism. After going along with a friend, Frankie McKitrick, to see a film called *The Story of Three Loves*, Joan became smitten with the film's theme music, Rachmaninov's 'Rhapsody on a Theme of Paganini'. The track had been released on a 78 record called *The Story of Three Loves* and whenever possible she'd go down to the department store and head for the listening booth, with the record clasped in her hand:

It was the most beautiful melody I'd ever heard ... when I heard that song, I really wanted to play the piano. I began to dream that I could play it beautifully. We bought one off the back of a truck one winter in North Battleford and I started lessons but at a rudimentary level. I wanted to jump immediately into playing the piano beautifully and you had to go through a lot of practising. I tried to make the jump and the teacher rapped my knuckles with a ruler. I took it personally but it turns out that it was something nearly every piano player I spoke to had experienced. It was part of the old system. She said, "Why would you want to play by ear when you could have the masters at your fingertips?" So creativity was not imagined in that culture. If you took piano lessons you were going to learn to play European classics.

The seven-year-old Joan had already come up with her first song, 'Robin Walk', and longed to play it, but the vigorous discouragement of improvisation and the strenuous use of the piano teacher's ruler destroyed her enthusiasm. The piano lessons ended. They had coincided with one of her favourite radio programmes – *The Adventures of Wild Bill Hickok* – so the punishment had been a double one: get your knuckles rapped *and* miss your favourite show. But while the precocious artistic child must have puzzled her parents at times, they did share her love of music. They listened to the music shows on the radio and the few records they had were much played. Her mother favoured classical nocturnes and melodies, Debussy's *Romantic Melodies* and Brahms' 'Lullaby', while her father indulged his love of the trumpet, with albums by world-class players like Harry James and Leroy Anderson. Beyond Rachmaninov, the next source of inspiration for Joan was a diminutive French chanteuse with an extraordinarily emotional vocal power, Edith Piaf: 'I remember the first time I heard her. It was a recording of "Les Trois Cloches" – "The Jimmy Brown Song" – and my hair stood on end. Her voice just thrilled my soul.'

As with the piano lessons, Joan bailed out of Bible classes, frustrated at the lack of logic and sense amid the fantastical allegories, like the story of Adam and Eve and their two sons, Cain and Abel. Cain killed Abel, and then he married. Who did he marry? His Mum? Well, who else was there? The Sunday school teacher's response did nothing to stop the questions but did halt the questioner; Joan stopped going to Sunday school. Disillusionment with the Bible stories was overcome by a stint in the church choir: 'I chose to sing descant because nobody else wanted to. I called it the pretty melody; everybody else called it the hard melody. It has a lot of fifths and fourths, singing over and under things. The leaps were easy for me.'

Artistic expression was not just an escape from boredom but a way of trying to belong: drawing and painting, pressed-flower scrapbooks, fancy dress costumes, small-town life transformed by make-believe, even if, as she recalled many years later, it was at times hard to fit in with the other children:

> All the [girls'] games are nurses, tea parties and dress-up. Sometimes we don't have clothes to dress up in, so we do imaginary dress. I'd say, 'I'm wearing a gold lamé dress, and I'm Ginger Rogers, and I'm descending a long staircase.'

'No you're not, I am!'

So even on the level of imaginary play, there was a lot of irrational competition. So then I try to play with the boys. The boys play Roy Rogers and war. Roy Rogers is the one that invents all the activities and chooses the site. They choose a new Roy every day.

So I say, 'Let me be Roy.'

They say, 'You can't 'cause you're a girl.'

So Christmas comes and I say, 'I want a Roy Rogers shirt and a Roy Rogers hat.'

'Oh, dear,' says my mother.

There's a big conference with my father.

'The girl wants a Roy Rogers shirt.' This is very bad.

My father says, 'Let her have it.'

So, come spring . . . here I stand in my red Roy Rogers shirt, [that] says 'Roy' right on it. And my red Roy Rogers hat, says 'Roy' right on it. And I've got all these places . . . I know this ravine that would be just great . . . And I say to the boys, 'Let me be Roy.'

'You can't!'

'Why not?'

'You're a girl.'

'But look, it says "Roy Rogers" right here!'

'That means you're Dale Evans.'

'Why?'

'Because you're wearing Roy's clothes.'

'Well, what does Dale do?'

'She stays home and cooks.'

An added advantage for her was having a cap pistol to go with the Roy Rogers outfit; that occasionally guaranteed admission to the boys' games, but they'd try to downgrade her role wherever possible. In war games, she'd be among the first to get shot and have to sit out the rest of the game as a dead body; in cowboys and Indians, she'd only be allowed as a lowly member of the sheriff's posse.

But having two best friends who were passionate about music – Frankie McKitrick, a classical piano prodigy, and Peter Armstrong, who was studying classical voice – offered a respite from the rough-and-tumble competitiveness of the boys or the frilly, fussy home-making of the girls: '[Frankie and Peter] were artists. And there was no role-playing, so play was able to happen. Had that play not existed, it would have changed my destiny.' Their play centred on artistic fantasies:

> We used to put on circuses together ... I used to dance around the room and say that I was going to be a great ballerina and [Frankie] was going to be a great composer, or that he was going to be a great writer and I was going to illustrate his books.

Even before music, painting and sketching had fired the child's imagination, Joan's mother had bought her a blackboard for her second birthday and later a set of crayons; paper and paints were never far away. The story of Bambi and her deer family, with all of its heartbreak and thrills, was an early artistic inspiration. As was Joan's Grade Five teacher, Miss Fulford, who was the unwitting subject of one of her first portraits:

> [she] wore her hair up high – all grey with combs at the side to hold it – and steel-rimmed glasses. I drew a picture of her. I really thought I caught her likeness. So I proudly showed her. She got really uptight about it. She thought I was being insulting and made me stay after school.

But her time in Miss Fulford's class was to come to an abrupt halt one day in October 1953, and it had nothing to do with her sketching skills:

> I vividly remember the day I got polio. I was nine years old, and I dressed myself that morning in pegged grey slacks, a red and white gingham blouse with a sailor col-lar, and a blue sweater. I looked in the mirror, and I don't know what I saw – dark circles or a slight swelling in my face – but I said to myself, 'You look like a woman today.' After I got outside, I was walking along with a school friend, and at the third block I sat down on this little lawn and said, 'I must have rheumatism,' because I'd seen my grandmother aching and having to be lifted out of the bathtub. I complained a bit more but still went

and spent the day in school. Next day, I woke and my Mum said, 'Get up! come!' I said, 'I can't.' She didn't believe me and yanked me out of bed, and I collapsed.

The child was rushed to the polio clinic at St Paul's Hospital in the nearest large city, Saskatoon. She was paralysed. During the first half of the twentieth century, the poliomyelitis virus spread panic and paralysis throughout the western world, especially the wealthier countries like Canada, the United States, New Zealand, Australia, Britain, Sweden, Denmark. In poorer countries like Ireland, the city of Cork became a pariah in the mid-1950s, because of the prevalence of the disease there. Polio is relatively rare today thanks to widespread immunisation, but epidemics raged from the late 1940s into the 1950s. The virus was no respecter of age or circumstance but children were often most vulnerable to what was also known as infantile paralysis. The polio epidemic of the late 1940s and early 50s affected a generation of young Canadians; Neil Young was also among them. The virus at first caused flu-like symptoms, aches and stiffness, and progressed rapidly; many people carried the virus without realising it, a factor which helped its spread in the early contagious stages. In those worst affected, the virus attacked the nerves of the brain and spinal cord, and could leave sufferers paralysed, usually in the legs, and often in the muscles that control breathing and swallowing.

In the early weeks, the polio virus mangled Joan's spine, forcing it to twist forward and then to the right, severely affecting one leg. Over the next few weeks, she underwent the conventional treatment of the time: deep massage of the paralysed limbs and the application of scalding compresses to her legs. The compresses were then removed, bringing the raw skin to the brink of blistering. Many doctors would later question the efficacy of this method, believing that its most lasting effect was not physiological but psychological: the memory of the searing pain. In the polio ward, the Emerson respirators – the 'iron lungs' – wheezed as they encased the most seriously ill patients, who were unable to breathe unaided. The respirators were two-metre-long steel cylinders, reminiscent of coffins, with bellows at one end. The bellows changed the air pressure inside the chamber; a vacuum forced the chest to expand to assist breathing. A patient lay inside each cylinder with only the head free, a collar fitted around the patient's neck to ensure an airtight seal inside the chamber. At the height of the epidemic in 1953, St Paul's Hospital had as many as nine iron lungs operating simultaneously.

After the initial infectious period had passed, Joan was moved to the children's ward, just a few weeks before Christmas. She'd been sent a colouring book to keep her occupied; the pictures were of old-fashioned English carol singers, with the lyrics printed alongside. Joan used cotton swabs – stained purple from the gentian violet used to treat her mouth ulcers – to colour the illustrations. Her mother visited, bringing a small Christmas tree decorated with lights and baubles. That night the nurses, many of whom were Roman Catholic nuns, let her leave the festive lights on until an hour after bedtime: 'I said to the little tree, "I am not a cripple!", and I said a prayer, some kind of pact, a barter with God for my legs, my singing.' She would sing hearty Christmas carols to cheer herself up, until the boy in the neighbouring bed complained:

> One time I was sitting on the edge of the bed with my legs exposed – I was nine years old – and I was singing a Christmas carol to a six-year-old boy who was pouting and picking his nose. He had also turned towards the wall and was telling me to shut up, when a nun rushed in and practically beat me up for showing my legs. A nine-year-old to a six-year-old!

Joan's tenth birthday was spent in hospital, pondering the prospect that the virus may have damaged her spine so severely that she would not ever walk again. At ten, you're still fizzing with that energy that hasn't yet propelled you out of childhood. The prospect of having it curtailed was not one to be considered for long. After weeks in hospital – and despite the gloomy prognosis – Joan felt ready to try to walk again. The test was whether she could get out of her wheelchair and make it to the end of a ramp, supporting herself by holding on to the railings and walking gingerly. She managed it, and was allowed to go home to North Battleford. There, Joan dispensed with corrective shoes, leg-braces and a wheelchair as her mother Myrtle devoted a year to rebuilding her daughter's strength and mobility. Myrtle had been a teacher during the 1930s, in a one-room rural school where she had had to make her own books. She now took on the task of teaching her daughter at home.

For months on end, the child's imagination – unlike her body – could run riot. The belief that inner resources and strong will could conquer almost anything slipped an armour of invincibility over the child's form that would be both tested and reinforced much later in adulthood. The worlds we construct as children are so often the ones we live in as adults. Her enduring self-belief may perhaps have its source in surviving this potentially fatal childhood illness that saw her struggling to regain her health:

> Polio probably did me good. Otherwise I would have been an athlete. I lost my running skills, but translated them into something less fast and more graceful; I became a dancer. I believe convalescence in bed develops a strong inner life in a young child. I think it solidified me as an independent thinker. [Friedrich] Nietzsche was a convalescent.

The often ailing philosopher Nietzsche believed that the creative process was stimulated by adversity, especially by ill-health, whether physical or mental. He regarded illness as a challenge which ought to strengthen a person's resolve – far from avoiding pain and failure, we should welcome and embrace them as challenges to be conquered and for the valuable lessons they can teach us.

In 1954, Dr Jonas Salk successfully tested a polio vaccine on school children in the United States. The following year, due to an error in the screening process, a faulty batch of the vaccine was administered, leaving 250 people stricken with polio and 11 others dead. After what became known as the Cutter incident – the name of the laboratory that dispatched the vaccine – Britain was among the countries reluctant to use it. But Canada and several others persisted with its use and did much to cut the future incidence of the disease. A British television producer and director, Ann Hawker, who made a programme on the British government's response to the polio crisis, said her interviews with polio survivors revealed a common characteristic: 'There was no self-pity or bitterness, they all just got on with life. Perhaps it was due to the fact it was all post-war and they were lucky to be alive, but they were all so pragmatic.'

Joan's childhood schoolfriend, Anne Bayin – whose father was the local minister in North Battleford – recalls that the youngster's brush with death only made her seem more glamorous to her classmates. Joan, she says, was 'magnetic and daring and inventive. She had the best husky laugh, even before cigarettes. As far as I was concerned, she had other major things going for her: she was blonde and she was an only child with her own bedroom.'

More upheaval came with another move: when Joan was eleven years old, the family packed up and left North Battleford for the big city, Saskatoon. She acquired a reputation as a talented artist, although this alone had been sufficient for one exasperated sixth-grade teacher at Queen Elizabeth Public School in Saskatoon to remark in the child's report card: 'Joan should pay attention to subjects other than art.' An auspicious meeting with a new teacher, who would encourage her passion for the arts rather than despair of it, came one day when Joan was in a corridor hanging pictures ahead of a parent/teacher day at the end of the school year:

> A good-looking Australian came up to me and said, 'You like to paint?' I said 'yes' and he said to me, 'If you can paint with a brush you can paint with words, I'll see you next year.' His name was [Arthur] Kratzman and he'd come to Canada with his teaching credentials kind of out of whack, so they'd punished him by sending him to teach on Indian reservations, which he loved. To send a teacher to the Indian reservations in Saskatchewan was like being banished to Siberia, but he took to it with relish and he was a very, very soulful man. He'd been a racing partner to [a] great gold medal winning racer in Australia at that time, so he was a really good runner and he was a teacher-maker and a writer-maker and an athlete-maker. He said, 'You know, I'm not going to teach it to you, I'm going to cram you in the last two weeks, you'll all pass with flying colours. I'm going to teach you what I know.'

Kratzman, who taught her in the seventh grade, encouraged an interest in poetry too, opening up a whole new world of words and their possibilities – as did the *Readers' Digest* column 'Improve Your Word Power'. The eleven-year-old Joan, inspired by seeing the film *Black Beauty*, chose to pepper a poem about a horse with words newly plucked from her parents' copies of *Readers' Digest*:

> I stretched vocabulary for an eleven year old and it was quite a precocious poem but he circled it all over 'cliché ["white as newly fallen snow"], cliché ["high upon a silver-shadowed hill"], good adjective, you've used this adjective, cliché', and he marked me harder than I think American college professors mark.
>
> He said to me, 'How many times did you see *Black Beauty*?'
>
> I said, 'Once.'
>
> 'What do you know about horses?'
>
> I said, 'Well, I go riding at the weekends, whenever I can. I like horses', and he said 'Well, the things that you've told me that you've done on other weekends are more interesting than this, you know. Write in your own blood!' . . . which was [from] Nietzsche I found out later.

Arthur Kratzman – a tall, kind-hearted Australian with a gold tooth, a spirited man who looked like the film idols Clark Gable and Gregory Peck – was to be among the inspirational figures who saw in the child something more than her artistic ability and a loathing of science subjects would indicate. Her art teacher, Henry Bonli, was to prove inspirational in another way: at the age of thirteen, Joan became Joni, 'because I admired the way [his] last name . . . looked in his painting signatures'. Bonli's passion for the abstract impressionists who dominated contemporary art at the time was also to have a lasting effect:

> Not to criticise Henry but he was a Barnett Newman proponent. Basically, all he did was to prejudice me against abstraction, particularly Barnett Newman who was his hero. He was trying to teach me the various shades of putty and beige, which are wonderful for upholstery, but at 13 I craved colour. So whatever it was that he had to teach was wasted, and basically it developed in me a contempt for modern art, which I ran into again at art school. I found it very disappointing.

As a student at Nutana and Aden Bowman Collegiate high schools, Joni's passions were art (the abstract impressionists notwithstanding), music, writing and fashion, with what were considered the more academic pursuits – maths and the sciences – lagging far behind. She joined a creative writing group that met after school, she painted backdrops for school plays, she wrote a column called 'Fads and Fashions' for the school newspaper, defining the meaning of 'hip' and offering fashion tips, and she became known as the local style guru. At 16, Joni pondered the value of celebrity, while sitting under a dryer at the hairdressers and reading movie star magazines full of gossipy features about the golden young couple of the time, Sandra Dee and Bobby Darin. That inspired 'The Fishbowl', a poem for a school assignment, denouncing the fame game:

> The Fishbowl is a world reversed
> Where fishermen with hooks
> That dangle from the bottom up
> Reel down their catch without a fight
> Pike, pickerel bass, the common fish,
> Ogle through distorting glass,
> See only glitter, glamour, gaiety
> Fog up the bowl with lusty breath
> Lunge towards the bait and miss
> And weep for fortunes lost
> Envy the goldfish? Why?
> His bubbles breaking 'round the rim
> While silly fishes faint for him
> And say, 'Look there!
> I think he winked his eye at me.'

What the poem lacks in mature literary style, it more than makes up for in prescient insight into her future. While poetry and prose came easily, Joni resorted to drawing portraits of mathematicians for her maths teacher and detailed charts for use in biology classes, as a way of appeasing her teachers for being so uninspired by their lessons. It was at this point that a less cerebral pursuit entered her life: ballroom and rock 'n' roll dancing. Among the first generation of teenagers, Joni and her friends discovered the soundtrack for their epoch: rock 'n' roll. They'd been listening to blues records, hits like Louis Jordan's 'Saturday Night Fish Fry', and embraced the new hybrid passionately. The other great attraction of the new music was that you could dance to it; for a teenager who'd been told at the age of nine that she may never walk again, dancing was a pleasure to be indulged at every opportunity. The teenage Joni won records in dance contests and had also evolved a blissfully simple barter system to get the records she didn't have the cash to buy:

> One year I did a Christmas card for a fellow who was a school leader, and he gave me a present of some Miles Davis albums. About that time my only musical interest, actively, was rock 'n' roll, Chuck Berry, and this was at the level of dance. I loved to dance.

Her collection of jazz albums – which by now included Miles's classic *Sketches of Spain* (recorded 1959–60 and still selling today) – received a further boost when she painted a mural of a bebop trio on a friend's wall; he too paid her in jazz records. Classical music and the blues had given way to rock 'n' roll dancing and jazz:

> Then I heard at a party, Lambert, Hendricks and Ross, *The Hottest New Sound in Jazz*, which at that time was out of issue up in that part of the country, in Canada. So I literally saved up and bought it at a bootleg price, and in a way I've always considered that album to be my Beatles because I learned every song off it. 'Cloudburst' I couldn't sing, because of some of the very fast scatting on it . . . I loved that album, the spirit of it . . . it came at a time when rock 'n' roll was winding down just before the Beatles came along and revitalised it. And during that ebb that's when folk music came to its full power.

Dave Lambert, Jon Hendricks and Annie Ross had caused a sensation in the jazz world when they released *Sing a Song of Basie* (Roulette) in early 1958. Springing from the bebop tradition, Dave Lambert had, along with Eddie Jefferson, been the first to put lyrics over established jazz works. In 1945 Lambert had arranged and recorded a group vocal with Gene Krupa's big band; the song 'What's This' was the first recorded bebop vocal. In 1952 Annie Ross (British-born Annabelle Short) had a hit with her song 'Twisted', based on a tenor improvisation by Wardell

Gray. Joni's affection for the song would result in its inclusion on her album *Court and Spark* in 1974; she would also incorporate the LHR hit 'Centerpiece' on the track 'Harry's House – Centerpiece' on her album *The Hissing of Summer Lawns* the following year. The other member of the ensemble, Jon Hendricks, was lauded by *Time* magazine as the 'James Joyce of Jive' and a 'poet of the jazz solo'.

The Basie works were their first ensemble recording and until the group broke up in 1964 – Annie Ross left in 1962, to be replaced by Yolande Bavan – they made the entire spectrum of modern jazz their own with their extraordinary style. Jazz writer Joachim E. Berendt said of Lambert, Hendricks and Ross, 'When these three sang solos by Charlie Parker, Lester Young, Sonny Rollins, Miles Davis, Oscar Pettiford, John Coltrane and others, to Jon Hendricks' lyrics, one had the feeling that this was what all those great musicians had wanted to say.'

As the 1950s sashayed into the 60s, Joni watched as 'the beer-drinking, cars in the country, dancing in the middle of a dirt field and kicking up dust with all the car radios blaring atmosphere died down to this more intellectual, civil rights-oriented, pensive college mentality'. The age of the earnest folkie had arrived, with groups like Peter, Paul and Mary in the vanguard. It was an evolutionary development that initially left Joni cold: 'I just thought it was pseudo-intellectual nonsense that you would sit around and talk about these dreary things when you could be dancing.' Joni's final year at Aden Bowman Collegiate had come to an end; along with her other classmates, her photograph was featured in the annual yearbook. The caption read: '"And her sunny locks Hang on her temples like a golden fleece". Joan's artistic hand has brightened many school functions. In whatever field she chooses for the future we wish her success.'

Back to the future

Joni had decided to go to the Alberta College of Art in Calgary and worked to save enough money for fees and living expenses. She worked in dress shops in Saskatoon, modelling women's wear:

> Travelling salesmen came through town and hired 'whole-sale models' locally, who were basically quick-change

artists exhibiting clothes for retail buyers. You wore a
black slip and changed behind a screen because you were
a young woman working in a hotel-room with a traveller.
You had to be a size eight, but the pay was pretty good.

She also got a job as a waitress at the Louis Riel coffee house on
Broadway Avenue and it was here, listening to the passing
parade of earnest young acoustic folkies, that she decided to
swap her apron for the microphone. She took the stage during
weekly open-mike or 'hoot' (hootenanny) night, accompanying
herself with the baritone ukelele she'd bought for $36, a bargain
compared to the guitars which were far beyond her means. Colin
Holliday-Scott, who had a brief stint as one of the owners of the
coffee house, recalls deciding against hiring one singer 'with a
terrible voice' – Joni Anderson. The Louis Riel was one of the
best-known places in town, named after the folk hero who had
been executed for treason in 1885 after he led his Metis people –
the mostly French-speaking descendants of early European fur
traders and Cree or Ojibwa Indians – in the Northwest Rebellion,
an armed uprising against the Canadian government in 1884–85.
The coffee house did not share the longevity of its namesake's
reputation; today another café is on the same site but hardcore
Joni fans still make the pilgrimage there.
    It was at the Louis Riel that she began to meet musicians and
singers, among them singer/songwriter Shawn Phillips. The son
of spy novelist Philip Atlee, the cosmopolitan Texan-born
Phillips was already an accomplished 12-string guitar player,
writing his own material and touring the coffee-house circuit.
Joni's own attempts to play the guitar had been literally painful:
she'd borrowed one from a friend but the strings were rusty and
so taut that they had lacerated her fingers. She later taught herself to play using Pete Seeger's *How to Play Folk-Style Guitar*
instruction record, which had in turn been inspired by the guitar-
playing of the Seeger family's housekeeper, Elizabeth 'Libba'
Cotten. Singer, songwriter and musician, Elizabeth Cotten
played guitar upside down and left-handed; with elements of
gospel and ragtime, her two-finger picking style became the
standard in folk guitar-playing. But because of Joni's residual
weakness in her left hand, a legacy of the bout of polio, she was
unable to master Cotten-picking – the sixth string, fifth string,

sixth string, fifth string – and ended up playing mostly the sixth string, banging it into the fifth string. She would later cite Cotten as an influence by default that forced her to develop an original approach and her own vast vocabulary of tunings.

A self-confessed party-girl, Joni had a wide circle of friends – earnest artistic types, rock 'n' roll dancers and the more exotic gregarious characters, like the Ukrainian and First Nations kids, then considered on the fringes of polite Saskatoon society:

> When I went back to my own neighbourhood, I found that I had a provocative image. They thought I was loose because I always liked the rowdies. I thought the way kids danced at my school was kind of . . . funny. I remember a recurring statement on my report card – 'Joan does not relate well.' I knew that I was aloof. Perhaps some people thought that I was a snob. There came a split when I rejected sororities and that whole thing. I didn't go for that. But there also came a time when my friends who were juvenile delinquents suddenly became criminals. They could go into very dull jobs or they could go into crime. Crime is very romantic in your youth. I suddenly thought, 'Here's where the romance ends. I don't see myself in jail . . . '

It came as a surprise then, to many of her friends, when she began to embrace the more esoteric world of traditional folk and left behind the rock 'n' roll of Elvis, Chuck Berry and Ray Charles. She remembers being drawn to the melancholy melody of folk:

> So this kind of joyous, fun-loving creature became this earnest creature. This transformation had taken place, and I think a lot of people had a hard time with that transition. I know some of my best buddies would say, 'Put that [ukelele] down. We're gonna drag you onto the dancefloor.' 'No, no, no!' I was clinging to it in the corner, saying 'Leave me alone!' I introverted into this intimate relationship with this stringed instrument.

Now armed with her baritone uke and a clutch of traditional folk songs and Kingston Trio standards, Joni would often sing at local parties and camp-fire barbecues. In between the bawdy drinking songs and the folkie favourites, guests listening to her at one party included people who worked for the local television station in the town of Prince Albert in northern Saskatchewan. They were impressed with Joni's looks, her voice and her poise, and booked her for her first television appearance – a one-off late night show – to replace the regular programme, on a favourite local pastime, moose-hunting: 'So I played my six-song repertoire with a baritone ukelele on my own half-hour TV special. People recognised me on the street the next day. So I was bitten by the bug.'

Her childhood friend, Anne Bayin, recalls the excitement that accompanied the prospect of seeing Joni on television:

> I'll never forget my mother's reaction . . . by this time, my Mum was conducting choirs and composing music as well as doing her theatre work. She knew her music. I was away at university, but home for the holidays. When we got wind that [Joni] was to sing on local TV that night we were glued to the set. Suddenly there she was, on the flickering screen in our living room, looking like a movie star. She sat on a stool and sang several songs in a lovely, lilting soprano, accompanying herself on a baritone ukelele. We were blown away. 'Well,' said my mother, astonished. 'Well.' We waited for it. 'She's *good*,' she pronounced. 'Joan can *sing*.'

The two teenagers would still see each other regularly before Joni left Saskatoon for art school in Calgary in 1963. Anne travelled from North Battleford by bus to spend weekends at Joni's parents' house, where the girls would swap clothes, drool over teen screen idols, and talk about their futures. They'd hang out with friends at favourite cafés. Bayin remembers a confident Joni, who 'not only had perfect hair but the answers to life's questions'. When she mused to Joni, 'Why did we get such square parents?', Joni responded, laughing, 'We needed something to rebel against!' The notion of parental disapproval and of rebellion would resound painfully in the year following Joni's departure from Saskatoon. But for now, Calgary held the promise of a life away from the familiar certainties, with a brave new world of art and music just waiting to be experienced.

2 Tears and fears and feeling proud . . .

Every fucking art student that plays out of tune
gets a record deal.
(Willy de Ville)

I F YOU CAN REMEMBER the 60s, the baby-boomers smirk, you weren't there. There may have been music in the cafés at night and revolution in the air, but there was also bigotry, prejudice and intolerance. If you *can* remember the 60s, it's also likely that you'll remember the divisions that seared race, gender and class, the pre-war attitudes that lingered in the postwar world. The sexual revolution revolved around new laws – spoken and unspoken – about old behaviours. The Generation Gap resembled less a gap than a gaping chasm, as young people rejected the old guard and their rules, without quite being able to dismiss entirely the uncertainty, insecurity and fear that often came as part of that unprecedented thrill of freedom. Young hearts may have run free, as the disco divas would bleat later, but their bodies often betrayed them.

At art school in Calgary, Joni, then twenty, became involved with fellow student Brad MacMath. She was not the first young woman to lose her virginity and jeopardise her future in quick succession. She became pregnant early in their relationship, keeping the news from her family. It's hard to imagine in these more tolerant times, when the permutations of family life and parenting are many and varied and largely accepted by society as a whole, that having a child outside of marriage was once considered shameful. Joni recalled ruefully many years later, 'To be pregnant and unmarried in 1964 was like you killed somebody.'

While at art school she sought out Calgary's coffee-house venues, but at the newly opened Depression she won few admirers at first among her fellow folk singers. One, Will Millar, who

later joined the Irish Rovers, recalled in Nicholas Jennings'
superb chronicle of the times *Before the Goldrush,* 'Joni came with
her uke and tormented us with a shrill "Sloop John B" and "I With
I Wath an Apple on a Twee".' But the coffee-house owner, John
Uren, was prepared to give her a chance:

> She looked just tremendous with all that blonde hair. I
> brought Peter Elbling in from Toronto to open the
> place. And he listened to Joni and said she should sing.
> She played the Depression for three and a half months.
> And she met a lot of people . . . it was a good scene in
> those days. And Joni was part of it. She did more for
> the uke than Tiny Tim.

She was able to earn $15 a weekend singing at the Depression,
which soon became one of the best-known coffee houses in the
city, and it helped provide a springboard for her to venture further
out on to the folk club circuit, to the Yardbird Suite in Edmonton
and the Bunkhouse in Vancouver. She also played in Winnipeg
where she recalls, good-naturedly, an audience once walked out
in mid-performance to watch a violent thunderstorm pass over-
head: 'The plains . . . the only place where I've been upstaged by
the rain. But I understand. When you are of the prairies, you know
that there's something very natural about that.'
    Joni and Brad left Calgary together in the early summer of
1964 at the end of the academic year. They bought one-way
train tickets to Toronto. Even the train journey itself was to
prove inspirational; she wrote her first song, 'Day After Day',
en route. The main impetus for the trip was the Mariposa folk
festival, the largest event of its kind in Canada. For Joni, the
biggest attraction at Mariposa was Buffy Sainte-Marie, whose
debut album *It's My Way* had just been released on the
Vanguard label. Sainte-Marie, a Cree Indian, was born on the
Piapot Indian Reserve in the Qu'appelle Valley, near Regina,
the capital of Saskatchewan. She'd been adopted as a baby and
grown up in the United States, living in Maine and
Massachusetts. Her first big hit was to be 'Universal Soldier',
included on the debut album and later to become an international hit for British folkie Donovan. She would also later
record Joni's own 'Song to a Seagull' and 'The Circle Game'.

The small town of Orillia, Gordon Lightfoot's home town 35 miles northwest of Toronto, hosted the festival. It was a gentler Canadian equivalent of Newport *et al*, but the summer of 64 brought some uncharacteristic tensions to Orillia. The towns-people were nervous. They had unhappy memories of the previous year's event – a weekend described by the local police chief as the worst forty-eight hours in the town's history: too many people, too much traffic, too few facilities to cope with the crowds, and some boisterous behaviour from the folkies and the long-hairs who'd descended on the normally sedate area. The town council opposed the previously agreed use of a local farm as the venue for the festival, and took its fight to the courts. A day before the festival was due to open, the court upheld the council's opposition. With their plans in ruins, the festival organisers managed to negotiate the use of the Maple Leaf baseball stadium back in Toronto as an alternative venue and set about dismantling the equipment and packing up for the trip back to the city. One of the festival organisers recalls Joni as being among those who helped load up the trucks.

Joni and Brad had arrived in Toronto penniless, and stayed in a hippie flop-house – chaotic, unsanitary and noisy – in the Annex neighbourhood of the city. Joni began working as a sales assistant in the women's wear department of the Simpson-Sear's department store. In the evenings she haunted the coffee-house circuit in the Yorkville area of Toronto, auditioning for performance spots. Toronto was at the heart of Canada's fledgling music scene, with numerous coffee houses and clubs, but most of the venue owners would only allow members of the musicians' union to perform. Joni simply couldn't afford the union membership fees of about $150 and, until she was able to save enough money to pay up, she performed in the clubs that didn't hold as steadfastly to pro-union principles.

One of the best-known of these was the Penny Farthing, the name chosen by its lateral-thinking owners John and Marilyn McHugh, because it was in a sprawling Victorian era building. And the penny-farthing was a bicycle invented during the Victorian era by the British engineer James Starley. It was no wonder that some confused souls sent mail to the building addressed to Miss Penny Farthing. The venue's reputation was further enhanced when the McHughs installed a swimming pool

38   SHADOWS AND LIGHT

for the use of their customers, and encouraged the waitresses to adopt a summer uniform of bikinis. For those patrons who went for the music rather than the waitresses, the venue's eclectic booking policy meant that most nights you could hear any combination of great blues, jazz or folk music. The venue spread over two performance spaces – upstairs for the more established acts, often American, and downstairs for the newcomers, most of them Canadian. Joni has described this as a period when, culturally, 'Canada had a tendency to eat its young. They would hire Americans, even though they were contemptuous of them, because they were exotic and imported But they didn't have much stock in the locals.' Nicholas Jennings, one of Canada's most prominent music writers, agrees:

What has plagued Canadian culture and Canadian music has been the residual effects of Canada's own colonial past and the fact that Canada is a former colony of Britain and at the same time living in the shadow of a giant like the United States. There has always been a kind of inferiority complex when it comes to culture. So when it comes to music it means that radio programmers and record company people have tended to not believe in Canadian talent the way they should, because there's no question that we've had tremendous musical talent right back to the 1950s and especially the 60s, which was really a Golden Age in Canadian music. There just wasn't the acceptance given at the club level, in the coffee houses, and there certainly wasn't in the music industry, such as it was in the 60s. There was always a feeling of 'well if it's Canadian, it can't really be that good'. It would have to play second fiddle to an American or British musician. It's the same thing that so many Canadian artists have felt, up until recently; it's very hard to get accepted here. Often what artists have had to do is leave and gain acceptance abroad and then come home. Joni left Canada at a time when there was no music industry to speak of . . . there weren't the managers or the promoters for an artist to hook up with and those that were around weren't very experienced.

Joni would soon exhaust the musical possibilities available in Toronto, but before then, living in hippie dives and subsisting on welfare cheques had quickly soured the taste of sweet freedom for MacMath. He left Toronto and later travelled to California. At the beginning of 1965, Joni moved out of the rooming-house and with her friend Vicky Taylor – a folk singer who had also been performing at the Penny Farthing – rented an apartment on Bloor Street, above the Lickin' Chicken restaurant, a few blocks from Yorkville. On 19 February, Joni gave birth to a baby girl, whom she named Kelly Dale Anderson. She had only been able to afford the cheapest medical facilities available, and years later recalled that the nursing staff had a policy of tightly binding the breasts of the unmarried mothers to suppress the milk flow. Living in poverty and without the support of family and friends, who knew nothing of the pregnancy, the fledgling family faced a bleak future. Taylor recalls the heartbreaking difficulty of Joni's decision to place Kelly with foster parents and eventually allow her to be adopted: 'It was particularly hard for her. I think that's something that has haunted her all through her life.'

For Joni, there seemed no way that she could afford to give Kelly the kind of life the child deserved. She had no job, no prospects and no one to turn to for help. Having any kind of success at a musical career was not even a remote dream at that stage – there simply was no musical career. A smattering of coffee-house gigs hardly presaged fame and fortune, and the singer-songwriter genre was only just becoming established around a coterie of male performers, with Laura Nyro and Buffy Sainte-Marie the only women gaining credibility for their writing. All of that was a world away from her life in Toronto. Joni returned to work in the clubs and coffee houses, earning a pittance but trying to save enough money to provide her and her daughter with a stable home. She and Vicky Taylor performed briefly together as a duo, Day & Night, singing traditional folk songs. Taylor says that it was around this time that Joni began to explore songwriting ideas:

> Of course, rooming together we sang together a lot so we put together some songs. But we were obviously going in different directions. I remember her getting up in the night all the time to work on her music. I said to her, 'You're lucky to be so talented,' and she said, 'No, it's awful! If I

have a melody going round in my head I can't sleep until I try to work it out'. I think it was therapeutic for her.

Taylor says that even in those early days, 'Anyone who knew her at that point could see that she was destined for greatness, there was just something about her.'

One night that June, after Joni had arrived for her gig in the Penny Farthing's downstairs room, a friend remarked, 'That song you've been trying to learn, there's an American upstairs and he's singing it!' The song in question was a Bob Dylan tune, 'Mr Tambourine Man'. The American in question was Charles 'Chuck' Mitchell, a 29-year-old singer from Detroit – the Michigan city known as 'Motortown', at the heart of the US vehicle-manufacturing industry, the city which had been dominated by Ford, Chrysler and General Motors, and which gave its name to one of the most recognisable sounds in popular music, Motown.

Chuck's repertoire centred around a mixture of new and traditional folk songs and Bertolt Brecht and Kurt Weill compositions. He was in Toronto for solo gigs and occasional duo performances with guitarist Loring Janes. Janes, who also taught classical guitar, was impressed with Joni's playing technique and when they saw her on stage he exclaimed, 'Look at that hand!' Chuck Mitchell replied, 'Look at those legs!' Compliments aside, Joni later admonished Chuck Mitchell for the changes he'd made by rewriting and reinterpreting the Dylan song. Their first meeting led rapidly into a relationship. They heard each other sing, they spent hours strolling through one of Toronto's most beautiful open spaces, High Park, feeding the ducks, sitting by the lake and talking, talking, talking. Thirty-six hours after they met, Chuck Mitchell proposed. Vicky Taylor recalls the speed of the courtship:

They met and fell in love instantly. It was very romantic. He finished his week [club residency] and went back to Detroit, and came back a week or two later. Then Joni came in and told me that she was going to get married and move to Detroit. Of course nobody has much wisdom when they're 21 years old! I just wished her well.

Chuck had encouraged Joni to go back to Detroit with him, reassuring her that he'd help her to find work in the clubs and coffee houses, a scene he knew well. She told him about the dilemma between persisting with the search for work that paid enough to enable her to keep her daughter, Kelly, and giving up the child for adoption before she languished too long in foster care, her future unresolved. Chuck Mitchell, older, more worldly-wise, well-educated and apparently dependable, held out the promise of a secure life and a fresh start, a possible mother and child reunion. Vicky Taylor remembers Chuck as 'a very nice man, but maybe a little too nice for Joni's taste, too dependable!' Joni would say years later: 'He kind of latched onto me at this very vulnerable time when I had no money, no work and a child in a foster home, which was tearing me up.'

Just weeks after meeting, in June 1965, they were married in a service held in the garden of Chuck Mitchell's parents' home in Rochester, Michigan. Chuck and Joni received $500 as a wedding gift; it was a small fortune to the struggling couple. Chuck Mitchell was late for his own wedding because he visited a car dealership and put the money down on a Porsche Speedster. The previous night, Joni's future mother-in-law had counselled her about marrying in haste and repenting at leisure. Her home-grown homily: 'The first waffle should be used to warm up the pan and then thrown out!' Eighteen months later, Chuck Mitchell, in a laconic comment to a radio journalist, said that Joni's acceptance of his marriage proposal 'shocked me some-thing awful!'

There had been an understanding that the baby would come to live with them after the couple married, and while the wedding was a rapid affair, with equal rapidity it became clear that Chuck had such serious misgivings about – as he saw it – having to bring up another man's child that they could not be resolved. The baby Kelly would not be coming home to her mother. The decision about the baby's future could not be delayed any longer; the older she got, the more difficult it could be to find a suitable per-manent home and settle her happily. Joni reluctantly signed the adoption papers, relinquishing the child for good. The painful paradox is that it can be a far greater act of love to give up your child than to keep her. The slow, agonising haemorrhage of loss began and it would not be staunched for more than thirty years.

The couple, attractive and talented, were embraced within the Detroit music scene, and featured in the local papers. With acute, albeit accidental perception, the *Detroit News* remarked in early February 1966 that 'In this era of computers serving as match-makers, it seems unlikely that Chuck and Joni Mitchell would have been paired off as matrimonial partners. But seven months after their marriage, they seemed to have beaten the machines.' With considerable understatement given the situation with the baby Kelly, the writer A.L. McClain commented blithely that 'their wedding required more sacrifice than the average couple's' and went on to detail the many differences in the backgrounds of the couple, with a particularly telling comment from Chuck Mitchell: 'We are both strong-minded people, and we both had our own ways of doing a number. There were some hectic times until we blended our styles.' Meanwhile, Joni, the writer notes admiringly, is a 'girl who bears a striking resemblance to Mia Farrow, of TV's *Peyton Place*', a reference to the soap opera drama that was hugely popular at the time. The article gives Chuck the last word: 'Joni and I have developed our act. We are not just folk-singers now. We do comedy, sing some ragtime and do folk-rock. We're ready for the big clubs now.' But the last line is the writer's: 'Joni nodded her approval, as any dutiful wife would do.'

A month later, in gushing 'Chuck and Joni invite you into their beautiful home' tones that predated the celeb-fest publicity-prose of *Hello* magazine by many years, a writer for the same paper vis-ited the couple's large inner-city apartment and detailed their decorating tips for creating the perfect artists' Bohemian retreat. Chuck Mitchell had moved into the apartment, in a sprawling old-style building called the Verona – nicknamed the Castle for its imposing facade – three years earlier. That part of the inner city had been earmarked for redevelopment but its low rents made it a favourite haunt for students, artists and musicians. The apartment – described variously in the article as 'mod', 'camp' and 'kookie' – was five floors above the corner of Cass and Ferry, in the area known locally as the Cass Corridor, near the Wayne State University campus.

Joni's creative influence on their home was obvious; the gloomy bachelor pad was being transformed into a bright airy space full of colour and light, in shades of red, gold and green. In the early hours of the morning the couple would often leave a club after their shows and wander the city, window-shopping for antiques and furniture. The apartment was furnished with discoveries from local antique shops and estate sales – a black-bear rug bought for five dollars, a fifteen-dollar couch, a trunk found dumped in an alley. Another trunk had belonged to Chuck Mitchell's grandfather during his student days; stained-glass windows, a gift to Joni, were set aside to be installed as a bathroom shower screen; a whisky advertisement, hanging in a red frame, was one of Joni's favourite belongings. She explained that she intended it as a 'protest at the rising tide of conformity'. The comment, the writer Jo Ann Mercer noted, brought 'a sparkle of rebellion in [Joni's] large blue eyes'. Chuck Mitchell mused that 'maybe we'll get rich and buy the building'. But that was not to be.

The building's lift had last seen service in 1942 but the rent was a bargain $70 a month. The couple kept open house for musician friends who were in town to play at clubs like the Chess Mate, among them Tom Rush, David Blue and Eric Andersen. Tom Rush recalls the couple's meticulous work on restoring the apartment's original features, like the oak woodwork, but has painful memories of how arduous the ascent to that fifth-floor apartment could be:

> I had had a collapsed lung while I was an undergraduate at Harvard; they fixed it up the quick and easy way but they said it could happen again. I was playing at the Chess Mate and closing every night with a song called 'Wasn't That a Mighty Storm' which really requires a lot of lung power, and it was getting more and more difficult. Climbing up those five flights every night, carrying guitars, was also getting more difficult. I was having chest pains that were getting worse by the day and I went to a doctor and he gave me some antacids and sent me home and I went to another doctor who did something equally ineffectual. Finally, at the end of the first week, I went to the hospital. Joni filled in for me at the Chess Mate for the second week; I remember [an audience member] telling me that they actually complained about that! They were very chagrined in retrospect that they had complained that they had had to listen to Joni instead of the person they had come to hear.

It was at the Chess Mate that Joni had first met Rush, who had regular headlining residencies there. Joni had played there often and came down one night when Rush was appearing, and asked the owner whether she could perform a set that evening, so that Rush could hear her songs. He agreed. Tom Rush picks up the story:

> She knocked my socks off! She did 'Urge for Going' that night and I was immediately smitten with that particular tune. I got her to put some songs on tape for me . . . subsequently she sent me another tape, with some really nice tunes on it. At the end [of the tape] she had put on a song, and said 'I've only just finished this song and it really sucks and you're going to hate it and I don't know why I'm putting it on!' And it was 'The Circle Game'.
>
> My colleagues and I at that time were mainly doing traditional folk tunes, which in my book is the only kind of folk tune there is, the ones handed down by ear. But I was getting restless because I hadn't found any new traditional tunes that really got me excited for a while, and here was Joni with these songs that had a folk sensibility to them yet were fresh and had a literate veneer to them. They were very exciting, they had a voice that had universal appeal. 'Urge for Going': as long as winter comes, that will be a relevant song. 'The Circle Game': as long as kids grow up that tune will be relevant.

If Joni's songwriting had begun in earnest in the weeks following her daughter's birth in early 1965, it was to intensify after she heard Bob Dylan's single 'Positively Fourth Street' later that year. For her, it represented an implosion of the boundaries of both poetry and song; lines like 'You've got a lot of nerve, to say you are my friend' represented a new way into self-expression:

> I wrote poetry, and I always wanted to make music. But I never put the two things together. Just a simple thing like being a singer-songwriter – that was a new idea. It used to take three people to do that job. And when I heard 'Positively Fourth Street' I realised that

this was a whole new ballgame; now you could make your songs literature. The potential for the song had never occurred to me ... but it occurred to Dylan. At first I thought he was a copycat of Woody Guthrie. For a while his originality didn't come out. But when it hit, boy, oh boy, I said, 'Oh, God, look at this.' And I began to write. So Dylan sparked me.

Within eighteen months she would be living only a dozen blocks from the street in Manhattan that had given the song its name.

With a clutch of her new songs, Joni had already returned for a second year to the Mariposa Folk Festival – this time as one of the performers and not among the crowd as she had been the previous year. Billed as Joni Anderson, she joined Ian and Sylvia, Phil Ochs, Gordon Lightfoot and Son House at the three-day festival. Mindful of the difficulties that had dogged attempts to hold the festival in Orillia a year earlier, the organisers decided to stage the event at Innis Lake, northwest of Toronto. The venue was perfect; the weather was appalling. Thunderstorms pounded the site and, at one point, Phil Ochs took the stage during a power cut, singing through a megaphone and with car headlights as stage lighting. The crowd reacted well to Joni, although there were some grumbles about her small but perfectly formed repertoire of songs.

One of the organisers, Estelle Klein, recalled that some people complained: 'They said, "She's really nice, but she's singing the same thing over and over again." So when I invited her back for the next year, I said, "Joni, I really like what you do, but could you expand your repertoire a little?"'

Mitchell was as good as her word – on the journey back to Toronto from Innis Lake, new lyrics were already forming for the song that would soon impress Tom Rush so much that he'd record it himself, 'Urge for Going'. Three years later she would describe it as the only protest song she had written: 'Those who like your songs agree with you. Those who don't won't listen. I've written only one protest song ... "Urge for Going", which was a protest against winter. And it certainly isn't going to stop winter.' Although the song would later be interpreted as a comment on her marriage to Chuck Mitchell, early drafts – including the words 'I've got the urge for going, but there's no place left to go'

– were also about the difficulties encountered by acoustic folk musicians looking for venues in which to play, as the tide turned against folk and even Dylan had seemed to abandon his acoustic folk roots.

Two months earlier, at the Newport Folk Festival, with musical backing from The Paul Butterfield Blues Band, Dylan had caused mayhem when he had 'gone electric'; to folk purists, he had gone insane. Earlier that year, his new album *Bringing It All Back Home* had featured one side each of electric, rock-oriented material and acoustic songs; the first single, 'Subterranean Homesick Blues', had been hugely successful. Dylan himself was to say in 1989: 'Folk music . . . got swept away by fashionable things . . . British invasions and pop art and medium-is-the-message type things. But it didn't die. All modern music is based on those forms and structural verses.'

Just as the boundaries between musical styles became blurred, Joni's songs were reaching a wider audience than the folkie followers who came to see her at the Chess Mate. The club also hosted after-hours jazz sessions – from 2 am to 6 am – and Joni got to know the musicians:

> I had to have my lead sheets done, so the jazzers did my lead sheets for me for a small fee, and they began to play my music in the sets. So the black audiences who would come for jazz would come a little earlier to see this apparition, this white chick playing kazoo! But in the set that would follow, the jazz musicians would play my music as if it were standard. These first songs that I wrote never even made it on a record; they sounded more like 1940s and 50s pop, because that was what I heard for the most part as a kid growing up . . .

Joni had bought her first six-string guitar in 1964 and played in standard tunings until she began to write her own songs. Just as, at seven years old, sitting through those literally painful piano lessons, she hadn't been able to find a way to express what she wanted to say through conventional methods, and as a teenager she hadn't been able to master the Cotten-picking style because of the post-polio lack of dexterity in her left hand, she devised her own tunings to translate what she heard in her head to her fingertips. She took blues tunings, Tom Rush's favoured open G, D and C, Eric Andersen's D modal, and began to explore.

With Detroit as their base, Joni and Chuck had regular bookings at the city's other clubs and coffee-houses like the Living End, the Poison Apple and the Cellar. They travelled in the Midwest, to the East Coast and back to Canada. In Toronto, Joni appeared at the Seven of Clubs and finally conquered the well-known Riverboat venue, run by Bernie Fiedler and Bernie Finkelstein, whose eclectic booking policy attracted blues and folk artists like Sonny Terry and Brownie McGhee, Odetta, Carolyn Hester, Phil Ochs, Tom Rush, Gordon Lightfoot and Eric Andersen. There is a much-retold anecdote – denied by Fiedler but affirmed by Mitchell herself – that when Joni first auditioned, he offered her a job in the Riverboat's kitchen rather than on the stage. A critic writing in *Variety* noted Joni's performance at the Riverboat in February 1967, describing her as a 'sensitive, original folk composer' before abandoning all pretence of musical deconstruction and salivating that Mitchell was 'an eyeful in a tight-fitting mini silver lamé dress, and sporting flaxen hair that falls below her shoulders'. He recovered sufficiently to highlight several of the songs she performed including 'The Daisy Summer', 'The Wizard of Is', 'Just Like Me', 'Blue on Blue' and 'Night In The City', with the recommendation that the songs 'rate recording by folk singers on the lookout for new material. They are quiet songs, sometimes forlorn and always evocative.'

In November 1966 Joni and Chuck had been in Philadelphia – Joni's first visit to the city – where they performed separately at the popular Second Fret club. One of the few times they would get together on stage would be to perform 'The Circle Game' during Joni's set. To promote the shows, they gave interviews to local radio journalists. One visited them in the dressing room at the club, and asked about their courtship and marriage. Chuck Mitchell appeared somewhat underwhelmed by romance, saying matter-of-factly: 'We've been married a year and a half and we're reasonably happy.' In truth, by this time the marriage was doomed, and it was obvious that despite the absence of a record deal, large-scale gigs, promotion or financial backing, Joni's solo career and her songwriting were becoming far more successful than Chuck Mitchell's. As her acclaim and earning power grew,

there was increasing friction between them. Even the radio journalist referred to Joni as 'the songwriter of the family', when
asking how she decided what to write about. She replied:

> I really don't decide. I just suddenly get an idea and
> write . . . In the beginning I wrote lyrics first and music
> afterwards, now most of the things I do come melody
> first and then I add the words. The song I'm working on
> right now is called 'Love is Like a Big Brass Band' and
> that's coming with the words first which is something
> that hasn't happened for a long time.

The obscure song was not destined to become a staple of the
Mitchell repertoire.

Two days later, Chuck and Joni were guests on the Folklore
radio show hosted by Gene Shay, on the local Philadelphia radio
station WHAT-FM (the interviews would be broadcast by Shay
again after he moved to another Philadelphia station, WMMR,
and recorded by bootleggers who mistakenly labelled them as
WMMR originals). They had come to the studio after performing at the Second Fret and Joni was wearing the short silver
lamé dress and matching high-heeled shoes that had so
enthralled the music critics in Toronto. Shay recalls that she
looked stunning, a world away from other singers associated
with folk music: 'Folkies in those days were wearing peasant
dresses and long flowing robes or jeans and dungarees. She was
very elegant.' He had already heard Joni's song 'The Circle
Game' through his good friend Tom Rush, who would soon
record it. Chuck and Joni performed the song on Shay's show,
with Chuck joining her on the chorus, and Joni sounding startlingly resonant of Joan Baez's vibrato – a recurring comparison
of vocal styles but one that would diminish rapidly. Joni had
explained in the previous radio interview why she'd felt the
need to distance herself from such comparisons:

> In the beginning I had a soprano voice so everyone
> compared me to Baez. I'd written a couple of songs but
> I just decided that the only way that I was going to be
> able to differentiate myself from any other of the
> singers was to have original material. Every time I'd

find a song, I'd find out afterwards that Judy Collins or
Joan Baez or somebody had recorded it. So with my
new material, I thought I was fairly safe and then I discovered some lower register [vocal] tones that I didn't
know I could use before.

With her own writing, liberated from standard melodies, tunings and phrasings, she had literally and figuratively found her
own voice. Gene Shay says Mitchell brought a distinctive style
to everything she did; it marked her out as being far above the
competition:

> [She had] . . . great melodies, a terrific wordsmith, this
> great use of language and a certain mystique and
> charismatic quality. I fell in love with her! It was easy
> to fall in love with her, her work, and this great look . . .
> she was always an innovator. She'd always carry a
> sketchbook and [coloured] pens and she'd work on trac-
> ing paper, so she'd make these great drawings and if
> you took the paper and held it up against a window it
> almost looked like stained glass because they were
> translucent.

By the end of 1966, Joni's days as a folkie interpreter were over
and her songwriting was establishing her as a vibrant new talent
on a wider scene. Tom Rush, Buffy Sainte-Marie, Ian and Sylvia
and American folk and blues singer and guitarist Dave van Ronk
were all performing her songs during their own gigs, which in
turn created a buzz among their audiences about this hot new
writer. The Canadian country music star George Hamilton IV,
who was well established in the Nashville country music scene,
had superb instincts about good writing, especially from the pens
of other Canadians like Mitchell and Gordon Lightfoot. He recognised the need to refresh the musical gene pool lest the torch 'n'
twang became too incestuous, and he recorded Mitchell's 'Urge
for Going':

> I think that Tom Rush and myself were the first peo-
> ple to record Joni Mitchell's songs ... Tom Rush
> recorded 'Urge for Going' ... But I was probably the

first country singer to do it. I first heard 'Urge for Going' on WBC in Boston. The DJ said 'Here's a tape we recorded in a coffee house here in Boston. A fellow named Tom Rush is singing a song by a new young writer called Joni Mitchell.' Gordon Lightfoot put me in touch with Joni. She sent me a demo tape, and we recorded it here in Nashville. It was a little radical in country music to do something that metaphorical.

Country music was obviously ready for some long overdue radicalism; Hamilton's faith in Mitchell's song was repaid with a Top Ten country hit.

Listening to that same Boston radio show that night in April 1966 was a fourteen-year-old boy from Philadelphia; a devoted guitarist even at that tender age, Joel Bernstein remembers vividly the first time he heard a song written by Joni Mitchell. He shared Hamilton's reaction to this new song and was desperate to hear more about Mitchell. He didn't have to wait more than a few months; unavoidably detained in his room doing his homework, Bernstein couldn't get to the Second Fret to hear Chuck and Joni's sets in November, but he was listening to his radio later that night when they were interviewed on Gene Shay's show and sang 'The Circle Game' together. Shay invited questions from the listeners. Young Bernstein phoned in to ask how to get lead sheets for her songs and Joni advised that he should write to her Detroit-based publishing company, Gandalf. He recalls:

I just thought it was fantastic music. I'd played guitar since I was five or six so by the time I was 14 I was fairly good for a 14-year-old, but I wasn't familiar with the world of open tunings let alone non-standard tunings ... I had recorded parts of the show on a dictaphone and stayed up all night trying to figure out how she was playing 'The Circle Game'.

It was to be a gentle start to an enduring working relationship and friendship that has seen Bernstein variously as one of Joni Mitchell's favourite photographers, her long-time guitar technician and, to this day, her musical and photographic archivist. He would take his first photographs of Mitchell at the Second Fret in March the following year.

Within months, Ian and Sylvia had released their version of 'The Circle Game' on their *So Much for Dreaming* album and Buffy Sainte-Marie had covered 'Song to a Seagull' and 'The Circle Game' on her *Fire and Fleet and Candlelight* album. Tom Rush was a great early champion of Mitchell's songwriting:

> I remember trying to get other people interested in her songs, including Judy Collins. I couldn't 'sell' her tunes to Judy at first. Later of course she had her biggest hit with 'Both Sides, Now'. The first I knew of the tune was when I heard [Judy singing] it on the radio. I remember being a bit miffed that Joni hadn't sent it to me first . . . some time later, she told me 'when I wrote that tune I thought, this will be perfect for Tom', but she didn't act on the impulse!

Dave van Ronk also covered 'Both Sides, Now' (changing the title to 'Clouds') and 'Urge for Going', but his enthusiasm for Mitchell's music had been late in coming. Appearing with Mitchell on a Canadian television programme, *Let's Sing Out*, he had been more enthusiastic about recommending an alternative career. Mitchell recalled:

> Van Ronk was saying things like, 'Joni, you've got groovy taste in clothes, why don't you become a fashion model?' . . . David did like 'Urge for Going' and he asked me for it, I remember. I wondered what ulterior motive he had in mind after saying all those dreadful things to me. I thought, 'He must just want to laugh at it or something.' I was that insecure about my writing.

She recalled getting even less support from the other star of the show, US folkie Patrick Sky, who was openly dismissive of her songs.

Given the lucrative nature of music publishing, especially when others are covering your songs, Chuck Mitchell had had one very good idea: at his urging, Joni had set up her own music publishing enterprise. A few early songs were registered under Gandalf, its name inspired by the wizard character in the fictional world of Middle Earth created by the British writer and academic J.R.R. Tolkien in his books *The Hobbit* and the trilogy *The Lord of the Rings*. These fantasy novels – peopled with hobbits, dwarves and strange magical creatures – achieved both cult status and mainstream popularity in the 1960s. Joni's first major publishing company was Siquomb – an acronym for She Is Queen Undisputably Of Mind Beauty, its title taken from a mythological story she had been writing as a possible children's book, and the subject of many of her sketches. It told the fanciful story of the land of Fanta ruled by the Queen, Siquomb, and her husband, Hwiefob (He Who Is Especially Fond Of Birds) and their subjects – tiny women known as the Posall (Perhaps Our Souls Are Little Ladies) and miniature men, the Mosalm (Maybe Our Souls Are Little Men).

But away from the fantasy-land fairy stories, life was deteriorating for the real woman and man at the heart of the tale. The gulf between them widened as Chuck, who had a degree in literature, became openly dismissive of Joni's comparative lack of education and intellectual sophistication and her attempts at writing. Their temperaments were as unsuited on-stage as off it, but Chuck insisted that the couple continue performing as a duo, singing a mix of their own songs and cover versions. The Chuck and Joni Show – they were billed by the Chess Mate as 'Detroit's Favourite Folk Singers' – was a more profitable enterprise than Chuck Mitchell's solo efforts. But nevertheless, as Joni's confidence and repertoire grew, their solo stints eventually became increasingly frequent. Tom Rush recalls that the couple's musical styles were noticeably different:

> Chuck's [music] was a little too cheerful for me, too upbeat and wholesome. Joni's was more quirky, both melodically and lyrically, so I don't think her voice would have fitted into that duo very well unless Chuck went through a really major identity change. I think basically that's what was happening to Joni, she was finding her voice, finding her identity.

In March 1967 Mitchell returned to Philadelphia for her second visit. By now she'd become good friends with Joy Schreiber, who combined managing the Second Fret with an interest in mysticism. Mitchell would stay with Schreiber when she was in Philadelphia; and it was in Schreiber's apartment that she had written one of her best-known songs, 'Both Sides, Now'. Schreiber would often read Joni's Tarot cards and they'd go shopping for the antique dresses that Joni loved. Gene Shay recalls Mitchell immersing herself in the then-fashionable trappings of mysticism, Tolkien, and the legends of King Arthur, his queen, Guinevere, the Knights of the Round Table and the wizard, Merlin: 'She was enchanting. She looked like some fairy goddess.' The Second Fret put up promotional posters describing her as The Enchanted Lady.

While in Philadelphia, Mitchell appeared again on Shay's radio show. During their interview, she performed a song she said she had only written three days earlier, but was so taken with it that she had already included it in her sets at the Second Fret, sometimes singing the song two or three times each night. The song, which she introduced as 'From Both Sides, Now', had been inspired by the hapless anti-hero of a book she was still reading at the time, Saul Bellow's *Henderson the Rain King*. One passage of the book had resonated with her: in it, Eugene Henderson peers down from an aircraft window somewhere high above the Egyptian countryside and reflects on what he sees below him:

> I dreamed down at the clouds, and thought that when I was a kid I had dreamed up at them, and having dreamed at the clouds from both sides as no other generation of men has done, one should be able to accept his death very easily. However, we made safe landings every time ... I kept thinking, 'Bountiful life! Oh, how bountiful life is!'

(The book would also inspire a musician who was not even born when Bellow wrote it: after reading *Henderson the Rain King*, Adam Duritz of Counting Crows wrote his song 'Rain King', featured on the Crows' debut album *August and Everything After*.) At one performance that week, she gently apologised for singing her two current favourite songs – 'Both Sides, Now' and 'The Circle Game' – in her first and third sets, asking first, 'How many people were here for the first show? Anybody?' It was usual for her to do three sets in an evening at the Second Fret. In between sets, the club showed underground films by film-makers like Kenneth Anger. Joel Bernstein recalls that Joni would sit out front with everyone else, darning her stockings and watching the short films.

Also on Shay's radio programme, she gave an affecting rare performance of the Neil Young song 'Sugar Mountain', which had inspired her own 'The Circle Game'. Young had written 'Sugar Mountain' as he approached his twenties, lamenting that he had to leave behind the things of youth. Mitchell would later point out that it also came to have more prosaic interpretations, after Young's twentieth birthday when he could no longer join his friends at their favourite teenybopper haunt in Winnipeg: 'His song was about being too old for the teen club and too young for the bar, so you had this terrible age of twenty when you were neither/nor.' Introducing 'The Circle Game' in concert for a BBC Radio broadcast in 1970, she said:

> That was about the same time that *Esquire* magazine was doing pictures of girls in trash bins, like once you were over 21, you'd had it. There was this strange philosophy going around at that time. I thought 'God, if we get to 21, and there's nothing after that, that's a pretty bleak future.' So I wrote a song for him and for myself, to give me some hope . . .

The title had other resonances in Canadian culture; the Canadian novelist and poet Margaret Atwood had published a volume of poetry in 1966 entitled *The Circle Game.*

Mitchell and Young had become friends after meeting at the 4D (Fourth Dimension) coffee house in Winnipeg in 1964; they shared a strong bond borne out of the similarities between them – their Canadian prairie roots, surviving the childhood polio that struck at their spine and legs, and the need to articulate their world through music. Mitchell would later say:

> I feel very kindred to Neil . . . we're caught between two cultures. We still salute the Queen up there, though Canada's becoming more independent . . . we grew up in the pre-TV era, and at that time radio was happening. There was more of an English influence

then, a lot of BBC humor. We went to J. Arthur Rank movies on the corner, Dr Seeley, that whole series. So we had an infusion of British comedy, which is a different sensibility than American humor.

Young wrote a song for her, 'Sweet Joni', which he would occasionally perform on stage in the early 1970s but which was never included on an official Neil Young recording and has only appeared on bootlegs:

> Sweet Joni from Saskatoon
> There's a ring for your fingers
> It looks like the sun
> But it feels like the moon
> Sweet Joni from Saskatoon
> Don't go, don't go too soon
> Who lives in an old hotel
> Near the ancient ruin
> Only time can tell
> Time can tell
> Go easy, the doorman said
> The floor is slippery
> So watch your head . . .

There has also been some speculation that Young's song 'Stupid Girl' on the 1975 album *Zuma* was about Mitchell, but there's no credible evidence to support this. It's one of those 'who's that song about' interpretations that began as fiction but came to be accepted as fact. As Johnny Rogan wrote in his biography *Neil Young: Zero to Sixty*:

> The song's subject was widely assumed to be Joni Mitchell, although this was most likely wishful thinking on the part of an over-imaginative critic. Beneath the insulting refrain lay the story of a girl's inability to vanquish the past and start afresh.

By early 1967, the Mitchell marriage was over, after less than two years. The end had come as suddenly as the beginning. Joni later recalled the night she left:

> I was in the middle of a poker game some place in
> Michigan late in the evening and I turned to a stranger
> basically, next to me and I said, 'I'm leaving my hus-
> band tonight. Will you help me?' We rented a U-haul
> truck. We drove back to Detroit . . . I separated what I
> considered was a fair split, fifty per cent of the furni-
> ture, and the stranger and I hauled it on our own backs
> down a fifth-floor walk-up in the middle of the night,
> and I moved out.

If she was to make anything of her musical career, the next
inevitable move was to a much bigger city, with greater opportunities. She chose the city that had moved the Swiss architect Le
Corbusier to write in 1944, 'A hundred times I have thought, New
York is a catastrophe, and fifty times: it is a beautiful catastrophe.' The American theatre director Joseph Papp – founder of
the New York Shakespeare Festival and the New York Public
Theatre – had said, 'Creative people get inspiration from their
immediate environment, and New York has the most immediate
environment in the world.' So, in April 1967, Mitchell moved
into a small apartment at 41 West 16th Street, in the Chelsea area
of Manhattan.

Just a short subway ride away was Greenwich Village –
Bohemia, the artists' haven and the centre of the coffee house
and folk club scene, where in the early 1960s struggling folk-
singers like Bob Dylan, Tim Hardin, Richie Havens and Jose
Feliciano had worked for little more than small change. A local
entrepreneur, Israel G. Young, had set up the Folklore Centre,
which played host to the early folkies, and later musicians like
Mitchell, Tim Buckley and Emmylou Harris.

Convinced that the folk era was on the wane, rapidly being
replaced by folk-rock, British pop and psychedelia, Mitchell
continued to tour energetically, thinking that at worst it would
simply allow her to build up some savings before returning to
modelling or designing women's clothes. Tom Rush invited
her along as a guest performer at his concerts. And she organised her own gigs along the eastern seaboard from Miami to
Boston, and back to Michigan, playing to a variety of audiences – clubs, coffee houses, military bases like Fort Bragg in
North Carolina:

As a hippie, I was playing Fort Bragg, I was playing to soldiers coming and going from the war and also in Charleston to the Navy. So I wasn't a normal hippie in that, singing 'Universal Soldier', I had sympathy for them. Some of them were just Southern boys who were going to kill a Commie for God and then they'd come back all broken up. My father was in the Air Force and I guess I was still romantic about being a comfort to the boys coming and going from the war, like Bob Hope. It seemed like a good thing to do. So while all of my friends were taking psychedelics and pretending to be crazy and avoiding the draft, one of my best audiences was Fort Bragg. The naval base was another thing because it was in Charleston and Southern women were really difficult to play to because they talked ... they didn't like their dates to pay any attention to me and they talked all through my set.

In June 1967 Mitchell was touring in Canada. She had a three-week residency in Ottawa at Le Hibou 'javary', a popular haunt that was to become the cultural heart of the city's coffee house and club circuit, under the management of Denis Faulkner and Harvey Glatt. The venue, then at Sussex Drive, is today a Hard Rock Café and the 1967 admission charge of one dollar 75 cents would barely buy a cup of coffee now. Back then it was money well spent for the *Variety* critic who described the guest act, Joni Mitchell, as 'a looker, 23, with extremely long golden hair, she has a remarkable vocal range plus fine quality, good guitar savvy and patter that's bright, pleasant and often bubbling with humor'. Songs that rated special mention included 'Song To A Daydreamer', which was introduced by Mitchell with an anecdote about overhearing teenagers talking, 'Chelsea Morning', described by the critic as 'quite upbeat', 'From Both Sides Now' (*sic*), 'Night Over the City' (*sic*), 'Play, Little David, Play' – inspired by David Rae, accompanist to Canadian folk duo Ian and Sylvia – 'The Circle Game' and an oddity entitled 'Dr Junk The Dentist Man', based on a person Mitchell had encountered during a visit to North Carolina. The critic acclaimed 'Dr Junk' as 'the first 6/8 she's ever tried writing and she's still working on it but it holds a lot of promise. So does she.' His instincts proved correct about the latter, unlike the former which has not shared its creator's resilience.

One of Mitchell's favourite venues at the time was a small coffee house called the Sipping Lizard in Flint, Michigan, an industrial city which during the 1930s was the scene of one of the most significant strikes in US labour history. Flint was also a university city, with a thriving Cultural Centre sponsored by the great and the good as well as many small clubs and coffee-houses. The regular music nights at the Sipping Lizard had started off as no more than a bunch of teenagers getting together to play folk music at a friend's house every weekend. Joni spoke fondly of it at the time:

> Soon they had about a hundred and fifty kids in their basement, and Jackie, the mother, had to start charging them admission because they were eating her out of house and home! So they moved the club into a pool-hall and it's marvellous, the enthusiasm. The thing that's great about it is the age breakdown because you get college professors and you get young kids and you get whole families. I had one little girl come up to me one night and she was part of a family that ranged from five years old; there was a five-year-old girl, a seven-year-old girl and a nine-year-old girl, and the mother and father. The nine-year-old came up to me and said, 'Would you play "The Urge for Going"?' And I looked at her and I said 'How do you know that song?' And she said, 'I'm learning it on the guitar.' The whole family are taking guitar lessons and the fellow who is teaching them guitar is a friend of mine, the son of the club-owner and he's teaching them how to play all my songs in the open tunings . . . So I have a following from 7 to 70 in Flint.

Mitchell's constant touring was giving her greater confidence in front of an audience but, listening to recordings of the shows from this time, it is hard to recognise the breathlessly giggly folkie girlie on the stage as the same woman who was writing songs with the perception, depth and maturity of 'Both Sides, Now', 'The Circle Game', 'Urge for Going' and her loving lament for her daughter, 'Little Green' (poignantly, when performing the song live, she'd often change the word 'Little' to 'Kelly', the name she'd given the child at birth). The cutesy hippie chick delivery of the rambling on-stage anecdotes about her travels, her impressions and the inspiration behind her songs seems almost set up to deny the intellectual energy of the work itself, the subtext being, 'I might be bright as hell but I can still be a cute non-threatening girl, you know!' The long anecdotes did have a practical purpose: they gave her time to retune her guitar to the intricate tunings she was already devising. Audiences were utterly charmed by her.

She'd often jokingly introduce an unrecorded song, 'Ballerina Valerie', as her Coca-Cola commercial: 'In this day and age of psychedelics, it's a psychedelic song that would make a natural Coca-Cola advertisement with few alterations.' Mitchell would sing the song, replete with drug references, adding lyrics to mimic a commercial:

> Down in the garden, under an oak she was drinking
> her Coke
> And she was looking at stardom,
> Everything's bright and she draws on the pipe, as the
> bowl grows redder
> Things go better, with Coca-Cola!

Mitchell had written the song after she'd seen an art-house film about an Australian dancer, Valli, a wild colonial girl who'd left Melbourne at seventeen to travel in Europe. The original flower child, Joni explained, Valli had embraced the Beatnik Bohemian life in Paris, dabbled in witchcraft, and moved to Italy with a man named Rudy. She went to England, appearing as a dancer in a concert by English folkie flower child Donovan, before retreating back to her Italian menagerie. (The song would appear later on bootlegs only, titled variously as 'Joni's Coke Commercial', 'Things Go Better', 'Ballerina Valerie' or 'Valli'.)

Her first trip to England, in autumn 1967, inspired another song to match her whimsy – a version of the nursery rhyme 'London Bridge is Falling Down', often introduced with an anecdote about visiting London and hearing that the bridge was for sale. She mused about how different the bridge would look if the

Beatles bought it and painted it in bright psychedelic colours just as they'd done with their Rolls Royce. She'd intersperse the nonsense verses with ad-libs:

> London Bridge is falling up
> Say the tea leaves in my cup, my fair lady-oh,
> London Bridge is up for sale,
> Booze heads put my friend in jail,
> Spent my bridge money on bail my fair lady-oh . . .
> If the bridge belonged to me I would serve you tarts and tea,
> Smiles that's all the tolls would be
> (No grouchy people would get across at all) my fair lady-oh,
> On the bridge there stands a car, painted with peculiar flowers,
> It's the Beatles', it's not ours . . . my fair lady-oh . . .

Mitchell had been invited to England by the wunderkind American producer and entrepreneur Joe Boyd, who had arrived in Britain in 1965 to run the UK division of Elektra Records. Still only in his early twenties, Boyd had come out of the New England folk and blues scene and had impeccable credentials; he'd helped to launch the Paul Butterfield Blues Band and had been production manager at the 1965 Newport Folk Festival where the PBBB had backed Dylan in his controversial 'electric' set. He left Elektra in late 1966 and when faced with the choice of going back to the US or staying in Britain, he opted to stay. He co-managed London's acclaimed underground club UFO, showcasing early gigs by Soft Machine and Pink Floyd (whose first single he produced in 1967). He set up his own management and production company, Witchseason, with a client list that would eventually include Fairport Convention and Nick Drake. Boyd booked Mitchell for a brief tour supporting his protégés, the Scottish folk duo the Incredible String Band, whom he managed, and for a few solo coffee house appearances. The ISB – Mike Heron and Robin Williamson – inspired a devoted following in British folk circles with their wistful mysticism and psychedelic folk. They were also gaining attention in the US after their appearance at the Newport Folk Festival that summer and Judy Collins's cover of their song 'First Girl I Loved'.

Joni enjoyed her brief stay and took in all of the tourist sights in London: 'I went around Piccadilly Circus in a red double-decker bus with no driver on the top', an echo of the line in the Wardell Gray/Annie Ross song 'Twisted' which Mitchell covered on *Court and Spark*: 'oh, they used to laugh at me when I refused to ride on those double-decker buses, all because there was no driver on the top'. She rode in the city's other trademark transport – black cabs – and figured out how much to tip the driver without insulting him. She went to Speaker's Corner at Hyde Park, where every Sunday there is a verbal free-for-all where rebels, rabblerousers and ranters, anyone with or without a cause, can stand up and have their say: 'I soaked up all sorts of speeches, black power speeches and white power speeches and flower power speeches and Irish power speeches, Catholic speeches, Protestant speeches.' She watched smartly uniformed nannies pushing babies in prams, learned to refer to trucks as 'lorries' and discovered that in Britain 'Wimpy' was a fast-food chain not an insult.

The trip had followed an eventful summer. Judy Collins had invited Mitchell to the Newport festival, where she was hosting a singer-songwriter workshop. Also appearing was Collins' friend, the Canadian poet and musician Leonard Cohen. He and Joni met for the first time and were instantly smitten with each other. Cohen had achieved more public fame with his poetry and prose – four volumes of poetry and two novels – than his music by the time he appeared at Newport. His debut album *Songs of Leonard Cohen* would appear later in 1967, but his brand of articulate angst and poetic lyricism – songs like 'Suzanne' and 'Avalanche' began life as poems – was already gaining him a wide following at festivals and clubs, and his appearance at Newport was no exception. The couple were together again at the Mariposa festival in Canada that summer, where Mitchell thanked the audience for their applause at the end of her set – and in a situation which would have felt unbearable only months earlier, upon hearing some catcalls from the crowd she repeated her fulsome thanks 'especially to the drunks out there in the back row'. Cohen led a songwriters' workshop at the festival, and Joni, Buffy Sainte-Marie and Canadian folkie Murray McLauchlan joined in.

The romantic relationship between Mitchell and Cohen was to be short-lived, but Cohen's poetry was to become an enduring inspiration, as Joni recalled:

> In my early twenties, I met two men who were best friends from childhood – one, a sculptor and one, a poet. My association with them was catalytic in opening my gifts in two areas. The sculptor, Mort Rosengarten, gave me a very simple exercise which freed my drawing – gave it boldness and energy. The poet Leonard Cohen was a mirror to my work and with no verbal instructions he showed me how to plumb the depths of my own experience.

Cohen's worldliness had played an important part in Joni's attraction to him, and it had made her question the maturity of her own songwriting and drawing. She wanted especially to be able to develop her drawing beyond the fanciful fairytale illustrations that would later appear on the cover of her first album. But her efforts to move away from a style that was feeling increasingly naïve had been frustrated – until Cohen introduced her to Rosengarten. The three were sitting in Washington Square in New York one day when Mitchell remarked to the sculptor, 'I don't like the way I draw.' Rosengarten's advice was simply, 'Draw me and don't look at the paper.' It worked.

The autobiographical intimacy of Leonard Cohen's poetry and lyrics would encourage Mitchell to mine her own experiences and emotions more intensively, but she sought to broaden her themes beyond that of a boudoir poet. By late 1967 Joni had been writing prodigiously and had completed almost all of the songs that would appear on her first two albums, and others that would feature on later releases or remain unrecorded but part of her performance repertoire. The cover versions of her songs had inevitably brought interest from the recording industry, but the offers were far from irresistible:

> Record companies offered me terrible slave labour deals in the beginning and I turned them down. I turned down [independent folk label] Vanguard. They wanted three albums a year or something. In the folk

tradition, they come and stick a mike on the table in front of you, and they collect it in an hour and that's the album. And that output – I already saw Buffy [Sainte-Marie] struggling under the weight of it. So I thought, no way. This'll take the fun out of it, there's no remuneration. It was a terrible contract, the high-light of which was they would provide little folding table-top cards that said I was a Vanguard artist, and it would have driven my price up slightly, I guess. To be a recording artist, I could have made a little more in the clubs, but not that much and it would have required that I have a manager.

If Sainte-Marie's experience was to prove a disincentive to sign-ing a deal with Vanguard, the two women's friendship was to provide the opportunity for a business partnership of a more beneficial kind. Sainte-Marie encouraged Elliot Roberts – who worked for her management company, Chartoff-Winkler – to go down to the Café Au Go Go in Greenwich Village where her friend was appearing one night, third on a bill supporting Richie Havens and a stand-up comedian. The quintessential wise-crack-ing New Yorker, Roberts (formerly Rabinowitz) had held a junior position at the William Morris talent agency, before his close friend and high-flying mentor there (and later business partner), David Geffen, encouraged him to leave for a better job at Chartoff-Winkler. Joni, meanwhile, was convinced that she didn't need a manager; she was autonomous, decisive about busi-ness matters and able to keep her hard-won gains without having to cut in a manager for a percentage. Soon after arriving in New York she had considered getting a manager, but a meeting with Dylan's manager, Albert Grossman, convinced her that she didn't need a Mr Ten Per Cent of her own:

> He was a very intimidating man. He smoked through his fist and he had these big, bushy grey eyebrows. One night he took me out for sushi ... the bean curd smelled like urine that night and I had such a hard time with it. And he was sitting there, smoking through his hand and looking at me like, 'Eat it all up, if you want me to manage you!'

They went back to her small apartment in Chelsea and Mitchell recalls Grossman was discomfited by the feminine trappings, the tasteful decoration and the lovingly restored vintage pieces retrieved from the Detroit home she'd once shared with Chuck Mitchell:

> He walked in and he couldn't believe it – it was fixed up really cute. He couldn't figure out how I did it and he tried to talk me out of [music]. He said I was too domestic to be in the music business. He took me to his place and all he had was a pallet on the floor with black sheets. He said, '*You* don't need a manager!'

But after Elliot Roberts had seen her show down in the Village, he was convinced that he and Joni could make a formidable pairing:

> I went back after the show and I told her how moved I was. She . . . was playing this incredible set and I told her that I wanted to work with her that night and she said, 'It's a coincidence, this is my last night here but I'm about to go to Detroit tomorrow,' and I said, 'Well hey, I'll go with you if you don't mind and just hang out with you for the rest of your tour,' and she said, 'Okay, you can come along,' and at the end of that tour Joni asked me to manage her and we had a lot of great adventures in this four-week tour and that's how we started working together. We worked together for about twenty years from then.

Roberts may not have seemed great managerial material at first glance. In his book, *David Geffen: A Biography of New Hollywood*, Tom King writes that Roberts had not been particularly adept in his initial role at Chartoff-Winkler – managing comedians:

> His first meeting with [major clients, Jerry] Stiller and [Anne] Meara showed that he was in over his head. 'Well what do you think, Elliot?' a dubious Stiller asked, curious to hear Roberts' plans for their careers. 'What do you think we should be doing now?' Roberts scratched his head, 'I

don't know. Did you *eat*? Maybe we should eat now?'
Within a month, all of the comedians on the Chartoff-
Winkler roster had rebelled and hired other managers.

If Roberts was unsuited to dealing with comedians, he was to
show far greater affinity with musicians. He and Mitchell hit the
road and their misadventures on tour were to seal the fledgling
partnership, as Mitchell recalled:

> We went to this town, Ann Arbor, Michigan. Pot was legal
> there and Elliot was a pot smoker but people were very
> secretive about that. He was also dressed in a suit with
> silk shirts with his initials on the pocket. So, we get to
> this hotel and it's before the gig, and we don't let each
> other know that we smoke pot. But I get to his room, and
> I can smell that he's been smoking pot, and he's got a
> towel under the door and everything. And I realise he's
> as bad as me, he has no mechanical aptitude. He can't
> find the light switch, he can't turn his TV set on. Anyway,
> we end up on our way to this gig. We get lost in the hotel.
> The hotel was kind of a square donut shape, and we lit-
> erally could not find our way out! We wandered through
> soup kitchens and all kinds of places and he was so funny.

When they finally got to the club, it was packed to capacity – the
biggest indoor crowd Joni had seen. She got up on stage, sang her
first song and was greeted by rapturous applause; as her face
creased into a wide grin, disaster struck:

> My upper lip stuck to my gums and I couldn't get it
> down! I had to peel it with my tongue. Elliot was doing
> loud schtick from the audience. He was making a lot of
> jokes and everybody was giggling 'cause everybody
> knew why. And so I said to him, 'Okay you're my man-
> ager.' I enjoyed his company on the road so much. He
> was good, and I was a great straight man for him. So, in
> this way we began.

On their return to New York, Roberts resigned from his job to
manage Mitchell full-time, a role that Roberts says just evolved

naturally. And he was rare in managerial circles for not wanting his management deal to include a share of his artist's publishing royalties. As he recalls:

> We were both very young, there were no rules at that time, you didn't go to college to study to be a manager. We made up what we felt was right and that's how I was guided. I was guided by Joan and we would have discussions on what should be her province and my province and we basically made it up as we went along, and what we felt was right. In the era of the singer-songwriter, we felt very strongly about publishing. When I finally did learn what was the money end of the business, I felt that her publishing had to be protected and that she should be keeping it at all costs. Our goal was to do this for a very long time, the role model was Bob Dylan and it wasn't a matter of radio play or hits, it was a matter of people being guided by your music and using it for the soundtrack of their lives, as it were.

Roberts had been a good tour sidekick but his big task lay ahead – to secure a recording contract that did not fall into the category of what Joni referred to as the slave-labour deals she'd already been offered. Major labels like Columbia – an obvious choice given that it was home to Bob Dylan – and RCA turned him down. Tom Rush – who was on Elektra Records along with Judy Collins – says he tried to get the label interested in Mitchell but without success:

> I remember taking a tape of her songs to Jac Holzman [label president] at Elektra Records and couldn't sell her music to him because he said she sounded too much like Judy Collins. And she did in the early days sound quite Judy-ish but so what? The songs were so fabulous that to me it was irrelevant. The danger for Joni at the time was that she would be branded as the next Judy Collins or the next Joan Baez or compared to them.

Elektra had another chance to sign Joni but again opted out. Danny Fields, an Elektra A&R man, had urged the company to take her on. Elektra's high profile and acclaimed roster of folk-rock and neo-folk artists seemed to hold out the promise of fame and fortune – until, says Fields, Joni asked to design her own album covers. The Elektra art department refused and the corporate hierarchy supported the decision. 'They said, no way. Our art department does the covers. You write the songs, you sing the songs. That's as far as it goes,' Fields recalled. Mitchell was, however, to gain recompense of a kind from Elektra when the royalties payments started flooding in after Judy Collins enjoyed great success with 'Both Sides Now' (the comma in the original title was deleted in the record and sleeve pressings).

Despite the rejections, Roberts was persistent and confident that, rather than Mitchell's music being seen as the last gasp of the declining folk era, it should be appreciated as part of an emerging genre of new music for a new society:

> Never for a moment did we think that we weren't going to get a deal, or [think] 'My God, I see something here and other people just aren't seeing it.' It was really not that. It was a transitional period in society and in history and you either *got* it or you didn't get it. We had to search for people who got it and once we did and found them, we found that there were an awful lot of them but they were just either underground or just coming [up], society was just changing, the long-hairs were just coming in, the war was just becoming a major issue, civil rights were [in] transition ... we didn't have a niche yet, there was a very small underground, [Greenwich] Village, everyone had their little quaint, Bohemian areas, but there were very few forums for artists like Joan or for poetry or poets. But we never thought that what she did wasn't unique and staggering. You just had to hear the songs and you went 'Wow, what great lyrics, that's timeless!' It's just a matter of time before other people see what we see, or we get to the audience. We just didn't know how to reach an audience yet.

Wider exposure was crucial to finding that audience. Roberts got in touch with a Warner Brothers Records executive, Andy Wickham, who he knew had seen one of Joni's shows at a club in

Greenwich Village. While on that first brief tour with Mitchell, Roberts had recorded the show she had done in Ann Arbor and sent the tape to Andy Wickham, who in turn played it for the head of Warner Brothers, Mo Ostin. They were impressed enough to invite Roberts out to California to discuss a possible deal. At that time, Warner Brothers was the only major label on the West Coast; all of the others were still in New York. But Roberts believes this geographical distance was a major factor in Warner Brothers' willingness to see Joni as a part of the musical future rather than the past:

> It was all happening sociologically [in California], the be-ins had started and flower power was starting, there was much more of a Bohemian scene. [Warners] were there while everyone else was in New York and they were exposed to the beginning of the [Jefferson] Airplane and the [Grateful] Dead, this whole type of music that was just starting in the West Coast hadn't reached the East Coast yet. And in the West Coast, what Joni did was in great demand, singer-songwriters . . . We could see that they were much more receptive there . . .

Elliot Roberts flew out to California armed with twenty of Mitchell's songs – almost all of the material that would later appear on her first two albums, including 'Both Sides, Now', 'Chelsea Morning', 'Michael from Mountains', 'That Song About The Midway', 'I Had a King' and 'I Don't Know Where I Stand'. He didn't have to do much persuading:

> Those are some of the greatest songs in history. How could you not hear that and go, 'I'd take a risk on that person'? And that's really what it was . . . the songs spoke for themselves literally, they really did.

The success of the cover versions of Mitchell's songs had also put Roberts in a strong bargaining position and he was able to negotiate an almost unprecedented concession, particularly for a new artist; his client was given complete artistic control over her albums, ranging from the cover art to sleeve notes and musical content:

That was the hard part. They were not used to anyone saying, 'It has nothing to do with the money, we need creative control.' We had a long-term goal, Joan had a long-term goal and knew how her record should sound. She hadn't learned the craft yet but she knew she was going to. It was new and a bit different for [Warners] to give up control but they could see that times were changing drastically ... Mo [Ostin] was an innovative man, he did the same for Hendrix and Van Morrison and Van Dyke Parks in that era, where he let them have pretty much creative control. No one understood the music, there were all these young kids, ... [the major labels] understood that there was a whole new generation and they looked a lot different to the generations they had previously been selling music to.

While Roberts was in Los Angeles, Joni continued on her tour. But a chance meeting in Florida was to start off a chain of events that would see, in quick succession, a romance, her first album and much more besides.

3 Places to come from and places to go . . .

> Formula of my happiness: a Yes, a No, a straight
> line, a goal . . .
> (Friedrich Nietzsche, *Twilight of the Idols,* 1889)

OR A BYRD IN FLIGHT, the Coconut Grove area of Miami was the perfect retreat from the stresses and tensions of an acrimonious departure from the pre-eminent folk-rock group at that time. The consciously rustic 'village' in the middle of a carefully planted mini-jungle is the oldest community in south Florida. The influence of its first settlers – black Bahamians, 'conchs' (whites from Key West, 240 kilometres from Miami, on the tip of Florida) and New England intellectuals – survives in a community that has always attracted artists, writers and musicians. By the end of the First World War, Coconut Grove was said to be the most-listed address of people featured in *Who's Who.* In the late 1960s–mid-70s it was the hottest of the cool places to be and it was where David Crosby had gone to escape the Byrds and Los Angeles. His major preoccupation, beyond the pursuit of fun, was the schooner he'd just bought, the *Mayan.* He was soon to acquire another passion. Thirty years later, in an interview with Wally Breese, the creator of the website www.jonimitchell.com, Crosby recalled his powerful first impressions of Joni Mitchell:

> I walked into the [Gaslight South] coffee house and was just completely smitten. She was standing there singing all those songs . . . 'Michael from Mountains', 'Both Sides, Now' and I was just floored. I couldn't believe there was anybody that good. And I also fell . . . I loved her, as it were . . . I was extremely fascinated with the quality of the music and the quality of the girl.

She was such an unusual, passionate and powerful woman. I was fascinated by her tunings because I had started working in tunings, and I was writing things like 'Guinevere'. So things like that made me very, very attracted to her.

Mitchell herself recalled in Crosby's autobiography, *Long Time Gone*:

I remember being introduced to him and thinking he reminded me of Yosemite Sam [Bugs Bunny's moustachioed cartoon foe]. I used to secretly call him Yosemite Sam in my mind. I don't think I ever called him that to his face, but I might have ... David was wonderful company and a great appreciator. When it comes to expressing infectious enthusiasm, he is probably the most capable person I know. His eyes were like star sapphires to me. When he laughed, they seemed to twinkle like no one else's and so I fell into his merry company and we rode bikes around Coconut Grove and the winds were warm and at night we'd go down and listen to the masts clinking on the pier. It was a lovely period and soon we became emotionally involved.

Mitchell phoned Elliot Roberts from Miami to tell him that she was returning to New York with Crosby in tow – and that he wanted to produce her first album. Given Crosby's reputation as something of a lovable rogue and his sudden and high-profile departure from The Byrds, Roberts was dubious at first:

They showed up at my office in New York and David ... had long hair flowing to his shoulder, he had the trademark moustache. He looked just like he did on his Byrds album covers. He was the first hippie that I met in that era. He didn't talk very much. He seemed slightly paranoid. He had gotten a bad rep. He was constantly being written about in the music papers as the Bad Byrd, the Byrd That Got Away.

Elliot and Joni packed up and moved west to Los Angeles. The three stayed initially with a friend of Crosby's, a well-known LA radio DJ, B. Mitchell Reed. Crosby may have had a stormy relationship with his fellow Byrds, but he was popular, good-natured and enthusiastic, and occasionally displayed a knack of being in the right place at the right time, as Roberts recalls:

> The very first day in the studio at Sunset Sound, about an hour into the session, an engineer comes in and tells David that the Buffalo Springfield were in the room next door. Joni says, 'You've got to meet Neil Young. He's from Canada. He's in the Springfield. He's so funny. You're going to love this guy.'

Warner Brothers was obviously confident that Crosby, given his past involvement with the Byrds, would – musically at least – be a positive and steady influence in the studio, steering his 'protégé' towards the undeniably lucrative waters of folk-rock. He, meanwhile, had decided that his technique as producer would be simply to let the music unfold with no intervention, no tricks, no gimmicks, no ostentation. Apart from Mitchell on piano and guitar, the only other musician was Stephen Stills, who wandered in from the Buffalo Springfield session next door to play bass on a single track, 'Night in the City'. Mitchell acknowledged that Crosby's encouragement of her autonomy helped to lay the groundwork for her future career:

> When it came time to make my record, David did me a solid favour for which I am eternally grateful, because the way you enter the game in this business is usually the way you stay ... David put me into the game at a certain level and helped me keep control of my work. In those days I resembled a folk singer to the untrained ear ... what David and Elliot did was to make me look like the new movement. The record company was going to 'folk rock' me up and David thought that would be a tragedy, that my music should be recorded the way I wrote it. He appreciated it the way it was and since he had been in the premier folk rock group, he could go to the record company with

some authority and say, 'I'm going to produce her', and the trick was that he was not going to 'produce' me at all! He said, 'It's like you're sitting on the patio of the Old World restaurant and a girl goes by in blue jeans and after she goes you think, "Did she have a little lace down the seams of her blue jeans?"' Anything we added would be minimal; that's the way we proceeded.

Crosby took genuine pride in Mitchell and her accomplishments and used every opportunity to promote her music. Visitors to his house would hear impromptu renditions of the songs being recorded for the album, and whenever they'd call on friends, Crosby would encourage Mitchell to sing for them, including B. Mitchell Reed, who mentioned the work-in-progress on his show and played songs from the album regularly after it was released. Crosby's eclectic circle included the actor Peter Fonda, who recalled the first time he saw Mitchell:

> She was brand-new, hadn't been heard by any of us. David came strolling in one day, having dropped by with Joni. . . . He said 'Fondle . . . ' That was his nick-name for me. He knew I liked to fondle women . . . he says, 'Fondle, I've got one for you.' I thought he had a groupie or something, you know, so I said, 'This is my house, David. My wife . . . ' He says, 'No . . . serious, man. Listen to this.' And Joni, kind of shy, appears. Staring at the ground for something to do, she sees my twelve-string guitar leaning against the wall and asks, 'Can I use that?' She grabs hold of my guitar and detunes the fucker and then plays thirteen or fourteen songs, warbling like the best thing I'd ever heard in my life. David's so proud and he says, 'That song's about me and that song's about so-and-so and isn't this great' . . . I was just bowled over by this fabulous person with a wonderful voice and a great style.

Mitchell would also on occasion grab Crosby's guitar and, as Fonda described it, 'detune the fucker'; Crosby would simply exclaim in mock despair, 'Oh, the Martians have been here!'

Elliot Roberts credits Crosby with giving the eponymously titled album (also known as *Song to a Seagull*)such great informal advance publicity that when it was released 'everyone in LA was aware of Joni Mitchell. The first club date we played, at the Troubadour, was standing room only for four nights, two shows a night.' But Crosby himself says that promoting Mitchell was the easy part, producing her was less so:

> I did bring her around to everyone I knew ... my favourite trick at the time was to invite everyone over, get a joint of dope that was stronger than they could possibly smoke and get her to play and they would walk out stupefied. They'd never heard anything like her and it was a lot of fun. It only stopped being fun when I started producing her first record. Joni is not a person that you stay in a relationship with. It always goes awry, no matter who you are. It's an inevitable thing. We were starting to have friction and at the same time I was starting to produce her record and I didn't really know how.

Despite his laudable hands-off attitude to producing Mitchell's voice and acoustic guitar, there were problems that Crosby could not have foreseen. The engineer, Art Cryst, was seriously ill and, although patient and diligent, most certainly found the sessions a struggle. He died soon after recording was completed. Mitchell and Crosby were the first to use what was then the newest studio at Sunset Sound. But technical problems and Crosby's lack of expertise soon cast a shadow over the project. Mitchell outlined the problems, in an interview a few months after recording ended:

> The album ... sounded beautiful in the studio as far as sound was concerned. When we finished it and took it out of the studio, there was a bit of noise on it but we thought it was in the speakers ... we took the tape off and we played it and we found out there was an incredible amount of tape hiss so when you came to the spaces on the bands, when the tape was clean, it was like silence, there was all of this noise underneath the track, crackling and things that the engineer had

insisted wasn't on the tape. So in order to save it because we'd worked all that time on it, this other engineer, a really good engineer, took it and cleaned the tape hiss off, though in the process of cleaning off the tape hiss took off a lot of the highs, which is the reason it sounds like it's under glass . . . under a bell jar, that's what Judy [Collins] said. You really need the words inside the book to follow my diction, which is pretty good usually. But that's not David's fault, he had some really beautiful ideas. One of the things that we did that was kind of fun . . . because of what had to be done to clean up the tape, a lot of it was lost, he had me sing a lot of it into a grand piano with the ringing pedal down. So . . . every note I sang repeated itself in the strings . . . if you sing into a grand piano, the notes on the strings reproduce the sound of your voice, that's the amazing thing. It was so beautiful. He had so many ideas. He had the idea too of doubling my guitar part so some of the guitar sounds like twelve-string. He was really good . . .

Crosby, speaking thirty years later, was satisfied with the conception of the album and Mitchell's performance, saying the thing he was most proud of was that he presented her music just as it was performed live, without misrepresenting it or embellishing it unnecessarily with anything but Stills's bass on 'Night in the City'. But he was largely critical of his own limitations as a producer and the technical aspects of his experimentation during the recording:

I hadn't recorded it well enough. I had allowed too much noise – too much signal-to-noise ratio – too much hiss. . . . I wanted to try and get the overtones that happen from the resonating of the piano and of course, it recorded at way too low a level. If you use those mikes at all you get a hiss, so we had to go in and take those things out. It was just an idea and it really didn't work . . . we went back in and remixed without all those tracks . . . I didn't know enough to know what I was doing but we did get the actual songs done without a bunch of other crud on it and that made me happy.

Mitchell had written all of the songs by the time recording started; she'd been performing some of them in her live shows for several months. But notably missing were her best-known songs, the ones appropriated by other artists before Mitchell had even recorded her first album – 'Both Sides, Now', 'The Circle Game' and 'Urge for Going'. She would record these on later albums, but some of the songs she'd been singing regularly during her live performances for the past eighteen months – including 'Ballerina Valerie', 'Just Like Me', 'Carnival in Kenora', 'Brandy Eyes', 'Eastern Rain', 'Blue on Blue', 'Go Tell the Drummer Man' and 'Winter Lady' – would be among 20–30 early songs that would never be released officially, although many appear on bootlegs. (Curiously, a participant in a website discussion list, who claimed to be a friend of Mitchell's during the Detroit days, insisted that her boyfriend had written part of 'Winter Lady', and that she herself had been the inspiration for the verse. When questioned by other participants at the time, the woman indicated that she did not want to discuss it further and my subsequent attempts to contact her to verify her claim went unanswered. A similar scenario unfolded over 'Urge For Going' with one website participant claiming that her father had written part of the song. Neither claim has been substantiated.)

When asked in a radio interview, later that year, why some of the 'old' songs had been sidelined, Mitchell had said:

> they're like old paintings. If you're an art student and you have a folio full of paintings and you look backward and you think my God, when did I do that . . . you can't identify with [them] after a while . . . some songs, I'm afraid, are lost until I re-identify with them . . .

The veteran Philadelphia broadcaster Gene Shay – who interviewed Mitchell on his show many times – says she simply outgrew much of her early material:

> She moved [on] quickly. She started to reject her [earlier] work as being too similar . . . and she probably said, 'Well I already did that, I want to try something else.' She was always looking for innovative devices . . .

the way she did 'Night in the City' with that falsetto voice, that was another musical device. Even the way she worked the microphone ... I remember seeing her in concert once and she would move her lips up close to the microphone to get a textural sound, a tactile sound. She was always progressing in different areas and experimenting, she never wanted to be held back. I remember once in an interview, trying to pin her down on something by saying, 'You're going through this phase'. She said, 'No, Gene! I just do what I want and whatever comes next is what's next but I don't say, I'm going to sit down and write songs about ... water!'

One significant early song that she did not outgrow – but which was not included on the album – was the painfully autobiographical 'Little Green', written for her daughter, who was by then settled with her adoptive family in Don Mills, a suburb of Toronto (although Mitchell would only find this out three decades later). Mitchell's own experiences did loom large in the song cycle running through the two themes of the album: 'I Came to the City' (Side 1) and (Side 2) 'Out of the City and Down to the Seaside'. (The titles of each side were echoed 32 years on, in P.J. Harvey's album *Stories from the City, Stories from the Sea*, released in 2000, which showed a similar geographical thematic journey.)

Joni Mitchell/Seagull could justifiably be acclaimed as the first concept album in pop/rock, long before the excesses of prog rock made the term one of derision synonymous with over-produced self-indulgence and pomposity. The album is near-perfect in its thematic execution: the songs clustered under 'I Came to the City' approximated the moves from Toronto to Detroit and on to New York. The opening track, 'I Had a King', came directly from the end of her marriage to Chuck Mitchell, the 'king in a tenement castle, Lately he's taken to painting the pastel walls brown', almost a literal description of the apartment which they'd decorated together, in a building known locally as the Castle. Chuck was the man who 'carried me off to his country for marriage too soon'; this man 'dressed in drip-dry and paisley' was a part of the past, still living in a fading world of traditional folk and Brechtian

art songs – 'ladies in gingham still blush While he sings them of
wars and wine But in my leather and lace I can never become
that kind.'

The second track, 'Michael from Mountains', was inspired too
by a man who would be in her life briefly, but long enough to be
remembered in song. Gene Shay recalls Mitchell introducing him
to her close friend Michael, around the time she wrote 'Michael
from Mountains', a song later covered by Judy Collins. Mitchell
said soon after recording it that it was the story of

> a real person. A child-man; he was always showing you
> his treasures, like a boy. I got a letter from him . . . it
> said, 'I found a cave at the foot of a mountain with a
> stone at the entrance where Neptune sits . . . '

'Night in the City', one of several songs inspired by New York,
reflects all of the romance and a little of the raucous realism of
the city, celebrating the liberating anonymity of urban life without giving in to any of the deadening loneliness that could also go
with it. The chorus 'Night in the city looks pretty to me Night in
the city looks fine Music comes spilling out into the street Colors
go flashing in time' is made even more engaging by the simple
technique of layering Mitchell's vocals.

Another city – swinging London, 1967 – provided the inspiration for the song 'Marcie', named after a woman Joni had
become friends with there. They discovered that they'd been
neighbours in New York, when Joni had lived at 41 West 16th
Street and Marcie lived a few doors down, at number 37. Mitchell
had begun to write a song at Marcie's flat in London, but what
began as a song about England became a song about Marcie and
'most girls who've come to New York City'.

Promoting the album months later, Mitchell said in an interview that the song had also been influenced by Leonard Cohen,
whom she'd met at the Newport Folk Festival the previous summer: '"Marcie" has a lot of him in it, and some of Leonard's religious imagery, which comes from being a Jew in a
predominantly Catholic part of Canada [Montreal, Quebec],
seems to have rubbed off on me too.' New Yorker and musician
Suzanne Vega believes this early song is one of the highlights of
Mitchell's work: 'The form is exquisite, it tells a story without

being confessional, the melody is pure and classic, the metaphors and images all ring true and are consistent through the song. I feel it's one of her best.'

Another New York song closed the first side of the LP. 'Nathan la Franeer' detailed an experience that will be familiar to anyone who has ever regularly taken cabs in New York City. It was based on a journey from Manhattan to the airport, with a driver named Nathan la Franeer: 'I asked him would he hurry, But we crawled the canyons slowly . . . he asked me for a dollar more, He cursed me to my face, He hated everyone who paid to ride, And share his common space.' Mitchell would say, somewhat ingenuously, around this time, 'When people listen to "Nathan la Franeer", which is about a real New York cab-driver, I hope someone who's been particularly greedy would hurt in his stomach, and say to himself, "Wow, what would she think of me?"'

The second side opened with the whimsical 'Sisotowbell Lane', its idealistic title taken from an acronym in the fairy-tale mythology that Mitchell was concocting (Somehow In Spite Of Trouble Ours Will Be Everlasting Love). It was written in one of Mitchell's original tunings that she'd labelled 'California Kitchen Tuning', after the very spot where she'd devised it. She later explained the tunings were 'the E string is natural, the second string is up a half tone, the 3rd string is down a whole tone, the 4th string is natural, the 5th string is down a whole tone, I believe, and I think the bass is down two tones . . . ' The setting of the story alludes to Mitchell's prairie upbringing, where the flatlands stretch as far as the horizon in every direction, 'the woodlands and the grasslands and the badlands 'cross the river . . . Go to the city you'll come back again, To wade through the grain.'

Canadian singer-songwriter Jane Siberry, who sees Mitchell as a role-model for a form of writing that is both personal and universal, says songs like 'I Had a King' and 'Sisotowbell Lane' resonated strongly with her when she first heard them:

> I think everyone writes from their own landscape, so to speak, but it depends on the individual. Someone else growing up in Saskatchewan could not see things in the way she has as far as the space goes. But her sense of space is broad and so inviting to people who for the most part feel cramped, and that's another

> wonderful thing she's given to people, is space to
> move out of their own tiny little worlds into land-
> scapes that she's created through what she sees. I
> guess an interesting question would be if she'd grown
> up in New York, would her writing have been really
> different?

There is also the flatlander's fascination with that other expanse
to the horizon, the ocean. David Crosby has always claimed that
the next track, 'The Dawntreader', was about him; there is much
seafaring imagery to which he could obviously relate, but
Mitchell maintained that he was not the inspiration behind it:

> He mistakenly thought I wrote . . . 'The Dawntreader'
> for him and was thinking of naming his boat
> *Dawntreader*. He ended up keeping the original name,
> *Mayan*, which was good because it had a history
> already. I guess people identify with songs that you
> write and think you wrote them just for them.

The oceanic themes, the safe harbour in stormy seas, the free-as-
a-seabird imagery run through the remaining songs: 'The Pirate of
Penance', again with a clever use of vocal layering in a call-and-
response story structure and its title, a play on the title of the
Gilbert and Sullivan light opera *The Pirates of Penzance*.

The final track, 'Cactus Tree', has at its core a determined
refrain of escape from men trying to contain and control: 'she
will love them when she sees them, they will lose her if they
follow . . . while she's so busy being free.' Among those men is
Chuck Mitchell; their divorce and settling of their financial
affairs including song publishing is described in the lines, 'He
has seen her at the office, With her name on all his papers,
Through the sharing of the profits, He will find it hard to shake
her, From his memory . . . ' Joni Mitchell saw the song as

> the song of *modern* woman. Yes, it has to do with my
> experiences, but I know a lot of girls like that . . . who
> find that the world is full of lovely men but they're
> driven by something else other than settling down to
> frau-duties.

Mitchell's intended title for the album was *Song to a Seagull*, but this was misinterpreted when the album and cover were being pressed and it became officially known as *Joni Mitchell*. There has been confusion ever since about the title, with some sources even listing *Joni Mitchell* and *Song to a Seagull* as two different albums. A recent CD pressing of the remastered recording is titled *Song to a Seagull* (although it is listed in the discography in the sleeve notes as *Joni Mitchell*). Her own psychedelic artwork shows lush life, vibrant flowers, trees and birds (one hatching an egg inscribed 'Love Life') and a golden-haired maiden with the words 'Joni Mitchell' woven into her flowing garlanded locks. In the background, a schooner at sea and a flock of seagulls in flight spelling out the words 'SONG TO A SEAGUL'. The last 'L' of seagull was dropped off the original cover art by a graphics department that may have been paying less than full attention. The city is a grim contrast, represented by unadorned photographs by Mark Roth showing Mitchell standing in the rain, clutching her suitcase on a dingy Lower East Side New York backstreet. Mitchell dedicated the album to her inspirational seventh-grade teacher in Saskatoon, Arthur Kratzman, who, the sleeve notes affirm, 'taught me to love words'. Writing in the *New York Times*, Ellen Landers was unimpressed, criticising the album's engineering – quite rightly – as 'uneven', the occasionally 'shaky' vocals and unsuitable arrangements. 'The effect is monotony, albeit a gentle monotony. Any one of these frailties would ruin an album of a lesser talent,' she wrote.

As Mitchell set off on tour to promote the album in early 1968, her producer was about to demonstrate his impressive talent for attracting trouble, particularly if two of his favourite things – drugs and guns – were involved. Elliot Roberts was to sample the hospitality of a Los Angeles jail in April, thanks to David Crosby, after police arrested the pair for drugs use and possession of a firearm. The drugs and the gun were Crosby's, but Roberts was smoking grass when their vehicle was stopped. Crosby was bailed by his lawyer the following morning and, having told the police that Roberts had nothing to do with the drugs or gun, they believed he would be released within an hour or two. Four days later, Roberts left jail after the charges were dropped. A puzzled Mitchell was left pondering the fate of a manager who had apparently gone AWOL after arranging to meet her in Canada three days earlier.

In March Mitchell went to Ottawa for a show at the Capitol Theatre – the other major drawcard at the venue that week was Jimi Hendrix. Mitchell recalled their first meeting:

> After his set, he came down and he brought a big reel-to-reel tape recorder. He introduced himself very shyly and said, 'Would you mind if I tape your show?' I said, 'Not at all.' And later that evening we went back, we were staying at the same hotel. He and his drummer, Mitch [Mitchell], the three of us were talking. It was so innocent. But [the hotel] management, all they saw was three hippies. We were outcasts anyway. A black hippie! Two men and a woman in the same room. So they kept telling us to play lower. It was a very creative, special night. We were playing like children.

Hendrix's own diary entry dated 19–20 March noted:

> Arrived in Ottawa – beautiful hotel . . . strange people . . . beautiful dinner. Talked with Joni Mitchell on the phone. I think I'll record her tonight with my excellent tape recorder (knock on wood). Went down to the club to see Joni, fantastic girl with heaven words. We all got to party. OK, millions of girls . . . We left Ottawa city today. I kissed Joni goodbye.

Many years later, when asked by *Rolling Stone* to describe Hendrix in three words, Mitchell said:

> His main concern at that time was that he wanted to drop the phallic aspects of his showmanship. The big, flamboyant dick stuff was offensive to him and he wanted to stop it. But every time he tried, the audience would boo. He wanted to take a different kind of band out, with a brass section. OK, three words? Sensitive. Shy. Sweet.

The Canadian tour included a two-week residency at the Riverboat; the cover charge each night was $1.75. Mitchell's return to the city was triumphant; three years earlier, poor and pregnant, she'd trudged around every non-union dive in town looking for work. Now her shows at the Riverboat attracted devoted crowds and media attention to match. Mitchell's potent mix of ethereal songs and blonde ambition was not lost on the (woman) writer from the *Toronto Daily Star* who'd attended the Riverboat gig and noted breathlessly the singer's considerable effect on the audience:

> The pleasantly round-faced girl in the Riverboat audience was watching her husband drink Joni Mitchell in. The singer's long golden hair floated around her doll's face while her shimmering voice chanted of flowers and sun-warmed shoulders and seabirds soaring out of reach. 'Call, and I follow, I follow!' cried the look on the husband's rapt face. 'And just who do you think would mend your socks, buster?' asked the pained, ironic smile on the face of his wife . . . she makes the men who hear her believe that a life without mended socks is still possible . . . man and boy, they are plainly thinking that if only they hadn't settled for their prosaic Maudes and Mary Janes, they could be taking flight with a naturally golden-haired Joni, one innocent yet wise, childlike yet knowing, half-buttercup, half-peony; one who would *understand*, and never sink their soaring souls with weights of darned socks and dental bills . . .

Her appeal was obvious: women wanted to be her, men wanted to be *with* her. A critic in *Variety* wrote approvingly of Mitchell's 16 April show:

> Much in the vein of another Canadian poet, Leonard Cohen, Miss Mitchell has a strong appeal to young people. Her songs go back to roots. They talk of the countryside and they deal with movement to either the city or the sea. They talk of more innocent days without bitterness and they leave an optimism that is rare from today's youthful talents.

The 'innocent days without bitterness' theory would soon be tested when British musician Graham Nash arrived in Los

Angeles on tour with his band, The Hollies. Nash and Mitchell had had the ill-fated beginning of a romance some time earlier, when both were in Ottawa for gigs, Nash appearing with The Hollies at the Capitol Theatre and Mitchell at Le Hibou coffee house, as Nash recalls:

> After the concert, the band was attending a party given for them by the local promoter. I noticed a beautiful woman sitting in the corner with an object on her knee. I walked up and introduced myself to her. The object turned out to be a nineteenth-century music box. We struck up an immediate friendship and she invited me to go back to her hotel and listen to some songs. The roof-top rooms at the Chateau Laurier are very special but none more so than Joni's room. Over the next few hours I not only heard some of the finest music I'd ever heard but I fell in love. That night is indelibly etched in my memory as one of the finest nights of my life up to that point.

The Chateau Laurier is one of the most beautiful buildings in Ottawa, with castle-like turrets and a burnished copper roof, in the same architectural style as the Parliament Buildings alongside it.

But if the location was perfect, the timing was not; they parted reluctantly and continued their respective tours. When they met again in Los Angeles, the attraction had not dissipated and there were already strains in the relationship between Crosby and Mitchell, as she recalls:

> [Graham] ended up at David's place and I was staying with David until my house was ready. Graham came down sick in David's house, and I took him home to my new house to play Florence Nightingale. At first it wasn't really for romance's sake ... I took him home and was looking after him and got attached – here was a mess. What was I going to say? I'm kind of going with David and we sort of staked claims, but I'd written all these independent songs, trying to explain my position to him; that I'm still in independent mode. But I got

really attached to Graham and I guess that's the first time I harboured the illusion of 'forever'. I really felt for the first time in my life that I could pair bond.

The couple shared the house in Laurel Canyon for the next two years.

The messages in the 'independent songs' on the album were clear; Crosby had been in the studio when they were recorded but whereas many listen to Mitchell's music and overemphasise autobiographical interpretations, Crosby obviously underestimated how acutely personal some were. The concept of freedom, of flight, of leave-taking, of arrival and departure in some form runs through every song on the album, notably on 'Cactus Tree' and on 'The Dawntreader', where she sings 'They'll say that you're crazy, And a dream of a baby, Like a promise to be free ... ' Crosby was to treat the relationship between his two close friends with some equanimity, as he explained in his autobiography:

> At that time in particular, I subscribed to the hippie ethic of non-ownership. I didn't feel that anybody owned anybody and I tried my level best not to be jealous or territorial about that kind of thing ... the thing with Joni and Graham was that I felt great about it. I wanted to be with Christine [Hinton, his former girlfriend] ... and Joni was a very turbulent girl and not an easy person to be in a relationship with, particularly then. I was very happy for them. They were in love and it was cool. Graham was then – and is now – my best friend and I didn't feel any jealousy about it. I loved him and I loved her and I couldn't see being angry at two people I loved for loving each other.

In 1972, Crosby and Nash would dedicate their eponymous album 'To Miss Mitchell' (although technically, of course, she was *Mrs* Mitchell).

The tour to promote *Joni Mitchell/Seagull* continued through the summer. Her appearance on the opening night of the Philadelphia Folk Festival in August was a triumph; the crowd sang along with her on 'The Circle Game', a song she had not yet recorded herself but which, like several others, had become popular through the cover versions by Judy Collins, Tom Rush, George Hamilton IV, Ian and Sylvia and Buffy Sainte-Marie. At the end of her set – 'Cactus Tree', 'Chelsea Morning', 'Both Sides, Now', 'The Circle Game', 'Little Green' – the enthusiastic crowd shouted for encores despite Mitchell's protestations that she couldn't overrun her allotted twenty minutes on stage. Writing in a local paper, the *Evening Bulletin*, Walter F. Naedele described Mitchell as 'the most exciting girl singer since Judy Collins, since Joan Baez', while in the same breath, acknowledging her as a phenomenon, he opined:

> Like the crashing surf, you have to feel her voice hitting you hard to gain the exhilaration of something yet unexperienced. The awful thing about Joni has been that she seemed to have two voices, a deep, open-throated tenor and a thin soaring soprano. She could not sustain a song without breaking across into what seemed a weakness. But last night, she was stronger than in her album, each of her voices a richness . . .

And yet Joni, he added mournfully, 'was in bad shape, suffering from the effects of hepatitis'.

In late September, Mitchell returned to Britain. She recorded a session for John Peel's high-profile BBC radio programme *Top Gear*, and on 28 September appeared at the Festival of Contemporary Song at the Royal Festival Hall in London. Also on the bill were Fairport Convention, American folkie Jackson C. Frank, and Al Stewart. Fairport Convention had, thanks to Joe Boyd, already added some of Mitchell's songs to their gig repertoire and to their debut album *Fairport Convention*. Her song 'Eastern Rain' would appear on their second album, *What We Did On Our Holidays*, which was released early the next year. But at the Festival Hall they left Mitchell's songs to her and instead performed a stunning version of her fellow Canadian Leonard Cohen's 'Suzanne'. Joni Mitchell, all serene distance and LA chic, could not have been more different on stage from Fairport's shambling, erratic and endearing Sandy Denny. Joe Boyd recalls Denny being:

> a real handful, [but] her manner on stage was a fumbling with her guitar strings, and tripping over

wires and laughing at her own clumsiness, making offhand, off the cuff, very funny one-liners, and making mistakes but laughing about them [while] maintaining a dialogue with the audience. She certainly wasn't somebody who got up there on stage [with] her long hair hanging over her face, and didn't look at the audience. That just wasn't Sandy at all.

Over the next three years, Denny's often shaky confidence in her talent developed enough for her to release her first solo album, *North Star Grassman & the Ravens,* in 1971. She'd written most of the songs on the album and many chronicled her own experiences yet she appeared determined to distance herself from a Mitchellesque self-revelatory writing style:

> I just take a story and whittle it down to essentials . . .
> I wouldn't write songs if they didn't mean something to
> me, but I'm not prepared to tell everyone about my pri-
> vate life, like Joni Mitchell does. I like to be a bit more
> elusive than that.

But Mitchell's success did appear to rankle over time as Denny went through agonies of self-doubt, despite the assurances of friends like Fairport's Dave Pegg:

> [Sandy] just didn't know how good she was, really.
> She never thought she sang well, and she never
> thought much of her songs. We all loved them. She'd
> go, 'Oh, you all love Joni Mitchell. She's much better
> than me.' We'd go, 'No, Sandy. You're as good as she
> is.' But [there was] this dreadful insecurity – about
> everything.

Mitchell meanwhile was countering criticisms that her lyrics and music were too bland, too out of touch with the real concerns of ordinary people, of those not privileged enough to be living the well-heeled bohemian LA lifestyle, and especially, of the 60s youth protest movements. During an interview in Toronto in April, she had said that it was the protesters who were out of touch with reality:

They're like the old fire and brimstone preachers who have you roasting in hell if you don't do what they say. They preach to the converted anyway. The preachers and teachers I remember best are the ones who pointed gently to where I was wrong, so that I felt naughty.

But within months, the brutal political realities of American life had intruded and the scales appeared to fall from her eyes. Mitchell had found the political situation so unsettling that it was difficult to concentrate on the personal themes of her own writing:

I'm too hung up about what's going on in America politically. I keep thinking, how can I sing 'Night in the city, looks pretty to me . . . ' when I know it's not pretty at all, with people living in slums and being beaten up by police? It was what happened in Chicago during the Democratic [Party] Convention that really got me thinking. All those kids being clubbed. If I'd been wearing these Levis, they'd have clubbed me, not for doing anything but this is the uniform of the enemy. That's what they are beginning to call the kids today, the enemy.

4 Songs to aging children come . . .

Where there are humans
you'll find flies
and Buddhas.
          (Kobayashi Issa, *c.* 1800)

IN THE FOLK-ROCK FIRMAMENT, Joni Mitchell was about to become a star. She would soon be cast in the role of the flower-child princess, the poster girl of the New Waif, the brainy beauty who seemed to reveal her life, her loves and losses in her songs. People listened to the songs and thought they knew her, listened to the songs and thought she knew *them*. One fan spoke for the many when phoning a radio programme on which she was a guest, asking the host to pose the burning question of the day: 'What's your sign?'

Unfazed, Mitchell responded: 'What is my sign? Partially with my moon in pliers! (laughs) . . . I am a dreaded Scorpio with Moon in Pisces and Sagittarius Rising, born of Gemini and Virgo . . .' This was, after all, the dawning of the Age of Aquarius.

She'd added many converts to her devoted following during a US and Canadian tour; the days of fifteen-dollar folk-club gigs were long gone. Now her concerts were earning her $3000 a night. An audience in Northfield, Massachusetts waited patiently for two hours after Mitchell missed a flight and had to be driven more than a hundred miles to make the show. The wait was enlivened considerably when a boisterous dog wrenched free of its owner and bounded around the hall, barking loudly. It was the nearest thing to a sound check; when Mitchell appeared on stage, there were problems with the microphone and a replacement had to be found. Canine equilibrium and sound levels restored, the crowd hung on every word, every chord. After the show a group of young disciples, most wearing jeans and duffel

coats, gathered outside the shabby dressing-room. When Mitchell
appeared one earnest young man said to her, 'I want you to
know, I've been on meditation. And I get good vibrations. I have
a message to give you. I've been told to tell you you're doing the
right thing. You're going to be all right. That's all. Peace.'

Mitchell was gracious in the face of such adoring intensity:
'Thank you. That's very important to me, because I get the same
feelings myself.'

The next gig saw Mitchell back in Canada. The show at the
University of Western Ontario, in London, Ontario, attracted similarly ardent fans. Afterwards, a girl wearing a paisley jumpsuit
and carrying a dove in a bird-cage came up to Mitchell: 'Joni, this
is Mr Peepers. He likes you. Won't you come away with Mr
Peepers and me. We love you, Joni. Please come.' Tempting as
the offer no doubt was, the object of her affection declined gently.
The ethereal soft-voiced folk-rocker could also, when the occasion demanded, prove herself capable of behaviour more associated with kick-ass rock-chick style, as exemplified by an incident
when Joni appeared at the State University of New York at Stony
Brook, on Long Island, as the support act for rehabilitated folkie
Tim Hardin, still best known for 'If I Were a Carpenter'. The
American science-fiction writer Spider Robinson, who was at the
gig, recalls that Joni got a standing ovation at the end of her set,
acknowledged the crowd's cheers and applause and left as Hardin
came on. Large sections of the crowd took that as their cue to
head for the exit doors:

> As far as they were concerned, the show was over. The
> star had already performed . . . They made no attempt
> to keep silent – didn't even bother keeping their voices
> down. Some shouted, the better to be heard over that
> guy onstage nattering on about carpenters and tinkers.
> Tim soldiered on. He finished his first song, to a smat-
> tering of applause, watched the doors open and a flood
> of people race to escape his music. He began another
> song, watched more chattering crowds form at his left
> and right as he sang, and flee the moment they were
> allowed to. He started a third tune; same result. He
> stopped in mid-song, unslung his guitar, leaned closer
> to the mike, said, very softly, 'How would you like it if

somebody pissed in your canteen?' and left. Some folks didn't even notice. But they sure noticed when an avenging angel swept down from the bleachers, trailing blonde hair like fire. Ms Mitchell sprang onstage, grabbed the mike, and for the next five minutes, she cursed that crowd. We were barbarians, pigs, reptile excrement; she profoundly regretted having performed for us, and would tell every act she knew not to come here because we didn't deserve to hear music; she maligned us and our relatives and ancestors until she ran out of breath, and stormed off stage. Leaving behind hundreds of baffled people . . . and a handful like me, cheering even louder than we had for her songs.

Robinson says he remains in awe to this day.

Mitchell's reputation had been enhanced even further by her appearance before 100,000 people at the Miami Pop Festival in December 68 – and the same month, her song 'Both Sides, Now' had given Judy Collins a Top Ten hit (and would later win Collins a Grammy for Best Folk Performance). Two months later, Joni gave her first performance at the prestigious Carnegie Hall in New York; among the audience were her parents, her new beau, Graham Nash, and her former boyfriend, David Crosby. That show and one at the Berkeley Community Theater in Berkeley, California, in March, were recorded for inclusion on a live concert album but the release was eventually dropped in favour of putting out Mitchell's third studio recording. However, two excerpts from these recordings would surface on a little-known Warner Brothers sampler album, then available for a couple of dollars by mail order. The tracks were described on the sampler packaging as being 'from Joni Mitchell's forthcoming live album'; one track was a story called 'Spoonie's Wonderful Adventure', an anecdote about Ian and Sylvia Tyson's son, and the other was an *a capella* version of 'The Fiddle and the Drum'.

The audience capacity at Carnegie Hall could not match that of the festivals but it was, at that time, the most high-profile venue of her career. It also represented a critical moment in the future of Philadelphia teenager and Joni fan, Joel Bernstein. Equally passionate about photography and guitars, Bernstein had endeared himself to Mitchell with his photographs of her and his

grasp of her complex guitar-playing technique. In January 1969,
she'd illustrated a hand-made notecard and sent it to Bernstein
inviting him to come along and photograph the Carnegie Hall
show. He accepted without hesitation:

> It was just incredibly thrilling, if you're in high school
> and that's what your world is, you're studying and all
> that, [then] to get this letter . . . I would have been not
> yet 17 at that point. I dutifully went to New York and
> had a life-changing weekend. I got to Carnegie Hall in
> time for the soundcheck, and met her manager, Elliot
> Roberts, who immediately said, 'I hope you have a lot
> of film tonight because we're recording this for a live
> album and it's going to be the cover.' That was the
> first I'd heard of it. So that was like . . . 'you're in the
> big-time now, you're photographing an album cover at
> Carnegie Hall, of this person who you've seen go in a
> very short time from obscurity – in the Second Fret
> shows, there were sometimes 12 or 14 people in the
> audience – [to fame] . . . the Carnegie Hall concert
> was a big turning-point for her and it was a big land-
> mark in my life.

Almost thirty years later, one of the photographs taken by the 16-
year-old Bernstein at Carnegie Hall was chosen by the Rock and
Roll Hall of Fame in Cleveland as the official still to accompany
its display on Joni Mitchell to mark her induction in 1997.

A week or two after the Carnegie Hall concert, Mitchell
phoned Bernstein and asked if, for publishing purposes, he could
make a tape of all of her songs that he knew, because she'd forgotten so many of them. Many were early songs that she'd
dropped from her set-lists and would not ever record. Bernstein
had already proven his knowledge of Mitchell's repertoire by
turning up at one show at the Main Point club in Philadelphia
and showing her a list of about thirty songs of hers. She
remarked, 'Are those the songs of mine that you've heard?', to
which Bernstein replied, 'No, those are the ones I can play!' He
recalls that she was taken aback that he'd been able to decipher
her idiosyncratic tunings. 'It was like her trade secret, not something that people were supposed to figure out and even if you

were a guitarist, it would take a lot to just follow her from one thing to another, particularly the tunings she made up herself.'

The Carnegie Hall show had indeed been a breakthrough and Mitchell's public profile was gaining momentum. In May, she was on the cover of *Rolling Stone,* the influential music and counter-culture Bible. Joni Mitchell was hailed as the rising star of a rein-vigorated folk resurgence that was threatening to batter the pop charts with gentle lyricism, pastoral allegories and acoustic arrangements. In the feature, Happy Traum wrote:

> Where Joan Baez is the embattled but still charming Joan of Arc of the non-violence crusade, and where Judy Collins is the regal long-time lady-in-waiting of the folk-pop world, Joni Mitchell is a fresh, incredibly beautiful innocent/experienced girl/woman. She can charm the applause out of an audience by breaking a guitar string, then apologising by singing her next number *a capella* . . . and when she talks, words stum-ble out of her mouth to form candid little quasi-anec-dotes that are completely antithetical to her carefully constructed, contrived songs. But they knock the audi-ence out almost every time. In Berkeley, she destroyed Dino Valente's 'Get Together' by trying to turn it into a rousing singalong. It was a lost cause but the audience made a valiant try at following. For one night, for Joni Mitchell, they were glad to be sheep.

Warner Brothers/Reprise had been clamouring for a new album. The company decided to try to capitalise on their artist's growing popularity and take advantage of Collins's success with BSN by launching an advertising campaign, devised by Stan Cornyn. Faced with two choices in promoting Mitchell – focus on the con-siderable quality of her work or on her considerable sexual appeal – he chose the latter. Abandoning imagination and intel-ligence in favour of irritating innuendo, he wrote an advertise-ment with the headline: 'Joni Mitchell is 90% virgin.' The apparent rationale behind the headline was more subtle than its execution – Judy Collins had sold ten times as many records as Mitchell had done; she'd achieved that with a Joni Mitchell song although Mitchell herself had not (yet) recorded it; the public were already familiar with the song through versions by Collins and others, etc., etc. It probably did seem like a good idea in a room full of perma-tanned weekend-hippie LA record company men. They seemed equally convinced that the follow-up slogans were positively Tolstoyesque in their ability to excite the imagination and conjure up a vision through the powerful use of an exquisitely crafted phrase – 'Joni Mitchell takes forever', i.e. she's too slow finishing that second album, and then, the campaign climax, the ad-men's wet dream fantasy realised: 'Joni Mitchell finally comes across', announcing the release of the album *Clouds* in May 1969. The advertisement declared:

> After lo these 14 months – it has happened. On our part, it's taken blood, sweat, tears and greed. Coaxing and cajoling. Even – yes – chicanery. But the blonde lady who only recently was the subject of a Reprise ad headlined 'Joni Mitchell takes forever' has finally, at long last, come across . . .

The ad copy urged people to buy the new album as well as Mitchell's debut, with an eager message for the wilful creator of the works: 'It might make Joni Mitchell come down from Laurel Canyon with her third album. But don't count on it.' The advertisement offered posters of the *Clouds* cover art for 25 cents; coupons were to be addressed to 'Joni Mitchell's Pretty Picture' at Warners in Burbank.

Given that her own record company was presenting her for public consumption in such a flippant manner, it's little wonder that, even at that early stage, Mitchell had begun to question the price of fame. She was receiving the public validation she had wanted for her work, but at heart was troubled by all the fuss and fever that went with it. She'd expressed her reservations in interviews during the year: 'Before I was a celebrity . . . I could just slip in and out of town without having to talk to anybody. I had to work hard on gaining confidence . . . I only started believing in myself this year.' She acknowledged that the first album had caused many changes to her life, and not all for the better:

> It's like being pressed by five suitors. And they're all pressing you hard. I began to feel really crowded, even

in my dressing-room. I had to start asking people, 'Please give me as much air as I had before.' But people don't understand. They say you've gone 'show business'. And they start to put you down. So you have to change. You really do change. And all I really ask is that people treat me like a person. I change as much as other people change. I feel more like a woman now. I used to think I was a teenybopper.

There was to be no respite from the attention with the release of *Clouds*; it had massive advance sales and peaked at number 31 on the US charts. Early the following year, its creator won the Grammy for Best Folk Recording. The promotional trail led her to Nashville and a guest appearance on *The Johnny Cash Show*, a short-lived but iconoclastic venture by Cash, who aimed for a broad mix of country, folk and folk-rock artists, many of whom were his friends. On the show with Mitchell was a nervous Bob Dylan, making a rare television appearance less than a month after the release of his *Nashville Skyline* album. It was the first meeting between Mitchell and Dylan, and the conversation continued later at the Black Poodle club, where Mitchell and Graham Nash, Dylan, Johnny Cash and his wife June Carter had gone to watch a performance by Cajun fiddler and fellow Cash show guest Doug Kershaw. Johnny Cash's sense of camaraderie and inclusiveness was not always shared by others in Nashville, where the hippie/hillbilly divide was alive and well and hollering insults from the sidelines. Speaking soon after arriving in Nashville with Nash and her manager, Elliot Roberts, Mitchell had said: 'In the hotel, we've been treated fantastically but the boys went out to get me a bouquet of flowers. They said everybody was hostile to them. People yelled, called them shaggy-hairs and hippies. They felt unsafe.'

Despite her male companions' momentary unease in Nashville, Mitchell herself had grown in personal and musical confidence. *Clouds* built on the lyrical themes of its predecessor and showed that over the past year, no longer the neophyte, she had become determined to do things her own way in the studio. She explained during recording why she had dispensed with a producer (apart from Paul Rothchild on 'Tin Angel'):

> I was working with a producer and we were pulling
> each other in opposite directions. I was working within
> this framework of sound equipment and the sound was
> fantastic, but I felt stifled. Now the sound isn't so good
> but at least I know I'm doing what I want to do.

Just as she would do for much of her recording career, Mitchell
dispensed with a producer and simply put the album together
herself, with Henry Lewy as her engineer.

Years later, she would describe her aversion to the interfer-
ence of an outside producer as having its roots in an art student's
sensibility:

> If you're in art school, nobody would come up and put
> a mark on your canvas. It is my work and be damned if
> anybody is going to put a mark on it. Whatever your
> reason to make it something else, it isn't my music and
> if it isn't my music, then I'm being slapped by my
> piano teacher again. You're going to kill my love of it
> and it won't go the distance. I knew what a good per-
> formance was, so in order to protect my music for the
> second time, I worked with just an engineer. He's like
> a print puller.

As with *Joni Mitchell*, the album used sparse instrumentation –
guitar and piano – but this time around, many of the tracks had
more obvious commercial appeal. Having watched others have
success with her songs in a market that was now clearly recep-
tive to her writing, Mitchell wisely included 'Both Sides, Now'.
The album title itself had been taken from the song, which was
to have extraordinary longevity, becoming that rare thing in popular music – a song that is universally familiar, that transcends
time and, circumstance and, occasionally, even translations. The
lyrics were at one time translated into Chinese calligraphy, then
back into English and entitled 'Joni's Theory of Relativity'. The
inspiration, Bellow's hapless Henderson, had been a man whose
life was a catalogue of misdeeds and mishaps, a pig farmer who
drove his tractor while drunk, fell off and ran over himself
(although not a fatal mishap); whose brother, Dick, took a pistol
and shot a pen out of a friend's hand in a diner, only for the bul-

let to pierce a coffee urn, spraying scalding coffee around, prompting the owner to call the police, forcing Dick into a car chase which ended when he crashed his car and tried to escape by swimming a river, only his cavalry boots filled with water and he drowned. But Henderson had peered from an aircraft window at the clouds below him and pierced that mystery of insight; Mitchell had shared it.

Back down to earth, the upbeat pop-ish 'Chelsea Morning' had been written during a visit to Philadelphia, after Mitchell and a group of women who were working in a club where she was performing had found chunks of brightly coloured glass discarded in an alleyway. They collected the glass and took it home to create mobiles with copper wire and coat-hangers. Mitchell took hers back to New York and hung it in the window of her small apartment in Chelsea; when the glass caught the sunlight, the colours shimmered around the walls:

> Woke up, it was a Chelsea morning, and the first thing that I saw
> Was the sun through yellow curtains, and a rainbow on the wall
> Blue, red, green and gold to welcome you, crimson crystal beads to beckon . . .

Within months of the release of *Clouds*, Judy Collins, buoyed by the success of her 'Both Sides Now' cover, released a single of 'Chelsea Morning'. It would be included on her *Living* album in 1971 and that version would later inspire a couple of young lawyers – Bill and Hillary Clinton – to name their baby daughter Chelsea.

Mitchell's former room-mate in Toronto, Vicky Taylor, believes she was the inspiration for the track 'I Think I Understand'. She recalls visiting Mitchell in Detroit and finding a haven there:

> I had had a nervous breakdown and I was taking all kinds of tranquillisers and sleeping pills. I think she wrote part of it while I was there visiting her in Detroit, and finished it later. . . I felt that was a great gift from her. Every person who came through her life was like

grist for the mill, but not in a cold way – she would try so hard to understand what they were feeling and then put that into words. Her musical talent is great but so also is her talent for empathy. I work as an addictions counsellor now, and so many of the young women who come through treatment will write in their journal, 'what I'm going through reminds me of [one of] Joni Mitchell's songs ...' She still has the voice of the heart of young women, it seems ... Emotions are very hard things to put into words, and I think that's what singers and songwriters do for people. [People] can listen to a song and say 'yes, that's exactly how I feel'. It's very comforting just to know that somebody understands what you're feeling.

Mitchell's empathy for the travails of her generation was also to the fore in 'Songs to Aging Children Come'. Where 'The Circle Game' had had its optimistic roots in encouraging Neil Young to think positively about entering his twenties, 'Songs to Aging Children Come' was a more sombre reflection, as illustrated in its use in a mournful scene from the Arlo Guthrie film *Alice's Restaurant.* The song could have led to Mitchell's feature film acting debut but a dispute over publishing rights meant that she turned down the role of a singer in the film. The producers of *Alice's Restaurant,* a film which celebrated 60s counter-culture and draft-dodging during the Vietnam war, had displayed a somewhat unhippyish materialism in their insistence on having a 50 per cent share of the song, a deal Elliot Roberts found easy to turn down. They had originally asked Mitchell to write a song for inclusion in a scene depicting a wake after the tragic death of one of the characters. They'd given her just one week to write the song but instead she had put forward 'Songs to Aging Children Come' as being appropriate to the theme: 'Some come dark and strange like dying Crows and ravens whistling Lines of weeping, strings of crying So much said in listening.' The song was used in the film; Mitchell was not.

Originally titled 'Song for America', the sparse hymn-like 'The Fiddle and the Drum' had been written late in 1967, before the civil unrest and turmoil of the months that followed, but it encapsulated the confusion and frustration of the times, with its variation on beating ploughshares into swords.

Clouds was dedicated to Sadie J. McKee, Mitchell's maternal grandmother. Young Sadie Henderson, of Scottish-French descent, had married James McKee, an Irish ploughman who was among the first settlers to come to the Saskatchewan flatlands after the railways had opened up the prairies. They became home-steaders in Creelman, a village in south-eastern Saskatchewan. Sadie played the organ and wrote poetry; she had her gramophone and opera records but was capable of kicking the kitchen door off its hinges, consumed with the frustrations of her life as wife and mother, with little outlet for her music and poetry. Her equally fiery husband once broke all of her records, believing his wife thought she had married beneath her. Sadie's granddaughter remembers her as being 'a fine musician who wrote poetry in thick Scottish brogue like Robert Burns, about lifestyles of the French and Indian traders'.

Back in Scotland, Sadie's great-grandfather had worked on the estate of one of the nation's best-loved writers, Sir Walter Scott, who had presented him with a medal for the speed and skill of his ploughing. Mitchell's paternal grandmother came from Norway and family legend has it that the last time in her life that she cried was at the age of 14, sobbing behind a barn on their farm in Norway, at the thought that she'd never have a piano of her own. She emigrated to the settlement of New Norway, in Saskatchewan, had eleven children, a deeply unhappy marriage and a lifelong frustration at not being able to express herself in music.

The album's cover art was dominated by a Mitchell self-por-trait – a fresh-faced prairie girl, the quintessential flower child holding a lush red amaryllis. In the sunset-streaked skyline behind her is one of Saskatoon's best-known landmarks, the chateau-style Bessborough Hotel on the banks of the South Saskatchewan river.

By the time the album came out in May 1969, Mitchell and Graham Nash were living in a house she had bought on Lookout Mountain Avenue in Laurel Canyon. Their life together there would famously provide Nash with the inspiration for his song, 'Our House'. It would also see Nash create one of the greatest folk-rock groups of the era, along with David Crosby, Stephen

Stills and, later, Neil Young, in CSN (and Y). Their impeccable musical pedigree ensured that the new band's first tour to promote the debut album, *Crosby, Stills & Nash*, would be a phenomenal success. As Graham Nash says, Mitchell was the obvious support act for the tour:

> When Joan came to play with us in 69, she was my girlfriend. CSN&Y always wanted to expose our audience to the best music possible. The problem was always, what kind of music would our fans like to hear before listening to us, and because of Joan's unbelievably fresh approach to music we believed that the audience for CSN&Y would love her music and her. Joan had always been 'one of the boys', had always been open to singing with us and to us singing with her. Our combined audiences got a great big helping of good music when they came to see the CSN&Y/Joni Mitchell show. We toured the USA together and did a couple of shows in Europe. I was an extremely fortunate man and couldn't have been happier.

Crosby, Stills, Nash and Young – the music world's newest supergroup – performed its first concert at the Chicago Auditorium Theatre on 16 August, with Mitchell as support. The following day they flew to New York for the onward journey upstate for their second live appearance. It was to be the biggest gig Mitchell *almost* attended: the Woodstock Music and Art Fair, held on Max Yasgur's farm in Bethel. She had been scheduled to play on Sunday night but conditions had worsened since the first day of the 'Three Days of Peace and Music'; massive traffic jams had caused gridlock in the surrounding area and torrential rain had left 300,000 festivalgoers wading through a sea of mud. Mitchell's manager, Elliot Roberts, and agent, David Geffen – who also had CSN&Y as clients – decided that they could not risk Mitchell being delayed in Bethel. She was scheduled to appear on Dick Cavett's high-profile TV talk show in New York the following day, and that was considered too good an opportunity to miss. Unlike Woodstock. Roberts and CSN&Y flew out by private plane; Geffen took a disappointed Mitchell back to his apartment in Manhattan where their experience of Woodstock was limited to television news reports.

Inspired by what she was watching and by the peace-love-music ethos of the festival, Mitchell saw it as a modern-day miracle, a Biblical loaves and fishes allegory of the multitudes, nourishing and nurturing each other. For her, Woodstock had come at the very time when she was trying to cope with her own growing celebrity, the media attention, and the role that was being thrust on her and her friends as the voices of their generation. She looked briefly for these answers in religion and saw a spiritual relevance in Woodstock:

> The deprivation of not being able to go provided me with an intense angle on Woodstock ... At the time I was going through a kind of born-again Christian trip, not that I went to any church, I'd given up Christianity at an early age at Sunday school. But suddenly, as performers we were in the position of having so many people look to us for leadership, and for some unknown reason I took it seriously and decided I needed a guide and leaned on God. So I was a little 'God-mad' at the time, for lack of a better term, and I had been saying to myself, 'Where are the modern miracles?' Woodstock, for some reason, impressed me as being a modern miracle ... for a herd of people that large to co-operate so well, it was pretty remarkable and there was tremendous optimism. So I wrote the song 'Woodstock' out of these feelings, and the first three times I performed it in public I burst into tears because it brought back the intensity of the experience and was so moving.

She wrote of 'bombers, riding shotgun in the sky, and they were turning into butterflies . . . ' after curious Air Force jet pilots flew their bombers low over the festival site to check out the 'happening'. The song became an anthem for the age:

> ... well, maybe it's the time of year
> Or maybe it's the time of man
> I don't know who I am
> But life's for learning
> We are stardust

We are golden
And we've got to get ourselves
Back to the garden . . .

Geffen's fears that Mitchell would have missed the Cavett show if she'd gone to Woodstock proved groundless; CSN&Y got back in time and Crosby and Stills appeared briefly on the show as well. Years later, Mitchell saw the segment repeated on television and was struck by an unconscious influence on her guitar-playing style, which came to employ percussive sounds, like tapping and slapping, as an integral element:

> I thought that slap came purely from [playing] the dulcimer until I saw [the] television show . . . Stephen slapped his guitar, which is a kind of flamenco way of playing it, so I would have to cite Stephen Stills also as an influence in that department. But it was latent and not conscious. It wasn't like I studied him and tried to play like him, but I admired the way he played.

CSN&Y might have had the physical experience of Woodstock but Mitchell had the song to immortalise it. On the flight back from Woodstock, Stephen Stills had tried to distil the experience into a song but ultimately gave up. He said later, 'Just as I was on the verge of getting it together, Joni came over and played us her song. I said I couldn't top it.' Early the following year the song became the first single released by Crosby, Stills, Nash and Young and peaked at number 11 in the US charts. David Geffen later successfully negotiated with the producers of a film about the festival to use the song, after making his position abundantly clear to them:

> I would not allow them to use the footage of Crosby, Stills, Nash and Young in the movie unless they used Joni's song with Crosby, Stills, Nash and Young singing it as a theme of the movie. That's how it happened. The producers were either going to give me what I wanted or that was it. And since I represented a lot of important artists on Warner Brothers and Atlantic and Elektra Records, they just weren't going to fuck with me . . .

The day after CSN&Y's Woodstock appearance they returned to Los Angeles with Mitchell for a sold-out show at the Greek Theatre. Robert Hilburn, writing in the *Los Angeles Times*, described CSN&Y's performance as 'a triumph of the first order ... a staggering display of individual and collective talent'. The support act didn't fare badly either:

> Though overshadowed by Crosby, Stills, Nash and Young, Canadian singer and folk-poet Joni Mitchell, best known for 'Both Sides, Now', drew a good response as she opened the show. In person as on record she is sometimes difficult on first listening. Her voice, haunting at times, can be distracting at other times as it changes rapidly from highs to lows. She is, I believe, foremost a writer. Her best songs, including 'The Circle Game' and 'Chelsea Morning', are intimate portraits of life. As the evening continues, however, the voice seems to make more sense. It begins to carry the words of her songs with a warmth that reaches out into the audience ...

It was welcome praise in a month that had begun in front of a vast and unreceptive audience at the Atlantic City Pop Festival in New Jersey, where Mitchell had left the stage after just a few songs because of the noisy and disruptive crowd.

A few days later, CSN&Y and Joni left Los Angeles and took the spectacular coastline Route 1 to Big Sur, a 75-mile stretch of eroding yellow-ochre cliffs, beaches, river canyons and redwood forests. The extraordinary unspoiled beauty of the area made it a favourite destination in the 1960s for those longing to drop in, drop out or just drop off. The village of Esalen, named after the local Native Americans, the first tribe in California to be made culturally extinct, was a favoured destination. The counterculture had created tribes of its own and many were drawn to the Esalen Institute which was then at the forefront of the New Age human potential movement. Built around natural hot springs on a clifftop high above the Pacific, it was an idyllic location for the Big Sur Folk Festival. Festivalgoers got to see artists like Mitchell, CSN&Y, Joan Baez and John Sebastian perform for free; they heard Mitchell sing 'Woodstock', which she'd written just weeks earlier, and they saw a volatile Stephen Stills in a slanging match with a heckler who had apparently taken exception to the band's folk-rock-star finery and wealth. The incident, as well as Mitchell's performance, would be included in a film of the festival, *Celebration at Big Sur*.

The celebratory mood of a hugely successful summer for CSN&Y had been shattered when David Crosby's girlfriend, Christine Hinton, was killed in a car accident. Fearful that a deeply depressed Crosby might attempt suicide, Graham Nash spent as much time as possible with his friend as Crosby sought to make sense of Christine Hinton's death. Eventually, in a bid to restore Crosby's spirits by taking to the ocean in his beloved *Mayan*, they went to Florida to pick up the boat and join friends who would help to sail it back to California, where Crosby wanted to scatter Christine Hinton's ashes at sea off San Francisco Bay. They set a course through the Bahamas, the Windward Passage between Cuba and Hispaniola (Haiti and the Dominican Republic), Jamaica and through the Panama Canal. Mitchell joined them in Jamaica but was to leave the schooner in Panama to return home. In his autobiography, David Crosby recalls going ashore at the Pacific end of the Canal to make arrangements for Mitchell's homeward journey; the yacht club was at an army base and he planned to use the telephone there to book her flight:

> I went to the bar, which is where they had the phone that they would let you use. In the bar was this big crew-cut drunk, a mean, obnoxious guy. When I walked by him, he said, 'Goddamn hippie son of a bitch. Why aren't you in Vietnam, you son of a bitch?' And more words to that effect. I remember thinking, 'Gee, there's a nice cliff right there. I wish he'd just walk over and step off. This is somebody the world doesn't need'. I ignored him. He got even more abusive, so I left. I remember distinctly thinking, 'I wish he'd die'. When I came back the next morning to pay my fuel bill, I asked the club secretary who the obnoxious guy was and she said 'He's the FBI head of security for the base.' I said, 'Thank God I didn't slap him with a beer bottle'. And she said, 'He died last night of a heart attack.' I wished he'd die and he did. Ever since then, I encourage everyone to be very careful about what they wish on other people.

Divine retribution or not, Crosby's brief but potent encounter with the gung-ho FBI man symbolised the 'us and them', hippie versus Establishment, liberal/conservative, anti-war/militarist dichotomy – if you are not for us, you are against us. The peace and love vibes of what came to be known as the Woodstock era would be matched by the brutality and nihilism of political assassinations, the Charles Manson murders and Altamont. The film-maker Oliver Stone said of the closing years of the 1960s:

> My generation had this tremendous surge of hope and idealism for a better world – a 'Peace Corps World', let's call it, for want of simplification. Then it just kind of caved in so quick. Bobby Kennedy went down in the bizarrest of assassinations. Martin Luther King Jr, again in the same year, 1968. I was in Vietnam at that time. All the blacks in my unit were so upset when King was killed, and they said, 'Never again! Don't trust whitey!' And it was over. You could just feel the 60s clattering down on top of you . . . it was a nightmare. And then we took drugs and dropped out, and then Nixon came in on this tremendous fear and everyone was so scared in 1968 that the world was going crazy with all these killings and assassinations. He was a face from the past and he came in and presented, like Hitler did, the concept of law and order to cure disorder. What did he give us? He promised us peace and he gave us four more years of war. He promised us order and gave us chaos. He gave us Watergate.

Richard Milhous Nixon, a lawyer from a Quaker background, had lost the race for the presidency to John F. Kennedy in 1960, in one of the most closely fought elections in American political history – its like was not seen again until the curious protracted Gore–Bush tussle in 2000 which ultimately put George W. Bush in the White House. But in 1968 Nixon had defeated his rival for the presidency, the Democrat Vice-President, Hubert Humphrey. His policy, the Nixon Doctrine, paradoxically abandoned close involvement with Asian countries while becoming even more involved in Cambodia through a massive bombing campaign that escalated the war there. Re-elected by a landslide margin in 1972, he was rewarded with a second term in office by an American electorate that had been saturated with images of the war, of its boys returning home in body bags and flag-draped coffins. He was credited with ending the war rather than prolonging it. While prepared to reward his foreign policy on the war in South-east Asia and engagement with China, the American public were to show less tolerance of his attitude to matters closer to home: Nixon's culpability in the cover-up of the Watergate scandal – in which Republicans bungled an attempt to bug the offices of the rival Democratic Party at the Watergate building in Washington – was to be his downfall. The attempted cover-up and subsequent inquiry finally pushed Nixon to the ultimate politician's dilemma: should I stay or should I go now? – with apologies to the Clash.

On 8 August 1974, Mitchell would walk on stage for a show at the Pine Knob Music Theater, north of Detroit, and announce to a jubilant crowd that Nixon had just resigned.

The hippie promise of the 60s, the marches, slogans, happenings, love-ins, the changes that were supposed to make real every American's constitutional right to the pursuit of happiness, now carried the hollow echo of Johnny Rotten's snarl, 'ever get the feeling you've been cheated?' Graham Nash:

> I don't believe that the 60s ended until Nixon was removed from office. The pendulum swings, very often in very non-plussing ways, and the swing from the idealism of the 60s to the conservatism of the Nixon and later the Reagan years was shocking to us. We thought that we would be able to change – when I say 'we' I mean the singer/songwriter community that I'm a part of – the world instantly and we were very naïve. This planet has a certain mass and it's very difficult to change the trajectory of that mass. Maybe one is able to do it in millionth of degrees, but we thought it would happen overnight and we were wrong.

5 Dreams have lost some grandeur coming true ...

Fame is but a fruit tree,
So very unsound
It can never flourish
Til its stalk is in the ground.
       (Nick Drake, 'Fruit Tree', 1969)

B E CAREFUL WHAT YOU WISH FOR, says the Chinese proverb, for you will surely get it. Having achieved the financial security that had seemed so far out of reach when her daughter was born, the fame and recognition of her artistry presented Joni Mitchell with a dilemma: she was a reluctant star, again pondering the value of life in the public gaze when it was exactly that gaze that had brought with it the rich rewards. In two years, she had recorded two albums and the release of a third was imminent; she was about to pick up a Grammy and had toured almost to the brink of exhaustion.

The intimacy of the folk clubs and coffee houses and the ease of interaction with the audience had been superseded by the anonymity and formality of large venues, stripping away any chance of a real rapport between artist and audience. The public gaze was particularly strong when it was fixated on a lone figure on a large stage, and it could at times be overwhelming for her:

> I really enjoyed playing clubs for about forty people. I liked being [the] centre of attention. It was like being the life of the party. That I could handle. When it got to the big stage, I found that I didn't enjoy it. It frightened me initially. I had a lot of bad experiences, including running off many a stage. I just thought it was too big for me, it was out of proportion. This kind of attention was absurd.

Doing live shows had become a stomach-churning ordeal for Mitchell, a fact not lost on her audiences. Writing in *Rolling Stone* in August 1971, Timothy Crouse recalled:

> The last time I saw Joni Mitchell perform was a year and a half ago at Boston's Symphony Hall, in one of her final appearances before she forswore the concert circuit for good. Fragile, giggly and shy, she had the most obvious case of nerves I have ever seen in a professional singer. Her ringing soprano cracked with stage fright and her frightened eyes refused to make contact with the audience.

In early 1970, while on tour with CSN&Y in London, Joni Mitchell announced that she would be taking an indefinite break from concerts. Even as a critic, Geoffrey Cannon, was panting in the *Guardian* of her show at the Royal Festival Hall, that he had 'never before experienced such a close communion between a singer and an audience. I believe that Joni Mitchell is better able to describe ... what it means, and should mean, to be alive today than any other singer. She, alone, of every singer I've heard, reclaims the sense of holiness of every human being ... '

She had decided she'd had enough of such close communion. On a personal level, it was exactly the right decision, allowing her time to recoup her energies and write. On a professional level, it was to be the first of many decisions that showed an admirable, indeed often awe-inspiring, defiance of the rules of career-making in the music industry. The decision not to perform in public had come virtually on the eve of the release of her third album, *Ladies of the Canyon*. And everyone knows the rules: record, promote, tour. The only thing stopping Reprise executives from despair must have been the fact that with or without a tour schedule, Mitchell's career was gaining unstoppable momentum. Within weeks of the release of *Ladies of the Canyon*, its predecessor *Clouds* won Mitchell a Grammy for Best Folk Performance and Crosby, Stills, Nash and Young released a single of their version of Mitchell's song, 'Woodstock', from their new album *Deja Vu*.

Ladies of the Canyon was a more lavish affair, musically, than its predecessors. Joining her again was engineer Henry Lewy but this time, no longer content with just her own guitar and piano, she'd drafted in other musicians on cello, percussion, clarinet, flute and baritone sax. Vocal support on 'The Circle Game' chorus was provided by the Lookout Mountain United Downstairs Choir, aka Crosby, Stills, Nash and Young. Mitchell's own multi-tracked bop vocals were credited to the Saskatunes. Lyrically, although she had outgrown the fey fairy-tale quality that had marked so much of the first two albums, the penchant for idealised storybook scenes was still evident, as in the opening track, 'Morning Morgantown', a song she'd first performed live more than three years earlier. It's a filmic excursion into a picturesque little place where the sun is always shining, jolly merchants and milkmen greet the day, ladies wear 'rainbow fashions' and there's always a spare café table just right for people-watching and sipping tea and lemonade.

Grittier by far is the contrast between her own success and that of a clarinet-playing street busker in 'For Free'. Here the sunny streets of Morgantown are far away as she walks through 'the dirty town' and Mitchell reflects on the opportunities allowed to her, the privilege and the luxury of fine hotel rooms and indulgent shopping. The talented anonymous busker, playing for love of the music in exchange for little more than a few coins, is contrasted with the 'star': 'Now me I play for fortunes And those velvet curtain calls I've got a black limousine and two gentlemen Escorting me to the halls And I play if you have the money Or if you're a friend to me . . . ' She was soon to turn her back on 'those velvet curtain calls'. Mitchell once said of 'For Free' that it was written when

> the money and success seemed distasteful. The fame and fortune seemed out of all proportion to what I was doing, although there were times when I felt I deserved every bit of it . . . I felt a little whorish about selling my soul, putting a price on it. I would get up and pour out fragments of it for money and applause, not only my life but the life of someone I was with in a close personal relationship.

Another early song, again featured in live shows more than three years earlier, was 'Conversation', although the album version is two verses shorter than the original. She would introduce it cryptically in her shows, 'Sometimes a best friend won't tell a best friend really anything near the truth, because they don't know it themselves. This is a song about a triangle.' The title track is a series of character vignettes of life down among the women in the Laurel and Topanga canyons of Los Angeles, the hippie chick, the earth mother, the 'circus girl' space cadet. Although well crafted, its images dated rapidly to become the equivalent of an old photograph in an album. Yet amidst the detail of fluttery antique lace and filigree, wampun beads, baking brownies and music pouring down the canyon, there is one extraordinarily powerful image: 'Songs like tiny hammers hurled, At beveled mirrors in empty halls'.

The gentle 'Willy' (or 'Willie' as it is noted in the US Library of Congress reference work) is a love song to Graham Nash thinly disguised by the use of his nickname. Theirs was a deeply loving relationship that was already foundering by the time the album came out. In June, the day before a CSN&Y show at Fillmore East, the couple separated. Writing in the sleeve notes to the CSN box-set, Nash wrote, 'my whole world fell apart. The afternoon of that show I wrote ['Simple Man'] and that evening I performed it for the first time with Joni sitting in the audience. I don't know how I got through that.' Theirs is now a lifelong friendship and Mitchell thinks of Nash with great affection:

> Graham is a sweetheart and we didn't part with any animosity. A lot of pain – there's always pain in pulling apart. Graham needed a more traditional female. He loved me dearly . . . there's still a fondness and everything, but he wanted a stay-at-home wife to raise his children. And I said that I could – a rash promise that I made in my youth – and then realised I couldn't.

Mitchell's early albums were occasionally criticised for overly romanticising love, for the hearts and flowers tweeness of the lyrics, but there was a strong sensuality running through each of them, and the frankly sexual in 'Blue Boy' – 'he would read to her, Roll her in his arms And give his seed to her'. The album's last three tracks alone justify its place in the history of music – all have become modern standards, contemporary classics that have been among the most 'covered' songs in popular music. The proto-environmentalist 'Big Yellow Taxi' was inspired by Mitchell's first visit to Hawaii. She'd gone to join Graham Nash who was on tour there with CSN&Y and the view from Nash's hotel-room window at the Royal Hawaiian Hotel provided her with one of her best-known songs:

> I came in at night and went directly to their hotel and when I woke up in the morning I threw back the curtains, we were on the 20th floor, and I looked and I could see green hills and beautiful white flying birds with long tails and as far as the eye could see below that, I saw a parking lot and I was heartbroken. We were in Waikiki, which is the most developed, and at that time was really paved over so I wrote that song then. The Hawaiians, because of their tradition of slack key, really loved the guitar on that piece and it's kind of leaked into Hawaiian music. If you listen to contemporary Hawaiian music, a lot of it sounds like 'Big Yellow Taxi' unfortunately! I think it kind of over-influenced the genre. I tend to like their music better before they heard 'Big Yellow Taxi'.

American popster Amy Grant had huge success with her cover version, and Janet Jackson sampled Mitchell's original on her own song, 'Got 'Til It's Gone'. Another unlikely cover version was Bob Dylan's; it appears on his 1973 *Dylan* album. Joni herself would later describe BYT as a 'powerful little song, because there have been cases in a couple of cities of parking lots being torn up and turned into parks because of it'. Just as had happened with 'Chelsea Morning', Mitchell's original version of one of her songs was out in the marketplace at the same time as a cover; both she and CSN&Y had included 'Woodstock' on their current albums. Stephen Stills's and Neil Young's electric guitars transported the song from Mitchell's original but her version here is peerless. *Rolling Stone* reviewer Gary von Tersch advised:

> Forget the hyperactive CSN&Y version and listen to this one. Joni uses a heavily-amped electric guitar [*sic*] and sings the hell out of each phrase, each syllable of this

soon-to-be-anthem of the 70s. She takes her time and
the song has its mellowing, quicksilver effect . . .

The album ends with 'The Circle Game', the song written as a
response to Neil Young's 'Sugar Mountain' some years earlier.
Her decision to wait until her third album before recording it is
intriguing. As early as 1967 she was talking about the differences
between her original and the cover versions:

> The way I sing 'Circle Game' . . . has evolved. The way
> Tom [Rush] sings it and the way Ian and Sylvia sing it
> is the same as it is on the lead sheet. Now I changed it
> because at one point, I went to Chicago and cut it as a
> single. And I was going to try and have somebody buy
> up the rights and promote it. And it didn't work out
> well because 'Circle Game' is not ever going to be a
> rock and roll song. Ian and Sylvia found that out with
> their version, and I tried to do the same thing. It has to
> be kept down. It has to be a ballad. It's very tempting.
> So in the process of rocking it up, we had to eliminate
> a couple of choruses, and when you put a verse back to
> back then the melody became tedious, so I did that
> (sings) 'So the years spin by and now . . . the boy is
> twenty'.

Mitchell's cover art was the simplest of the three albums to date;
an unadorned incomplete line drawing self-portrait with a paint-
by-numbers-style snapshot of a steep canyon road, dotted with
houses. Sting has said that when *Ladies of the Canyon* came out,
he was smitten immediately:

> I wore it out. I played those songs and played them and
> played them. Her ability as a story-teller is second to
> none. But she doesn't get sufficient credit as a musi-
> cian. She's under-rated. She's a fabulous guitarist and
> everybody knows she's a great singer.

Musicians who were barely babies when the album first came
out were to discover it years later, among them Speech, the co-
founder of the rap group Arrested Development:

She is definitely one of my greatest influences. What I like most about her is, her lyrics are so real-life. She notices the simple things in life and makes them sound so profound. I imitate that in my own songwriting. If someone wanted to run out today and get what I think is the best introduction to Joni Mitchell, I'd say get *Ladies of the Canyon*. You can't help but come away from that with a definite appreciation for her vocal arrangements and her vocal and lyrical ability.

The ever-inventive Reprise advertising department had decided on a slightly different tack to promote *Ladies*; they abandoned the sexual innuendo of the *Clouds* campaign, designed to catch the attention of men, and took aim at Mitchell's aspirational women fans who saw themselves as artistic lovelorn ladies of the canyon – or suburb or small town. A full-page advertisement in *Rolling Stone* told the fictional story of one such young woman and reads like an encyclopaedia of popular cultural reference points of the time. We join Amy Foster, a 'quietly beautiful' 23 year old, as she sits in her orange inflatable chair, toying with the enormous antique ring on her finger, listening to Neil Young's second album and pondering the prospect of spending an evening tie-dyeing some curtains for her 64 Chevy camper van. Amy, alas, is blue. Her ex-boyfriend had left her a month earlier and married 'some chick he met at the Jeans West shop he managed'. She wonders whether she should just get in that van and hit the road to 'get her head back together'. Poor Amy. 'I'm incredibly down, man,' she says to herself as she lifts the turntable stylus off 'Down by the River'.

There is a knock at the door; it's Barry, the delivery boy from the local store, dropping off her groceries. He pauses to admire the Van Morrison collage she's just made. They share herbal tea (with orange honey mixed in) then a joint which Barry has thoughtfully provided and listen to Side 1 of CSN&Y's *Deja Vu*. Amy is now 'mellow'. Barry notices her stereo player:

'Hey, you have a really far-out system here,' he enthuses. 'Do you think we could listen to some of Joni Mitchell's new album on it?'

He had bought the album that very afternoon and being a delivery boy who is clearly always prepared for any eventuality, he has it with him.

'Hey, groovy,' murmurs Amy in assent.

The narrative continues:

> As much as they downed her for reminding her all too
> vividly of her now-irrevocably consummated relation-
> ship with David, 'Willy' and 'Conversation' were some-
> how reassuring – there was someone else, even another
> canyon lady, who really knew. Amy began to feel a lit-
> tle better. By the time 'Circle Game' had finished, Amy
> was no longer dejectedly contemplating splitting for
> Oregon. In fact, she could scarcely wait for the sun to
> get through setting so she could drive up to the top of
> Lookout [Mountain] and watch Los Angeles twinkle
> beneath the indigo April sky.

Life, it seems, is not always easy for a lady of the canyon but it's
nothing that a little Joni first aid can't fix.

Mitchell herself, meanwhile, had decided to 'split', and set off
on sabbatical spending the next several months travelling, writing, getting a life. She went to Europe, stopping in Greece, Spain
and France, taking only a few clothes and two easily portable
musical instruments – a flute and a dulcimer she had bought at
the Big Sur Folk Festival the previous summer:

> I'd never seen one played before. Traditionally, it's
> picked with a quill, and it's a very delicate thing that
> sits across your knee. The only instrument I ever had
> across my knee was a bongo drum, so when I started to
> play the dulcimer I beat it. I just slapped it with my
> hands.

She wrote most of the songs that would appear on her next
album, *Blue,* around the dulcimer while in Greece, which was
then under military rule. A military coup in 1967 had forced King
Constantine into exile and installed a hard-line regime, known as
the 'Colonels':

> I was craving a guitar so badly in Greece. The junta had
> repressed the population at that time. They were not
> allowed public meetings; they were not allowed any

kind of boisterous or colourful expression. The military was sitting on their souls, and even the poets had to move around. We found this floating poets' gathering place, and there was an apple crate of a guitar there that people played. I bought it off them for fifty bucks and sat in the Athens underground with transvestites and ... the underbelly running around – and it was like a romance. It was a terrible guitar, but I hadn't played one for so long, and I began slapping it because I had been slapping this dulcimer. That's when I noticed that my style changed.

Mitchell had hoped to spend time living with a Greek family, to truly experience the country in a more authentic way than simply being a tourist allowed, but her plans foundered and she headed for the island of Crete, centre of the sophisticated maritime trading empire of the Minoans in 2000 BCE and a stopping-off point for invaders from ancient Greece and Rome, the Saracens, the Byzantine Empire, Venice, Turkey and modern Greece. Another wave of invaders came in the 60s – no hippie-trail voyager would consider a trip to Greece complete without a visit to Crete, where a hippie community had sprung up in the coastal village of Matala. It was here, according to Greek mythology, that the supreme god Zeus, in the guise of a gentle white bull, fooled the lovely princess Europa into allowing him to carry her to shore on his back, only to resume his normal shape and ravish her in a most ungodly way. In more contemporary times, westerners seeking Nirvana or simply a cheap place to live had come to Matala and made their homes in dozens of caves that had been carved out of the compacted-sand cliff overlooking the beach. They were only the latest in a long line of occupants – the Minoans may, or may not, have set up home there but the Romans or early Christians are believed to have used the caves as burial chambers; locals had lived in them for centuries and, during the Second World War, the caves were commandeered as munitions dumps. It took the 60s to make them chic. And as would happen in so many parts of the world, travellers in search of unspoiled natural beauty, isolation and tranquillity stayed just long enough to ensure that they destroyed the very qualities that had drawn them there.

The rustic charms of rural Crete were romanticised – quaintly authentic farmers leading citrus-fruit-laden donkeys, the enforced simplicity of a peasant family's lifestyle, seen as very Zen, very minimalist when in truth they were just poor. But the reality of everyday life occasionally proved disorienting for the hordes of pampered brats whose parents were paying for them to go slumming among the peasant folk of Europe, as Mitchell recalled:

> Matala was full of kids from all over the world who were seeking the same kind of thing I was, but . . . they may as well have been in an apartment in Berkeley as in a cave there because the lifestyle continued the same wherever they were. And the odd thing to me was that . . . we came to this very scene – the very scene we were trying to escape from – and it seemed very attractive to us. There were so many contradictions . . . like, the kids couldn't get used to seeing all the slaughtered meat hanging up in the shops – they'd only ever seen bits of meat wrapped in cellophane, and to see it there on its frame turned their stomachs.

Mitchell and her companion, Penelope, a friend from Ottawa, stayed for five weeks in a cave at Matala. Mitchell recalls the cave dwellers were eventually evicted by the police as their excesses came to outweigh the lucrative benefits of their presence to the local economy: 'It was getting a little crazy there. Everybody was getting more and more into open nudity. They were really getting back to the caveman. They were wearing little loin cloths. The Greeks couldn't understand what was happening.' Joni would later immortalise her friend, Penelope, in a poem with the words 'Penelope wants to fuck the sea . . . '

Through the summer, Mitchell reconsidered her self-imposed ban on live performances and agreed to appear at the Isle of Wight festival in southern England, in August. She may have missed Woodstock the previous year but this was her chance to experience the British equivalent. It became a vivid reminder of why she'd decided to stop performing live in the first place. The festival attracted some of the biggest names in music; it was to be the last great music 'happening' of the era. The Beatles were indisposed and the Rolling Stones were still reeling from the tragedy of Altamont the previous year, but the Doors, Jimi Hendrix (who, tragically, would be dead less than a month later), the Who, Jethro Tull, Miles Davis, Procul Harum, Chicago, the Moody Blues, Joan Baez, Leonard Cohen, Kris Kristofferson and Donovan were among those who were also there, along with 600,000 people who'd turned up to see them, only a fraction of whom had actually paid the ticket price of three pounds.

The lush fields of East Afton Farm, near Freshwater, had been chosen for the festival site. The area was overlooked by a hill – which came to be known as Devastation Hill – that was to provide the perfect vantage point and makeshift camping ground for the non-paying multitudes. Agit-prop pamphlets urged people to set up camp on the hill and enjoy the festival for free. The promoters had set up perimeter fences and security patrols to prevent freeloaders gatecrashing the site as had happened at Woodstock but it proved to little avail. The organisers tried a variety of methods to restore a semblance of lucrative ticket-buying order but these only served to strengthen the crowd's resolve: the volume was turned down to deprive the hillside residents of the sound, but it also meant that legitimate ticket-holders were missing out so that was abandoned; a searchlight was trained on the hill at night but achieved little more than lighting the way for those who were stumbling or stoned or both, and alerted others to places that hadn't yet been taken. Finally, the organisers resorted to threats, saying the festival would be cancelled if the hill wasn't cleared. It didn't happen. One activist, allowed on stage to have his say, denounced the set-up as a psychedelic concentration camp. The organisers finally relented and eventually a festival that was already unofficially free was declared officially free. Speaking to reporters, protest veteran Joan Baez had said:

> The question of kids now wanting everything to be free is very hard to handle, because it's hard to talk to those kids, but I am not going to be forced into giving a free concert because they insist upon it. That doesn't make sense either. I mean these kids have been handed down an evil stinking rotten world, and they're rebelling against it. They're sick of it and one of their ways of saying it is 'I'm not going to pay for it.'

The move didn't, however, stop the resentment among sections of the crowd, over the fences, the security patrols, the technical problems and appalling sanitary conditions, which would have upset them even more if they'd actually paid to be there. There was also the constant carping, threats and entreaties of the organisers who, it was felt, seemed happy to lavish vast amounts of money on the superstars and their guests but resented a few – or indeed, a few hundred thousand – people seeing their musical heroes for free. Stories abounded of financial excess and profiteering – stars were flown in by helicopter or driven to the site in limousines; there was a motorcycle escort for Leonard Cohen and his entourage; agents and managers demanded cash up front before their clients would perform. Mitchell herself had turned up with Neil Young and their manager, Elliot Roberts, in a vintage red Rolls Royce, complete with chauffeur. But when workers for the charity Release went backstage to take up a collection for people who'd been arrested, they came away with only a few pounds.

Kris Kristofferson was so threatened by the noise from the crowd pounding on the corrugated-iron fences that he walked off stage without finishing his set, saying to his band, 'I think they're gonna shoot us.' When Joni came out on stage, she was overwhelmed by the size of the crowd and commented, 'It looks like they're making *Ben Hur* or something!' Her hour-long set began with 'The Gallery' and contained songs from her previous two albums, and some that would soon appear on *Blue*. Despite a restive audience, including a man near the front experiencing a drugs-induced meltdown, and the sound of small airplanes taking off from a field nearby, she got through 'That Song About The Midway', and part-way through 'Chelsea Morning' she stopped and told the audience, 'I don't feel like singing that song very much. Let me play you one on the piano.'

After singing 'For Free', she could ignore the crowd's raucous interruptions no longer. Only a year earlier, she had walked off stage for far less. But an emboldened Mitchell declared: 'You know maybe I'm kinda weird but when I'm sitting up here and playing and I hear all those people growling out there and people saying, "Joni, smile for Amsterdam" and stuff, it really puts me uptight and I forget the words and then I get nervous and it's really a drag! I don't know what to say ... Just give me a little help, will ya?'

Help arrived from an unexpected quarter. At that moment, a hippie friend she'd met in Matala, Yogi Joe, bounded on to the stage, gave Joni the peace sign and settled in next to her for an impromptu session on the congas he'd brought with him. Mitchell and the stage managers, fearing they might antagonise the crowds if they threw him off, allowed him to stay onstage, and while she sang 'Woodstock', he played along – badly. Mitchell recalls:

> He looks up at me and says 'Spirit of Matala, Joni!' I bend down off-mike and say, 'This is entirely inappropriate, Joe.' It was 'Woodstock' of all the songs to be singing, because this was so different – it was a war zone out there.

As the song ended, Yogi Joe stood up and took the microphone from Mitchell to say, 'I have an announcement that I've been asked to make. Desolation Row is this festival, ladies and gentlemen.' Security and stage hands eventually had to wrestle him off stage but the incident further incensed the crowd, who jeered as Mitchell attempted to play the piano intro to 'My Old Man'. Faced with a choice of either abandoning her set and fleeing the stage or facing a vociferous crowd that now seemed to be baying for blood, a visibly upset Mitchell turned on the several hundred thousand people in front of her:

'Listen a minute, will ya? Will ya listen a minute? Now listen ... A lot of people who get up here and sing, I know it's fun, ya know, it's a lot of fun. It's fun for me, I get my feelings off through my music, but listen ... You got your life wrapped up in it and it's very difficult to come up here and lay something down when people ... It's like last Sunday I went to a Hopi ceremonial dance in the desert and there were a lot of people there and there were tourists ... and there were tourists who were getting into it like Indians and there were Indians who were getting into it like tourists, and I think that you're acting like tourists, man. Give us some respect.'

Astonishingly, it seemed to work. As she described it years later, 'the beast lay down'. Both she and the crowd relaxed, and she went into 'Willy' followed by two new songs, 'A Case of You' and 'California', then finished her set with 'Big Yellow Taxi'

before returning to encore with 'Both Sides, Now'. Backstage,
Yogi Joe – who had taught Mitchell yoga in Crete – was telling
anyone who would listen:

> I believe this is my festival. If I had been allowed to go
> on stage, we might have discovered that I was one of
> the most coherent people around here ... coming to
> talk to an old friend of mine, Joni Mitchell. 'We are
> stardust, we are golden, we got to get ourselves back to
> the garden, we are caught in the devil's bargain.' Rikki
> Farr [one of the organisers] or whatever his name is,
> came to me on Wednesday. He gave me a hundred
> tickets and made me the head of the official committee
> to paint the fences invisible. OK, he wanted to paint
> the fence invisible at the time because it was embar-
> rassing him. At that time I suggested to him that he put
> a few swivel panels on it. Since then we've discovered
> that it isn't a question of money. We're all middle class
> children and we can afford to have our festival.
> Basically this was all a plan. It was a plan of friends of
> ours to meet Joni Mitchell on stage, get stoned and
> make music ...

While visiting Britain, Mitchell recorded a concert for BBC television which was broadcast shortly before she returned to
London in November for a show at the Royal Festival Hall. By
then the British group Matthews' Southern Comfort, led by Ian
Matthews of Fairport Convention, had had a British Number 1
with their version of 'Woodstock'. The omens could not have
been better for the Festival Hall concert. After a shaky start,
Mitchell settled in and for two hours played the guitar, piano and
dulcimer, to accompany songs from all three of her albums and
newer ones like 'River', 'Carey' and 'California' that would
appear months later on her next album, *Blue.* For her encore,
'The Circle Game', her manager, Elliot Roberts, and former beau,
Graham Nash, emerged from the wings to join her on stage as
back-up singers. Her concert 'comeback' was greeted with rave
reviews, even in normally staid publications: the *Financial Times*
noting that in an 'atmosphere heavy with awe and adulation',
Mitchell had held the audience 'in her hand, massaged their

souls and then released them fulfilled'; the *Daily Telegraph* felt that Mitchell's 'occasional hesitancies served only to reveal the depth from which she draws her inspiration and the uncompromising standards she sets herself'. The critic writing in the music magazine *Sounds* believed that:

> Few other performers today can strike such a rapport with an audience, yet few others are prepared to expose themselves, their private loves and fears, to the public gaze. Unlike her countryman Leonard Cohen and other contemporaries who enact their emotions against a background of human desperation, Joni sings of hope, of love and joy. Of dignity in despair.

A few days later, Mitchell recorded a concert at the BBC's Paris Theatre in London, hosted by John Peel, for broadcast later in December. Appearing with her was James Taylor, with whom she was having a passionate though turbulent relationship. Taylor's second album, *Sweet Baby James,* had already gone platinum in the US, boosted by the success of the single 'Fire and Rain', and by the time he and Mitchell arrived in London his album was at Number 7 in the British charts. At the Paris Theatre, Mitchell sang a number of songs solo including 'That Song about The Midway', 'The Gallery', 'Hunter (The Good Samaritan)', 'River' and 'My Old Man'. Taylor sang his own 'Rainy Day Man', then introduced 'Steamroller Blues' with an anecdote about his band, Flying Machine, playing a residency at the Night Owl Café in Greenwich Village, and hearing all the suburban white kids pretending to be bluesmen, with testosterone-fuelled songs declaring 'I'm a man!' or 'I'm a jackhammer!' or 'I'm a steamship ... the Queen Mary!' Not to be outdone, he explains that he wrote what he jokingly referred to as 'the heaviest blues tune I know, ladies and gentlemen', calling it 'I'm a Steamroller'. It was back to Mitchell for 'The Priest' and 'Carey' (playing a dulcimer) before Taylor returned for a song from *Sweet Baby James,* 'Carolina In My Mind' (the single, featuring Paul McCartney on bass, peaked at Number 67 on the US charts). Taylor stayed on stage to accompany Mitchell on guitar for 'A Case of You', 'California' and 'For Free', which, he explained, he'd first heard at the Newport Folk Festival when they were both involved in a songwriting workshop, 'it's kind of a cowboy-type tune'. They sang together on 'The Circle Game' and Taylor's 'You Can Close Your Eyes'.

The show was a triumph. Their romance lent an air of intimacy and warmth to the proceedings, they were immensely comfortable together and enjoying the experience, and Taylor's presence encouraged Mitchell to be more relaxed. Musically, their voices and styles are highly complementary, and for Joni it was the first time that she had duetted on several songs on stage, since she and Chuck Mitchell were together. A charming, patrician New Englander, Taylor was an intriguing mix of ambition and self-effacement. Talented and troubled, he was already grappling with a serious drug problem that would blight his life for years. The album *Sweet Baby James* would be to his career what Mitchell's next album would become for hers – the incandescent moment against which all others are compared, fairly or unfairly. Their work for decades to come would be measured against an album from the opening years of the 1970s, creating a filter that would often distort the view that critics and fans would formulate of all that would follow.

6 Just when you're getting a taste for worship . . .

> Is your cucumber bitter? Throw it away. Are there
> briars in your path? Turn aside. That is enough. Do
> not go on to say, 'Why were things of this sort ever
> brought into the world?'
> (Marcus Aurelius, *Meditations,* 2nd century)

ERNEST HEMINGWAY ONCE WROTE, in a letter to his friend F.
Scott Fitzgerald, 'When you get the damned hurt, use it.
Use it and don't cheat.' Use it, don't let it use you.
Hemingway knew a thing or two about the 'hurt'; it dogged him
for much of his life, ran like a seam through many of his fictional
characters. Self-mythologising old curmudgeon he may have
been at times – his former wife, the acclaimed journalist Martha
Gellhorn, once described their five-year marriage as 'life-darken-
ing' – but he never cheated, even when he pulled the trigger of
the gun that ended his life.

Deep emotional pain is a condition that allows immunity to
no one. Hemingway won the Nobel Prize for Literature in
1954; Nelson Mandela won the Nobel Peace Prize almost forty
years later. Yet, in 1996, Mandela, then president of South
Africa, stood in a Johannesburg courtroom and gave
testimony about a struggle – but not the political struggle that
had seen him imprisoned for almost thirty years, or the battle
to undo decades of apartheid and rebuild his country. It was
the struggle to overcome the unhappiness of his fractured
marriage to his wife, Winnie. In a statement to the court hearing their divorce proceedings, he said, 'I was the loneliest
man during the period I stayed with her.' It was a poignant
yet startlingly simple declaration – one of the great political
figures of the twentieth century, humble in his loneliness and
emotional isolation.

Life can seem painfully bleak when the 'hurt' comes calling
with its soulmates – loneliness, depression, anxiety, fear and
inertia – but when you meet adversity head on, when you do use
the hurt and don't cheat, as Hemingway exhorted, there can be
an extraordinary richness in the experience. Mandela transformed pain and adversity into political and personal action;
Hemingway, like so many other artists, channelled it into his
work. Virginia Woolf said that the closest she came to undergo-
ing psychoanalysis was writing *To the Lighthouse*. She invented
her own therapy – the narrative – and exorcised her obsession
with both her parents. Yet for all the loss and grief in the book, it
still begins and ends with sentences starting with the positive,
affirmative 'Yes'.

With her 1971 album *Blue,* Joni Mitchell also invented,
almost instinctively, her own therapy to try to assimilate her
experiences, particularly those of the several months preceding
its release, and make sense of the longings and needs that
often seemed to be pulling her in different directions, of the
conflicts in love, romance, passion, desire, freedom and creativity. Battles with deep depression have been a well-docu-
mented hallmark of many creative personalities, but the
eminent psychiatrist Dr Anthony Storr says that these struggles
can prod sufferers into undertaking the solitary and painful
work of exploring their own depths and recording what they
find – and that this process, in turn, protects them from being
overwhelmed by depression. In his book *Solitude,* he observes
that the creative process can provide a means of regaining a
sense of mastery in those who have lost it, and to an extent,
repairing the self damaged by bereavement or the loss of confidence in human relationships which accompanies depression.
For Joni Mitchell, this process of self-healing took the place of
conventional psychotherapy which had already failed her:

> I got very depressed – to the point where I thought it
> was no longer a problem for burdening my friends with.
> But I needed to talk to someone who was very indiffer-
> ent. I had done a lot of thinking beforehand as to what
> was eating me, so there wasn't a lot of uncovering to do.
> I went to see him . . . and just started to rap from the
> time I came in through the door – which turned out to

be forty minutes of everything I thought was bothering me, which included a description of myself as being a person who never spoke, which naturally he found hard to understand! But it was true that in day-to-day life, I was practically catatonic. There were moments when I thought I had nothing pertinent to say, but there I was blabbing my head off to him. So in the end, he looked at me and said, 'Well, do you ever feel suicidal?' and I said, 'Sometimes I feel very bad but I have to make another record ...', telling him I had all these things to live for. So he just handed me his card and said, 'Listen, call me again some time when you feel suicidal.' And I went out into the street – I'd come in completely deadpan, my face immobile ... and I just felt this grin breaking over my face at the irony of it all, at the thought that this man was going to help me at all.

With *Blue*, there was this same compulsion to confront, to be honest, to strip away the persona that was being thrust on her by fans and critics and reveal what was true and authentic, however intimate the findings :

I was at my most defenceless during the making of *Blue*. Now, to be absolutely defenceless in this world is not a good thing. I guess you could say I broke down but I continued to work. In the process of breaking down there are powers that come in, clairvoyancy and ... everything becomes transparent. It's kind of an overwhelming situation, where more information is coming in, more truth than a person can handle. So it was in the middle of all this that I wrote the *Blue* album. It is a very pure album; it's as pure as Charlie Parker. There aren't many things in music that pure. Charlie Parker played pure opera of his soul – especially the times that he was extremely sick. He had no defences. And when you have no defences, the music becomes saintly and it can *communicate*. As one group of girls in a bar that accosted me put it, 'Before Prozac, there was you!', and especially that album. Somehow it had more power than an aspirin for the sufferer,

and I think part of it is because it's extraordinarily
emotionally honest . . .

It was an attitude that moved her friend Kris Kristofferson, upon
hearing *Blue,* to urge her to be more self-protective, 'save something for yourself'.

Recording was done in near-seclusion in a bid to minimise the
pressures on a fragile and distressed Mitchell: 'At the time I was
absolutely transparent, like cellophane. If you looked at me, I
would weep. We had to lock the doors to make that album.
Nobody was allowed in. Socially I was an absolute wreck.'
Perhaps more than any other of her albums it was the one created by using Nietzsche's dictum, 'I have at all times written my
works with my whole body and my whole life.' She would later
describe herself as emulating Nietzsche's poet-penitents writing
in their own blood in *Thus Spoke Zarathustra.*

Blue is often portrayed as Mitchell's bleakest work, the title
seen as not just a disguised name for a lover but also describing
the mood of feeling blue, having the blues. Even the album cover
is a wash of blue, Mitchell's gaunt face withdrawn in the half-
light, her gaze downcast in a close-up photograph by Tim
Considine (a former actor who found fame as one of the sons in
the vintage US sitcom *My Three Sons*). The word 'blue' itself
crops up in numerous songs, 'My old man, keeping away my
lonesome blues', ' So you write him a letter and say, "her eyes are
blue"', 'Blue, songs are like tattoos', 'all the news of home you
read, just gives you the blues' and 'in the blue TV screen light'.
But an over-emphasis on shades of blue, the colour, the
metaphor and the mood, is to ignore the romance and sense of
fun that runs in parallel with the introspection, aching ambivalence and longing.

The title itself was not even Mitchell's first choice; she had
intended to call the album *River* after the song of the same name.
The original name and the song itself had inspired her photographer friend Joel Bernstein:

> From the song I had this image of her all in black, skat-
> ing down the middle of a river disappearing off to the
> horizon, where she's looking back over her shoulder at
> me; it was a very clear kind of image that I had, with

pine trees on either bank. That's how I envisaged it but by the time she was finished in the studio, winter was gone. She just thought, 'Okay, we're not going to be able to do that shoot' . . . Elliot [Roberts] went through a drawer that she had of photos that had been sent to her and picked out the shot by Tim Considine, which I believe was taken at the Troubadour in 1967 or 68.

Bernstein's idea would be revived more than five years later and create some of the most striking artwork of Mitchell's career.

By early March recording was complete and the master tapes were sent for processing. But soon after, Mitchell urged Reprise to halt production so she could change two of the tracks – the original running order was: Side 1, 'Carey', 'Little Green', 'A Case of You', 'Hunter (The Good Samaritan)' and 'Blue'; Side 2, 'California', 'My Old Man', 'Urge for Going', 'This Flight Tonight' and 'River'. The tracks 'Hunter' and 'Urge for Going', both of which pre-dated the writing of new songs for *Blue,* were deleted – the former has not appeared on an official studio release and the latter (which had been such a big success for Tom Rush) would be recorded the following year as a B-side to the single 'You Turn Me On, I'm A Radio' and would also appear on the *Hits* compilation in 1996. Two new songs were included at the beginning and end of the original *Blue* – 'All I Want' and 'The Last Time I Saw Richard', respectively. They comprise her equivalent of Virginia Woolf's affirmative 'Yes' narrative bookends: 'All I Want' reflects the ambivalence of a love affair, 'Oh, I hate you some, I love you some, Oh I love you when I forget about me', but also highlights the impeccable intentions that accompany the doubts: 'All I really really want our love to do is to bring out the best in me and in you too'. Her soon-to-be-ex beau, James Taylor, plays guitar on the track. A love affair without regrets and doubts is celebrated in 'My Old Man', affirming that a lasting marriage of true minds doesn't need the sanction of City Hall officialdom.

Fans and critics have always been eager to ascribe autobiographical connotations to so much of Mitchell's writing and the songs on *Blue* provided them with fertile ground in which to plant the seeds of intense speculation. Thirty years after it was released, her fans still have heated debates about the subjects of the songs, equally adamant that the song 'Blue', for instance, can only have been written about one man: James Taylor/David Blue/Graham Nash/Leonard Cohen, pick a name, any name. Each 'relationship' song is held up to the light, scrutinised, examined for clues and hidden secrets, energised by a reluctance to accept mystery, to accept that it's good to be puzzled sometimes, that it's a gift not to be presented with the transparently obvious time and time again, because in that space created by not knowing, we can imagine, we can relate, we can endow the work with the value, if any, that it holds for us. Significant writing uses mystery, abstraction, subtlety and skill to enable us to do that. As the writer and critic Susan Sontag observed, interpretation is the revenge of the intellect upon art and the world: 'To interpret is to impoverish, to deplete the world – in order to set up a shadow world of "meanings"'.

In the coming years, Mitchell would express her frustration at the often wildly inaccurate theories about her lyrics and their subjects, theories that destroy the listener's ability to make the song their own. Michael Stipe of R.E.M. has articulated the same frustration:

> I really don't want to reveal anything about a character or a song because I can remember, as a teenager, a record falling into my lap, and how magical and mysterious and revolutionary and unbelievably life-altering even one song on a record like that can be. I would hate to diminish or be unfaithful to that notion. Plus, I maintain that my take, my interpretation of what my songs are about, is, in the whole world, the least important take. I wrote them but that does not give me some divine insight into their meaning.

The best possible response, however, to the question 'What are your songs about?' was vintage 60s Bob Dylan: 'Oh, some are about four minutes, some are about five, and some, believe it or not, are about eleven or twelve,' he replied.

Given the obsession with creating a who's-who of Mitchell's work, one important song seemed to evade the net of scrutiny for years: 'Little Green', recorded on *Blue* but written some years earlier, is the loving lament for her daughter Kelly/'Green', full of promise for a happier life ahead than the one Joni felt she could provide for the child. In the song, she does not shy away from articulating her decision to have the baby adopted: 'child with a child pretending Weary of lies you are sending home So you sign all the papers in the family name You're sad and you're sorry but you're not ashamed . . . ' She had been performing 'Little Green' in her live shows long before her first album was released, but it did not appear on record until four albums into her career. Given that *Blue* was recorded at a particularly troubled time in her life, the inclusion of the song was both cathartic and challenging, defying the listener to offer an insightful and accurate analysis. Reviewing the album in *Rolling Stone,* Timothy Crouse wrote of 'Little Green', 'the pretty, "poetic" lyric is dressed up in such cryptic references that it passeth all understanding'. It was also the first of her songs to lay a trail for her daughter to follow, a message in a bottle thrown out into the waves in the vain hope that someone will find it, open it and understand.

There are reminiscences over her adventures in Crete in 'Carey', a pre-reggae calypso played in what she labelled 'Matala tuning' in honour of the place where she'd devised it. The song title had been inspired by a friend she met there, Carey Raditz:

> Some of the people that have remained in my life entered my life in a colourful way. Carey Raditz blew out of a restaurant in Greece, literally. *Kaboom!* I heard, facing the sunset. I turned around and this guy is blowing out the door of this restaurant. He was a cook; he lit a gas stove and it exploded. Burned all the red hair off himself right through his white Indian turban. I went, 'That was an interesting entrance – I'll take note of that.'

Raditz is the 'bright red devil' of the song, who shared the wine-fuelled nights in the Mermaid Café even as the attractions of the relatively rudimentary living conditions were starting to wear thin. Stephen Stills' bass and guitar and Russ Kunkel's drums, recreated the spirit of Matala partying.

The 60s hippie trail provided distractions on the beaches of Europe or the foothills of the Himalayas but the elegiac 'Blue' presents a cautionary tale of the other diversions sought by the Me

Generation, 'acid, booze and ass, needles, guns and grass', flirting with the notion that 'hell's the hippest way to go'. The mood changes with the upbeat 'California', detailing her European travels of 1970 and the welcome return to her adopted home. The beach-bum days and nights in the caves of Crete and her friendship with 'red rogue' Raditz are recalled when she sings, 'I met a redneck on a Grecian isle Who did the goat dance very well He gave me back my smile But he kept my camera to sell Oh the rogue, the red red rogue He cooked good omelettes and stews . . . ' The 'make me feel good rock 'n' roll band' of the lyrics has a mirror image in the musicians who played on 'California' – James Taylor (guitar), Russ Kunkel (drums) and 'Sneaky' Pete Kleinow on pedal steel guitar.

The haunting 'River' is the saddest 'festive' season song imaginable, with the dull ache of longing – 'I wish I had a river I could skate away on' – and self-reproach – 'I'm so hard to handle, I'm selfish and I'm sad, Now I've gone and lost the best baby That I ever had . . . '. There's also the incongruity of the preparations for a northern hemisphere Christmas in sunny southern California, where Christmas trees, reindeer cutouts and carol-singing do nothing to imbue the season with joy and goodwill. The insatiability of romance is both mocked and celebrated in 'A Case of You', one of Mitchell's most sensual and visceral songs, with its allusion to the religious rite of communion, turning the lover's essence into sacred wine coursing through the bloodstream. Nearing the end of an affair, protestations of fidelity ring increasingly hollow: 'Just before our love got lost you said, "I am as constant as a Northern Star", and I said, "Constantly in the darkness? Where's that at? If you want me I'll be in the bar."'

A love less passionate is recalled in 'The Last Time I Saw Richard', a song that breaks all of the rules of lyric-writing; there's too much to say and too little time to say it but it works remarkably, becomes more like a spoken-word prose poem than a song. It's the other book-ended 'Yes' wherein the 'dark café days' of her life in Detroit in the mid-60s and marriage to Chuck Mitchell are revisited without regret as 'only a dark cocoon before I get my gorgeous wings and fly away Only a phase, these dark café days'. Richard/Chuck accuses her of overly romanticising love, only to have the accusation turned on him: '"Richard, you haven't really changed," I said, "it's just that now you're romanticising some pain that's in your head, You got tombs in your eyes, but the songs you punched are dreaming, Listen, they sing of love so sweet. . . "'

Timothy Crouse, in his *Rolling Stone* review, described *Blue* as the 'free-est, brightest, most cheerfully rhythmic' of Mitchell's albums to date:

> But the change in mood does not mean that Joni's commitment to her own very personal naturalistic style has diminished. More than ever Joni risks using details that might be construed as trivial in order to paint a vivid self-portrait. She refuses to mask her real face behind imagery, as her fellow autobiographers James Taylor and Cat Stevens do. In portraying herself so starkly, she has risked the ridiculous to achieve the sublime. The results though are seldom ridiculous; on *Blue* she has matched her popular music skills with the purity and honesty of what was once called folk music and through the blend she has given us some of the most beautiful moments in recent popular music.

The British music magazine *Sounds* highlighted the strengths and weaknesses of the 'confessional' style of writing, in a review by Billy Walker:

> You feel that each composition is a piece of the artist herself and that each new segment is exactly true to life, nothing however painful or personal has been left out . . . Joni Mitchell wears her heart on her sleeve and doesn't care who knows it, and this fact alone has alienated her to many who feel that such emotions, because of their apparent openness, must be false. But whatever you like or dislike, her artistry is unquestionable . . .

The British singer and songwriter Sandy Denny – perhaps best known for her work with Fairport Convention – expressed unease at Mitchell's facility with the genre in almost identical terms when interviewed in the mid-70s:

I adore Joni Mitchell but I do think she went around wearing her heart on her sleeve. I adore listening to those songs but I wouldn't like it to be me who's painting it around for everyone to know. The last thing I'd want everyone to know is my business.

Much of Denny's own material could be interpreted as autobiographical, and she had referred to *Blue* in her song 'Makes Me Think of You' which was only ever recorded as a demo. The song is shot through with Denny's sadness at her deteriorating marriage to Trevor Lucas:

> ... The albums strewn without their clothes
> Gather dust among the grooves
> The only one I play is *Blue*
> It makes me think of you ...

Blue is the Joni Mitchell album most likely to appear on those 'Top Ten', 'Top 100', 'all-time favourite', 'classic album' lists. There's no doubt that the attention is merited; for a relatively young artist – she was 27 when it was recorded, but much younger when some of the songs were written – it is a work of great maturity, skill and insight. It's the album most often cited as her seminal work, the benchmark for all that came before and after. More than a quarter of a century after it was recorded, people are still making value judgments about her music and referring back to *Blue*, never quite allowing her to step out of the shadow of that album. And therein lies the rub. *Blue* was a great success and not only consolidated her fanbase but broadened it immensely. But it also became a form of honey-trap because it wooed many people into wanting nothing more from Joni Mitchell: they believed she'd reached her apogee and could climb no further. The only way to go was down. Typically, if Mitchell herself had ever for a moment considered that she had reached her creative peak with *Blue* she simply looked around, saw another metaphorical mountain range to climb and set off to explore the far distant hills.

The album was a turning-point; she would be angrier on future works, more introspective and questioning but never quite as nothing-left-to-lose openly vulnerable again. Emerging from *Blue* and the experiences and relationships that had inspired it, Joni Mitchell developed a measure of emotional detachment, a protective outer layer that would allow her to explore pain and loss without being terminally wounded by them. Crucial to developing that was creating a retreat back in her homeland. She decided to sell her house in Laurel Canyon and set about clearing out its contents. She gave Joel Bernstein – later, her guitar technician and archivist – boxes full of acetates and audio tapes. They included live recordings of the Carnegie Hall and Berkeley Community Theatre concerts that had once been destined to end up on a live album, studio out-takes, sonic doodlings she'd done at home, multiple versions of 'Both Sides, Now', publishing demos, a recording of Mitchell writing 'The Fiddle and the Drum' on piano. There were unique discoveries like an audio tape recorded during Buffalo Springfield sessions, with a rough mix of Stephen Stills as well as a recording of other musicians experimenting with a jazz riff on the Neil Young song 'Broken Arrow'. Joni, it seems, may have been looking for a spare tape on which to record at home, and had simply put this one into her tape recorder, using the reverse side to the Springfield sessions.

Mitchell left Los Angeles and returned to Canada. She settled at Half Moon Bay on the Sunshine Coast, north of Vancouver in British Columbia, drawn to what she described as the 'rich melancholy' of the land: 'Not in the summer because it's usually very clear, but in the spring and winter, it's very brooding and it's conducive to a certain kind of thinking.' It was to become a refuge, away from the distractions and demands of LA and the music industry. With the help of a friend she built a house by the bay and over several months, losing herself in the physical labour of construction, she rediscovered her equilibrium. She began to take tentative steps back into the world, after feeling bruised and bereaved during the recording of *Blue* and the end of her relationship with James Taylor.

Most of the songs for her next album, *For the Roses,* were written at the house in Canada:

In the process of building and being alone up there when it was completed – I had written a lot of new

songs. And it seemed to me that [they weren't] like a
completed art until they were [performed] in front of a
live audience . . . there's a need to share them.

She joked that when she phoned the owners of a local bar and
asked if they wanted to hear her play some songs, they'd say
'That's really nice – know any Gordon Lightfoot?'
   She'd begun to change her attitude about what she'd once seen
as the limitations of performing:

> When I retired I felt I never really wanted to do it again
> – ever . . . I gained a strange perspective of performing.
> I had a bad attitude about it . . . I felt like what I was writ-
> ing was too personal to be applauded for. I even thought
> that maybe the thing to do was to present the songs some
> different way – like a play or classical performance
> where you play everything and then run off stage and
> let them do whatever they want, applaud or walk out.

Mitchell's sojourn in Canada had restored her energies and her
enthusiasm and she returned to Los Angeles. She began recording early tracks for the album, which would be her first release
on her co-manager David Geffen's new record label, Asylum.
Leaving Reprise and joining Asylum was Mitchell's gesture of
support for Geffen and Elliot Roberts, who had formed a management venture, The Geffen Roberts Company. Indeed, they
even shied away from the term 'management', preferring to
describe themselves in more caring, sharing, nurturing terms as
providing 'direction' for their artists. They were now able to
realise a long-held dream of Geffen's to have his own label. He
had originally planned that Asylum would be a hot new company, set up to record new singer-songwriters: in July 1971, he
gave an interview to *Record World*, saying that Joni Mitchell and
another client of his, Laura Nyro, were to be the jewels in the
label's crown. Mitchell's contract at Reprise was about to expire
and she did want to join Asylum. However, Geffen would soon
lose Nyro both as a client and potential Asylum artist after acrimonious disagreements with her.
   No other fledgling label, or indeed many established ones,
could have hoped to attract Joni Mitchell; the acclaim for her

most recent albums, *Ladies of the Canyon* and *Blue,* and the strength of her writing talents as showcased by the successful artists who were covering her songs, had confirmed her as one of the most significant singer-songwriters of her generation. But her move did not mean she had left the Warners family entirely; it was only a generous deal with Atlantic Records – one of the three labels, along with Warner Brothers/Reprise and Elektra, owned by Warner Communications – that had enabled Geffen to launch Asylum. Within a year, Warner Communications would pay Geffen several million dollars for the 50 per cent stake in Asylum that it did not already own. (A condition of the deal was that, to prevent a possible conflict of interest, Geffen had to withdraw from the management company he ran with Elliot Roberts.)

Mitchell approached the tour schedule with more gusto than she had in years, relishing the chance to play the new songs for fans who had keenly felt her absence from the concert stage. It was this adoration-in-waiting that caused Michael Watts to write in *Melody Maker* in May 1972, in a review of Mitchell's show at the Royal Festival Hall in London:

> To those who attend her concerts ... she's much more than a singer and a songwriter. She's some kind of high priestess, virginal and vulnerable, not to be vilified. The effect was heightened on Friday by her appearance in long flowing culottes that dazzled white in the spotlights. It seems almost heresy to criticise her, but one fault to my mind is that the mood of her performances tends to be excessively devotional ... she becomes not just a performer but a kind of icon.

The restorative effects of her lengthy absence from performing and her time in Canada were evident in the equanimity with which she greeted the sound problems that dogged the evening. The support act, Jackson Browne – making only his second appearance in London – had manfully struggled with a sound system that rendered much of his performance all but silent.

Playing guitar, piano and dulcimer, Mitchell performed her more popular songs like 'Big Yellow Taxi', 'Woodstock', 'Carey', 'Both Sides, Now' and 'Blue' and previewed several new ones that

would soon be recorded on her next album, *For the Roses* –
among them was a future single, 'You Turn Me On, I'm a Radio'
as well as the title track, 'Lesson in Survival', 'Cold Blue Steel and
Sweet Fire' and 'Judgment of the Moon and Stars (Ludwig's
Tune)'. Jackson Browne joined her on stage for an encore of 'The
Circle Game', with the audience joining in, happy to forgive the
recalcitrant sound system. Browne was a rising young star in the
folk-rock milieu; like Mitchell, his early work had found a stal-
wart champion in Tom Rush, who recorded three of his early
songs. While living in Los Angeles, Browne had briefly joined the
Nitty Gritty Dirt Band before decamping to New York. There, the
preternaturally pretty singer-songwriter had caught the eye and
ear of the sometime Velvet Underground chanteuse, Nico. As
love interest and guitarist, he joined Nico's band and she
recorded three of his songs on her album of cover versions,
Chelsea Girl.

The Browne had been signed to Asylum in 1971 after Geffen's sec-
retary Dodie Smith had urged her boss to listen to the demo tape
Browne had sent to their office. Smith had opened the envelope
and found the attached publicity shot – a sepia-tinted photograph
of an undeniably photogenic Browne – as engaging as the accompanying letter, which began, 'Dear Mr Geffen, I write to you out
of respect for the artists you represent . . . ' Browne's self-titled
debut album (sometimes referred to as *Saturate Before Using*,
after the words emblazoned on the cover shot of a cloth water-
bag) was released early in 1972. By the time the US and
European tour with Joni Mitchell was underway, Browne's first
single, 'Doctor My Eyes', had reached Number 8 in the US charts
– and he and Mitchell were romantically involved. His album
was to be Asylum's first big success, to be followed soon after by
a band made up of several of Browne's friends, the Eagles. It was
a vindication of Geffen's 'artists first' policy, after the label's first
two releases – by Judee Sill and David Blue – had failed to set the
waiting world alight when they appeared in October 1971.

The head of Atlantic Records, Ahmet Ertegun – one of the
industry's elder statesmen – had hosted a party for Asylum at the
St Moritz Hotel in New York, on 23 February, the night of a triumphant return to Carnegie Hall for Joni Mitchell. She and
Jackson Browne – who again played support – were among those
to attend the party at the Sky Garden roof restaurant. The

Carnegie Hall concert had been a sell-out: the industry magazine *Variety* calculated approvingly that at a price of $6.50 per ticket, the promoter had grossed $16,000 for the evening. In a brief review, the magazine noted:

> The Canadian gal, whose programmes used to consist mainly of numbers backed by her guitar-playing, has improved at grand piano and added dulcimer. She spends about as much time tuning the latter as she does her guitar but her friendly visage helped these moments pass ... Jackson Browne ... was a good opener for one of today's top femme folk-style artists.

The tour continued through the spring and summer, as did the recording sessions. Now that she was back living in LA, Geffen and Mitchell began spending more time together, and he introduced her to his brand new best friends, Warren Beatty and Jack Nicholson. Mitchell and Geffen joined the two noted Hollywood Lotharios, to go to a celebrity fundraising concert for the Democratic Party candidate for the presidency, Senator George McGovern. Mitchell's former boyfriend, James Taylor, was among those performing at the show; they exchanged pleasantries, the tensions of their break-up seemingly resolved. The relationship with Taylor had undoubtedly influenced the writing on *For the Roses*; it was no departure for Mitchell to examine romantic entanglements in her lyrics but the album's musical departure was to build on the rock 'n' roll band touches that had been hinted at on several tracks on *Blue*.

Mitchell and her engineer, Henry Lewy, had again returned to the A&M studios in Los Angeles and set to work with Wilton Felder on bass, Russ Kunkel on drums, percussionist Bobbye Hall, James Burton on electric guitar, Tom Scott on woodwinds and reed and even Graham Nash on harmonica; Stephen Stills is credited with 'rock 'n' roll band' on one track. Mitchell and Tom Scott had met indirectly through Quincy Jones, one of the few great Renaissance men of popular music. Scott was signed to Jones's label, Qwest:

> Quincy suggested that I record 'Woodstock' and I said, 'Oh, yeah, the one CSN&Y do.' Well, Quincy played me Joni's version and I was floored. Especially with her

voice. So I did the tune using a recorder, kind of imi-
tating Joni's voice. She heard the track and asked me if
I'd like to play on her new album [*For the Roses*]. A few
nights later we went to the studio and struck up a very
rewarding relationship.

The folk tag had continued to follow Mitchell around many years
after it had become redundant, but this album showed that she
could rock if she had a mind to. It helped to minimise, although
not entirely put an end to, the perception of her as a girlishly
romantic wordsmith, which had prompted a writer in *Sounds*
magazine to sigh a year earlier, 'her frail, helpless, feminine
approach has an appeal that is hard to resist'. Mitchell's time
away from the music business, during her retreat in Canada, had
if anything sharpened her instincts about the industry's traps
and temptations, and the title track is one of several of her songs
over the years to have perceptively and persuasively chronicled
that world, and her attitude to it – 'I guess I seem ungrateful,
With my teeth sunk in the hand, That brings me things . . . ' – and
it's a cautionary tale on the nature of celebrity: 'Just when you're
getting a taste for worship, They start bringing out the hammers
And the boards And the nails. . . '. The impetus for the song had
come as James Taylor teetered on the brink of impending star-
dom, as she described:

> I was watching his career and I was thinking that as his
> woman at that time I should be able to support him. And
> yet it seemed to me that I could see the change in his
> future would remove things from his life. I felt like hav-
> ing come through, having had a small taste of success,
> and having seen the consequences of what it gives you
> and what it takes away in terms of what you think it's
> going to give you – well, I just felt I was in no position
> to help. I knew what he needed was someone to sup-
> port him and say it was all wonderful. But everything I
> saw him going through I thought was ludicrous, because
> I thought it was ludicrous when I'd done it. It was a very
> difficult time and the song was actually written for that
> person: 'In the office sits a poet and he trembles as he
> sings and he asks some guy to circulate his soul around

On your mark red ribbon runner'. Like, go after it, but remember the days when you sat and made up tunes for yourself and played in small clubs where there was still some contact, and when people came up and said they loved a song, you were really glad they loved it.

The theme of Taylor's growing success and the price he would pay for it is reprised in 'See You Sometime', a gentle lament of the feelings that lingered after their relationship had ended. The in-joke puzzle of Mitchell's cryptic lyrical reference 'Pack your suspenders, I'll come meet your plane ... ' was solved when Taylor posed proudly for the cover of his *Mud Slide Slim* album, wearing a pair of braces. *Rolling Stone* ran an interview with Taylor in January 1973, during which he was asked about 'the suspenders' reference; he replied diplomatically, 'Joni's music is much more specifically autobiographical than a lot of other people. Everyone who writes songs writes autobiographical songs, and hers are sometimes disarmingly specific.'

If musically *For The Roses* was a move away from the sparse arrangements that dominated much of *Blue*, her lyrical absorption in exploring the pains and pleasures of love relationships was undiminished. And for a woman whose romantic life was dominated by fellow musicians, her authority is beyond dispute when, in 'Blonde In The Bleachers', she declares:

She tapes her regrets
To the microphone stand
She says, 'You can't hold the hand
Of a rock 'n' roll man ...
Compete with the fans
For your rock 'n' roll man ... '

Struggles elsewhere in Taylor's life – his drug abuse – provided the impetus for 'Cold Blue Steel And Sweet Fire', with its refrain of dealer and heroin user, supply and demand, 'bashing in veins for peace'. Mitchell described it as 'a real paranoid city song – stalking the streets looking for a dealer'; James Burton's electric guitar gives it an appropriate edginess. Drugs are de-romanticised here into the reality of 'Red water in the bathroom sink, Fever and the scum brown bowl' but given that drug use was – and is – so commonplace among musicians, including many of Mitchell's friends at the time, another song on the album, 'Banquet', acknowledges without any judgmental intervention that drugs can also hold the promise of escapism and enlightenment, in the way that others see religion or travel.

As a member of the first generation of women to be liberated by the Pill, the sexual revolution and feminism, Mitchell high-lighted the residual longing for enduring love, for the happy-ever-after ending that was not incompatible with the new freedoms – even if they might, at times, have made uneasy and restless bedfellows. In 'Woman of Heart and Mind' she described herself, and so many others, 'With time on her hands, No child to raise', confronting a commitment-shy man while declaring 'I'm looking for affection and respect, A little passion, And you want stimulation – nothing more'. The rebellion of this generation of women against the strictures of their parents is examined in 'Let the Wind Carry Me', where Mitchell, the only child of loving parents, details her own rebellious streak as a teenager obsessed with rock 'n' roll dancing, earning the worried disapproval of her mother and the benevolent indulgence of her father.

The track chosen to be released as a single, 'You Turn Me On, I'm a Radio', is an irresistible country-rock jaunt that Mitchell admitted was an only half-mocking attempt to court AM radio airplay. Friends like Graham Nash, David Crosby and Neil Young and his band came along to help her concoct the perfect radio single but, despite the extraordinary line-up of talent, it didn't quite come off. Mitchell described the scenario as 'too many chefs . . . we had a terrific evening, a lot of fun, but . . . it's like when you do a movie with a cast of thousands'. It may not have conquered AM radio but it moved the *New Yorker* rock critic, Ellen Willis, to declare it a 'metaphysical poem' in the tradition of John Donne. The single reached a respectable Number 25 on the Billboard singles charts, while the album itself peaked at Number 11.

The album ended with a glimpse far beyond the world of LA folk-rockers and singer-songwriters, to Ludwig van Beethoven, in 'Judgment of the Moon and Stars (Ludwig's Tune)', which Mitchell wrote after reading a book about the composer.

Beethoven struggled with encroaching deafness to reinvigorate and reinvent the music of his time. Where Mitchell's previous albums had largely examined the inner world, *For the Roses* saw her looking increasingly outward. Several critics highlighted this with something akin to relief. Among them was Toby Goldstein, who wrote in *Words and Music*,

> Unlike many of her other compositions, these songs deal with themes of the universal, carrying her out of the Hollywood Hills and into the thick of other people's problems. Selfishness, criminality, freedom, all are fit themes for her now bittersweet voice. The sometimes shrieking indulgence of past years has all but vanished . . . her voice is now captivating . . . stating exactly what she means with a deliberateness that is shocking.

Writing in *Sounds*, the BBC radio icon John Peel proclaimed:

> When I first heard Joni Mitchell all those years ago, I was bewitched by her. As time passed, I became less enchanted, feeling that she, in common with so many artists, had fallen back on making money by making the noises people expected of her. Her *For the Roses* LP reconverted me. She has become, once again, a leader.

Stephen Davis ended a hyperbolic review in *Rolling Stone* by saying,

> Got a hole in your heart? *For the Roses* will cost you about four bucks and it won't cure you, but shit, it's good salve. If it came in a can, was a little greasy and smelled OK, I'd rub a little on my forehead over the prefrontal lobe, where the third eye lives.

The album artwork gained a little gentle notoriety for its uncharacteristically candid depiction of Mitchell; the cover was a photograph of her, clad in woodlands shades of green and brown, taken by Joel Bernstein in the woods at her home in Canada. The inner sleeve was also a photograph of her – nude and with her back to the camera, standing on rocks looking out across the bay near her home. Bernstein says his intention was to express a line from 'Lesson in Survival' about just such a view across a stretch of seawater:

> I thought that it was really in keeping with the album as an image in terms of the music because it's so painterly . . . the thing that I always liked about it was the line 'I'm looking way out at the ocean, Love to see that green water in motion' and just to the left of her is this emerald-green wave in the photo and I liked that it illustrated that so literally. I just loved the album, I thought it was a fantastic advance for her and thought her songwriting was getting better and better.

Far from being prurient or titillating, there is an unstudied innocence about the shot, although Mitchell recalled that it raised eyebrows back home in Saskatoon:

> I remember my mother putting on glasses to scrutinise it more closely. Then my father said, 'Myrtle, people do things like this these days', which was a great attitude. It was the most innocent of nudes, kind of like a Botticelli pose . . . Joel Bernstein [was] the only photographer I would feel comfortable enough to take my clothes off for.

The original title for the album had been *Judgment of the Moon and Stars* and the nude photograph had been part of the concept for the cover. The photograph was originally going to be set in a circle, with the daylight sky replaced by a starry night in the style of Magritte. Joel Bernstein did a mock-up of the cover design and presented it to David Geffen and Elliot Roberts, whose concerns were more for the financial bottom-line than the fine traditions of a Botticelli nude:

> They were horrified at the idea of this naked image of her on the cover and immediately [said] 'Well, Sears won't display it and the rack jobbers won't put it out and we'll lose immediately, right off the top,

forty per cent of our possible sales because of outlets
that won't carry it because it's a nude photo.'

Roberts thought that, at best, other retailers might censor
Mitchell's nether regions with the price sticker. He said, 'Joan,
how would you like to see $5.98 plastered across your ass?'
They decided to swap the shots planned for the cover and gate-
fold, and the Mitchell rear view was consigned to the inside of
the album. One of her own colourful marker-pen style
sketches, an impressionist portrait of Judy Collins in semi-
profile, was placed on the back cover. Joel Bernstein recalls
that Tim Buckley was among the many men who compli-
mented Mitchell effusively about the nude shot: 'He said, "Joni,
I loved your new album, really loved that cover, really loved
that picture on the inside!" And she was [thinking], "But did
you listen to the *music* at all?!"' Mitchell's willingness to appear
naked on her album sleeve showed a healthy distancing from
people's expectations of her; in the past, she had stripped bare
her feelings and experiences in her songs and would continue
to do so in subsequent work. But she would do it with a
boldness and confidence that would be much needed in the
years to come.

7 Anima rising, queen of queens . . .

> My role in society, or any artist or poet's role, is to try and express what we feel. Not to tell people how to feel. Not as a preacher, not as a leader, but as a reflection of us all.
>
> (John Lennon, radio interview on the day of his murder, 8 December 1980)

LENNON ONCE GAVE JONI MITCHELL some sage career advice: 'Why do you let other people have your hits for you? You want a hit, don't you? Put some fiddles on it.' He was talking about her 1974 album *Court and Spark*. Lennon gently chided Mitchell for being a 'product of your own over-education', in her efforts to write literature within the pop genre – although, apart from her year at art college, she'd had no formal education beyond high school. What she did have was a fierce intellectual curiosity and an inability to accept complacency – her own or anyone else's – and critics and fans were to be left in no doubt of this when they heard *Court and Spark*. And Lennon's advice was to prove unnecessary – even in the absence of fiddles, *Court and Spark* was to give Joni the greatest commercial success of her career at that point.

The album also gave Bob Dylan the chance to display some boyishly bad manners. A triumphant David Geffen – by then president of the merged Elektra/Asylum labels, to which Dylan had just been signed – had gathered together some friends, including Mitchell and Dylan, to hear tapes of their newly completed albums. When Dylan played his, *Planet Waves*, it was praised rapturously; when Mitchell played her own *Court and Spark*, it was all but ignored. Dylan affected indifference and promptly fell asleep. Geffen shrugged off his own apparent disinterest, saying that given that Mitchell was staying at his house at the time, he had heard the songs repeatedly anyway. A month after Geffen's 31st birthday, the top three albums in the *Billboard* chart were Elektra/Asylum releases: *Planet Waves* was at Number 1, followed by *Court and Spark*, with Carly Simon – now married to James Taylor – in third place with *Hotcakes*. Geffen's commercial courting of Dylan was to be short-lived, however; *Planet Waves* was Dylan's only recording for the label before he returned, disillusioned and disappointed, to the Columbia stable from whence he came.

David Geffen's reputation as a ruthlessly ambitious business-man was not entirely undeserved, but he could also be a loving and generous friend (despite rumours to the contrary at the time, Mitchell and Geffen – who is gay – were only ever platonic friends, although Geffen did have a romantic relationship with Cher). Months earlier, he had offered Joni a room in his house, when she was bereft after the end of her affair with Jackson Browne. Geffen suggested a trip to Paris to raise her spirits. The two joined forces with Robbie Robertson of the Band and his French wife, Dominique, and headed for Paris, where they stayed in the Ritz Hotel.

The trip was a welcome distraction for both Mitchell and Geffen. As her friend and label boss relaxed visibly away from the pressures of Los Angeles and the industry, he admitted to feeling unfettered and liberated, free of the demands and deals that dominated his working life. Their time in Paris inspired one of her best-known songs, 'Free Man in Paris', which would appear on *Court and Spark*. Geffen, however, was not comfort-able with being seen as vulnerable, as a man wearied by the movers and shakers, dreamers and deal-makers he encountered every day of his working life. He implored her to leave the song off the album. Sensibly, she ignored him; the single peaked at Number 21 on the US charts.

The evolutionary process of musical and lyrical development that had marked each album was at its most evident on *Court and Spark*; all of her influences, all of her explorations were embraced here. The deep subjectivity of *Blue* and its predecessors remained, with revelations personal enough to be authentic yet general enough to enable the listener to identify. Unlike D.H.

Lawrence's character Richard Lovatt, wrestling with the problem of himself and calling it Australia, Mitchell struggled with the problem of herself and her relations with the world yet never confused the source. This is the rebuttal to those who accused her of self-obsession, of only ever focusing on her own concerns, of being another drop in that ocean of white whine that so intoxicated elements of the 70s singer–songwriter genre. Unlike so many 'love-gone-bad' songwriters, particularly women of that era – or indeed, sadly, every musical era – she was never the victim, never bleating 'he done me wrong' without also looking at her own role as an active participant.

From the album's coyly romantic title, evoking more genteel days of courting than the bang-and-blame of contemporary times while at the same time savouring the casual-affair temptations of the title track, she neither lets herself off the hook nor encourages anyone else to do so. Through the insightful honesty of 'Help Me', with its refrain of 'we love our lovin' But not like we love our freedom' and the 'Same Situation' tale of a Warren Beattyish Hollywood bachelor and the parade of women through his life, there is the narrator's absolute clarity of knowing how it feels to be 'caught in my struggle for higher achievement And my search for love that don't seem to cease'. There resignation is tempered with hope; insecurities brush against certainties and don't feel the need to apologise.

By now, the rock band in evidence on *For the Roses* had metamorphosed into a jazz ensemble, to stunning effect. Mitchell had taken the advice of drummer, Russ Kunkel (who had played on *Blue* and *For the Roses*) and found jazz musicians who were less likely to be fazed by her anarchic tunings and complex musical vocabulary. She had gone to see Tom Scott's new jazz venture, the LA Express, at a North Hollywood club, the Baked Potato, and asked the band to play on the new album. They agreed and the album would feature Tom Scott on woodwinds and reeds, bass-player Max Bennett, Larry Nash on piano, guitarist Larry Carlton and drummer John Guerin, with whom Joni would soon become involved. Their work on tracks like 'Help Me', 'Free Man in Paris' and 'Down to You' gave Mitchell's sound the jazzed-up pop clout it needed, the bass and drums beloved of pop radio playlists.

The passion for rock 'n' roll that Joni had felt in her teenage years is revisited in the rousing 'Raised on Robbery', with her own multi-tracked vocals and guests Dr John and Robbie Robertson (during their trip to Paris, Mitchell had discussed the song with him and he'd been eager to play on it). The song is entirely observational rather than personal, the story of a hapless prostitute Mitchell had once seen coming on to a man in a bar; the potential client is more interested in the performance of the Maple Leafs hockey team than that of his new acquaintance. The album ends with two very different reflections on emotional collapse. The elegant musical arrangement of 'Trouble Child' does little to dilute the despair of knowing that there is no one left to rely on, of the slow but sure implosion of 'breaking like the waves at Malibu'. The final track is a counterpoint: Joni's first officially released cover version, 'Twisted' is the catchy, quirky Annie Ross song (written to an instrumental by Wardell Gray) that she had discovered when, as a teenager, she began listening to Lambert, Hendricks and Ross. The comedy duo Cheech and Chong are unlikely but inspired choices to accompany her as scat singers, 'the chick is twisted!' Tom Scott recalled, 'Singing without her own instrument is revolutionary for Joni. The first time we rehearsed "Twisted", she said, "Oh, I feel like Helen Reddy!"' In an odd coincidence, middle-of-the-road chanteuse Bette Midler had also covered the song on her own album released around this time, but made it a more campish send-up.

For all the song's upbeat humour and jokey punchline, its theme – psychoanalysis – mirrored Mitchell's own experience. In a cover feature for the Canadian magazine *Macleans*, Mitchell was interviewed by her friend, the folk-singer Malka, and explained how her time in analysis had made the song feel even more relevant:

> I figured that I earned the right to sing it. I tried to put it on the last record but it was totally inappropriate. It had nothing to do with that time period and some of my friends feel it has nothing to do with this album either. It's added like an encore.

Mitchell then spoke of her ambivalence about the therapeutic process – she had left an appointment with an analyst some years earlier, bemused by his attitude – even as she recognised that her later psychotherapy had helped her:

I felt I wanted to talk to someone about the confusion which we all have ... and I was willing to pay for his discretion. I didn't expect him to have any answers or that he was a guru, only a sounding-board for a lot of things. And it proved effective because simply by confronting paradoxes or difficulties within your life several times a week, they seem to be not so important as they do when they're weighing on your mind in the middle of the night, by yourself, with no one to talk to, or someone to talk to who probably will tell another friend who will tell another friend, as friends do. And I went through a lot of changes about it, too. It's like driving out your devils – do you drive out your angels as well? An artist needs a certain amount of turmoil and confusion, and I've created out of that. It's been like part of the creative force, even out of severe depression sometimes there comes insight. It's sort of masochistic to dwell on it but you know it helps you to gain understanding. I think it did me a lot of good.

Upon its release in early 1974, Robert Hilburn, in the *Los Angeles Times*, described *Court and Spark* as a virtually flawless album, saying:

Part of Miss Mitchell's strength has always been her ability to explore and then honestly reveal – rather than filter, soften or glamorise – her emotions and experiences, both the pleasure and pain. Too many artists filter experiences to make themselves appear wiser, stronger, more confident. Miss Mitchell, however, allows the vulnerability to be seen.

But other critics fell into the trap of assuming that everything Mitchell wrote was autobiographical. Charlotte Greig, writing in *Mojo* twenty years after the album was released, said, '[Mitchell's] mercurial, if self-absorbed reflections charmed a generation in the 70s and that, along with her immense musicality, let her get away with adopting the role of spoilt minx in songs like "Free Man in Paris".' The 'spoilt minx' of the song was in fact David Geffen.

The album eventually peaked at Number 2 on the US charts, with the single 'Help Me' reaching Number 7 – Mitchell's first and only Top Ten single. It would receive four Grammy award nominations: Record of the Year, Album of the Year, Best Female Pop Vocal and Best Arrangement Accompanying Vocalists. Joni won only the last of these, with Tom Scott for 'Down To You', and lost out to Australian pop warbler Olivia Newton-John in Record of the Year and Best Female Pop Vocal (for 'I Honestly Love You') and to Stevie Wonder's *Fulfillingness First Finale* as Album of the Year. The then little-known LA Express had joined her on tour to promote the album, as both support act and backing band (with Robben Ford substituting for guitarist Larry Carlton, who wasn't available). Speaking to Barbara Charone – then of *New Musical Express* and eons later a UK publicity supremo for Warner Brothers, the label to which Mitchell would return in the 1990s – Tom Scott described the run-up to the tour:

> We rehearsed for ten days before the tour, mostly learning Joni's material because it's so intricate. Her music is very delicate and needs to be treated very carefully. We worked hard to be as true to her tunes as we could. It evolved very spontaneously. Maybe instead of just playing the melody on sax, we'd try guitar and sax. That really seemed to click so we've done several tunes constructed around that tension. Joni's lyrics aren't as easily accessible as Dylan's. Dylan's lyrics are universal messages at his best, but Joni's are more transparent – you have to look a little deeper.

The result was hardly a Dylanesque electrified Newport Folk Festival revisited but the new jazzed-up amplified Joni took some audiences by surprise. Several venues on the US tour resonated with demands for solo, acoustic Mitchell, as she ranged through material from all of her previous albums as well as *Court and Spark*. At a show in Chicago, someone shouted, 'Turn down the volume!', to which she replied with mock innocence, 'What's the matter, do we have a hall full of purists? I thought Chicago liked to boogie.' In St Louis, a heckler urged, 'Let's hear her *without* the band', to which another voice responded, 'Let's hear her *with* the band.'

As if prepared for mutterings that she'd sold out, with a bunch of LA jazzers and a new tour wardrobe of elegant evening gowns, Mitchell was quick with a response when one member of the audience demanded the Jefferson Airplane song 'White Rabbit'. To cheers and laughter, Mitchell retorted, 'I'm slick but not that Slick!' The rapport with the audience and the confidence to engage with them in that way were signs that she'd come to terms with the ambivalence she had once felt about live performance, still aware of its limitations but more able to enjoy the unique atmosphere. With the LA Express, she joined Crosby, Stills, Nash and Young on their summer tour and, in September, appeared with them, the Band and Jesse Colin Young at Wembley Stadium in London. Annie Ross – one of Mitchell's early musical influences, as part of Lambert, Hendricks and Ross – joined Joni on stage for 'Twisted'.

Live recordings from three venues on the 1974 tour – the Berkeley Community Center on 2 March, LA Music Center on 4 March and the Universal Amphitheater, 14–17 August – appeared on the live double album *Miles of Aisles*, which was released in November. The album was the nearest thing to a 'best of' compilation that Mitchell would release for years: of the 18 tracks, two new songs ('Jericho' and 'Love or Money') co-exist happily enough with some of her best-known from each of her albums. But perhaps the most revealing feature of the entire work is not the two new songs, or the new arrangements of many of the older ones, or the superb sound quality created by engineer Henry Lewy, or the success of the LA Express in merging with Mitchell's vision of her work.

The most revealing moment comes as she retunes her guitar against a barrage of shouted song requests from the audience. She pauses just long enough to muse:

> That's one thing that's always been a major difference between the performing arts to me, and being a painter. A painter does a painting and ... that's it. He's had the joy of creating it, and he hangs it on some wall, somebody buys it, somebody buys it again, or maybe nobody buys it, and it sits up in a loft some-where 'til he dies. But nobody ever says to him ...

nobody ever said to van Gogh, 'Paint a *Starry Night* again, man!'

That spontaneous comment encapsulates exactly the dilemma of the 'serious' artist and it's one that has dogged Mitchell throughout her career: how to remain a vital and inspired creative force in the face of attempts to keep you rooted in the past as a musical curio. Do you keep the customers satisfied by turning yourself into a human jukebox or do you continue on your own exploratory path, letting the chords fall where they may and hope people listen without prejudice? How many times can you keep hearing and reading that your best work was done decades earlier without losing heart and spirit? Charles Mingus – with whom Joni would later work on the *Mingus* album – when faced one night with repeated shouted requests from someone in the audience, urging him to play an old song, walked up to the man and thrust the bass into his face, and said '*You* play it!' It was the same with Miles Davis and the pressure on him to keep playing ballads when he wanted to stretch his musical boundaries. His attitude was: go back and listen to those records; I'm not going to but you can.

Despite the dreams of some fans and ageing critics, Joni Mitchell will never create *Blue* again, just as Bob Dylan will not write another *Blood on the Tracks,* Neil Young won't reproduce *After the Goldrush* and the Beatles could never have recorded another *Sergeant Pepper's Lonely Hearts Club Band*, no matter how long they'd stayed together. Those albums amounted to one scorching moment in a career – now it's time to *move on,* as the psychobabblers say. Don Henley, speaking in 1989, recalled this process at work when the folk-rock royalty that was the Eagles started to implode: 'We just kept going until we burned out. 'Cause there was that pressure from record companies and ourselves to follow up *Hotel California*: "Give us another one of those!" You can't do that again.'

Even in the mid-1970s, with her recording career less than a decade old, Mitchell was aware of that pressure to repeat a winning formula, to come up with another *Blue,* to change the jazz-influenced course she'd embarked on and take her seat again in the acoustic confessional. It was to be more open-minded critics and fellow musicians who could see the logic in musical adventuring. Among them was Jimmy Webb, who, in an interview with Peter Doggett of *Record Collector* in 1993, spoke of his personal and professional debt to Mitchell:

> I was tremendously influenced [by her]. She was a good friend and I was fortunate enough to be around her when she was working on *For the Roses* and *Court and Spark*, right here in London, because she sang background on *Land's End* [his 1973 solo album] with my sister. We were just part of each other's lives for a while. I definitely envied that part of her work: that this is just a conversation you're listening in on. If it's poetry, then yes, it is, but not as a self-conscious, forced thing. I just got extremely under her spell, influenced by her writing; in fact, I still am. She's probably responsible for a lot of that change of style about then. I used to go to the studio and just listen to her record, sit quietly in the back of the control room. After Lennon and McCartney, Joni was the next big blip on my radar screen in terms of 'Hey, pay attention! This girl is doing something a little different.'

As 1974 drew to a close, Joni Mitchell was the subject of a respectful cover feature in *Time* magazine. She was described as rock 'n' roll's leading lady,

> the rural neophyte waiting in a subway, a free spirit drinking Greek wine in the moonlight, an organic Earth Mother dispensing fresh bread and herb tea, and the reticent feminist who by trial and error has charted the male as well as the female ego.

The writer, David DeVoss, describes an evening spent with Mitchell and John Guerin at the home they'd just moved into in Bel Air. It's a revealing aside to the very dilemmas with which Mitchell battled in so much of her work: the disparate longings for personal freedom and romantic permanence, the desire for independence and the deeply felt traditionalism that were at the core of many of her relationships and the complications of celebrity, when love affairs are played out under the intensity of the public gaze.

DeVoss is clearly impressed at her role as the perfect hostess, extolling the virtues of home-cooking, making her own Yorkshire puddings and spiced apple dumplings. After dinner, Guerin retreats, beer in hand, to watch football on television while Mitchell reinspects her kitchen for traces of dust. Mitchell takes DeVoss to see her painting studio and he notes there is no mirror in the room, without, it seems, asking himself why there *would* be a mirror in an artist's studio. He confides, 'Joni will not have one in a room in which she writes and paints – too distracting.' As she plays him a song on her cassette recorder, the phone rings. It's a friend inviting her and Guerin to a party; without hesitation, Mitchell says 'We'd love to', and then, 'But why don't you ask John. If I suggest it, he'll think I want to see my old boyfriends.'

Rock trivia misconceptions 1: In 1975 *Rolling Stone* named *The Hissing of Summer Lawns* the worst album of the year. Wrong. It was branded worst album *title* of the year. But the former interpretation has become part of the accepted wisdom about Joni Mitchell's work and is oft-repeated in articles about her.
Rock trivia misconceptions 2: Joni Mitchell only ever writes about herself and her own emotional world. Wrong. The move to a more external narrative to replace the largely internal focus began in earnest with *The Hissing of Summer Lawns* – the observed became the observer and used a poetic reportage to describe what she saw. Without abandoning autobiography entirely, personal philosophy extended to the realm of social philosophy, a lovers' quarrel became a lover's quarrel with the world, examinations of the power balance in romantic relationships were interspersed with vignettes on other power structures: the old world and the new, the primitive and the 'sophisticated', the dealer and the user, the trophy wife and the corporate husband.

For a woman who has always disavowed any link with feminism, Mitchell would have been a powerful asset to the movement in the 70s, if she could only have overcome her resistance to that F word. She showed herself willing and able to write deeply insightful works on the female condition, on the dynamics of relationships where the power is immensely weighted towards the man's superior financial status and the woman's dependence on it, and on the real or imagined victimhood of many women and their capacity to escape that. As the narrator/writer, she has few illusions about life down among the women but depicts their tales compassionately, neither damning nor making excuses.

Feminist in all but name, Mitchell created an elliptical mystery play in 'Don't Interrupt The Sorrow', rich in religious imagery that invokes both Madonna and goddess as well as the 'prophet witches' who perished needlessly at the stake, in a denunciation of Bible-belt patriarchs, of weak men who can only gain strength by blaming and controlling women and its celebration of defiant women: 'Anima rising, Queen of Queens . . . she's a vengeful little goddess, With an ancient crown to fight.'

A more dubious brand of female wisdom – the one that has worked out the benefits to be gained by relentless exploitation of one's sexuality – runs through 'Shades of Scarlett Conquering', where the modern equivalents of Scarlett O'Hara and Blanche DuBois step from the scenes of *Gone With the Wind* and *A Streetcar Named Desire*, armed with girlie guile and womanly wiles: 'Any man in the world holding out his arm, Would soon be made to pay.' That observation resonates through the title track (a collaboration with John Guerin) and 'Harry's House – Centerpiece' where trophy wives trade their independence, and more than a little of their integrity, for the financial security offered by a corporate-clone husband.

In the former, the woman acknowledges – even as she walks from the rooms full of Chippendale furniture 'that nobody sits in', to the well-tended garden and hears the hissing of sprinklers on the manicured summer lawns of her upmarket suburb – that 'she stays with a love of some kind, it's the lady's choice'. But in 'Harry's House – Centerpiece' the Stepford wife ultimately rebels, throwing it all back at her husband, telling Harry just where he can shove his house and his take-home pay. We also glimpse the marriage from the husband's viewpoint, the man hopelessly trapped in the paper chase through boardrooms and airport departure lounges, to his tastefully decorated *House and Gardens* home, where his unhappy, frustrated wife in a single breath shouts at the children – 'I said, get down off of there!' – and demands of him, 'When will you be home, Harry?' He finds her unrecognisable now from the glistening young beauty he'd married, the girl who shone as she reeled him in. The piece segues into one of Mitchell's favourite Lambert, Hendricks and Ross songs, 'Centerpiece', with the drooling lounge-lizard arrangement highlighting the disappointment at the core of the marriage, the clash of the romantic fantasy in 'Centerpiece', with the everyday reality of life at 'Harry's House'.

The role of the power/money equation in a woman's downfall is explored in the cautionary urban tale of 70s sexploitation and drugs, 'Edith and the Kingpin', where cocaine strengthens the hold that the pimp/dealer has over women like Edith, women who are 'romantic and snow-blind'. The drug imagery surfaces with the 'poppy snake' opiate of 'The Jungle Line', the complex, heavily percussive track which features the Warrior Drummers of Burundi, one of the earliest experiments in sampling 'world' music. It predated by many years the world music 'discoveries' of Paul Simon, Peter Gabriel, Sting, Talking Heads *et al.* At once hypnotic and unsettling, the drums snake with menace to lyrics inspired by the paintings of Henri 'Le Douanier' Rousseau, slavery, the power of the primitive in the face of Western exploitation, and the evolution of jazz and the blues.

Rousseau had retired as a customs officer in 1893 and devoted himself to painting, although – like van Gogh – it was only after his death that he gained recognition. A master of nineteenth-century naïve art, Rousseau's exotic jungle fantasy landscapes and the lush, bold sensuality of his colours are contrasted in the lyrics with the grimy bland tones and hard edges of a concrete jungle of high-rises and the survival of the fittest in urban life – the heart of darkness in the heart of the city.

A powerplay of another kind – that between Art and Commerce – weaves through 'The Boho Dance', based on *The Painted Word*, Tom Wolfe's slim volume that charts the erratic course of the social history of modern art from its revolutionary beginnings to the point where it has become almost as mannered, packaged, commercialised and cliché-ridden as the salon art against which it first rebelled. In the book, Wolfe describes the mating ritual between artist and art establishment which begins with the Boho Dance and ends with the Consummation. The former takes place during the artist's Bohemian loft/garret days, when s/he's working and exhibiting only within that indie sphere, determined to stay far from the madding crowd of the commercial mainstream. The Consummation comes when the mainstream gallery owners and critics invade arty Bohemia and make off with what they perceive to be the hottest new artists and new movements, showering them with the rewards of success and celebrity. Picasso saw it all for what it was and enjoyed it anyway; Jackson Pollock went to all the right parties but peed in the fireplace in feeble defiance of selling out his Boho credentials. Mitchell uses the analogy in relation to her own days as a struggling musician playing in small clubs and coffee houses before she became aware of the dubious seduction of commercial and critical Consummation.

Those carefree pre-Consummation times are recalled in Mitchell's remembrance of her rock 'n' roll dancing days – the teenage hormonal thrills, girls in tight dresses and push-up bras, wooed by Brando-like boys – on 'In France They Kiss On Main Street', as she protests to her mother that kissing a boyfriend in the street was about love, 'not cheap display'. (Mitchell has always displayed that rare gift of remaining good friends with ex-lovers: Graham Nash, David Crosby and James Taylor provide background vocals on the track.) The years spin by and now the girl is 32 and beginning to confront the prospect of ageing and the brevity of youth despite 'all these vain promises on beauty jars' in 'Sweet Bird' – its title taken from the Tennessee Williams play *Sweet Bird of Youth*. It's a gentle meditation on transience and inevitability. The album ends with the hymnal 'Shadows and Light' which picks up on the theme that all things must pass, the incantation heightened by a ponderous synthesiser (Mitchell herself on Arp-Farfisa).

The current and former members of the LA Express – Guerin, Max Bennett, Victor Feldman, Robben Ford, Larry Carlton – and the other jazz musicians featured had helped to crystallise Mitchell's jazz inflections from *Court and Spark,* but their musicianship was criticised for not always matching the strength of her writing. In *Rolling Stone,* Stephen Holden described the album as substantial literature set to insubstantial music, denouncing what he called the 'pseudo-avant-gardism' of the drum and synthesiser-dominated arrangement for 'The Jungle Line'. He advised: '*The Hissing of Summer Lawns* is ultimately a great collection of pop poems with a distracting soundtrack. Read it first. Then play it.' Mitchell's sleeve notes amounted to an intriguing manifesto:

> This is a total work conceived graphically, musically, lyrically and accidentally – as a whole. The performances were guided by the given compositional structures and the audibly inspired beauty of every player. The whole unfolded like a mystery. It is not my intention to unravel that mystery for anyone . . .

She would later say that while she loved the title of the album, it was too oblique for most people's tastes.

Mitchell's painting on the cover uses the New York City skyline as a backdrop, towering above suburban houses, while in the foreground a group of Amazonian Indian tribesmen carry a massive anaconda: the reassuringly bland hiss of lawn sprinklers gives way to something primal and menacing. The image of the tribesmen is taken from a photograph featured in an article on the Amazon in *National Geographic* in the early 1970s. On the back cover, far removed from the city, the suburbs and the snake, is the oasis-like retreat of Mitchell's home in Bel Air. The work was chosen by Q magazine in 2001 as among the 100 Best Album Covers of All Time. On the inside sleeve, Mitchell is photographed in a bikini, swimming in the pool at her home. The photographer, Norman Seeff — who worked with Mitchell often – explained how the shoot progressed:

> I thought it was a very powerful co-creation between the two of us. It was a rather sensuous – not sensual, but a sensuous shoot. To me, they were just beautiful images, rather than trying to go for the very in-depth personality type of stuff.

The illustrative quality of the artwork was largely missed by some fans who interpreted the images as haughty and superior, a show of wealth and privilege. They felt that Joni had already distanced herself by minimising the first-person narratives in her writing and, with that, their ability to identify so closely – and now she appeared happy to stay in Bel Air and immerse herself in her pool rather than their projected angst.

The photographs and the album they adorned came out at a time when Mitchell and other musicians and singers like the Eagles, Jackson Browne and Linda Ronstadt were strongly associated in the public consciousness with the conspicuous consumption and glory days of 70s California hedonism and the eventual souring of the dream, but Don Henley, solo artist and now back in a re-formed Eagles line-up, denied that they were ever inextricably part of that: 'We never glorified California! We were running it down from the beginning. [Jackson, Linda and Joni] are three of the hardest-working people I know! If living in California and making records is hedonism, then I'm sorry . . . '

While Mitchell was on the West Coast recording *Hissing,* Bob Dylan was on the East Coast putting together ideas for a long-cherished notion of getting together a musical revue, a travelling circus with a changing line-up of performers, poets and partners. The Rolling Thunder Revue hit the road with an eclectic cast of characters including Dylan's band, Joan Baez, guitarist Mick Ronson, who was more used to touring with David Bowie, Roger McGuinn, poet Allen Ginsberg, singer/actress Ronee Blakely, and playwright Sam Shepard, who was initially taken on as a writer to help Dylan create a film during the tour, *Renaldo and Clara,* using the Rolling Thunder guests as improvisational actors. Shepard later chronicled the tour in his *Rolling Thunder Logbook.*

Part-way through the tour Mitchell joined simply for the experience, as an observer, but quickly became a participant appearing at a number of shows including an impromptu appearance during a visit to the Tuscarora Indian Reservation in New York State. Joni threw herself into the anarchic, improvisational spirit of the ensemble as it travelled, making up songs on stage or singing in fractured French. She refused to let footage of herself appear in the final cut of *Renaldo and Clara,* reportedly unhappy with her appearance, although later admitted that when she saw how ragged everyone else looked, she'd had second thoughts. The filmmaker Larry Johnson, who had come along to shoot the film, described the edginess between Joni, Baez and Blakely as the 'Battle of the Berets' – a reference to the headwear favoured by the three women. Dylan-scribe Larry Sloman, who wrote about the tour in *On the Road with Bob Dylan,* said tensions among the women were palpable:

> Joan Baez . . . was not encouraging to anybody on that tour . . . she was like a huge prima donna and felt

incredibly threatened: one, that Ronee Blakely was on that tour, and two, that Joni Mitchell came in. There was all this horrible behind-the-scenes shit going on.

Throughout the tour, Dylan had touted his advocacy of Rubin 'Hurricane' Carter and his campaign to have the African-American middleweight boxer freed from jail, after being convicted for committing a triple-murder in a bar in New Jersey in 1965. As disquiet grew over evidence alleging an unfair trial, Dylan and others believed that Carter had been victimised, an innocent scapegoat who had been denied justice because of racism and corruption. Using a large measure of poetic licence, Dylan had written his own version of the case in his song 'Hurricane', soon to surface on the *Desire* album – and, years later, to be rebutted line by contentious line by a former news reporter, Cal Deal, who had covered the case and has since set up his own website dedicated to a more factual account.

On 6 December, the Revue musicians performed to inmates at the Correctional Institution for Women, a medium-security prison in Clinton, New Jersey. The 'guest' of honour at the show was Hurricane Carter, one of the hundred or so male inmates who were housed separately from the women prisoners. The Revue musicians were more accustomed to playing to a white middle-class audience and some were ill at ease in a room full of prisoners, most of them black. Roberta Flack immediately broke through any social and musical barriers and was rewarded with enthusiastic standing ovations for her three-song set; Joan Baez – a veteran of both political benefit gigs and prison visits, who had herself been arrested before for her anti-war and civil rights protests – came a close second.

Baez thanked the prison authorities for 'making it so easy for us to get in', then remarked ruefully that 'I just wish they'd make it a little bit easier for you to get out.' The other musicians and singers joined Dylan on the song 'Hurricane', as its subject looked on. The Beat poet Allen Ginsberg, dressed in sober suit and tie, was greeted with cheers as he delivered his poem 'Kiss Ass', which included the lines 'America will have to Kissass Mother Earth, Whites will have to Kissass Blacks, for Peace and Pleasure ...' But within minutes of Joni Mitchell taking the stage, some of the inmates grew restive during her pared-down acoustic word-plays and began to heckle her. She stopped just long enough to say, 'We came here to give you love. If you can't handle it, that's your problem.'

Undeterred, she appeared the following night at Madison Square Garden in New York as the Rolling Thunder Revue ended its tour with a benefit concert for Carter. But by now, Mitchell felt growing unease about the campaign to have him released. She had spoken to Carter several times on the telephone and concluded that he was a violent opportunist making the most of being courted by what Mitchell herself described as 'white patsy liberals'. So when Joan Baez asked her to introduce Muhammad Ali at the Madison Square Garden concert, she made her feelings known:

> I was in a particularly cynical mood – it had been a difficult excursion. I said, 'Fine, what I'll say is . . . ' – and I never would've – 'I'll say, "We're here tonight on behalf of one jive-ass nigger who could've been the champion of the world, and I'd like to introduce you to another one who is!" She stared at me and immediately removed me from this introductory role. I thought then, 'I should go on in black-face tonight.' Anyway, Hurricane was released and the next day he brutally beat up this woman . . .

The Dylan campaign was largely instrumental in gaining Carter's release in 1976, pending a retrial. New Jersey prosecutors offered Carter a deal – they would drop the charges if he took and passed a lie-detector test; he refused. He faced a second trial and was again found guilty. In 1985, a federal judge ruled that the convictions be set aside – not overturned – and Carter was released from prison. Fifteen years later, there was more controversy when a highly fictionalised and sympathetic account of the case, *The Hurricane*, with Denzel Washington playing the Carter role and Norman Jewison as director, was nominated for the film world's most prestigious awards, the Oscars. Cal Deal was so incensed about the inaccuracies in the story, and what he believed were gullible media which accepted the film's claims without question, that he launched a publicity campaign which many believe was successful in ruining the film's Oscar chances.

At the same time, Carter was on a publicity tour promoting his new autobiography. A particularly flattering feature in the *Kansas City Star* newspaper described him as a global freedom fighter, making much of his unsubstantiated claims to have been a gunrunner for Nelson Mandela's African National Congress while it was outlawed during the apartheid years in South Africa, to have befriended South African activist Steve Biko and been a part of the US civil rights movement led by Martin Luther King. The *Irish Times* writer George Kimball, in a piece criticising the unquestioning partisan tone of the feature, described as ludicrous Carter's claim to have smuggled guns to the ANC and mused:

> Perhaps that would explain the live .32 calibre bullet and shotgun shells – both precisely matching the weapons used in the [New Jersey] killings – found in Carter's car literally minutes after the murders. Presumably the ammunition rolling around under the seat that night was on its way to Nelson Mandela.

Joni Mitchell's experience with Dylan's Carter campaign was to reinforce her wariness of the rent-a-cause celebrity band-wagon of radical chic and ill-informed sloganeering, and in the future her involvement in political issues would be confined to a carefully considered few. But her stint with the Rolling Thunder Revue had been a good warm-up for her own tour with the LA Express, in support of *The Hissing of Summer Lawns*.

In January 1976, as the tour got underway in Dylan's home state of Minnesota, Elektra/Asylum described *Hissing* as Mitchell's fastest-selling studio album. The year also began with a ringing endorsement from the readers of *Playboy*, who had voted her the top jazz and pop female vocalist of 1975 – complete with a curious cartoon illustration of Mitchell, who was depicted as a sexy chanteuse, wearing an entirely uncharacteristic get-up of skin-tight midriff-baring trousers and a tiny top that only just covered her cartoon breasts. It was this kind of projected image of her – as opposed to the real one – that had led *Melody Maker* writer Michael Watts to pant:

> Joni Mitchell is disturbing in a very real way because after watching and listening to her for awhile you start

thinking she's not just a woman, she's WOMAN, embodying all male desires and expectations ... like the White Goddess of mythology, she beckons, elusive, virginal and not a little awe-inspiring.

It would prove to be a hard cliché to live up to.

8 Dreams and false alarms . . .

Courage is the price that Life exacts for granting
peace, The soul that knows it not, knows no
release From little things; Knows not the livid loneliness of fear, Nor mountain heights where bitter joy
can hear The sound of wings.
(Amelia Earhart, *Courage*, 1927)

FURRY LEWIS WAS PISSED OFF and telling anyone who'd listen:
friends, neighbours and even a reporter from *Rolling Stone*.
As he held court in the bedroom of his three-room apartment in Memphis, Tennessee, his indignation rose in proportion
to the amount of Ten High bourbon he was drinking. At eighty-
three you've earned the right to be cantankerous, but this time
Furry was in bad spirits after being reminded of 'that woman'.
The one who wrote a song about him and called it 'Furry Sings
The Blues' and put it on her new record.

It had all begun peaceably enough, when Joni Mitchell was in
Memphis for a show in early February 1976. She'd gone down to
Beale Street, the once proud home of the Memphis blues, and
found it reduced to little more than a derelict site, crumbling in
the wreckage of the old buildings on either side of the street, and
just waiting for the developers to move in – a far cry from the
restored historic area/tourist mecca it is today. A statue of the
father of the blues, W.C. Handy, presided over what was left – a
couple of pawnshops and a modern movie theatre. Joni was
taken aback when a man standing outside one of the pawnshops
recognised her:

He looks at me and says, 'You Joni Mitchell?' I think,
'Culturally, this is impossible. This guy should not
know my name.' However I had heard that Furry

Lewis lived in Memphis, so I mentioned it to the pawnbroker. He says, 'Oh sure, he's a friend of mine. Meet me here tonight and we'll go over and see him. Bring a bottle of Jack Daniels and a carton of Pall Mall cigarettes.' Furry was in his eighties ... and senile at this point. Lived in a little shanty in the ghetto there. It was quite a nice visit until I said to him – meaning to be close to him, meaning 'We have this in common': 'I play open tunings too'. Now, people must have ridiculed him about it or something, because he leaned up on the bed and 'Ah kin play in Spanish tonnin!' Real defensive. Somehow or other I insulted him. From then on, it was downhill. He just said, 'I don't like her.'

Furry was a part of blues history, had been all over the South in a travelling medicine show, worked with W.C. Handy himself, hoboed on the railroads and lost a leg in the process, came to Memphis where he swept the streets and made records, famous for his slide-driven guitar blues. But now, after his encounter with Joni Mitchell had gone into a song – right down to his expressed dislike of her – he wanted a piece of the action. And he was telling the *Rolling Stone* writer Mark Seal exactly why:

The way I feel is that your name is proper only to you, and when you use it you should get results from it. She shouldn't have used my name in no way, shape or faction without consultin' me 'bout it first. The woman came over here and I treated her right ... She wanted to hear 'bout the old days, said it was for her own personal self, and I told it to her like it was, gave her straight oil from the can. But then she goes and puts it all down on a record, using my name and not giving me nothing!

Mark Seal later asked Mitchell's manager, Elliot Roberts, whether Furry was right to feel exploited, and Roberts denied that the old bluesman had been used in any way:

All [Joni] said about him was 'Furry sings the blues', the rest is about the neighbourhood. She doesn't even mention his last name. She really enjoyed meeting him, and wrote about her impressions of the meeting. He did tell her that he didn't like her but we can't pay him royalties for that. I don't pay royalties to everybody who says they don't like me. I'd go broke.

By the time Furry Lewis died in 1981, the song by 'that woman' had brought him and his earlier work to the attention of people who'd never heard of him before Mitchell had sung, 'While our limo is shining on his shanty street, old Furry sings the blues . . . ' Almost twenty years later, she would describe writing the song as one of her happiest creative moments in music: 'When the second verse came that was a thrill, 'cause it all just poured out at once.' It became one of the new songs she performed during the rest of the tour, along with ones from previous albums, traditional folk songs like 'Yarrow' and works in progress including 'Talk To Me'. She'd been writing while on the Rolling Thunder excursion: the fruits of this were 'Coyote' and the song she described as its sequel and usually played as a companion piece, 'Don Juan's Reckless Daughter'. The six-week tour ended in a wintry Madison, Wisconsin, in late February, and after a troubled tour together, Mitchell's relationship with drummer John Guerin was also over. Amid the turmoil, the original plans to extend the tour to take in Asia and Europe were scrapped and Guerin returned to Los Angeles. Joni and her tour photographer, Joel Bernstein, stayed on in Madison.

It was here that Bernstein revived his original plans for the *Blue* sleeve shots that he'd devised more than five years earlier:

> We were staying in a lovely hotel on the lake there and it was still deep in winter. I said to her, 'Listen, Joan, before we send the trucks back with the costumes and all of that stuff, I've got my cameras, we're looking at snow here, let's do that shot, this is our chance. I see you in all black which means a) we're going to have to get you some men's skates and b) you're going to have to pick out some stuff that's all black to wear. I'm seeing your silhouette on the whiteness of the snow . . . '
> So she went to her wardrobe trunk and she pulled out the stole that she is wearing [in the photos] and black

top and a black skirt and black tights and we went to a skate shop and got her black men's skates, because there were no black women's skates, and went on to do this series of photos in a snowstorm and I did get the 'Hans Brinker' one that she and I had discussed [years earlier]. It was just like I imagined except it was a lake instead of a river. It was a real thrill to just do that.

Some of the photographs would be used on the cover and sleeve of her next album, *Hejira,* released in November that year. One image is particularly striking: Mitchell is skating with her arms outstretched behind her, the heavy black shawl spreading like a crow in flight. For Joni Mitchell, the symbolism was important, as Bernstein says: 'It's so bird-like and of course she had just [named] her publishing company Crazy Crow Publishing and had just done the song "Black Crow" as a new song. To have that image of her was key, visually.' Joni has professed a strong affinity with Native American culture and philosophy and saw the crow as a totem – an animal or bird which, Native Americans believe, holds special significance for each individual, as both a protector and a source of power and wisdom.

The cover of *Hejira* is dominated by a monochrome studio shot of a black-clad Mitchell taken by Norman Seeff, but the rest is an intricate composite of a number of images including elements of some taken by Joel Bernstein in Wisconsin, as well as stock shots of a desert road and a cloud-filled sky. Mitchell pieced together a collage of the images she wanted and these were then enlarged or reduced, fitted together again, re-photographed and then airbrushed to make it a seamless whole, smoothing out the edges and differing light sources. To get a thematic continuity, Mitchell wore the same clothes for Seeff's studio shots as she did in Wisconsin. Bernstein also took some of the photographs on the inner sleeve, which continued the snow/skater theme:

> She asked me to do pictures in a skating rink she took me to. She was fascinated by the skating of [Olympic figure-skater] Toller Cranston. We went to an ice show of his in Buffalo and afterwards she decided that she wanted to rent a rink and have me photograph him on the rink. So the shot of the skater is him and the bride

[in the shot] refers to the bridal gown in [her song] 'Song for Sharon'.

That song was written at the end of a day spent in New York, when Mitchell and Joel Bernstein had gone to Staten Island so she could buy a mandolin. Less a song than an epic poem, for eight-and-a-half minutes it ranged over Canadian prairies, small towns, big cities, lost loves and life's choices, in a conversation-in-song with Mitchell's childhood friend Sharon Bell. Bernstein says that the New York verses were almost like a diary entry of that day:

> We were in a taxi passing a bridal shop, with an elabo-rate bridal gown in the corner of the display, and she said, 'Joel, did you see that? that bridal gown over there? some girl is going to see that and go crazy. She's going to want to get married, she's going to want to be that bride.' It ended up just like that on the song. Then we took the ferry over to Staten Island.

That too is detailed in the song. Years later, when asked in an interview about her drugs experiences, Joni Mitchell would say that she'd done some good writing while taking cocaine – notably 'Song for Sharon'.

For most of the other songs, Mitchell had reverted to another favoured method to encourage her writing. She travelled. The album was originally called *Travelling* but Mitchell found the Arabic word *hejira* in a dictionary and was taken with its mean-ing of exodus or migration, a breaking of ties. The word is used in Islam to refer to Mohammed's flight from persecution in the seventh century, when he fled Mecca to reach safety in Medina, where he founded the first Moslem community.

The imagery of departure, flight and travel, literal and metaphorical, reflects the writing of most of the songs, as Mitchell drove across the US with two friends and deposited them in New England. There one of her companions, a former boyfriend from Australia who had arrived in the US for a three-week trip, planned to carry out his scheme to kidnap his young daughter, who was in Maine with her grandmother. Mitchell left him to it and set off alone for the return journey, travelling down the coast to Florida and around the Gulf of Mexico coastline through the southern states until heading inland for California. In song she would describe it as finding 'the refuge of the roads', as she stayed in small-town motels, enjoying the freedom of anonymity, assuming a different persona whenever she chose, meeting locals and drifters alike and shrugging off her Mercedes by saying that she was simply delivering it for a friend.

Amid the solitude of the return journey westwards, Mitchell found a spiritual fellow traveller in Amelia Earhart, whom she described as 'a ghost of aviation' in the song named for her. She saw the song as a message 'from one solo pilot to another . . . sort of reflecting on the cost of being a woman and having something you must do'. The more reflective road songs like 'Amelia', 'Refuge of the Roads', 'A Strange Boy' and the torchy 'Blue Motel Room' contrast with the teasing playfulness and dry humour of 'Coyote', written late the previous year. On *The Hissing of Summer Lawns*, the focus had moved to a large degree away from the experiential 'I' to the observational 'you', but now she was back in a writing mode with which many of her fans felt most at ease – positioning her emotional experiences and romances in such a way that there were enough clues to allow them to specu-late endlessly about the who, the where, the why of it all, but too little evidence to be transparent. Speaking twenty years later, *Hejira* still held meaning for her: 'To me, the whole *Hejira* album was really inspired. I feel a lot of people could have written "Chelsea Morning" but I don't think anyone else could have writ-ten the songs on *Hejira*.'

The restlessness and spartan simplicity of the road-trip is mir-rored in the arrangements for *Hejira* – there are no songs for piano, for instance, because she was travelling only with what she could throw in her car. Back in LA and ready to record her new songs, Mitchell again enlisted jazz musicians, including the LA Express: guitarist Larry Carlton, drummer John Guerin, with whom she remained friends after their break-up, percussionists Bobbye Hall and Victor Feldman, and Max Bennett sharing bass duties with a newcomer to Mitchell's musical line-up, Jaco Pastorius, the gifted, flamboyant but ultimately doomed musician who was to redefine the role and power of bass in 70s jazz fusion.

Pastorius had released his Grammy-nominated self-titled debut album in 1975 and by the time he came to Mitchell's attention he

Joni at home in Laurel Canyon, Los Angeles, 1968. (Baron Wolman/Retna)

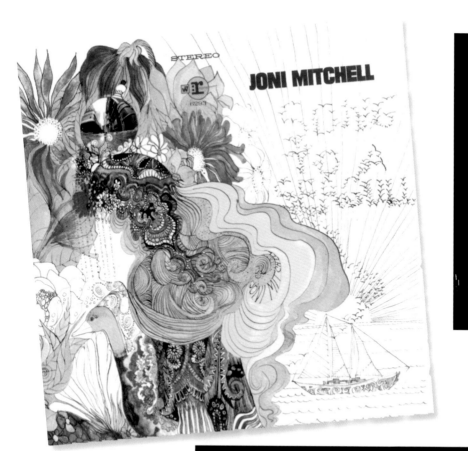

Above Lush '60s pastoral psychedelia inspired Joni's first album cover painting for her 1968 debut *Joni Mitchell*, also known as *Song to a Seagull*.

Right Joni performing at the Isle of Wight festival, August 1970.
(Tony Russell/Redferns)

Above (from left) Joni Mitchell, Stephen Stills, David Crosby, Neil Young and Graham Nash performing at Wembley Stadium, London, September 1974. (Barrie Wentzell/Star File)

Below The Rolling Thunder Revue at Madison Square Garden, New York, August, 1975 including (front, from left) Joni, Joan Baez and Bob Dylan. (Bettmann/Corbis)

JONI MITCHELL

Left Norman Seef photography and Joni's race-and-gender-bending brought her alter-ego 'Art Nouveau' to the cover of *Don Juan's Reckless Daughter* in 197

Right Joni in '70s glamour mode, Boston, 1976.
(Ron Pownall/Star File)

Joni with Peter Gabriel after receiving the Billboard Century Award
in New York, December 6, 1995.
(Kevin Mazur/LFI)

Left and below Vincent by Vincent: van Gogh's *Self-Portrait with Bandaged Ear*, 1889. (Courtauld Institute Gallery, London) and Joni by Joni: *Turbulent Indigo*, 1995.

right Suffering for her art? Joni with self-portrait, based on a photograph taken for an advertisement for The Gap in 1990. The words 'self promotion' are written across the middle of the painting.
(Guido Harari/Katz)

below Joni in front of her painting, *Scuba* (1990), at a news conference at the opening of *voices: Joni Mitchell* at the Mendel Gallery, Saskatoon, June 30, 2000.
(Glen Berger/Canadian Press)

Left Joni and her daughter Kilauren Gibb, at Joni's Bel-Air home in Los Angeles, March 23, 1997. This was their first meeting since Kilauren's adoption in 1965. Photographer Edward 'Ted' Barrington was Gibb's then-boyfriend. (Sygma/Corbis)

Below Joni with some of the artists featured in the tribute concert in her honour at the Hammerstein Ballroom in New York, April 6, 2000. Artists pictured include (from left, second row) k d lang and James Taylor; (front row, centre) Joni; (front row, from right) Elton John, Shawn Colvin, Larry Klein and Cassandra Wilson. (Gene Shaw/Star File)

had already recorded with Weather Report, the seminal jazz fusion outfit led by Wayne Shorter and Joe Zawinul; a guest spot on their *Black Market* album was the beginning of a musical relationship that would span Weather Report's best work. The LA Express guitarist Robben Ford had played Jaco's album to Mitchell, and she liked it so much she wanted to work with Pastorius, seeing his eclectic, free-spirited approach as a refreshing change from the folk-rock bassists she had worked with in the past:

> For the first eight albums or so, I was directing bass-players and annoying them to death with it. I wanted them to stop putting dark polka dots all over the bottom and instead treat it like a symphony. When you listen to a symphony, the bass is not always in, it gets light and airy for a while and then *boom*! It anchors again. And most bassists go plodding along there at the bottom like all pop music does. Finally someone said, 'There's this bass-player in Florida, he's really weird, you'd probably like him ...' So Jaco was a natural for me. We were on the same wavelength as far as that went.

The sense of a reinvigoration of the bass in her music was heightened by Jaco's unfamiliarity with her work and what had preceded *Hejira*. He came to it unencumbered by its connotations with folk-rock or pop, but armed with his iconoclastic skill on both electric and fretless bass. The latter, at the time unusual among jazz and rock bassists, would be an integral part of *Hejira* and the three albums that followed it. Speaking in a BBC radio interview in 1978, Pastorius said:

> I didn't know [Joni's] music but it was really fun coming in from nowhere, and adding this thing. It was a nice combination, especially on the *Hejira* album. The cut, 'Hejira' itself, I really like. I think it was the first thing I played with her.

Twenty years later, Jaco's widow Ingrid spoke to Wally Breese, the founder of the official Joni Mitchell website, about her late husband's work with Mitchell:

I think his whole meeting and experience with Joni was a totally positive experience . . . I think he was inspired. She opened up new doors for him, career-wise and also music-wise. Jaco was raw. He was not a musician who ever took lessons in music. He didn't learn how to read [music] until much later . . . I think Joni was definitely one of the main people in his life.

While Mitchell's move away from arrangements that centred on her own guitar, piano or dulcimer, and what was perceived as largely autobiographical writing, into the more incidentally radio-friendly and jazz-rock tones of *Court and Spark* and *The Hissing of Summer Lawns,* may have caught some critics and fans by surprise, her move back appeared equally unexpected. Sam Sutherland, writing in *High Fidelity,* said:

Hejira is a risk for Joni Mitchell even in the afterglow of international acceptance at the broadest level, for the subdued intensity of these new performances demands far more from her audience than the heady romantic bloom that made *Court and Spark* so attractive to radio programmers as well as confirmed fans. Yet the risk is well-taken.

Reviewing the album in *Sounds* Tim Lott declared: 'On a commercial level, this is manifestly the most non-instant album she has ever produced', but he praised her singular use of ideas, 'the way components are introduced and discarded without overkill devaluation, is specifically what makes Mitchell unique in her genius as a composer'.

The one constant in Mitchell's career to date had been change – with each album, her music had progressed, opening up new territories without losing sight of what was of value in the old musical landscape. *Court and Spark* had marked a dramatic shift that would dominate her output for most of the 70s and leave her folk-rock days a distant memory – and her appearance at the Band's farewell concert, affectionately dubbed The Last Waltz, showed the growing gulf between her own increasingly jazz-influenced music and the blues/folk-based roots rock of the Band.

Despite rehearsals with the Band ahead of the 25 November show at the Winterland Ballroom in San Francisco, and the efforts of their friend and sometime producer John Simon, who had painstakingly transcribed the songs in her set, Mitchell was still wary of the Band's aptitude for turning into a jazz combo. Their robust but somewhat ragged performances as her backing band on 'Coyote', 'Shadows and Light' and 'Furry Sings the Blues' proved her right. Robbie Robertson would say later, 'It was "so far, so good" as we were going along. I mean we had to learn some twenty-odd songs we'd never played before in our lives, so every time out of the chute it was like throwing the dice. It seemed hard enough to remember our own stuff, let alone everyone from Muddy Waters to Joni Mitchell.' She returned to the stage again after Van Morrison's blistering set – which included his joyous impromptu Belfast version of the can-can – to join Neil Young on harmony vocals when the Band played 'Acadian Driftwood'.

The only song from Mitchell's own set to end up in the Martin Scorsese film of the event was 'Coyote'. The film ends with one of the most affecting moments of the seven-hour show, the Band and their guests – Mitchell, Young, Bob Dylan, Morrison, Eric Clapton, Ron Wood, Ringo Starr, Ronnie Hawkins, Paul Butterfield, Bobby Charles, Neil Diamond, Ronee Blakely and anyone else who could cram onto the stage – performing Dylan's 'I Shall Be Released'. The Last Waltz felt almost like a last gasp for bands founded on roots-based authenticity and credibility at a time when slick southern Californian supergroups like the Eagles and Fleetwood Mac dominated the US music scene. And by 1977, the manufactured punk boy-band, the Sex Pistols, was snarling its safety-pinned way to chart-topping glory and artists like Patti Smith and Elvis Costello were mixing punk and poetry to make New Wave, punk's eloquent and arty perfect cousin, with influences as diverse as the French poet Arthur Rimbaud (Smith) and Joni Mitchell (Costello).

Mitchell herself seemed impervious to all else that was going on around her in contemporary music and was widening her explorations of the boundaries of jazz and lyric-writing with the double-album *Don Juan's Reckless Daughter*, released in December 1977 – its title a wry comment on her own romantic history and a homage to her favourite Carlos Castaneda books about his mystical adventures with the shaman, Don Juan. Mitchell's growing identification with Native American and black culture, and the imagery of both, sprawl across *Don Juan's Reckless Daughter*.

At the beginning of the title track, she declares her position – 'I'm Don Juan's Reckless Daughter' – and using the serpent/eagle symbolism of Native America, details her battle to reconcile opposites: the serpent of blind desire and the eagle of clarity, self-indulgence and self-denial, yes and no, woman and man. Ambitious and complex, the album displays a subtly challenging schizophrenia of style and subject matter. Although not conceived originally with a thematic progression – 'Dreamland' for instance was written two years earlier – one nevertheless emerged, coursing its way from the jazz joint jive of 'Cotton Avenue' and the anticipation of a wild night of music, dancing and drinking, through the drunken regrets and hung-over recriminations of 'Talk to Me' to the loving determination and good intentions of 'Jericho'.

The cinematic semi-autobiographical stream of consciousness work that is the sixteen-minute part-orchestral interlude, part-vocal 'Paprika Plains' picks up these themes, moving through a rainy-night bar scene to Mitchell's first childhood memory of refracted light through a window blind and later, in Saskatchewan, growing up surrounded by the prairies among the 'sky-oriented people' for whom reading the skies could signal either crop devastation or resurrection, and of seeing the local Indians come to town, dispossessed, with little left to do but drink and fight and daydream. The song itself was partly inspired by a dream Joni had while travelling with the Rolling Thunder Revue, and the printed lyrics on the album sleeve included unsung lines that described the dream and carried the storyline through the orchestral piece, to be picked up by Mitchell's voice several verses later.

The narrative moves on in 'Otis and Marlena' to take an acerbic look at bloated Middle America wintering in Miami Beach, working on its tan in between appointments for nips, tucks and lifts – while back home, 'Muslims stick up Washington', a reference to racial tensions of the time. Tourists winter further away in 'Dreamland', where planeloads of well-heeled colonisers are seen as ruinous invader-descendants of Christopher Columbus and Walter Raleigh – and again, back home the scene is radically different, as the snowdrifts pile up on 'Myrtle's lawn' (a reference to Mitchell's mother).

The two tracks are separated by the acoustic percussion instrumental 'The Tenth World', an Afro-Latino hybrid equivalent of the Burundi drummers on *The Hissing of Summer Lawns*, featuring a specially assembled collective of percussionists and vocalists including Chaka Khan, Airto Moreira, Mitchell's new lover and drummer Don Alias, Alex Acuna, Jaco Pastorius, Manolo Badrena and two crows (on tape). The musical cast on *Don Juan* also included saxophonist Wayne Shorter of Weather Report, who would become a staple of Mitchell's touring and studio work in the years to come. The album ends with an unexpected return to neo-folk and romanticism in 'The Silky Veils of Ardor', reminiscent of English and Scottish folk ballads with its appeal to 'fair and tender schoolgirls' to beware of courting young men who, like stars, disappear with the dawn's early light.

Critics were more polarised about this album than any of her other work to date. In *Rolling Stone,* Janet Maslin described the album as, at best, 'an instructive failure', and at worst, 'a painful illustration of how different the standards that govern poetry and song lyrics can be, and an indication that Joni Mitchell's talents, stretched here to breaking point, lend themselves more naturally to the latter form'. But in *BAM,* Blair Jackson hailed it as a major work:

> The significance of this album is easily explained: it's ambitious as hell; a double-record set of staggering depth, complexity and musical scope from one of the most talented artists working in pop music. It is also the album which will reveal Joni Mitchell's 'singer-songwriter' tag to be shamefully inadequate ... we must add 'composer' and 'musician' ...

Within a decade, Joni Mitchell had completed the metamorphosis from folk-rock singer-songwriter ingenue to sophisticated jazz explorer and at one point became – literally – unrecognisable: the woman who had once joked that she was married to a possessive guy called Art (just as when Andy Warhol was asked to describe the meaning of Art, he shrugged, 'Isn't that a man's name?') – so Joni *became* a man called Art. In a way.

One Halloween Night, she had watched costumed partygoers carousing in the street and longed for inspiration for her own costume – and at that moment, inspiration sauntered past, a sharp-dressed black Los Angeleno doing the kind of 70s blaxploitation film-style pimp-strut walk that can still be seen on inner-city streets from Los Angeles to Lower Hutt, New Zealand. Oozing high spirits and confidence, the man nodded approvingly as he passed Mitchell and drawled, 'Lookin' good, sister!' Smitten with his swagger and image, she went to the nearest downmarket menswear shop, choosing a polyester suit and garish accessories; she shopped around for an Afro-cut wig, a stick-on moustache and the darkest pancake make-up she could find – and transformed herself so completely that she turned up to a Halloween party hosted by comedy duo Cheech and Chong, and no one, including friends and a former lover, recognised her.

The night belonged to her new alter ego, Art Nouveau; 'he' was to make a more public appearance on the cover of *Don Juan's Reckless Daughter*. At one point during the photo session with Norman Seeff, Joni had disappeared into a dressing-room to change her outfit. S/he walked out to a nonplussed photographer and had become Art Nouveau, in full-on dude style, black-face make-up, Afro wig, heavy gold accessories, three-piece suit and feather-trimmed hat. Art became the cover star, along with her Joni-self more characteristically attired in an elegant diaphanous black dress. Deciding that the plain black dress needed a makeover, Mitchell modified a design she'd just seen on a postcard – a nude woman wearing a Mickey Mouse hat and surrounded by balloons. She superimposed the images on the photograph of the black dress, which was transformed with a design of mouse-faced balloons (though not Mickey, for Disney-related legal reasons) and the full-frontal nude – with the pubic area partly obscured, with some gentility, by flying doves. In the shot, Mitchell is wearing a magician's top hat and appears to have conjured the doves as part of a magic trick performed for a formally dressed young boy (both the shot of the boy and the doves were superimposed on the artwork). It was a pastiche of the symbolism of magic that ran through the album.

The Art Nouveau character left critics puzzled; some thought the imagery was inappropriate, harking back to the minstrelsy era, the musical variety genre in which white performers would paint their faces in a bizarre approximation of blackness and sing songs recalling a sentimentalised and often cruelly inaccurate view of nineteenth-century plantation life in the deep South of the United States. Al Jolson was its prime twentieth-century exponent and reached an international audience far beyond the US vaudeville circuit. As late as the 1960s, *The Black and White Minstrel Show* was shown on British television but was eventually dropped because it was deemed to be clumsily inappropriate at best and offensive at worst. The debates around minstrelsy, racial stereotypes and the appropriation of black musical styles by whites also complicated the issue of the cover image. Some critics wondered whether Mitchell was implying simplistic racial 'they got rhythm' stereotypes. She explains:

> I remember they wrote, 'What is she trying to say – that blacks have more fun?' Regardless of what I was trying to say – because a lot of it is instinct – the important point is the chain of events. I was just going on the hottest impulses I had, the creative ideas.

The critic and author Greg Tate, a co-founder of the Black Rock Coalition, agrees with Mitchell that her ruse was neither inappropriate nor insulting: 'I've heard only praise for what a great drag performance she put on there.' Her black-face idea also had its roots in the Rolling Thunder Revue tour when Dylan and Joan Baez had appeared on stage with faces painted in a chalky white mask. After Baez had removed Joni from her role introducing Muhammad Ali at the benefit concert for Hurricane Carter, for fear that Mitchell might make a facetious comment, Joni had then considered going on in black-face make-up that night as a retort.

The imagery of the cover and the complexity of much of the music on *Don Juan's Reckless Daughter* may have done little to win over the critics or persuade those of her fans hankering for a return to a more melodic and accessible Joni that they should stick with her – but they did intrigue one man enough to seek her out as an inheritor of his own brand of iconoclastic jazz and

uncompromising artistry. Charles Mingus had a lust for life, a
defiant attitude to death and a gift for conflict – with himself, his
past, his country, his fellow musicians, his music and, finally,
with his own mortality. When Dizzy Gillespie ran his spoof pres-
idential campaign in the early 1960s, his Cabinet nominees
included Mingus as Minister of Peace – 'because he'll take a piece
of your head faster than anybody I know'. A cultural and musical
melange, Mingus was born on a US army base in Nogales,
Arizona, in 1922; his mother, Harriett, who died when Charles
was six months old, was the daughter of an Englishman and a
Chinese mother. His father, Charles senior, was the son of a
Swedish woman and a black farm worker. In his novelistic autobiography, *Beneath the Underdog*, Mingus wrote of his evolutionary
journey from this complex ancestry, describing himself as
Mingus One, Two and Three. In the early 1960s he'd explained:

> I am Charles Mingus. Half-black man, yellow man –
> half-yellow – not even yellow, nor white enough to pass
> for nothing but black and not too light enough to be
> called white. I claim that I am a negro. I am Charles
> Mingus – I am nothing. I am Charles Mingus, a famed
> jazz musician but not famed enough to make a living in
> society, that is in America, my home. I cannot even sup-
> port my family, honestly, that is, from the fame that I
> gain to the right of being a negro musician. I am a
> human being born in Indian territory, conquered by
> white skins, or invisible skins, transparent skins, peo-
> ple who killed and robbed to inherit the earth for them-
> selves and for their children. Charles Mingus is a
> musician, a mongrel musician who plays beautiful, who
> plays ugly, who plays lovely, who plays masculine, who
> plays feminine, who plays music, who plays all sounds,
> loud, soft, unheard sounds, sounds, sounds, sounds . . .

Mingus's capacity to surprise stretched towards the infinite; his
voracious appetite for music, knowledge, experience, food, love
was near-limitless. Passion fired everything. When he played at
the Village Vanguard club in downtown Manhattan, he once got
so angry when the audience talked that he smashed his bass, and
flying debris broke a ceiling light. Visiting tourists always looked

around for the Mingus Light. But by the end of 1977, Charles was forced to come to terms with the finite in a diagnosis that the intermittent unresponsiveness of his body, the unfamiliar rubbery nature of his hands, the leaden weight in his legs, had a name – amyotrophic lateral sclerosis, or Lou Gehrig's disease. It had by then become better known for its association with a different kind of American hero, Lou Gehrig, the New York Yankees baseball star who died of the illness in 1941. Doctors had told Mingus in November 1977 that he had between three and six months to live; his body and the unforgiving calendar were both conspiring against him. Mingus was already seriously ill by the time he asked Joni Mitchell to collaborate with him on a project based on T.S. Eliot's *Four Quartets.*

A few months earlier, Charles's friend Daniel Senatore had played him some of Mitchell's albums, thinking he would be interested in the literate lyrics, her vocal style and jazz influences. She caught Charles's eye but not in the man–woman way in which he had become so adept over the years: he'd seen the cover of *Don Juan's Reckless Daughter* and was intrigued that she'd had the audacity to present herself as a black man. After hearing the album – especially the sprawling 'Paprika Plains', with its seven minutes of improvisational jazz – he was equally intrigued at what this white woman more commonly associated with pop and rock was prepared to explore in the name of musical adventures.

She'd also caught his ear: the improvisational section of 'Paprika Plains' was recorded in four different versions, months before the verses that precede and follow it on the track. Joni edited the versions together, although some were separated by several months, and the re-tuning of her piano in that time had lent a subtle difference. An arranger then added strings to the piece, and when the entire song was orchestrated the strings and piano begin in tune together, then the strings hit the piano that was recorded months later in a different tuning, as Mitchell explains:

> With a fine ear, you notice. So somebody was playing this piece for Charles, and Charles is a stickler for true pitch and time, and he kept saying, 'It's out of tune, it's out of tune!' But when the piece was over, he said that I had a lot of balls.

The out-of-tune string section was the first thing he mentioned to
her the moment they met.

By this time, Mingus was in a wheelchair and since he was no
longer able to control his fingers enough to play the piano,
singing into a tape recorder was his only way of composing.
Determined to defy the doctors' gloomy predictions of the time
left to him, Charles wanted to wring as much out of whatever
remained of his life. He embarked on several new works, including what was to be his last, with perhaps his most unlikely collaborator. The omens were good: Mitchell wanted to extend her
journey into jazz and working with the iconoclastic Mingus was
a unique opportunity; she wasn't familiar with his work so came
to it without preconceptions. Indeed, her former lover, John
Guerin – who had once played Joni the Mingus classic 'Goodbye,
Pork Pie Hat' and got almost no reaction from her – was aston-
ished that Mingus should ask her to collaborate; his response
when she told him was good-natured but spirited: 'You unconscious motherfucker! You don't even like his music. Why didn't
he come for me?'

For his part, Charles's interest had already been raised by *Don
Juan's Reckless Daughter* and his record company was encouraging him to work with Joni, thinking that the highly regarded
Mitchell would help bring his music to a different audience in
the rock and pop world. A friend of a friend told Joni that Mingus
wanted to meet her; she phoned him and he invited her to come
to New York. Joni agreed but her plans got changed and instead
she sent a tape of her music to Charles. He listened to the songs
on it and remarked to his friend, the musician and arranger Paul
Jeffrey, 'She's trying to copy Billie Holiday a little, so maybe she
can do something with me.'

Charles was already ruminating on what that 'something'
would be. His plans centred on T.S. Eliot's poetic examination
of Christianity in four parts, with each representing the four
seasons and the elements. Published in 1943, these were
among the first of Eliot's poems to reach a wide audience and
reflected his own spiritual explorations and search for an eternal reality. There was something in this search that Mingus
could relate to as he painfully faced his own mortality, and in
Eliot's words, 'the end of all our exploring'. Mitchell takes up
the story:

Charles discovered he was dying and called a friend of his over to the house to talk to him about God. Well, his friend was an Italian film producer and he said, 'Charles, I think you've come to the wrong guy to talk about God you know,' and so he went out for some reason and got the *Four Quartets* . . . I found it at that time, on a few readings, lacking in meat. I thought there was a lot of verbiage here but if I was dying I wouldn't be getting any help out of this.

(Years later, the Canadian-based conductor Richard Bradshaw was drawn to the *Four Quartets* because he felt it evoked strong parallels with the search to understand the essence of Mitchell's homeland, Canada, and the vast potential it represents. People who do not 'cease from exploration' are drawn to Canada from all over the world, and hopefully discover at the end of that exploring that there is something extraordinary about the nation and all that it holds. The key, says Bradshaw, is that final awakening in which one comes to 'know the place for the first time'. Inspired by Eliot, he believes, 'You think, [Canada] is where I can do something'.)

Mingus's own exploration of the Eliot work involved a full orchestra playing one strand of the composition, bass and guitar playing another strand of the composition, a formal literary voice reading Eliot's words and, interspersed with that, he wanted Mitchell to distil Eliot down to street language, and sing it mixed in with the reader. It would be, he explained, in the tradition of the Baptist church, where one reader presents the Bible in the original form and another interprets it colloquially. Joni concluded that it was too dense a project to attempt and tactfully declined. Charles was persistent and despite the shelving of his Eliot plans, he wrote six melodies, entitled 'Joni 1-6', and phoned Mitchell, asking her to set them to words and sing them. She came to New York to meet him and, at the time, spoke of the friendship that developed:

He has a reputation for being a very violent and ornery person but I seem to like those kind of people. I always suspect there's a heart beating under there that's very sensitive, which turned out to be true. He has a wide emotional spectrum. Our relationship has been very sweet.

Joni spent several months in New York, seeing Charles often; she was attentive and warm, friendly but respectful, and appeared to relish the chance to work with and learn from him. She was painstaking in trying to understand his intentions for the project; she listened to the themes running through his earlier recordings and discussed his newer works, trying to get to the essence of Mingus.

Charles liked Joni immensely and enjoyed her company, referred to her affectionately as the 'hillbilly' for her rural Canadian roots. She recalls that, although weak in body, his spirit was full of vitality and his humour teasing:

> We started searching through his material and he said, 'Now this one has five different melodies.' I said, 'You mean you want me to write five different sets of lyrics?' He said 'yes', then put one on and it was the fastest boogiest thing I'd ever heard, and it was impossible! So this was like a joke on me; he was testing and teasing me, but in good fun.

Earlier, Mingus had asked Paul Jeffrey to transcribe and arrange the material he'd written but Jeffrey felt it was an impossible task: 'I can't think of how you'd do it, man,' he told Charles. The pieces were then sent to a number of different musicians but Charles was unhappy with the results. His friend, trombonist Jimmy Knepper (who once sued Mingus for punching him so hard in the mouth that he lost two teeth, an octave of range on the trombone and some mobility), recalls that Mingus was in despair when he told him:

> 'They're ruining my music': he was half-paralysed by that time; he could lift his hands but couldn't do anything with them, so he couldn't play the piano. So Susan [Mingus' wife] had set up a metronome and turned a tape recorder on and he sang about five different pieces. One of those pieces, 'Sketch Number Five', became 'A Chair In the Sky'. He was right – the arrangers were ruining his music. They'd figured he was a strange writer, so they gave it the strangest harmonies they could come up with. But he wasn't *that* strange a writer.

Mingus was eager to hear his arrangements in a studio setting and several were recorded at Electric Ladyland in Manhattan, the studio originally set up by Jimi Hendrix. These early recordings kept faith with his initial vision for the *Four Quartets* project – his longtime drummer, Dannie Richmond, read parts of *Beneath the Underdog* to bass and drums, with a big band overdubbed. Three or four versions of each song were recorded by established jazz players including saxophonists Phil Woods and Gerry Mulligan, bass-players Eddie Gomez and Stanley Clark, guitarist John McLaughlin, drummers John Guerin and Tony Williams, and Jan Hammer on mini-Moog. Although she wanted Mingus to like the album, Joni consciously tried to avoid producing a conventional jazz work; her ambition was to create a hybrid – keeping the musical integrity of the jazz idiom while staying accessible to a pop audience. Charles was there for the first sessions but ultimately it came down to her decision, and she felt that something integral was missing, a sense of innovation to take the early versions away from twenty-year-old jazz history. And so her own players were brought in – Jaco Pastorius on bass, Wayne Shorter on soprano sax, Herbie Hancock on electric piano, Peter Erskine on drums, Don Alias on congas and percussionist Emil Richards – and theirs were the recordings that appeared on *Mingus*.

Charles had already outlived the doctors' predictions of a few months but, as his condition worsened, that brief time-scale appeared chillingly realistic. He and his wife Sue left New York for Mexico, where they rented a large villa and Charles put his faith in alternative healing treatments. Joni flew to Mexico and spent several days with Mingus and Sue at the villa in Cuernavaca; she painted their portraits, as well as some of the artwork later featured on the *Mingus* album, which was being prepared for release the following year.

By that time, Charles' speech had deteriorated severely and he struggled to convey his thoughts. Every night he'd say to Joni, 'I want to talk to you about the music,' but it would be too difficult. Charles' problems in communicating meant that it was impossible to convey all of his hopes and intentions for the project, and Mitchell says it wasn't possible to use all of the music that he had in mind:

> Of the melodies he gave me, two I never could get into,
> they were too idiomatic for me. They were modern

enough for my own sense of what is modern – they were
reminding me of something back there, and I couldn't
find any new way I could transcend them . . . [a third]
one was extremely beautiful, but I couldn't get into it
because the theme was very difficult.

The latter was based on a passage in Charles' autobiography in
which he and the trumpeter Fats Navarro talk about God.
Navarro died in 1950, at the age of 26, after years of heroin abuse.
In his book, Mingus makes the doomed trumpeter, who was his
friend and mentor, into an emblematic figure for modern jazz.
Mitchell recalls that this section proved impossible to adapt:

It was his own metaphorical description of God and
relationship to God. I just couldn't lift that literally and
make it adhere to his melody. That threw me into my
own confrontation with my own metaphors about God
and it boggled my mind – it fried my brain. So those
three never got finished. The four I did complete were
all inspired: either I came across pieces of the poetry in
the street, or they came to me in mysterious ways –
they were meant to be.

That 'poetry in the street' inspired part of the lyrics to 'Goodbye,
Pork Pie Hat'. Charles had played Joni several different recorded
versions of the work and she chose the one she liked best.
Charles had written the song as a gentle tribute to his great friend
Lester Young, who had died in 1959, and Joni wanted the lyrics
to reflect the friendship the two men shared, and their lasting
legacies. The first verse came easily but she struggled with the
rest until one night she and Don Alias were walking down a New
York street and saw two young black boys tap-dancing for spare
change. A group of men had also gathered to watch; nearby there
was a bar with its name in bright neon lights. It was called
'Charlie's' and Mitchell felt that the song had come at last:

All of a sudden I get this vision, I look at that red [neon]
script, I look at these two kids, and I think 'The generations . . . '. Here's two more kids coming up in the street
– talented, drawing probably one of their first crowds . . .

to me, it's like Charlie and Lester. That's enough magic for me, but the capper was when we looked up on the marquee that it was all taking place under. In big capital letters, it said 'PORK PIE HAT BAR'. All I had to do was rhyme it and you had the last verse.

Of the two songs that were not Mingus compositions, one was inspired directly by his autobiography: 'God Must Be A Boogie Man' is based on the first four pages of the book, with Mitchell's own melody. It was the only track he didn't hear completed; Joni finished it two days after his death. The other was a song that she'd been writing before she and Charles had met: 'The Wolf That Lives In Lindsey', a musically anarchic piece full of bright bursts of rhythmic passages and no linear musical progression, that began life as a live studio duet between Joni and drummer Don Alias. At the time, Joni had left her engineer, Henry Lewy, with the task of finding some effects to complete the track – wolves and water-gongs – and gone to Berkeley, California, to appear at the Bread and Roses charity concert, organised by Joan Baez's sister, Mimi Farina.

She'd arrived at her hotel, ready to have a drink with Tim Hardin, who was also appearing at the benefit, when she had a chance encounter with a drunk in the lobby – and he just happened to have a tape of a wolf family howling to each other. It fitted her own 'Wolf' track uncannily, and the following night at the concert Joel Bernstein hooked up the tape and for an encore Joni came out and performed the song, with the wolves mixed in and the audience howling back in call-and-response. The wolves became a permanent part of the track and although the song is seemingly unconnected with Mingus' oeuvre, Mitchell believed it had a place on the album:

> I felt that the wolves constituted part of Charles' musical concept of cacophony. There was still some natural, beautiful cacophony; those wolves are singing in a chorus, hitting every note on the keyboard, but it's beyond dissonance, it transcends dissonance. So I thought it was kindred to Charles' way of thinking.

During her appearance at the Bread and Roses concert, she also played other songs from the work in progress – 'A Chair In the

Sky' and 'Goodbye, Pork Pie Hat', with Herbie Hancock on keyboards, and 'Fool's Paradise' (later retitled 'The Dry Cleaner
From Des Moines').

One of Mitchell's favourite melodies was 'A Chair in the Sky'
and when she asked Charles what kind of a theme he would like
it to reflect, he turned to her with a wry look on his face and said,
'Things I'm gonna miss.' The album was going to be named for
that song but Sue Mingus felt uneasy about it, believing that it
would fix Charles as an invalid in people's minds, forever associated with his wheelchair. For Joni it had other connotations –
when she first met Charles he'd been like a superior being, substantial and regal, enthroned in his armchair dozens of floors
above the New York city streets in his Manhattan apartment
building.

Sue had given Joni a number of tapes and interviews and she
was thrilled as she listened to them: much of what Charles felt
and described was kindred to her own feelings. Excerpts from
some of the tapes, including conversations between Mingus and
his friends, would be interspersed through the album and used as
links between the songs. The album opens with his friends and
his wife, Sue, singing 'Happy Birthday' on his fifty-third birthday
(though Charles, on tape, insists to Sue that he is fifty-four). In
other conversations, he talks about his plans for a traditional
Vedanta Hindu funeral ceremony rather than a huge church service, although at the same time vowing to live longer than Duke
Ellington, who had died in his late seventies. He muses about the
luck and happiness he's had in his life and, on one track, he and
Joni briefly scat-sing together.

As the project was unfolding, Ben Sidran interviewed Joni for
an article in *Rolling Stone* – she had only just begun talking to the
magazine again, seven years after it had published the largely
inaccurate family-tree-style diagram of her supposed lovers. But
when Sidran asked for an interview with Charles, Sue Mingus
said that her husband was away; he was, in fact, extremely ill and
having enormous difficulty communicating. In the piece, Sidran
observed:

> Mingus' reputation in the music world is based not only
> on his musical virtuosity but also on his unrelenting
> criticism of whites. He hasn't simply been voluble on

the subject; he has been volcanic. To think now, so late in Mingus' life, his music will be heard in hundreds of thousands of homes interpreted by a leading white female pop singer is perhaps the ultimate twist in an extremely stormy career ... [He has] a volatile personal style that often seemed more noteworthy than the music itself.

It's always later than you think. The article appeared in late December 1978; just days later – on 5 January 1979 – Mingus died in Mexico at the age of fifty-six. Sue Mingus noted that the following day, fifty-six whales perished after beaching themselves on a stretch of the Mexican coastline. Local people burned the whales' bodies where they lay and the remains washed away into the ocean. Mingus himself was cremated the same day; Sue later travelled to India where she scattered his ashes in the Ganges, the river sacred to Hindus, a faith in which Charles had found some meaning. In the album liner notes, Joni wrote: 'Sue and the holy river, Will send you to the saints of jazz, To Duke and Bird and Fats, And any other saints you have.'

The album was released a few months after Charles' death, and became a form of epitaph, right down to the packaging. Painting had helped Mitchell out of the writer's block that had hit her when she was trying to write the lyrics to 'Goodbye, Pork Pie Hat' and two of the artworks on the cover and sleeve had come out of that fallow writing period. Joni's paintings included three of Charles, painted in Mexico.

The back cover is the poignant 'Charlie Down In Mexico' (also known as 'Mingus Down In Mexico'), showing Mingus in his wheelchair, on a patio of the Mexican villa he'd rented. For all the clarity of light and colour in the piece, there is a sadness about it: Charles has his back to the viewer/painter, and is facing away as if already withdrawing from life and the people around him. There is also an inevitable melancholy in the portrait entitled 'Chair In The Sky', with a shadow of both despair and resignation flickering across his face. Joni says she painted almost constantly for two days to complete the work:

I had his features down, so the likeness was there, but there was no real emotion coming off. I just kept pushing the paint around on the board, waiting for the right expression to appear; then suddenly it was there. The emotion is a very complex one in a way. I'm hesitant to say the emotions I think it embodies but if I were in his place I think I know what he would have been feeling at that time in his life and I think I've captured it.

The third Mingus portrait, 'I's a Muggin', is taken from a photograph and shows Charles, face creased with laughter, and Joni, a smiling semi-abstract form behind him. The cover is a work entitled 'Sweet Sucker Dance (Abundance and Decline)', a far more abstract piece than any of her previous cover paintings, and typical of the paintings she did for pleasure rather than the more commercial cover art done specifically for her albums.

When faced with the marketing campaign for *Mingus,* the Elektra/Asylum chairman, Joe Smith, had said:

> [Joni] has taken a chunk out of her career and accomplished something monumental. When we received this album, I got on a conference call and talked with all our promotion men. If any radio station calls itself a trend-setter, it must recognise this album and Charles Mingus. I'm also having a contest for my promotion men: first prize is they get to keep their jobs!

The promotions staff could eventually rest easy – even with nonexistent airplay, the album peaked at Number 17 on the *Billboard* charts. But Mitchell recalls her manager, Elliot Roberts, telling her not to expect universal acclaim:

> I was warned by [my] management that it would cost me, that by doing this I would have betrayed an orthodoxy and [no one] would know where to place me. I thought that's ridiculous. This was an opportunity for musical education and so it was, with the collaboration that came out somewhere in the middle. It was neither his nor mine and this was very misunderstood. Also, in certain jazz circles the old-timers thought that I was an opportunist because they'd never heard of me, trying to

tailgate on Charles. And in pop circles . . . it was vastly misunderstood but it was challenging because I had to write from his perspective.

The jazz bible *Downbeat* urged Joni to forget her fears about how the album would be received, declaring '*Mingus* is so ambitious, so painstakingly constructed, and so special that even in those moments when the deed fails, the thought carries the day.' The reviewer singled out 'Goodbye, Pork Pie Hat' as emblematic of the entire album: 'what Mingus did for Lester in writing that song, Joni has done for Mingus in making this album. She gave her best on this one and it's proved to be good enough.' In the *Los Angeles Times,* Robert Hilburn announced himself pleasantly surprised, describing it as an uncompromising artistic statement – 'warm, confident and engaging'. Jazz author Joachim Berendt described the work as

> the most beautiful, moving memorial to this great jazz musician ... Critics have called Mitchell's singing much too ethereal and fragile to have anything to do with Mingus' music; and yet this very fact makes it clear how far Mingus' message carries.

The pre-eminent American jazz saxophonist Branford Marsalis has said *Mingus* is one of his favourite albums but not for its jazz influences: 'It is funny that people consider it a jazz record, and nothing could be further from jazz. But it is a great record.'

Critics and Mitchell fans alike finally had to come to terms with folk-rock Joni going missing in action, to be replaced by a woman determined to have musical adventures, who clearly put more store in her own artistic evolution than her commercial career development. Many – along with the jazz purists – were not best pleased. Writing in *Melody Maker,* Michael Watts opined that 'Few records can have been made with as much underlying affection, nor received with so much goodwill; but music cannot be judged only by its intentions. *Mingus* unfortunately doesn't enhance his legend, and it diminishes hers.' A *Sounds* reviewer declared it a beautifully recorded, self-consciously precious, maddeningly white attempt at blackness. And in *Stereo Review*, Noel Coppage predicted that '*Mingus* is going to catch considerable flak for being ponderous where [Mingus himself] was light-hearted, for being uptight where he was loose, and for being un-Mingus-like in general.'

Producer and bass-player Larry Klein – whom Mitchell married in 1983 – says that the reaction to *Mingus* left Joni in a no-win situation:

> She certainly felt that no one was happy that she had gone into that area, the jazz people considered her to be a carpetbagger and the rock audience, the pop audience, felt betrayed and couldn't understand what she was doing. So the feedback that she got, not to mention the critics and the record company stuff . . . [was negative]. Her way of doing that kind of record, which certainly in retrospect makes absolute sense, was that if she was going to do it she had to do it in a way that was fresh and didn't have any elements of a kind of dilettante playing around with jazz. But the down side of that was that she made a record that was hard for people to understand and I think that it's really come to be much better understood with time.

The critical backlash seems hard to understand now: some of it smacked of putting an 'uppity' woman in her place, that she had presumptuous ideas above her folk-rock station; some was resentment from jazz purists who couldn't understand why Mingus would anoint a rich white woman from Canada. She lost a few more fans, those who felt let down, just as they had with *The Hissing of Summer Lawns*; they'd always relied on Joni to articulate their feelings and emotional traumas but once again she'd become a storyteller rather than a diarist, talking about old jazz cats playing Birdland and the colour bar and pork pie hats and a dry-cleaner from Des Moines punching coins into a fruit machine. But although Mitchell would later affectionately describe her *Mingus*-era musical explorations as her 'Jackson Pollock period', the album was to be a precursor, not just in the evolution of jazz fusion, but of a greater integration of jazz influences in the pop and rock sphere.

Where Mitchell had been pilloried by many critics and traditional jazz fans, she had also enabled other musicians coming after her to tread the same path without watching it turn into a musical minefield beneath their feet. Twenty-two years after *Mingus* was released, former Police guitarist Andy Summers recorded an album of Mingus works, *Peggy's Blue Skylight*, featuring Deborah Harry, hip-hopper Q-Tip (who recites 'Where Can A Man Find Peace?' over 'Goodbye, Pork Pie Hat'), trumpeter Randy Brecker and the Kronos Quartet. Not a single reviewer attacked Summers for having the temerity to reinterpret Mingus so liberally and from the viewpoint of a white middle-class Englishman who had made his fortune in a band which dominated pop charts from the late 70s with catchy reggae-inspired pop classics.

Mingus may well have approved of that too. He was highly politicised and spoke out more fiercely about the exploitation of black musicians than anyone else – but he also spoke out against restrictions of other kinds, the ones we impose on ourselves:

> People are getting so fragmented, and part of that is that fewer and fewer people are making a real effort anymore to find exactly who they are and to build on that. Most people are forced to do things they don't want to most of the time, and so they get to the point where they feel they no longer have any choice about anything important, including who they are. We create our own slavery.

Charlie Parker had said, 'They teach you there's a boundary line to music. But, man, there's no boundary line to art.' It's in that spirit that an album like *Mingus* should be assessed.

While preparations were getting underway for gigs to promote *Mingus,* Joni appeared at an anti-nuclear rally in Washington along with a number of high-profile figures including Jane Fonda, Graham Nash, Jackson Browne, John Sebastian and John Hall. An impromptu news conference followed a day of speeches and singing, and when Mitchell was asked how long she'd had strong feelings about nuclear power she said:

> Since the early 50s. 'The Crow on the Cradle' [a song she'd performed that day] comes from the Ban the Bomb movement. Since that time, I think that

> everybody, either consciously or unconsciously, has been disturbed about potential destruction ... but I don't think they expected it to come on friendly territory, from their own government.

Unlike the Hurricane Carter campaign, Joni had no reservations about politicising her celebrity for the no-nukes cause. She had already helped Greenpeace raise funds to send a vessel to Amchitka island in Alaska, to protest against American nuclear testing there.

The *Mingus* works were premiered at the University of California Jazz Festival in Berkeley, with a band comprising Pastorius and Alias, who were joined by Herbie Hancock and Tony Williams. Joni headlined the Playboy Jazz Festival in Los Angeles in June, to coincide with the album's release, and the following month she assembled a touring band – with Jaco Pastorius on bass and as musical director (despite his legendary tardiness at rehearsals), drummer Don Alias, Pat Metheny on lead guitar, Lyle Mays on keyboards, saxophonist Michael Brecker, with vocal group the Persuasions as the support act. The tour began in Oklahoma City and ended six weeks later in Los Angeles. One of the last shows, at the Santa Barbara County Bowl, was recorded and filmed; the film of the tour, *Shadows and Light*, was shown on television at the end of the year and the live double album was released the following year.

The album was less of a career retrospective than her previous live double album *Miles of Aisles* had been; of her original songs on the album, all but 'Woodstock' and 'Free Man in Paris' were from the previous five years. It opens with a manifesto of cool, a sound collage blending parts of the song 'Shadows and Light' with Frankie Lymon's 1957 UK hit, 'I'm Not a Juvenile Delinquent' – with not a little irony, he died of a heroin overdose at the age of 26 on his grandmother's bathroom floor – and the scene from *Rebel Without a Cause* in which a defiant James Dean is told 'You can't be idealistic all your life, Jim' and replies, 'Except to yourself, except to yourself!' Through the course of the album, jazz gives way only to rock 'n' roll as the legend of Frankie Lymon is reprised in the cover version of his hit 'Why Do Fools Fall in Love'. With impressive backing from the Persuasions, this track was released as a single. The album ends

with an impressionistic solo version of 'Woodstock', the arrangement transformed from the original 60s anthem. It was a fitting
final track. Although the album was released in September 1980,
it marked the end of the 70s in terms of Mitchell's recording
career and musical direction. And it was to be her last album for
Elektra/Asylum.

Mitchell had started the year by going to a party at musician
Stephen Bishop's house – the theme: 'Be nice to the 80s and the
80s will be nice to you.' On the way to the party she'd stopped off
at a record store and returned moments later to discover that her
ageing but much-loved car, a 69 Mercedes she called Bluebird,
had been stolen. Things can only get better. And very soon they
would.

9 Love's the greatest beauty . . .

The great question that has never been answered,
and which I have not been able to answer, despite
my thirty years of research into the feminine soul,
is 'What does a woman want?'
(Sigmund Freud)

THERE ARE WOMEN WHO COMPILE wish-lists of men, grading their prospective partner's psyche, bank account, character and genetic inheritance. Then again, there are women who dispense with all that and have just one or two requirements that are not negotiable. Just before Joni Mitchell met her future husband in 1981 she expressed her hopes in a simple, silent prayer: let him (whoever *he* might turn out to be) play pinball and be a good kisser. A few days into recording her album *Wild Things Run Fast,* the bass player on the sessions, Larry Klein, wandered up to Mitchell during a break and asked if she'd like to go down to the pinball arcade on Santa Monica pier. A prayer answered. Although it would be some months before she could vouch for the second part of her wish, it's like the old saying goes, 'From your lips to God's ears'.

Klein challenges every stereotype, every cliché ever uttered about sun-drenched, psycho-babbling Californians. Erudite, articulate and ferociously well-read, with a Renaissance sensibility not commonly associated with the home of the California raisin – Nietzsche rather than *National Enquirer*, Buddhism rather than *Baywatch* – he entered Mitchell's life at the perfect time. Klein, at 25, was an acclaimed jazz bassist with an impeccable pedigree – while still at college, he'd played with Willie Bobo's band and at the age of 19 he'd left his studies to begin his odyssey through the jazz world. For the next six years – as Mitchell was taking her own iconoclastic route through jazz – Klein toured extensively with the jazz trumpeter Freddie Hubbard and also played with other luminaries including Joe Henderson, Jack De Johnette, Bobby Hutcherson and Carmen McCrae. The constant touring eventually became wearing and, feeling a gnawing disaffection with jazz, Klein resolved to make some changes in his working-life:

> I became disenchanted with the whole narrowness of the jazz world which has its own set of 'this is good, that's not good' [attitudes], like the people who think that bebop is the only jazz and that anything else is inconsequential. I became more interested in rock and pop music. After bands like Weather Report had done what they set out to do as far as opening up territory in jazz, the energy started to shift to rock and pop. The Police were starting to happen, the Blue Nile had just started. A lot of these bands that were incorporating the structural sophistication of jazz into pop music were starting to spring up. So I segued out of the traditional jazz world because it became boring to me and started staying [in Los Angeles] more and doing studio work.

Klein had come to know a number of people who had already worked with Joni, including Victor Feldman, Roger Calloway, Joe Sample and of course Guerin, with whom he'd formed a dynamic rhythm section on several projects. Larry had only a passing knowledge of Mitchell's work – *Court and Spark*, *Mingus* and a smattering of individual songs – when John Guerin invited him along to the first sessions. The recording of *Wild Things* was episodic, and there would be a respite while Joni went back to her homes in British Columbia and New York, where she would continue to write. The more time Klein spent with her in the studio, the more he was impressed at her method of working:

> I had never worked with anyone who was that dedicated to finding the right way to approach songs, that incessant and unfailing way of seeking out how to get to the core of a song and really make something that was fresh and new and true. I was fascinated with the way that she worked and found it really inspiring . . .

that idea of the magical coincidence and the magic of
unconscious intent that she [had]. For me, as a bass
player, it's very rare that coming into a session, you
find people who are so dedicated in that way. I can
count them on one hand, out of all the people that I've
played with. Certainly, Peter Gabriel was like that and
Lindsay Buckingham. It's just extraordinarily stimulat-
ing. It was the first time I observed that kind of dedica-
tion to finding the right thing, where if it doesn't work
initially you try it again another way and you try it until
you find the right formula. When I first started working
with Joni, I thought, 'That's the way that you're supposed to do it!'

It was Mitchell's first studio album in three years – an unprecedented gap for an artist who, for the first decade of her recording
career, had put out virtually an album a year. She came to the
early recording sessions at A&M Studios in Hollywood with a
handful of songs – 'Ladies Man', an acerbic look at the predatory
male of the title, preferring cocaine to commitment; 'Man to
Man' with its refrain of 'how come I keep moving from man to
man to man', later made especially pertinent by the presence of
two of Joni's former lovers on the track (Guerin on drums and
James Taylor on background vocals) and Klein on bass; 'You
Dream Flat Tires', which would be recorded with Lionel Ritchie
on background vocals.

The other song was 'Love', which she had written for a short-
film series commissioned by producer Barry Levinson, in 1980.
He had asked several women to write and produce a work on the
theme of love. Simone de Beauvoir, Rebecca West, Jacqueline
Kennedy Onassis and Gloria Steinem all turned him down but
those who agreed included director Mai Zetterling; writers Edna
O'Brien and Antonia Fraser; the actor Liv Ullmann and the academic and social commentator Germaine Greer.

Joni had initially been asked to do the music for the films but
instead she asked to write a screenplay and star in it – she
revived her black alter-ego, Art Nouveau, and Zetterling directed
the film, a fantasy about a rejected lover who meets an old flame
at a costume party. Art/Joni carried around a huge portable cassette player, blasting out favourite Miles Davis songs. The song

'Love' was inspired by Liv Ullmann's film about an elderly man tending to his bedridden wife; at the end of the film he reads the Biblical passage from St Paul to the Corinthians 1:13, 'Although I speak with the tongues of men and of angels . . . '. Joni found the ubiquitous Gideon's Bible in a hotel room and began adapting the verses. She eliminated some of the more archaic phrases and imagery and added another verse of her own – the last, which concludes that, of faith, hope and love, 'Love's the greatest beauty'. It would be the final track, an eloquent and definitive statement of the meaning of love.

As the album evolved, so did the friendship between Klein and Mitchell, 13 years his senior. Within nine months of meeting, their friendship had evolved into romance and on 21 November 1982 – a month after the record was released – they married in a ceremony at Elliot Roberts' home in Malibu. Their growing closeness during the recording sessions had contributed to the feeling of ease in the studio. Joni was playing with gifted musicians who were also her friends – including Guerin and Vinnie Colaiuta on drums; saxophonist Wayne Shorter – and the atmosphere was relaxed and supportive. They were joined by guitarists Steve Lukather (of Toto) and Mike Landau, and on synths Russell Ferrante and Larry Williams (who also played tenor sax).

The veteran British-born jazz pianist and percussionist Victor Feldman – who had played on *The Hissing of Summer Lawns* and *Hejira* and had worked with Klein – also came in. But this virtuoso musician, writer of music textbooks, was struggling with Mitchell's idiosyncratic open tunings on one track, 'Moon At The Window' . Klein recalls Feldman's unaccustomed discomfort:

> He was playing on this piece and just had this grimace on his face, and I remember Joni going out into the studio and saying, 'What's the matter, Victor?' She thought he didn't like the words because they were about a friend of hers who had become agoraphobic somewhat and was haunted by memories, and Victor was such an Englishman, such a happy man. So she said, 'Victor, do you not like the song?' and he said, 'No actually, I hate it!' What he meant was the way the chords moved was – and I explained this to her after the fact – so antithetical to the logic of Tin Pan Alley

songwriting, which really formed the basis of what jazz
theory was, that he just didn't know what to think
about it. The way the chords moved was so strange to
him that it just felt absolutely wrong. Joni was never
conditioned from a theoretical standpoint by that Tin
Pan Alley logic in regard to chord movement. She's not
hemmed in by it at all and she moves the chords just in
the way that they feel right to her. She was the James
Joyce of guitar tunings.

Joel Bernstein, who has published several books of Mitchell's
transcribed tunings, says that while she was not the first player
to explore the world of alternative tunings, she has explored them
more thoroughly and more prolifically than any other guitarist:

These unique, 'non-open' tunings, i.e. those which do not
sound an easily named chord when open, are very important innovations in the guitar-players' universe. Each of
them represents a 'world' in which each of the chords are
composed by her to be played only in that tuning – even
if the shape of the chord can be used in another tuning,
it would there make a different chord. Many of the
tunings only have had one or two songs written in them
ever, for instance 'Black Crow' or 'Talk To Me'.

Bernstein estimates that Joni originated at least 35 unique tunings, with many more being variations on those tunings. She
originally wrote 'Clouds', for instance, in open E tuning – much
favoured by blues musicians – but as her voice deepened with
age and her prodigious smoking habit, she began performing
the song in open D tuning, placing it in a lower register in
which she could sing more easily. Later, she performed the
song in open C, lower still. Mitchell's tunings are so numerous
that she has often relied on Bernstein to remind her of them.

Musically, the album alternated between jazz, pop and rock 'n'
roll, collating all of Mitchell's influences since her teenage years. A
map of the past had been dusted off and referred to again in Lieber
and Stoller's hit for Elvis Presley, '(You're So Square) Baby I Don't
Care', which was released as a single and was one of the very few
cover versions she had recorded at that point. After several years of

abandonment by radio programmers, a critical drubbing for some of her most adventurous work and professional and personal turmoil, Joni wanted to have some *fun*.

The *Mingus* project had signalled the end of an experimental cycle that had started when Mitchell became disillusioned with the backbeat inherent in pop and rock music. Now the cycle was returning to the point at which it began. And who better to help her back than the classic pop-meisters, the Police, whose music she'd heard every night blaring out at a disco while on holiday in the Caribbean? It was vintage reggae-fied Police – their 'De Do Do Do, De Da Da Da' phase – and it so impressed Joni that she asked the band to work with her on her new album. It wasn't to be because of scheduling problems but she took the memory of their tuneful pop into the studio with her.

For a woman who'd become so closely associated with the world of jazz and the rarefied air at the heights of *Don Juan's Reckless Daughter* and *Mingus*, she was now listening avidly to bands like the Police and stadium rockers Journey, and embracing them as influences: the reggae and rhythm hybrids of the former and the sonic boom of the latter, which she said taught her a thing or two about EQ and sonic frequencies. Larry Klein too was a factor in broadening her listening perspective; while his jazz background would be an important element of a shared musical language, at 25 his formative musical years had been quite different to Joni's as a result of growing up and discovering music in the diversity of the 60s and 70s. He had a more defined sense of the lower end of the music, the bass and drums, and like the best of his generation of musicians, he was not essentially a specialist but could adapt to a range of genres – rock, pop, jazz, funk, electronica or neo-folk.

Mitchell's long-time trusty sidekick, her engineer Henry Lewy, was again with her in the studio and recalls that her relationship with Larry Klein had a positive effect on recording:

> She was very happy while she was making this album. The records are always reflections of her mental attitude and she really found the groove for this record about halfway through, when she got a new boyfriend and everything in her life solidified.

During the months of mixing the album, Joni, Klein and engineer Larry Hirsch retired to Paramount Studios, where they divided up the duties, with Joni handling the treble aspects and placement of the vocals and horns, and Klein and Hirsch handling the rhythm section.

Some music writers were to sideline the musical strengths in favour of concentrating on events in Mitchell's private life and *Wild Things* came to be seen as her 'Joni Loves Larry' album, inspired in part by their courtship. Joni had found a new man to 'court and spark' and the music writers were not going to forget it. Joni herself described it as a romantic album for an unromantic time. Larry Klein admits that writing about romantic love can present difficulties, especially when the writer is a woman whose fans have become accustomed to hearing her sing about romantic woes:

> It is a pretty tough thing to write about without pissing people off, because if you're not happy in that way you don't necessarily want to hear about people who are. The record came out in a time that was characterised by a superficial fascination with dark imagery. Billy Idol was really at his peak and every time you turned on MTV, you saw Billy Idol and a girl with a stiletto heel stomping on the guy and there was a lot of this post-punk imagery around. So the climate at the time was difficult, aside from the fact that people a lot of times don't want to hear happy songs about romance, especially from someone like Joan who they've come to use as their analgesic or their tool to open the gates of sorrow inside themselves. They really don't want to hear it from someone who's been their sacrificial lamb. The problem would have been there regardless of when it came out. I think that people just wouldn't want to hear about her being happy.

Mitchell confessed that writing overtly happy love songs like 'Solid Love' and 'Underneath The Streetlight' and declaring joyously and genuinely 'I love you!' in song also caught her by surprise:

> It made me nervous as a cat to write like that, because I've always had a hard time tapping into my joy. It was

always, 'This is nice now *but* . . . ' Always a *but*. Now I
sing, 'Yes I do, I love you!' You never heard a comment
like that out of *me* before. But I had the up-tempo music,
the feelings were genuine. I was in New York having a
good time and I missed my boyfriend, so I just screamed
it out to the skyscrapers. Why not?

The genre of the love song, in all its guises and reinterpretations,
is the most enduring theme in popular music – virtually the only
theme – and it was perhaps inevitable that it would lead her back
to walk the green pastures of pop. But the blissful state of being in
love – 'whatever that means', as the heir to the British throne,
Prince Charles, had noted perceptively on the occasion of his
engagement to Lady Diana Spencer the previous year – was not
the only sentiment expressed on *Wild Things*.

There is much else besides, with microscopic examinations of
nostalgia for the passing years, coming to terms with ageing, fail-
ing relationships and personal limitations. The longing for the
daughter Joni gave up 17 years earlier surfaces again (as it had in
'Little Green') in 'Chinese Café – Unchained Melody', one of her
most painfully acute songs about women of her generation – she
was then 39, and there's both reassurance and resignation in the
line 'nothing lasts for long'. Interwoven in the song are lyrics
from 'Unchained Melody', the gorgeously slushy 1955
Zaret/North song that was revived by the Righteous Brothers in
1965 – the year her daughter was born.

If the references to a child in 'Little Green' slipped by unre-
marked, the same was not so of 'Chinese Café'; in an interview
with the *Sunday Times* during promotion for the album, Joni was
reluctant to discuss the issue in deference to her parents but
when pressed by the writer, Michael Watts, she bristled at the
intrusion, 'You're thrilled, like it's Watergate or something, and
here I am, stuttering and stammering.' But she did tell Watts
about an encounter with a couple and their young daughter, at a
music festival in 1968:

> The child said, 'Hello, Kelly.' I said, 'My name isn't
> Kelly, it's Joni.' The mother looked at me and said, 'No,
> *her* name is Kelly.' All these years I've assumed it was
> my child, and I've always thought, 'She's well taken

care of.' It has liberated me from any remorse I might have had.

Many of Joni's fans may have thought they'd lost her when she ventured into jazzland but *Wild Things Run Fast* would lure them back, reassured that she could still articulate their hopes and dreams like no one else. Mitchell described 'Man to Man' as a personal song but also one that was indicative of the attitudes of many women her age, looking back on a series of doomed relationships:

> I remember thinking, 'Oh my God, maybe this is too much', when I wrote one line. It says 'I don't like to lie, But I sure can be phony when I get scared, I stick my nose up in the air, Stony, stony when I get scared.' I didn't know if I wanted to confess to that. I know it's universal, but *I'm* the one who has to sing it, and I'm liable to have it thrown back at me. I sang it . . . at the Bread and Roses Festival in Berkeley . . . and I was creeping on that line, wondering if I wanted to deliver it. So I spat it out. When the line came out, there was a little moan. I could hear people sucking in their breath.

She had not lost her touch.

Just as *Wild Things Run Fast* marked a musical return to what in visual art terms would be the more 'representational' pop and rock, with less of the 'abstraction' of jazz, Joni's artwork for the album followed the same path. She returned to self-portraiture but the flower-child ingenue of *Clouds* in 1969, who had gazed hopefully into the future, had matured into a worldly woman, comfortable in her own skin, and more than capable of taking the future on her own terms. The 'wild things' motif – horses pounding through the surf – is shown on a television screen beside her and picked up in a separate illustration. There is an engaging portrait of Joni and Klein together – one of many that would be painted over the years, a large-scale painterly equivalent of relaxed family snapshots. She had dedicated the album to him with 'Special thanks to Larry Klein for caring about and fussing over this record along with me'. The artwork also includes a witty and highly accomplished neo-Impressionist still-life,

'Homage to Matisse' – a cleverly executed painting-within-a-painting, where the main subject is an artbook, left lying open to display an illustration of one of the two decorative panels produced by the French painter and sculptor Henri Matisse in 1909–10 entitled 'Dance I' and 'Dance II'.

Writing in the *New York Times*, Stephen Holden described *Wild Things* as the most exhilaratingly high-spirited of Mitchell's career: 'the album features several vibrant rock 'n' roll performances that communicate a rare joy in being alive'. The *NME* took a different view, with Richard Cook believing that:

> *Wild Things Run Fast* seems such a palpable retreat from the vantage point she'd grafted towards for so long that its appearance is a severe anti-climax in a progression that should have dispensed with highs and lows. There seems nothing of consequence to remark on.

Even as the album was being recorded, boardroom battles were underway with Joni Mitchell at the centre of them. Her former label boss and Asylum founder David Geffen – who had wooed her away from Warner Brothers/Reprise to Asylum, only to merge his company later with Warners' label Elektra – had left Warner Brothers at the end of his five-year contract in 1977. He took a long sabbatical and pondered his future. Before long, he was yearning to return to the music industry. By 1980, Geffen had figured out how he would do it. He approached the head of Warner Communications, Steve Ross, and asked for backing to set up a new label, with the faintly vainglorious title Geffen Records. Having made a fortune with Asylum, Ross did not need much convincing, even when Geffen insisted that Warners put up all of the money – $25 million – in exchange for a 50 per cent share in the company.

But the deal was not without its detractors: Joe Smith, then head of Elektra/Asylum, discovered to his dismay that one of his label's most prestigious artists – Joni Mitchell – was being transferred to Geffen Records. It was hardly a surprising move – Geffen and Joni had a long history as friends and former business associates and she was still managed by Geffen's friend, his one-time business partner and protégé, Elliot Roberts. Geffen was promising her artistic freedom and lifetime distribution of her work. But Joe Smith believed that Mitchell was moving simply because Geffen was putting her under extreme pressure. Smith says he also saw the terms of Warners' deal with Geffen as taking vast amounts of money out of Warners' own coffers:

> I tried to explain to Steve Ross what it meant when Geffen took Joni from me at Elektra. First, you're financing that label with Geffen, and second, it's a joint venture with Geffen, so you're only getting half the profit. So you're financing somebody who's stealing from us. He shrugged. He didn't want to take on Geffen.

For her part, Joni acknowledged that Elektra/Asylum had kept faith with her and put out some of her most commercially daunting work yet she also felt that the company could have probably exerted itself more to promote the albums. Where Geffen had created Asylum as a sanctuary for gifted singer-songwriter poets, he wanted to make Geffen Records as mainstream as possible – and quickly signed Elton John and Donna Summer. John Lennon and Yoko Ono came to the label with the much-anticipated 'comeback' album, *Double Fantasy* – a little over a week after its release, Lennon was dead. Neil Young left Reprise and joined Joni on the new label – two of the most revered writing talents in contemporary music were now under Geffen's roof.

Within a year, Geffen would be sueing Neil Young for $3 million, alleging that Young had behaved fraudulently and deceitfully by making 'uncommercial records' (the techno-pop *Trans* and the rockabilly *Everybody's Rockin'*). The case was eventually settled amicably. Mitchell's album had peaked at Number 25 on the US charts but sales were not as significant as Geffen had hoped, and he lamented that he'd lost money on the album. The same was true of his other artists, Elton John and Donna Summer, as well. It was only Don Henley's *Building the Perfect Beast,* released at the end of 1984, that would rescue Geffen's ambitions and restore the gleam to his Midas touch.

While David Geffen fretted over sales units back in Los Angeles, Joni set off on tour with a new band at her side – Refuge was a collection of musicians who'd played on *Wild Things*: Larry Klein, Vinnie Colaiuta, Mike Landau and Russell Ferrante. It was her first extensive tour in several years, and began in Japan in

March 1983, and took her through Australia, New Zealand, Europe and the United States. Larry Klein has fond memories of the tour:

> It was a great group of musicians and the playing was of such a uniformly high level. We were out for almost a year and it was really a great tour. It was very tightly knit, not only the band but the whole crew that worked with us and it was an extraordinary group of people, in retrospect . . . Whenever [Joni] plays, I think there's a sense of importance that is given to the occasion because of the fact that she's not prone to doing a lot of touring.

A film of the tour, *Refuge of the Roads*, was released on laserdisc the following year. Even after high-profile shows at Wembley and other large venues, the tour was expensive to maintain and although Mitchell didn't lose money on it, she made relatively little. A long tour was also gruelling; her childhood bout of polio had left her with a weakness in the spine which meant it was difficult to stand for long periods holding a guitar. The 83 excursion would be her last major tour. When it ended, she and Klein returned to their new home at Malibu Beach with their cats and paintings and music. Joni took Klein to Canada to retrace the steps of her childhood and teenage years, seeing the places of her memory made real again.

Meanwhile, in bars, cafés and clubs, near and far, the music industry's Next Big Thing was about to surface and be greeted as Joni Mark II: the cliché was that they were young women with short hair and sensible shoes, acoustic guitars and a penchant for Dylan, Cohen and Emily Dickinson or Lou Reed, Patti Smith and Sylvia Plath. Too cerebral for the ambitious attention-grabbing Madonna template and too grounded for the reclusive and eccentric Kate Bush model, they had much more in common with Joni Mitchell and Laura Nyro.

The first wave of this new generation had appeared in the mid–late 70s with Rickie Lee Jones and Joan Armatrading, who helped to reclaim the singer-songwriter title from the California-based heavyweights. The repetitive 'new Joni' refrain soon became tiresome for both the original and the women who were seen as her imitators. Jones was hailed as the Crown Princess to Joni's Queen Bee and has admitted that there was a sense of rivalry between them. She says this was inspired in part by her frustrations at emerging onto the music scene, feeling vibrant and original, only to hear herself constantly being referred to as a clone of someone else:

> Joni and I did have a kind of war going on, just a quiet war – she called it the War of the Berets – and whilst making *Traffic from Paradise* [in 1993], I worked with Julie Last, Joni's engineer, and I was a bit nervous about hiring her because I knew ... I'd heard from mutual acquaintances that Joni was not fond of me because of things I'd said earlier in my career. I don't remember it but it was detrimental, the kinda thing people say when they've just come out and they try to discredit everyone who came before them.

Jones – like Mitchell herself – has expressed surprise that she was always compared to other women when her musical influences have been men. She sees inherent sexism as being at the core of such comparisons:

> It's like 'Joni Mitchell spawned all women' and I find that really offensive. As creative as she is, she did not spawn all women and I get tired of seeing everyone ultimately compared to her. In the man's world, Bruce Springsteen was obviously heavily influenced by Van Morrison but ... [reviewers] don't mention Van every time they review him. It has nothing to do with Joni Mitchell, it's just me going, 'Hey, this is really sexist. Two blondes look alike and play guitar so you've decided ... ' I listened to Laura Nyro and Van and you can hear it, but I didn't listen to Joni Mitchell. People wrote that because of the physical similarities. I couldn't find any other reason. And I don't think it's fair to her. It's pissed her off but not as much as me. Because it's more horrible to be compared to.

Shawn Colvin – who attracted Mitchell comparisons from the time of her first album, the Grammy award-winning *Steady On* in

1989 – has a different view of the Joni link, seeing it as a compliment rather than a curse:

> I don't believe I was a born songwriter, like she was
> and so many people are. For me that was an aspect I
> had to work hard at. I truly still feel that if anyone were
> to say 'you are the next Joni Mitchell, you were influ-
> enced by Joni Mitchell' I'd say 'yes!' That to me would
> be complimentary. It wouldn't bother me. If that's
> what people get from what I do, they're one hundred
> per cent correct . . . The diversity of followers that she
> has is phenomenal. When people say 'who influenced
> you?', Prince says 'Joni Mitchell', the Police said 'Joni
> Mitchell'. She was one of the first women, if not the
> first, to be so massively wonderful that there should be
> no gender about it, she's just one of the most phenom-
> enal musicians that our generation and beyond has
> had. The fluidity with which she changed direction and
> did it beautifully has been inspiring to people, the
> diversity with which she drew from things. It's deep
> enough to extend to all boundaries of music.

Colvin met Joni when Larry Klein produced her 1992 album *Fat
City*. Much of the recording was done at Mitchell and Klein's
home-studio, the Kiva; Joni was put to work on one track, 'Object
of My Affection', providing percussion and hand-claps. The two
women became friends:

> She was very much how I thought she would be,
> extremely intelligent, very spirited, great sense of
> humour. As a listener she just enthralls you. It's won-
> derful to listen to her talk – and talk she does! She was
> always very gracious to me. She just lives in the
> moment, is deeply enthusiastic about existence even
> though within that she has many emotions. She's angry
> about certain things, even bitter about certain things but
> it's all out there and she doesn't pretend about anything.

When *Fat City* was released the liner notes included a cryptic
thankyou: '. . . and to Joni Mitchell – me wimp, you master.' It

was a reference to a comment Colvin had made during a television interview. When asked whether she considered her music as folk, she said she felt that when people hear the word, 'they think you're wimpy and I'm not!' Joni had watched the interview and when she saw Colvin again, she challenged her playfully: 'Are you calling me a wimp?!' Colvin demurred. 'I said "not at all! You are the antithesis of that and you taught me to do what I do and that's why I think I'm not wimpy." Some mention was made of "you are the master". She didn't like that either! She doesn't want to be the guru . . . '

Suzanne Vega – who led the second wave of women singer-songwriters – has often found the over-use of lazy comparisons both irksome and inaccurate. She had emerged unscathed by punk to embrace urban neo-folk, with quirky tunings and literate writing, inspired by Leonard Cohen and Lou Reed. She recalls that it was Mitchell's artwork, not her music, that had first made an impact on her:

> I was about six years old or seven, and I saw a cover of her *Clouds* album in our house somewhere. My hair was cut the same as hers on that album, so I thought, 'Oh, she looks like me.' Someone told me that she had painted that picture herself, and I was impressed by that. I don't remember actually listening to her albums until later.

Although not directly influenced by Mitchell's music, Vega believes that Joni has stretched the boundaries in ways that have lasting significance:

> She has had an enormous impact on not only music but on culture in general – everyone knows who she is – she is the archetypal 'poet woman with guitar'. I can't think of another person who typified this image the way she did. Maybe in the medieval days when troubadours travelled, there was someone who did. Carole King came before her but she had a different feel – her music was less introspective, and everyone knew she had written songs in the Brill Building so she was considered more of an inspired craftsman than a poet. But

[Joni] was also experimenting with song forms on *Don Juan's Reckless Daughter* and with using African rhythms as far back as the mid-seventies, which is something everyone does now with hip-hop, fusing folk narratives with a groove.

Vega's own music had seemed so out of step with punk, New Wave and disposable pop that record companies simply heaped rejection upon rejection. It was only the persistence of Nancy Jeffries at A&M that finally persuaded the company to change its mind – and Vega's debut album was a million-seller. The floodgates opened and a torrent of record deals swept over women as diverse as Jane Siberry, Mary Margaret O'Hara, Tanita Tikaram, Shawn Colvin and Syd Straw, soon to be followed by Tracy Chapman, Tori Amos, Sinead O'Connor, Sarah McLachlan *et al*. Intelligent, creative women became the Hot New Thing. It couldn't last. But while it did, almost every one of them was compared to Joni Mitchell in some way – even when the differences between them far outweighed any similarities, even when all they had in common was blonde hair or a guitar.

Mitchell's Canadian compatriot Jane Siberry says Joni cut a direct trail through a mode of writing that encouraged others as well:

> She gave the go ahead to a lot of people, to explore a different way of expressing their Muses ... for me, that's what [role] models are, they are people who give you permission to have confidence to do what you were going to do anyway but were unsure about. A lot of people had things in their heart to talk about and no one had spoken with a certain slant, a certain honesty. I would say she avoids the pitfalls of [being] maudlin, too sentimental, those are pitfalls that other people have fallen into, who have been working along the same lines as Joni Mitchell. She, to me, was very cool ... my definition of cool.

Rosanne Cash experienced a similar feeling of liberation:

> She gave us all permission. Until Joni, I felt like all these feelings and all of that artistic expression and

working out your sexual selves and your emotional selves and your power selves in a public and creative forum – I thought that was all the province of men until Joni did it. And then I saw how possible it was for a woman to explore [that] in a public arena. And it was completely inspiring. It changed my world.

Mitchell was deeply unimpressed when a fan once called her the 'best female singer-songwriter of all'; he thought it was a compliment, she thought the word 'female' was redundant: would he have called Bob Dylan or Neil Young or Bruce Springsteen the best *male* singer-songwriter? Clearly not. Her irritation with the gender label extends to the word 'feminism' – and this has caused consternation among many women, who have far more positive associations with the word and see its use as a matter of personal pride. Musician Ani DiFranco interviewed Joni for the *Los Angeles Times* in 1998 and was discomfited at what she felt was a paradox within Joni – the woman whose entire career and creative path have been the model of feminist strength, who has acknowledged that sexism lies at the heart of disrespectful treatment of her within some sections of the media, yet who is openly critical of feminism and its adherents.

DiFranco's frustration is almost palpable when she writes of Mitchell:

> She even cites the breakdown of the family and says children are not 'playing in backyards anymore' because their 'mothers are not at home', implicating feminism and no other social or economic circumstances, as the cause of the problem. This seems ironic coming from a woman who, at a young age, made the difficult decision of adoption for her child, when confronted with the choice between motherhood and career.

When the article appeared, that comment drew a swift response from Mitchell's managers, Sam Feldman and Steve Macklam, who wrote to the *Los Angeles Times* to say 'Notwithstanding the emotional impact of this comment, it happens to be wrong. There are a number of infinitely more significant reasons for Joni to have made the difficult decision that she did.'

If the clichés of blonde, ethereal, high-cheekboned, introspective, acoustic-guitared self-absorption and female rivalry could be pushed far enough aside, there would be room to look at the real strengths that Mitchell has bequeathed women musicians – whether or not they have chosen to acquire them – and most were gained in the 1960s when respect, power and opportunities for women in music were infinitely more limited than they are today: she has maintained complete artistic control over her music and album artwork from the very beginning of her career; she has retained all of the rights to her own publishing; she has made most of her albums without the intervention of a producer, believing her own vision is strong enough to carry her work; she has never been afraid to take risks, to look foolish, to make mistakes, to lose money, fans, radio play and video exposure, to do the very things that the industry insists you must not do – or else. And – old enough to be Britney Spears' grandmother – Joni is a living experiment in how women can maintain a creative career in popular music through their forties, fifties and beyond. So too are Chrissie Hynde, Deborah Harry, Marianne Faithfull, Bonnie Raitt and Joan Baez. As Chrissie Hynde said so eloquently:

> One thing I'm glad about if I was a role model at all: I never had to take my pants off or take my tits out 'cos I think that's really vulgar. There's this silicone brigade. To me it's really crude and unattractive and I don't know how that must pressurise the unformed mind. I never liked tits because they didn't look cool with the guitar.

No less an authority than Bob Dylan had told *Rolling Stone* in 1987, 'I hate to see chicks perform. Hate it . . . because they whore themselves.' When the interviewer, Kurt Loder, asked him whether this included Joni Mitchell, Dylan responded:

> Well, no. But then, Joni Mitchell is almost like a man (laughs). I mean, I love Joni, too. But Joni's got a strange sense of rhythm that's all her own, and she lives on that timetable. Joni Mitchell is in her own world all by herself, so she has a right to keep any rhythm she wants. She's allowed to tell you what time it is.

Mitchell has declared herself weary of the plethora of 'women in rock' magazine and newspaper features, which invariably include her only in relation to other women and not in a wider gender and genre context. She believes that the black press has a far less restrictive approach to her work. Writing in *Vibe* in 1997, cultural critic, musician and co-founder of the Black Rock Coalition Greg Tate urged hip hop artists to emulate Joni Mitchell, Miles Davis and Carlos Santana if they wanted a career of longevity and artistic integrity. He said of Mitchell:

> She's got more African-American fans than maybe even she realises and has been a major influence on black artists as diverse as Cassandra Wilson, Seal and the Glyph Formerly Known as Prince. Mitchell is someone who's made a career of putting musical progress ahead of the ring of the cash register ... there's a lot in Mitchell's music for hip-hop musicians to learn from, particularly the quality of her lyrics, which match the inventiveness of the best rap writing but which delve deeper ... If hip-hop is going to remain a form of exploration and expression, more brothers and sisters are going to have to follow Joni Mitchell's example. Why settle for right now when you can have eternity?

Mitchell's work in jazz, the collaboration with Charles Mingus, her admiration of the genius of Miles Davis, Billie Holiday, Charlie 'Bird' Parker and Jimi Hendrix have strengthened the affinity she feels with black culture:

> I find it offensive to see certain white artists praised and called geniuses, when the person they're emulat- ing went to the grave poor and hardly recognised. Look at Bird. You hear a lot of white saxophonists being called geniuses and you say, 'No, man, they're not the one who started it'. I hurt for Bird. I hurt for all the great ones who were never fully appreciated.

Miles Davis was a major inspiration and Joni asked him many times to work with her. He always refused and they'd end up talking about painting rather than music; he liked her artwork and she once gave him a print that he placed by the side of his bed. After Miles died, Mitchell met his brother Eugene and told him, 'Miles would never play with me because I was white.' Eugene told her she'd got it all wrong; his prejudice was always against *singers* because 'they got *words* to do it with!' Miles' son told Joni that his father had every record she'd ever made.

Joni has said that the first line of her memoirs will be 'I was the only black man at the party' – a likely reference to her Art Nouveau creation. She believes black musicians are drawn to her work – and more willing than their white counterparts to credit her as an influence – because she writes like a black poet: 'I frequently write from a black perspective.' Authenticity and appropriation are difficult waters to negotiate but Greg Tate feels that Joni has a point:

> As problematic as this construction might sound, I think of Mitchell as a black person turned inside out, projecting vulnerability and sensitivity from a steely inner core, as opposed to projecting the image of an armoured tank from a socially traumatized and stigmatized interior. In her work she openly, nakedly, publicly dares to portray the fissures, cracks, fragility and walking-wounded quality that most black people might only reveal to their most trusted and intimate friends ... Her voice is indelibly white and incredibly non-ethnic at the same time – it's not a folk sound or a Celtic sound but a Joni sound, a pure poet's sound. Reverence for poets and poetic language is considerably high in African-American culture ... Mitchell's profusive and effusive way with sensual language even more than her way with melody and song has made so many black people unabashedly embrace her. Her gift of allusive tongue combined with her fearless, frank revelation of her interpersonal disasters makes her irresistible to many black people who wish they could be so forthcoming.

Greg Tate believes that Joni, Leroi Jones (in his pre-Amiri Baraka incarnation) and the painter Jean Michel Basquiat are the only jazz poets worthy of the name. For her part, Mitchell says it was a young black piano player who paid her the greatest compliment she's ever received. He told her, 'I love your music. You make raceless, genderless music.'

10 It's dog eat dog – I'm just waking up . . .

> If ever I would stop thinking about music and politics, I would tell you that music is the expression of emotion and that politics is merely the decoy of perception.
>
> (Disposable Heroes of Hiphoprisy, *Music and Politics*, 1992)

W HEN RONALD REAGAN was in the White House during the 1980s, his fans included Neil Young and the British prime minister at the time, Margaret Thatcher. Those less impressed by him ranged from Joni Mitchell to the Soviet leader, Mikhail Gorbachev – Reagan had famously joked during a pre-broadcast microphone check in 1984, 'My fellow Americans, I'm pleased to tell you I just signed legislation which outlaws Russia forever. The bombing begins in five minutes.' To add insult to injury four years later, he fell asleep during a lavish state dinner in his honour at the Kremlin, just as Gorbachev proposed a toast to him.

Gorbachev, in his own foreign policy and the attitude of *glasnost*, or openness, recognised the need to hasten the end of the Cold War; Reagan often appeared eager to escalate it by seeing Commies under every bed in Central America. Ronald Reagan had presided over California as its governor, before taking the helm of the western world. The United States in the 1980s was in thrall to the floundering former actor whose time in Hollywood had been distinguished by co-starring opposite an engaging chimp called Bonzo and, as head of the Screen Actors Guild, doubling as an FBI informant whose area of expertise was Communist influence in post-war Hollywood. Under his Republican presidency, the forces of conservatism enjoyed a strong platform in American political and cultural life.

Never the most political of artists, Mitchell has chosen her causes carefully – ecology, the anti-nuclear movement, support for Native Americans. But in the early 80s, she'd become increasingly politicised as she watched many of the hard-fought social gains of the 60s come under threat from the conservatives, with Reagan's blessing. Conservatism had spawned groups like the right-wing Moral Majority and allowed a meteoric rise in the fortunes of evangelist ministers like Jerry Falwell, Jimmy Swaggart (an unlikely cousin of Jerry Lee Lewis) and Pat Robertson, who was planning to run for president – fundamentalist preachers whose preferred pulpit was a television studio, whose parish was Middle America and whose spiritual endeavours brought handsome financial rewards. Larry Klein says he and Mitchell watched with a mixture of horror and fascination as Swaggart – one of the most outspoken – appeared each week on television: 'We were amazed at the whole spectacle of this thing, this guy who was claiming to represent Jesus Christ and who was advocating all kinds of wild things, including bombing Cuba.' When Joni began writing for her next album, *Dog Eat Dog*, the broadcasts came to be an inspiration – although not in the divine way that Swaggart would have liked.

Mitchell and Klein originally planned to sample some of Swaggart's most outrageous pronouncements but, mindful that he would inevitably have launched a massive lawsuit, opted to find someone to play the role of a fire and brimstone evangelist. They asked Robert Duvall but he was involved in a film in which he played just such a role and he felt there'd be a conflict between the two appearances. They then approached Mitchell's friend, Jack Nicholson, who was delighted to do it. Nicholson may be a household name among cinemagoers but he drew a blank with the security guard at the Hollywood studio where they were recording. The man didn't recognise Nicholson and refused to allow him into the building. Nicholson's film commitments meant another date was impossible but they soon found someone closer to home – their neighbour in Malibu, Rod Steiger. Famous for his Hollywood hard man roles, Steiger took to the task with vigour. Klein says:

> It wasn't the easiest thing in the world to get him to do
> what we wanted because he just wanted to do it his

way. I remember Joni going out into the studio to talk to him and him coming on the microphone saying 'Larry, would you please get her out of here!' But it was great that he did it. He was very good although I think the best version still was Jimmy Swaggart as himself.

The track, 'Tax Free', with words by Joni and music by Klein, was a stinging attack on the cosy relationship between church and state and the evangelists who preached love and charity but promoted hate and intolerance.

The album became largely a work of social commentary, fuelled by a barrage of television images of the evangelist zealots and advertising slogans, by newspaper headlines and slick soundbite politics, global conflicts and domestic happiness, fame and famine. It was unlike anything she had done before: Mitchell's lyrics had become politicised, where in the past politics had barely featured; her anger at and distrust of the corporate culture appeared more strongly than at any time since the broadsides against the music industry on *For the Roses* many years earlier. She now confounded many of her jazz, pop and acoustic fans by embracing technology – drum machines, synthesisers, a Fairlight music computer and special effects, with Mitchell's trademark guitar and piano transformed. Songs like the title track were written on acoustic piano and guitar and then translated into electronics.

The change had come about partly as a result of Larry Klein's growing interest in the machine music of the time; he'd become dissatisfied and depressed with the session work he was doing, feeling that much of it left him uninspired. He set about reviving his interest in music, getting up at five in the morning to take lessons in the use of the Fairlight and taking university classes in mathematics and computer programming. He'd then come home to experiment with what he'd learned:

I started writing, using these instruments, and a lot of these things somehow ended up shifting the record's direction into that area – not in a self-conscious way but in the way you go where things are leading you. We didn't sit and say, 'Okay, let's work on this record together and make it a technological record.' It just became the way to execute these songs and a lot of the songs were conceived on synthesisers to begin with, because [Joni] started experimenting, sitting down at the keyboards and writing. Some of the songs that we co-wrote began as pieces of music that I was working on, on these keyboards. She'd hear something and say 'Let me write a lyric to that. It sounds really good to me.'

They equipped a small home studio in the Malibu house, with an eight-track recording deck, a basic drum machine, the Fairlight and a couple of other keyboards. Two of the songs they co-wrote would be included on the album: 'Tax Free' and 'Fiction', the latter a return to rock form but with some of the most minimalist lyrics Mitchell has written. For a writer whose lyrics have often tended to be constructed more like elaborate prose poems, most of these lines consisted of only three or four declarative, definitive words with the recurring refrain declaiming 'truth!' and 'fiction!'

As her love affair with music technology became more ardent, Geffen Records and Elliot Roberts encouraged her to work with British electro-popster Thomas Dolby, who had his only two real hits in the early 80s – 'She Blinded Me With Science' (1982) and 'Hyperactive' (1984). Mitchell had been hugely resistant to having a producer foisted upon her – she'd made 13 albums without one, including Crosby's non-interventionist nominal role on her debut. Soon after the first album, Crosby had introduced her to Henry Lewy and over 12 albums she and Lewy had made a formidable studio team. At the time, Crosby had told Lewy that Joni did not want or need a producer, but simply 'a third ear', someone to act as a catalyst between her and her music, and over the years, Lewy says, this method of working proved to be the most natural and effective:

I was a teacher and a listener at first. When we first got together, she didn't really know anything about the studio. When we'd over-dub vocals, for instance, she was so insecure that she had to hold a guitar. As the years went on, she picked up the engineering aspect more and more and today she knows what a studio can do for her and she knows how to get what she wants.

Joni has to be free to try things out. That's how she makes records. She'll come into the studio with a song one way and it'll end up being completely different when the record comes out. In between there are all the different ideas she tries out. Some of them are good, some of them aren't. She has the intelligence to know when something is or isn't working.

Lewy's customary role amounted to little more than a guest spot on *Dog Eat Dog,* on the novelty track 'Smokin' (Empty, Try Another)' – the sound effects were of a cigarette machine at the studio where *Wild Things Run Fast* had been recorded. Mitchell liked the clanging industrial sound of the machine as it dispensed a packet of cigarettes and it was recorded then, along with Klein's basslines, but not used on *Wild Things*. The new album had a new engineer, Mike Shipley, and Mitchell could see no reason why she, Klein and Shipley could not see the album through, just as she and Henry Lewy had done for so long. But she was aware that they lacked the necessary speed and facility with the new equipment and began to seriously consider using Thomas Dolby. For his part, he had expressed an interest in producing the album – and Joni approved of his undoubted technical skills and of the fact that he was conversant enough with her music to have recorded a cover of 'The Jungle Line'. But from the start, Mitchell says, there were misgivings abut Dolby's role:

> We called Thomas and I explained to him that what we needed was really a more menial position than the one he had vied for – to take a back seat on the project and to be more supportive than a producer who has the last say. He said that would be fine with him, it would be lovely, and that he was tired of people looking to him for all the answers. While he said that I thought, 'Wait a minute, this guy's had three or four years of being in the foreground . . . Can a person who's used to having control do that?'

As it happened, no. Mitchell was used to having total artistic control in the studio and self-mockingly described herself as a benign dictator – she'd had the freedom and confidence to become, by her own admission, impossible to produce. Her autonomy led to frequent arguments with Thomas Dolby, who, despite his earlier protestations to the contrary, began to assume the role of producer rather than technical adviser and assistant. There were predictable consequences. Dolby would become engrossed in creating a track and be reluctant to relinquish it, despite Mitchell's urgings, until he'd finished putting his own signature on it. Being reminded that he'd simply been brought in to set up sounds on the computer clearly rankled. More heated debates would ensue, with Dolby declaring testily, 'I'm not getting anything out of these adult talks, Joan.' Mitchell says the way she was used to working was largely incompatible with Dolby's:

> The problem was that in all my records, the structure of the song is usually laid down by acoustic guitar or piano first, and then I bring in other players and just give them the freedom to blow and counter-melody against that. Sometimes I edit them, sometimes I just take their parts and move 'em around. I gather all this material and then collage it in afterwards. The advantage is that it keeps up spirits in the studio and saves me from having to give a lot of verbal instruction. So when Thomas came in and immediately started building and building tracks, it just drove me crazy.

The tracks Dolby constructed in that way were not used on the album.

The 'two's company' set up that Joni had enjoyed for so long with Henry Lewy in the studio was replaced by the 'four's a crowd' working arrangement that evolved when she, Klein, Shipley and Dolby struggled to form a consensus. Eventually, all four would share some production credits. She had often used samples and effects in the past and while the new technology made even more experimentation possible, she was confident about her instincts in using them to embellish particular songs. One, 'The Three Great Stimulants' (enumerated as 'artifice, brutality and innocence'), contained a number of effects including a helicopter blade in motion and the sound from a Super-8 film that Mitchell had shot in New York with background noise of hammering and a burglar alarm. It proved to be the most troublesome track, after all three men decided they didn't like her ideas, particularly her plans for the rotor-blades.

Joni finally insisted and grudgingly they set to work – and came up with an altered version of the sound but one she liked better. Her plans for the hammering/alarm were dismissed as not 'hi-fi' enough and no one but Joni seemed to like the elements she used to illustrate the song's concepts of 'innocence' (a harp), 'brutality' (a fragment of Stravinsky) and 'artifice' (a beat from Madonna). It's not hard to see why she once described *Dog Eat Dog* as one of the most difficult albums she'd ever made. Dolby has said of Mitchell that she is at her best when throwing out the old conventions:

> Her best moments in music have come when she's cut through everything that's going on, transcended that hippie-folk mentality and done something that couldn't have been anything else. The *Hejira* album, that's completely timeless. You'll never find it in some musical museum as an example of a particular era.

For all the tensions, the album did remain true to Mitchell's initial vision. She had joked that it should have been called 'Songs of a Couch Potato', given that much of its inspiration came from spending so much time at home, happily with Klein, watching television and doing everyday things. But the external politics did impinge on her life in direct ways – her ire at Reagan's Republican government and the apparatus of the state was also fired by being one of a group of twelve musicians (including Neil Young and the band America) singled out by the California state authorities for a new tax levy – the musicians all had artistic-control clauses in their recording contracts and this was used as the basis of the new law. They were required to pay tax on their album from the point at which it was handed over to the record company, as Mitchell recalls: 'Somehow or other, to these people who knew nothing about the music industry, this clause technically made us seem like independents and therefore taxable.' Mitchell was issued with a demand for 15 per cent of her income between 1972 and 1976 in back taxes. It would take a decade for her to win the case to have the levy dropped.

The political and cultural climate she was writing about left few people unaffected – whether it was big government, the United States' gung-ho dreams of a Star Wars space-based missile defence system, the litigation culture, organised religion, Christian fundamentalism, the resurgence of the Right, corporate power and capitalism, famine relief or censorship. The Christian Right had – not for the first time – pronounced the music of the young to be the music of the devil. They would soon launch an insidious campaign that quickly gained ground, first against heavy metal and then rap, rock and pop – although serious moves to censor song lyrics and musicians came not only from the Right but the centrist politics of Tipper Gore (wife of Democratic Party politician Al Gore, the man who later became US vice-president) and her ladies-who-lunch friends in Washington. The Parents Music Resource Center – to which Mike Love of The Beach Boys donated money – gained a victory in having a system of labelling introduced, to warn of 'explicit' lyrics. As the PMRC pushed to have even more restrictions imposed on artists and their work, and as the tele-evangelists grew more powerful, musicians were slow to organise against them.

In his book on political pop, *When the Music's Over,* Robin Denselow wrote that the only musicians who seemed to care were Joni Mitchell and Frank Zappa. He singled out Mitchell's 'Tax Free', saying it 'sounded a little far-fetched in 1985, but she was ahead of her time with the reminder that "you get witch-hunts and wars when Church and State hold hands"'. Frank Zappa launched a campaign of his own to try to counter the anti-rock lobby and appeared before a Congressional committee. He told the hearing, 'There is no conclusive scientific evidence to support the claim that exposure to any form of music will cause the listener to commit a crime or damn his soul to hell.' In the end a compromise was reached between the industry and the PMRC. Soon after, Zappa's new album, *Frank Zappa Meets the Mothers of Prevention,* was released, with a warning sticker of its own:

WARNING GUARANTEE: This album contains material which a truly free society would neither fear nor suppress. In some socially retarded areas, religious fanatics and ultra-conservative political organisations violate your First Amendment Rights by attempting to censor rock and roll albums . . . The language and concepts contained herein are GUARANTEED NOT TO CAUSE ETERNAL TORMENT IN THE PLACE WHERE THE GUY WITH THE HORNS AND THE POINTED STICK CONDUCTS HIS BUSINESS.

By the time the Washington wives were fighting to restrict the power of music, Bob Geldof and friends had already proven its force. The Live Aid concert on 13 July 1985, organised in response to a devastating famine in Ethiopia, and the shows and records that both preceded and followed it, focused global attention on musicians and the enormous power they could wield. As British anarcho-popsters Chumbawamba sang, 'Pictures of Starving Children Sell Records'. Radical had never been so chic. Mitchell had taken part in Northern Lights for Africa, the Canadian equivalent of the Band Aid collective of musicians who had first gathered together to make the fund-raising record 'We Are The World'. The Canadian group sang a song co-written by Bryan Adams, called 'Tears Are Not Enough'. Joni wrote 'Ethiopia' soon after and donated the royalties to charity:

> 'We Are The World' is a beautiful idea. I believe we *are* the world – it's a very idealistic idea, but a good one. I just felt that in singing the words, that the general overtone of these albums was self-congratulatory . . . in all the big charity events of the past – [the concert for] Bangladesh, No Nukes – a lot of self-congratulation went on, and everybody that appeared in these things was 'the new consciousness' and inevitably it did all their careers some good – and the money never got to the people. It got stripped off by the government, by the inevitable expenses of presenting such a thing.

The Hunger Business can indeed be a very lucrative one, depending on your place in the food chain. Corruption, misman-agement and political posturing often sap the vital reserves of food aid and funds. Fifteen years after Live Aid raised two hundred million pounds, the United Nations warned that twelve million people in the Horn of Africa – most of them in Ethiopia – were facing famine, following prolonged drought and continued conflict.

When Woody Guthrie scrawled 'This machine kills fascists' on his guitar he could not have known the absurdities that would mark much of the 'social comment' in popular music – American singer Crystal Waters had a massive dance hit in the 90s, yelping 'she's homeless, yeah, she's homeless!'; Spice Girl Mel C lamented about homelessness and how she'd cope without her mobile phone. Musicians have so often given social comment a bad name. Larry Klein:

> A lot of pop stars or celebrities are so lacking in knowledge of all of the ramifications, of all the elements that are afoot in these issues, invariably it becomes, 'God, aren't we great, we're saving the world.' I think that an artist's talent is to touch people through their art and where [Joni has] chosen to focus her effort when she feels passionately about something is to write a song like 'Ethiopia' in the hope that people hear it and that it makes them feel something strongly and in that way they might endeavour to help someone that they can actually help – maybe a person down the block or something like that.

Mitchell was asked to appear on the anti-apartheid record 'Sun City', which denounced the South African government's apartheid policy and its programme of relocating blacks to so-called homelands. It singled out western rock and pop stars like Rod Stewart, Queen, Linda Ronstadt, Julio Iglesias and the O'Jays for defying a United Nations cultural boycott and going to South Africa to appear at the Sun City resort – a temple of opulent kitsch, built on the back of black labour in the homeland of Bophuthatswana. Stars like Elton John, Ray Charles and George Benson were also paid exorbitant amounts to play there. Mitchell refused to take part in the recording, and defended her friend Linda Ronstadt, saying she would only have appeared at Sun City in the interests of showing that 'art should cross any border'. It's possible that the enormous fee Ronstadt was paid may also have been a factor. (Mitchell was to prove herself a loyal friend to Linda Ronstadt; she once wrote a letter to the editor of *Musician* magazine, taking Rickie Lee Jones to task for criticising Ronstadt's recent foray into jazz. In the letter, Joni asserted that jazz wasn't 'a private sidewalk'.)

The climate seemed more conducive to creating a greater receptivity to Mitchell's music than it had been for years. The 'new Joni' women were making their presence felt, so her name was ever-present in that debate; male artists like Elvis Costello and Prince were openly acknowledging her as an influence. Prince often played her songs as the pre-show music before he took the stage and he told *Rolling Stone* that the last album by any artist that he loved all the way through was *The Hissing of Summer Lawns*; Boy George declared his passion for *Court and Spark*. (More than 15 years later, George would quote Joni's lyrics from 'For the Roses' in a poignant tribute to Paula Yates, the ex-wife of Bob Geldof, who died of an apparent accidental drugs overdose: 'Just when you're getting a taste for worship, They start bringing out the hammers, And the boards, And the nails'.)

Mitchell's lyrics on *Dog Eat Dog* were utterly contemporary, detailing the issues that were inescapable at the time. There were even a couple of love songs to keep her more traditional fans happy. But there may have been just a little too much reality and too little romance for most tastes and some critics felt that embracing the new machine music was simply pandering to popularity. Reviewing the album in *High Fidelity*, Rosemary Passantino sniffed that the songs 'avoid examining Mitchell's recent transition from wandering romantic to married woman, an exposé many of her devotees may rightfully expect'. She did, however, praise the 'cool precision of sequential Fairlight samples and percussion patterns ... tempered by warm, deftly-layered jazz and folk accompaniment ...' *Newsweek* declared the audio special effects 'simply intrusive – aural flash for its own sake' and *Rolling Stone* lamented that 'while Joni's venom is an encouraging sign, its clumsy expression is unnerving'. The album peaked at Number 63 on the US charts and fared marginally better in Britain. A line from the title track – 'nothing is savoured long enough to really understand' – would become an epitaph for *Dog Eat Dog*.

The 80s had started on a low note then improved immeasurably with her marriage to Larry Klein – but now what would become the decade of difficulties had taken hold. During the recording of *Dog Eat Dog*, Joni and her long-time manager, Elliot Roberts, parted company. They'd left the East Coast together in the late 60s to join the California musical gold-rush and had mined an extraordinary seam of success and recognition; they'd been comrades in arms, confidants and fellow travellers for 17 years. But like any long relationship, the strains were beginning to show. The closeness they'd shared had other outlets; both were now married, and Roberts had children. There were differences over their respective jobs: Joni resented Roberts' insistence that, for the first time ever, she *needed* a producer and felt it was part of moves to laminate her to Dolby simply because he was popular at the time. Arguments ensued. Roberts also had increasing commitments to his other clients including Neil Young and Bob Dylan. Elliot Roberts, for his part, was aware of the changes in Joni's work and studio production since her marriage to Larry Klein, and felt she was not concerned enough with regaining the power and attention she had held within the industry. When he'd heard the songs she was writing for *Dog Eat Dog*, he'd remarked only halfjoking, 'I don't know about these songs, Joan. Don't you have anything about sex and parties?' It was a difficult and hurtful split for both of them but the friendship has been an enduring one.

 Mitchell reverted to managing her own affairs as she'd done when she first started out but soon realised it was impossible. She contacted Peter Asher, who'd enjoyed a taste of fame in the 60s singing duo Peter and Gordon before starting up his own management company. His long-time clients included Mitchell's friends James Taylor and Linda Ronstadt and she now joined them. Asher was supportive and encouraging of her new project although acknowledging that his new client would not always be the easiest to 'sell':

> I loved *Dog Eat Dog*. Other people didn't. Of course Joni was disappointed when it didn't do well. The thing is, every artist has a reluctance to accept that, basically, not enough people liked the record. Then anyone who's around gets blamed, which is usually the record company. But Joni doesn't have any of this even vaguely on

her mind, not for an instant. In the studio her objectives are purely artistic. And I don't say that is a virtue. She doesn't even *think* of pleasing the public. In that sense, she's lucky she's as popular as she is. At least, around the world, she still does half a million every time.

About a month before the album came out, Mitchell and Klein were driving along the Pacific Coast highway when their vehicle was hit by a drunken driver; their car was a total wreck but, astonishingly, they walked away with only minor injuries. There had been almost an element of prescience in Joni's writing months earlier: in an early draft of the ebullient synth-pop song 'Good Friends', she'd written 'Sometimes change comes at you Like a broadside accident You get minor cuts and bruises that's all You could hammer out the dents.' In the final album version – a duet with former Doobie Brother Michael McDonald – Joni kept the first two lines but dropped the other two, only to remember their relevance after the accident.

The release party for the album was held in October 1985, as a benefit for the Museum of Contemporary Art in Los Angeles. The walls of the venue, the James Corcoran gallery, were lined with Mitchell's paintings. The artwork for the album showed a baying wolf pack circling Mitchell and on the prowl. The wolves imagery was significant, symbolic of the travails of the time: the politicians, the state tax authorities, the right-wing evangelists, and the drunken driver who could have killed her and Klein. She was even in trouble back home in Canada: Joni's neighbours up in Half Moon Bay had asked her to join their protest against a salmon hatchery being built in the area amid fears that it would damage the environment. She did so, only to come in for flak from the media and the company involved, accusing her of opposing jobs for local people, when she spent so little time there herself. The *Alberta Report* newspaper published an unflattering cartoon depicting her bludgeoning innocent salmon with her acoustic guitar.

Initial thoughts of touring to support the album were dismissed, given its lacklustre sales performance and relatively poor chart positions, although Joni did take part in the Farm Aid benefit in Illinois in September 1985. Nine months later, in June 1986, she gamely took the stage again for the Amnesty International

'Conspiracy of Hope' benefit at the Meadowlands in New Jersey. Mitchell had gone on as a last-minute replacement for Pete Townshend with the crowd more anxious to see U2 and a re-formed Police. Joni launched into her brief set – a solo acoustic 'The Three Great Stimulants', the new song 'Number One', with backing from a woman from Sting's band, and then 'Hejira', joined by Larry Klein. The crowd were getting fractious and started pelt-ing the stage; when her water-glass went flying, Joni rebuked them saying, 'Save the bombs for later! I'm not that bad, you dig? Quit pitching shit up here!'

By then, though, she'd begun writing for her new album and the crowd's displeasure was little more than a momentary dis-traction. It would soon be time to find out whether she'd be caught again in the cleft stick that is so often used to entrap many artists: damned if they change, damned if they don't. No musical genre or lyrical theme had ever seemed out of bounds; the only issue that had lost the urgency of old was the search for romantic love – marriage to Klein had solved that. With *Dog Eat Dog,* she'd been criticised for venturing out into the world and reporting back from the frontline, just as a few years earlier she'd been accused of being far too insular, preoccupied only with her inner world.

It had been a trip to England that coaxed her back into the studio. Klein was there producing a solo album for Cars bass-player and vocalist, Benjamin Orr; they had installed themselves at the Wool Hall studio in Beckington, near Bath. Peter Gabriel had set up his own studio, Ashcombe House, in Bath and Klein found time to play bass on some songs that Gabriel was record-ing for his new album, *So.* When Joni arrived, Gabriel offered her the use of his studio. In the meantime, Klein had met Robert Plant – Led Zeppelin's front man and along with Zep guitarist, Jimmy Page, a major Joni Mitchell fan – and they discussed the possibility of working together. Klein began to work on a couple of songs that he thought would suit Plant but, when Joni arrived and heard his work in progress, she was eager to write lyrics for them; the songs became 'Lakota' and 'Snakes and Ladders'. When Klein told Plant that his wife had inadvertently hijacked the songs, Plant's response was, 'Has she nicked any more of *my* songs?!' Plant was to make a valiant effort to get one of Joni's own compositions, 'Number One', a scathing look at the tread-mill that is the pursuit of fame and success above all else. Plant declared it to be a gender-specific song and one he should have; he told her, 'You can't play that song, it's a man's song!' She wasn't convinced.

Plant's playful comment did highlight the thread running through the songs that would become *Chalk Mark in a Rain Storm*: the album was more like a collection of short stories, each one a sketch from a particular character's life, fleshed out with a hand-picked cast to play supporting roles. When Peter Gabriel came to visit Mitchell at his studio one day, she put him to work on the romantically suggestive duet 'My Secret Place'. Benjamin Orr provided backing vocals for 'Number One' and 'The Beat of Black Wings', which was inspired by a soldier – 'Killer' Kyle, a paratrooper medic who had witnessed appalling scenes during his time in Vietnam – whom Mitchell had met in the mid-60s when she did a show at the Fort Bragg military base in North Carolina. Joni wrote the song as a dramatised version of Kyle's story. Militarism was much on her mind at the time; Gabriel's studio was worryingly close to an airbase that had been used to launch air strikes on Libya and she feared that if there were retaliatory attacks, they could be in the firing-line.

Musically, drum-machines and synthesised keyboards were much in evidence – Thomas Dolby even had a cameo appearance with a Fairlight Marimba – but Mitchell had been hankering after the sound of real, live musicians playing real instruments so old comrades like Wayne Shorter joined her in the studio (for 'A Bird That Whistles', her arrangement of the old song 'Corrina, Corrina'). Recording back in the US, Mitchell began to cast around for bit-part players to illustrate her songs and she came up with an eclectic ensemble: she met Prince's former protégés Wendy Melvoin and Lisa Coleman at the studio coffee-machine and invited them along to sing backing vocals on 'The Tea Leaf Prophecy (Lay Down Your Arms)'. The song was loosely based on a tea-leaf reader's predictions to her mother and her parents' subsequent courtship, but also drawing in elements of wartime history – her father had been in the air force – and Native American folklore. Mitchell's fascination with the latter is explored further in 'Lakota', an examination of the Lakota Sioux tribe's struggle to preserve Native American lands in the uranium-rich Black Hills of the south-western US and to stop the erosion of tribal values. Mitchell had cast herself

in the Lakota role and included chants as part of the background vocals, but she wanted reassurance that she had not
crossed some invisible line between honour and dishonour.

When she heard that there was going to be a big tribal community meeting in Los Angeles, a pow-wow, she longed to go. A
sudden breakdown in equipment in the studio meant she was
free. She went along and was introduced to Iron Eyes Cody, a
tribal leader and actor who jokingly referred to himself as the
'Hollywood Indian'. She explained her concerns and he came
back to the studio with her. Just as they arrived, the equipment
fault seemed mysteriously to disappear – and Cody's chants were
recorded. After hearing 'Lakota', the chief of the Lakota Sioux
invited Mitchell and Klein to visit the reservations and join the
tribe on a protest march. She accepted, later describing the visit
as 'a high honour and a good experience'. In October, Joni performed at the 'Free Leonard Peltier' benefit in Costa Mesa, along
with Willie Nelson, Jackson Browne and others. The money
raised was to be used to fund a new trial for Peltier, who'd been
convicted of killing two FBI agents during a dispute over Native
American rights.

Another of *Chalk Mark's* inspired 'castings' was a double-act of
Billy Idol – whom Mitchell had seen at the Grammy awards; she
thought his demeanour made him perfect for the role – and Tom
Petty, playing two street toughs in 'Dancin' Clown'. Willie
Nelson, whom Joni had met at Farm Aid, gives the perfect coun-
try-tinged twang to her adaptation of the classic 'Cool Water', a
song she remembered from her childhood. He called into the
studio in the early hours of the morning after a gig, parking his
huge Winnebago camper-bus outside.

The album was co-produced by Mitchell and Klein (who also
took the photographs of Joni used in the artwork), and when it
was released in March 1988 it was generally greeted as being
more accessible than its predecessor: there was no over-reliance
on technology and much of the writing expanded on themes that
Mitchell had explored in the past – fame and success, Native
American lore, romance and the power struggles it often
involves, which she'd dissected so acutely on *The Hissing of
Summer Lawns*. A duet with Don Henley, 'Snakes and Ladders',
charted an 80s version of the 70s marriage of 'Harry's House –
Centerpiece' and 'The Hissing of Summer Lawns'.

Nicholas Jennings, writing in *Macleans*, hailed *Chalk Mark in a Rainstorm* as 'an artistic landmark that re-establishes Mitchell as one of pop music's premier talents'. Mitchell's home-town paper, the *Saskatoon Star-Phoenix*, described it as 'the most ambitious and complex recording project she has undertaken in her twenty-year career'. *Rolling Stone* writer J.D. Considine wrote:

> To her credit, the sound of *Chalk Mark* is slick and entic-
> ing, with Mitchell making the most of her wide-ranging
> guests. Alluring as its surface is, the album doesn't invite
> repeated listenings; in that sense [it] is all too aptly
> named, for its pleasures simply wash away with time.

The album peaked at Number 45 in the US charts; 26 in the UK. Mitchell was nominated for a Grammy for Best Female Pop Vocal Performance – she lost out to the rising star of Elektra/Asylum, Tracy Chapman, and her single 'Fast Car'.

The lure of a life outside the music business, devoting herself to painting, writing poetry and short stories, had exercised a strong pull ever since her recording career had begun; Joni had succumbed to the temptation many times for short- or long-term sabbaticals. But her doubts were now getting deeper. Life in the public eye and status as a celebrity meant that even media coverage of a heavy storm at Malibu brought unwanted attention on Mitchell and Klein's home there. Joni had become painfully conscious of the security of her homes, after a five-year campaign by an obsessive fan who had camped outside her house in Bel Air in the mid-70s. Forced to live under armed guard, Mitchell had implored the man's parents to persuade him to leave, and finally, two days after John Lennon's murder in 1980, he did. Her wealth had also emphasised the industry cliché that 'with the hits, come the writs' – and the writs can come from many different quarters: in the late 80s, Mitchell was being sued by her house-keeper after an altercation during which she kicked the woman in the shin. Joni felt that she'd been ripped off – she had twice paid for the woman to return home to see her family in Guatemala, but on the second occasion the woman had instead gone on holiday in Europe. The woman felt her shin should have remained unmolested and was seeking a multi-million-dollar settlement; she eventually lost the case.

If the personal price had often seemed too high, so too had the professional one. Geffen Records, increasingly concerned about recouping the enormous costs of her albums, had imposed a lien on her publishing royalties. That was eventually lifted – only to have the label threaten to put out a money-spinning greatest hits album if *Chalk Mark* didn't pay its way. Joni had long resisted any such suggestion, believing – possibly, with good reason – that shops would simply stock that and not bother with her less commercial work. That threat too receded but it did cast serious doubt over David Geffen's assurances when she left Elektra/Asylum that she would have a happy home for life with his label. With what seemed like indecent haste, the company deleted her two previous albums from its back-lists. As he had done with Neil Young in their dispute over money, Geffen did not easily let an old friendship get in the way of commerce. Less than eighteen months after the release of *Chalk Mark*, Geffen sold his company to MCA, making a huge profit.

In early 1988, buoyed by the new album, Mitchell and Klein set off on a promotional tour through the US, Canada, Britain, Japan and Australia, doing interviews and television performances. While on a British TV programme, Joni gave the first public performance of a new song, 'Night Ride Home' – it would become the title of her next album. In May she went to Japan, where she opened an exhibition of her paintings; it was the first time her artwork had gone on sale to the public directly. In the past, the few paintings, photographs and lithographs that had come on to the market had been sold by people to whom she'd given them as gifts. Now, there was an incentive for her to sell: Geffen Records would not allow her a budget for videos and, without them, there was even less chance of getting radio play and television exposure. As Tom Waits once lamented, 'Marcel Marceau gets more airplay than I do.' The $120,000 Joni received from the sale of her paintings paid for the production of two videos but interest from MTV and VH-1 was negligible.

There were a small number of shows and benefits in the coming months – Joni received a songwriters' award at the San Remo Song Festival and again tentative plans to arrange a tour came to nought; in March 1989, she took part in the recording of a single, 'The Spirit of the Forest', to raise funds for the Brazilian rainforest. In a United Nations-organised benefit performance in

June, Mitchell joined a specially formed mini-supergroup, 'Herbie Hancock's Super Band', along with Larry Klein, Wayne Shorter and Andy Summers (ex-Police). And in September, she appeared – lip-synching 'Night Ride Home' – in the unaccustomed company of a bunch of Muppets in the Jim Henson series *The Ghost of Faffner Hall*. Mitchell and Klein settled into their studio at the Bel Air house, the Kiva, and began recording some early tracks for the new album. By the time 1989 drew to a close, *Dog Eat Dog* had defied the critics who thought of it as an unfocused synth-fuelled rant. Ronald Reagan was about to leave the White House – only to be replaced by his Republican successor, George Bush. Many would say with hindsight that Reagan had long been showing signs of the Alzheimer's disease that would eventually manifest itself. The power of the TV evangelists was on the wane, eroded by financial and sexual scandals.

Political events were transforming the face of Europe. The Berlin Wall had crumbled in the face of popular protest, poor economic conditions in the East, and the inevitability of change. Eastern Europe was opening itself up to democracy, McDonald's and capitalism. In July 1990, the Wall that had been the focus of international tensions and the symbol of the Cold War became the setting for a charity concert organised by Roger 'Pink Floyd' Waters. Waters revived Pink Floyd's 1980 epic stage production *The Wall* – a study in alienation, centred around the construction of a huge wall between the audience and the band, which was then ceremoniously toppled after the intermission.

He gathered together an eclectic cast of characters to sing or play the costume roles, including actors like Albert Finney and Tim Curry, Joni Mitchell, Van Morrison, Sinead O'Connor, Bryan Adams, Cyndi Lauper, Marianne Faithfull, Phil Collins, the Scorpions, Ute Lemper, Thomas Dolby and members of the Band. The Red Army Marching Band, the East Berlin Rundfunk Symphony Orchestra and hundreds of 'extras' from the British and East and West German armies also took part as the 'Wall' (made of Styrofoam bricks) was built over two hours and then destroyed. More than 200,000 people gathered in Potsdamer Platz to watch the eight-million-dollar production as it was broadcast around the world.

Despite the huge budget, the inevitable technical difficulties caused sound problems; they were resolved as Joni came on with flautist James Galway to perform 'Goodbye, Blue Sky'. She reappeared at the finale to sing 'The Tide Is Turning'. Proceeds from the concert went to the Memorial Fund for Disaster Relief, a new charity to aid victims of national disasters, set up by the British Second World War hero Leonard Cheshire.

In September, Mitchell travelled to London for the opening of a retrospective of her artworks: 'Diary of a Decade 1980–1990' was held as part of a festival of Canadian culture, art and music. Back home, she attended a performance revue of an entirely different kind several months later in Los Angeles, when the LA Theatre Center launched a three-month run of a show based around her songs, *The Joni Mitchell Project*. A few days after it opened, Joni went along and briefly joined the cast, singing a song she'd written for her new album – 'Cherokee Louise' was loosely based on the experiences of a young First Nations girl she'd been friends with in Saskatoon, who had run away from home after being sexually abused by her foster-father. It's not an easy topic to write about without either sounding flippant or foolish, but Mitchell manages it with some sensitivity – unlike Toad The Wet Sprocket's seemingly well-meaning but ludicrous 'Hold Her Down', with its male-voice chorus repeating those words to a pop riff.

Where *Chalk Mark* had seen Mitchell take a more observational role, scripting and casting characters in song vignettes, she was back firmly in the narrative on *Night Ride Home*. The title track is a memory of driving with Klein on a deserted road, heading towards a house they had rented, late on a perfect Hawaiian night – the track is complete with a summertime cricket; one flew into the studio during recording. Joni's Saskatoon teenage years are revisited in 'Ray's Dad's Cadillac' and the opening of 'Come In From The Cold', where the strict martinets at school dances – wielding rulers to ensure the dancers remained the regulation ' foot apart' – could still not repress the fizzing circuitry of teenage hormones. There's a return to the indignation of *Dog Eat Dog* in 'Passion Play (When All The Slaves Are Free)' and 'The Windfall (Everything for Nothing)', as Mitchell herself became embroiled in the parasitic litigation culture that has become such a feature of American life. Facing the lawsuit filed by her housekeeper, Mitchell sang 'I'm not going to be the jackpot At the end of your perjured rainbow'.

Happier times are recalled in 'The Only Joy In Town', a snapshot from a holiday in Rome, when Joni and a woman friend

noticed a beautiful young man on the Spanish Steps. She muses
that as a younger woman she'd have pursued him but now feels
no need, appreciating his beauty without having to possess it –
the serene maturity behind that decision comes under scrutiny
in 'Nothing Can Be Done', when Joni, at 47, asks herself 'Must I
surrender With grace The things I loved when I was younger . . . '
It's a poignant piece, certain to resonate with any woman of a
certain age – and many men as well. Klein's music gracefully
underscores a lingering sadness and resignation. Mitchell spoke
about the feelings that inspired the song:

> I'm 47 and I guess I've come through my middle-age
> crazies, which are as predictable as the terrible twos.
> You wake up one day and suddenly realise that your
> youth is behind you, even though you're still young at
> heart. You've got to get through this lament for what
> was. The song was based partly on *The Desiderata*
> which says 'Surrender gracefully the things of youth'.
> When I play the song for my middle-aged friends they
> either won't look at it or they look at it and weep.

Longing for the things of one's youth haunts the central character in 'Two Grey Rooms', a story of unrequited passion and
obsession: a German aristocrat finds the man he loved decades
earlier, working in a dockyard. Content to long for him from afar,
he leaves his luxurious home to live in two shabby rooms on the
street where the man passes every day on his way to and from
work. Mitchell had written the music back in 1982, but it had
taken years for the lyrics to take shape.

The most surprising work on *Night Ride Home* is her adaptation of William Butler Yeats' poem 'The Second Coming'. With
the approval of the Yeats estate Mitchell set to work on her own
version of one of his best-known works:

> I love Yeats. The poem that I set to music, though . . . I
> corrected . . . there were parts of it I added. They let me
> do it which was amazing. Because I think they sued Van
> Morrison for setting something. They just said, 'You
> have to put, "adapted by . . . "' And I think I did it pretty
> seamlessly because I understand his style – the third

stanza is mine, and it's very much in the style of the first
one, more so than his second stanza.

Changed, but not utterly. The title echoed that of Joan
Didion's essay, published in 1967. This was not the first time
Yeats' words had entered the realm of poetic pop – in 1972
Leonard Cohen had opened a concert in Dublin with a reading of 'Under Ben Bulben'. And in 1997 a collection of Yeats'
poems set to music would be released; *Now and in Time To Be*
featured Van Morrison, Christy Moore, Sinead O'Connor,
Shane MacGowan, Waterboy Mike Scott and an excerpt from
Yeats himself. Yeats had once written to a friend, 'I think that
a poet, or even a mystic, becomes a greater power from
understanding all the great primary emotions & these one
only gets out of going through the common experiences &
duties of life.' In a single sentence, it seems to sum up the
creative journey that Mitchell herself had embarked upon in
the mid-1960s and had pursued doggedly ever since. With a
return to more personal lyrical themes, Mitchell had also
returned to more traditional studio arrangements – the technology of the last two albums was barely recognisable,
replaced by the guitars, bass, keyboards, subtle percussion and
Wayne Shorter's haunting sax that added much more than any
synth could to the new songs.

With the album's release in March 1991 came a special edition of 15,000 copies in a gift-wrapped package that included
four of Mitchell's double-exposure self-portrait photographs.
One, which included Klein in profile, adorned the album cover.
Entertainment Weekly writer Linda Sanders pronounced it the
most graceful record Mitchell had ever made:

> The 'I' of Mitchell's songs is a half-real, half-fantasy
> character, which has evolved over time into a gen-
> uinely modern romantic heroine, a feminist devoid of
> cant, who's trying to figure out, not how to live a polit-
> ically correct autonomous life, but how to live a *deeply
> fun* autonomous life.

Recalling the scope of her past work, a *Rolling Stone* reviewer,
Tom Sinclair, said:

Old-time Mitchell fans may well prefer the incandescence of her *Blue* period or even the abstract impressionism of *Mingus* or *Shadows and Light*. Still, *Night Ride Home,* if not the masterpiece some have hoped for, is a convincing demonstration of her continuing validity as an artist.

Robert Hilburn, in the *Los Angeles Times,* greeted the album as 'her warmest and most accessible collection since *Court and Spark* in 1974 – an album that joins recent works by Paul Simon and Sting as an example of pop's growing ambition and maturity'. The reference to Simon and Sting is interesting given that Mitchell had long since cleared the world/jazz musical paths that their new albums were treading. The album peaked at Number 41 in the US charts but fared better in the UK charts, reaching Number 25. Again, there were no plans to tour so there was the usual round of promotional interviews. The video for 'Come In From The Cold' aired on VH-1 and was followed by other video releases featuring Joni – Roger Waters' production of *The Wall,* a combined video and interview, *Joni Mitchell: The Original Returns,* and a collection of videos from *Night Ride Home* and *Chalk Mark in a Rainstorm,* entitled *Come In From the Cold.*

The album would be her last for Geffen Records. As she neared the end of her contract, it would soon be time for a change. In February 1992, Mitchell ran into David Geffen at Elizabeth Taylor's lavish sixtieth birthday celebrations at Disneyland. He peered into her face in the unforgiving California sunlight and proclaimed, 'We're old!' But as the novelist Isak Dinesen (Karen Blixen) once observed, 'Women, when they are old enough to have done with the business of being women, and can let loose their strength, may be the most powerful creatures in the world.'

11 Part of this is permanent, part of this is passing . . .

> Women should be tough, tender, laugh as much as possible and live long lives. The struggle for equality continues unabated, and the woman warrior who is armed with wit and courage will be among the first to celebrate victory.
>
> (Maya Angelou, *Wouldn't Take Nothing For My Journey Now*, 1993)

IN TWELVE YEARS, Mitchell and Klein had probably spent more time together than most couples do in a lifetime. Living, working and travelling together, they had survived intact through the decade of trials and tribulations that was the 1980s, through lawsuits and car crashes, natural disasters and personal ones, Mitchell's health problems (and untrue reports that she was dying of lung cancer), a miscarriage in her late forties and through Klein's own struggle with depression. While they would remain close friends and musical collaborators, their marriage was over. It had been the most enduring romantic relationship of their lives. With a handful of songs written for the new album, they began recording in early 1993. Within days, the couple separated at Joni's instigation:

> My main criterion is, am I good for this man? If at a certain point, I feel I'm causing him more problems than growth, then if he doesn't have the sense to get out, I have to kick him out! The 'Mr Mitchell' thing of course is prevalent . . . I started in the business kind of ultra-feminine, but as I went along I had to handle so many tough situations for myself – had to be both male and

female to myself. So it takes a specific kind of man who wants a strong, independent woman. Klein did, but at the same time there were things about living with 'Joni Mitchell' – not with me – that pinched on his life in a certain way that made me think he needed a break. Our separation, I think, was wholesome – painful and occasionally a little mean, but never nasty or ugly.

Although, years later, she would say, 'When I married Larry Klein he was a bass player, but inside our marriage he became a producer. Then he started hanging around in my sessions and that's the main reason why we divorced', there was never any question of abandoning recording together for the new album. Their working partnership appeared creative and strong and they maintained co-production credits on what would become *Turbulent Indigo*. Larry Klein:

> I don't even have to say it was a difficult record to do. Although we certainly never were really acrimonious toward each other and there was never any hatred or that extreme thing that happens with people when they split up, there was a lot of tension and certainly it was a very intense, emotional period for both of us. So the record was a pearl to come out of an extraordinarily difficult time in both our lives. Also, we knew it was possible that it might be the last time we worked together on a record in that kind of way, where we're in a studio for months [together].

Although most of the songs were written after their separation, there is little blood on the tracks, beyond the regretful 'Last Chance Lost'. Mitchell has said that the relatively gentle nature of the break-up left no gaping wounds that needed healing in song, so it did not become a topic for her writing. But there is a more melancholic and reflective air about this album; there are no joyful love songs, no passionate celebrations of romance. In its sadness it may also have won back some of the fans who had been hankering for a return to the Joni-as-Therapy-Session of the old days. The social commentary was as forceful as that of *Dog Eat Dog* only this time the predators were often closer to home, not the government or state decision-makers, or the corporate sharks in their high-rise offices, or the evangelists on the television screen. The guilty ones were in the street outside, or one's own home and workplace or down at the local swimming pool. They were people in positions of trust – lovers, lawyers, doctors, clergy. And their victims were invariably women.

The most powerful songs are the ones in which Mitchell speaks for brutalised women – a stance she took even while still insisting on a disavowal of feminism. 'The Magdalene Laundries' was inspired by a newspaper article she'd read about an institution run by Roman Catholic nuns in Ireland. After their land was sold, graves were discovered there with only simple markings, 'Magdalene of the Sorrows' or 'Magdalene of the Tears'. The women buried there had simply not merited their real names; all were considered to be versions of the Biblical harlot, Mary Magdalene – 'fallen' women, unmarried mothers or simply unruly girls who were forced to live there and work off their sins scrubbing other people's clothes. There was no attempt to emulate Jesus' humanity towards the original Magdalene. Joni's own experiences as a pregnant and poor young woman added poignancy to the lyrics: 'I could identify because when I was pregnant and looking for an institution to hide away in, I went to places like the Salvation Army and I was refused.'

The accusatory 'Not To Blame' took shape after Joni met a number of women over several months in Canada who had all suffered violence at the hands of a husband or lover. The song was to be her most controversial – many interpreted the lyrics as referring specifically to Jackson Browne, with whom she had been involved more than twenty years earlier. Browne's often troubled relationship with actress Daryl Hannah had ended in 1992 after she accused him of beating her, an allegation he denied. Mitchell told journalists that the song was not about him but rather about any number of men but Browne continued to assert equally adamantly that it *was*. He cited numerous passages that he believed were direct references to Hannah's allegations, his social activism and his wife's suicide and in turn accused Mitchell of hitting him twice during their affair in the early 1970s and dismissed her as nothing more than a woman scorned:

> Joni Mitchell is not really well. At this point in her life,
> she has deep fallings out with many people in her life.
> She's not a happy person, and what she says is
> absolutely, one hundred per cent wrong. And it's really
> very nasty ... very bad spirited of her to make this
> kind of conjecture when in fact as she and every one of
> her friends knows ... it's all about carrying a torch for
> twenty years.

The whole debate about 'is it Jackson, isn't it Jackson' hijacked
attention away from the subject at the core of the song – bat-
tered women – and meant that an opportunity to acknowledge
an enormous social problem was lost. (The opportunity would
reappear, in the US at least, when O.J. Simpson later went on
trial for the murder of his wife, Nicole.)

There is no doubt, however, about the presence on *Turbulent
Indigo* of another former beau, David Crosby. He and Mitchell
co-wrote 'Yvette in English'. She explained the process to
singer/songwriter Stephen Bishop in his book *Songs in the
Rough*:

> The only reason I [wrote] with Crosby was because he
> was making his record and he wanted me to produce
> him. I didn't want to produce him. He wanted me to
> co-write with him, but I didn't have any ideas. [He
> asked] Did I have any songs that I hadn't recorded?
> No, I didn't. So then he said, 'If I fax you this, will
> you look at it?' So I looked at it, and there were some
> good lines in it, but it needed structure, rhymes.
> There was just a premise and a little bit of language.
> The amazing thing was, with the little bit of stimula-
> tion he gave, that thing was done in a couple of days.
> I took what he had and I paraphrased it a lot ... and
> then I gave her a name – Yvette.

Crosby's version appeared on his 1993 album, *Thousand Roads*.

On the title track of *Turbulent Indigo*, Joni had invoked the spirit
of Vincent van Gogh to help fight attitudes she'd encountered when
asked to address a high-profile conference on arts education, held
in Saskatoon. The Canadian Conference of the Arts had called the

summit 'Educating Van Gogh' – artists, administrators, teachers, academics, writers and bureaucrats discussed how to create creators. But how do you make an artist? Mitchell's view, based on her own experience and arts education, was simple: discouragement. That, she believed, was the key: 'Discouragement makes artists flourish. You need just a little bit of encouragement to keep you from slashing your wrists . . . '

That opinion may have taken some of the 175 delegates by surprise, given the prevailing emphasis on the importance of affirmative action programmes and giving students access to art. But if exposure were all, Mitchell argued, everyone in Florence would be an artist. She spoke passionately and spontaneously about how she believed artists are created – the artist is born, not made; the artist embraces the irrational and the mystical, feeling a compulsion to create, no matter what the obstacles. She urged Canadians to get over their sense of cultural inferiority, saying it had taken her years to get the same chip off her shoulder.

She told the audience that her fellow Canadian, the rocker Bryan Adams, had once said to her, 'I can't believe you come from Saskatoon.' Why shouldn't she come from Saskatoon? She was frustrated at the delegates' well-intentioned plans to 'make Van Goghs out of women, native Canadians and other ethnic groups', and argued that artists could not be created by government decree in that way. Many in the audience were young enough to know her music and were possibly even fans. Others, mainly the visual artists, were not so impressed; some left the room conspicuously while she was speaking, for urgent deliberations in the bar. In the song, she railed against the production-line artistry that gets the bureaucrats' seal of approval: 'You wanna make Van Goghs, Raise 'em up like sheep . . . Make 'em nice and normal, Make 'em nice and neat . . . ' The title refers to what she described as the 'turbulent blues of this warring, frenzied climate that we live in, riddled with plagues and wars and divisionalism'.

Writing about the conference, a *Toronto Globe and Mail* reporter, Liam Lacey, speculated that the artists were perhaps irritated by Mitchell's confidence that she was a serious painter as well as a musician: 'They did not need a rich pop star who left the country twenty years ago to rehash clichés about the Canadian inferiority complex . . . What does Joni Mitchell know about surviving as a Canadian artist today?' Lacey and a friend next saw

Mitchell at Calgary airport when she was on her way back to Los Angeles. His friend commented, 'I'm glad you're back', referring to the recent release of *Night Ride Home*. Mitchell said simply, 'But I never left. You did.'

Inspiration for other new songs was just as varied. On the last day of the 1992 riots in Los Angeles, Mitchell had stopped at traffic lights when she noticed the licence plate of the long white limo in front; it said JUST ICE. She sat there seeing the word 'justice' transformed into something chilling – and the observation became the opening of the song 'Sex Kills'. The song sprawls across social and legal justice and finds it lacking, into society's ambivalent obsession with sex –'Sex sells everything, And sex kills' – and the incidental rage that permeates modern life. That rage is reflected in 'Borderline', where the sharp edges of envy, cruelty and intolerance only serve to carve boundaries of all kinds – whether in relationships, gender, nationalities or the arts.

Mitchell included one cover on the album, the James Brown song 'How Do You Stop' – with backing vocals by Seal – because, she said, there weren't a lot of good 'middle-age' songs around. 'How Do You Stop' is a cautionary tale about chasing success and novelty at the expense of love. The album ends with the epic 'The Sire of Sorrow (Job's Sad Song)', based on the Old Testament Book of Job. It's a painful anthem of disappointment, betrayal and undeserved punishment. After her experiences throughout the 80s, Mitchell had earned the right to ask 'What have I done to you, That you make everything I dread and everything I fear come true?'

Mitchell's guitar and keyboards were sounding stronger than they had in years. Klein played bass and guest players included Wayne Shorter on sax, drummers Jim Keltner and Carlos Vega and guitarists Steuart Smith and Michael Landau. Recording finished long before the album was released. Mitchell had decided that she did not want to stay until the end of her contract with Geffen Records; she described it as a 'slavery with tenure' deal. She and Geffen do not agree on the specifics of who said what to whom and why, but suffice to say, it was eventually agreed that she could leave. Joni returned to the company that had first signed her in the late 60s, Warner Brothers' label Reprise, which released *Turbulent Indigo* in October 1994.

The reviews were some of the best she'd had in a very long time. Timothy White wrote in *Billboard* that it was 'one of the most commanding statements of a peerless seventeen-album career that has itself questioned most accepted precepts in popular music'. *Rolling Stone* described it as 'Mitchell's best album since the mid-70s and a work that is highly musical, poetic and very, very sad'. *Acoustic Guitar* declared it 'a masterpiece of instrumental understatement that ranks as some of the most haunting work of her career'. But in *Stereo Review,* Alanna Nash wrote, 'Sombre, disillusioned and fatalistic in middle age, the Joni Mitchell of today sounds like the embittered mother of the dreamy Joni Mitchell of yesteryear.' The album peaked at 47 on the US chart. Woody Allen declared it one of his favourite albums of the year: 'It's one of those records that hardly anyone talked about, but I thought it was great.'

The album cover, a self-portrait, showed Mitchell in a homage to Van Gogh, modelled on his *Self-Portrait with Bandaged Ear*. In December 1888, Vincent had severed part of his right ear and offered it as a gift to a prostitute. Within a month, before the wound was even healed, he had painted the self-portrait. Van Gogh committed suicide a little over a year later. Mitchell's take on the cover was a dark joke at her own expense: the tortured artist, unappreciated and undervalued until it's too late. She expanded the joke by including tiny paper ears in 500 CDs; when the packaging was opened, the ear fell out. She had wanted to have tin ears in 10,000 CD cases but it was too expensive. Joel Bernstein says it was vintage Mitchell:

> I love stuff like that where she's tweaking – as she is in the song – this serious art education establishment. Would she love to be Van Gogh? Of course. Would she say that she's at that level? Never. In terms of having something that's at least half-humorous, the idea of doing a portrait in emulation of or as a parody of an Old Master's work, of a famous piece that also means something to her, has a kind of multi-layeredness to it that she would enjoy.

A number of Mitchell's paintings – including an endearing one of Larry Klein nuzzling one of their cats – were also used as album artwork. The *Turbulent Indigo* launch party was held at the Ruth Bloom Art Gallery in Santa Monica, where several of Mitchell's paintings were put on display.

Turbulent Indigo was later nominated for two Grammys – for Best Pop Album and in an artwork category. In early 1996, it won both. Larry Klein says the competition from more commercial pop artists was so strong that a win seemed out of the question:

> Both of us felt like there was not a chance in hell that we were going to win anything because we were up against records that sold more and certainly artists who were so high profile, Madonna and Annie Lennox. Particularly in the Best Pop Album category, all the records sold at least twice what we had sold and in most cases exponentially more. So neither of us expected to win and it was quite a surprise and really a very touching thing for both of us. It did feel like a vindication because we had been making these records together for years at that point and for one reason or another, [they] would come out and attract a certain amount of attention, but in the record business, on one level people don't take notice unless something sells a million copies and certainly none of those records had done that. Joni had continued her way of being relentless and uncompromising in making the record that reflected how she felt, with no concessions towards singles and radio [but] the price for that often is not being able to feel the impact of a record in terms of the mass public appeal and the kind of frenzy that accompanies a record selling a million copies.

It was Mitchell's first Grammy since 1975, and a much-needed affirmation after years of feeling neglected, undervalued and invisible. By the time *Turbulent Indigo* came out, it had been ten years since her last full tour. Her promotion for the past three albums had been reliant on interviews, the occasional concert guest appearance and infrequent video releases. Her recurring health problems ruled out a major tour – she still suffered from post-polio syndrome, allergies, and throat problems – the latter being a legacy of bleeding lesions which she says were finally cured by a mystic healer. But she did make several appearances to promote *Turbulent Indigo* in the months before and after its release.

In May 1994 she travelled to Japan for the three-day Great Music Experience concert, the first of a planned international series of such events especially staged for global TV broadcast. It was held in Nara, once the country's ancient capital, and home to the eighth-century Todaiji temple – at ten storeys high, the largest wooden structure in the world. Also appearing were Bob Dylan, INXS, the Chieftains, Ry Cooder, Jon Bon Jovi, Wayne Shorter and a host of Japanese musicians. Japanese and Western performers were encouraged to jam and perform together. When asked about a possible contradiction between the staging of a Western-style rock gig and the sacred nature of the Buddhist site, Mitchell – who has an interest in Buddhism – said, 'This temple has always been the site of festival. When it opened 1,300 years ago, musicians from all over Japan, China and Korea gathered to play together. We're part of that tradition.'

Accompanied by Wayne Shorter and a Japanese flute player, her set included 'Sex Kills', 'The Magdalene Laundries', 'The Crazy Cries Of Love' – co-written with her new boyfriend, Donald Freed – and 'Hejira'. She joined Dylan and the other artists for 'I Shall Be Released' as the finale. On the third night, Joni and Dylan shared a microphone and that was the segment chosen for broadcast, as Mitchell recalls:

> If you look closely at it, you can see the little brat, he's up in my face – and he never brushes his teeth so his breath is like . . . right in my face – and he's mouthing the words at me like a prompter, and he's pushing me off the mike. It's like he's basically dipping my pigtail in ink. The press picked up on it and said, 'Bobby smiles!' Yeah, sure, because he was having a go at me up there.

Games aside, their mutual respect for each other and the unique nature of their roles in the evolution of popular music have made them friends. Just before they were both due to travel to Japan for the concert, Dylan had phoned Joni at home. In the course of the conversation, he said, 'I forgot how to *sing* – but I remember now. The trouble is they want me to do all these Bob Dylan songs – and they're so heavy.'

That summer, Mitchell turned down an invitation to play at the Woodstock 94 concert celebrating the 25th anniversary of the original festival, describing the event as a silly idea. She went to Canada instead and headlined the Edmonton Folk Festival, playing to an audience that included her parents and several elderly relatives who'd never seen her perform before. Introducing her new songs, she told the crowd:

> One of every two women in North America is raped. I'm not a feminist – believe me, I've been with the boys all my life. But it makes you wonder if it was always that way or is something accelerating. That [the] O.J. [Simpson case] should come up in the middle of this is kind of symbolic.

During a promotional stop in Toronto, she did a showcase for the Canadian music-video channel, Much Music. The channel waived its no-smoking policy and supplied quantities of warming sake, to help Joni feel at ease. The format of the 'I and I' – 'Intimate and Interactive' – show was of a live performance, interspersed with questions from the audience and the viewers. One young boy phoned and said in pure Canadian-ese to everyone's delight, 'Joni, thanks for the music, eh?' A woman phoned to ask whether Joni was proud to be a Canadian. The answer appeared to show some ambivalence when Mitchell said, 'The cold (Canadian) winters and Scottish and Irish blood create an emotionally withholding people.'

She introduced a number of songs with background and anecdotes – 'Sex Kills', 'Moon At The Window', 'The Magdalene Laundries', 'Cherokee Louise', 'Hejira', 'Night Ride Home', 'The Crazy Cries Of Love' and 'Just Like This Train'. Before singing 'Facelift', she talked about the complexities of the mother–daughter relationship; the song is based on an argument with her mother, after Mitchell and Freed had stayed in a Saskatoon hotel together. Joni's mother, Myrtle, had introduced her to Freed, the son of a family friend, but Myrtle felt uncomfortable about her not-yet-divorced daughter being in a new relationship. Mitchell had written the song to reassure her mother that being happy was the most important thing, that 'happiness is the best facelift'. Before singing it in the TV studio, she said, 'Mama, if you're listening tonight, I love you so much.' Her parents, both in their eighties, were watching the programme and were not best pleased; they felt she'd embarrassed them in front of millions – smoking, singing songs with swearwords in them. The comments about Canada may also have smarted; Mitchell's mother is of Irish-Scots descent. At 51, their only child was still young enough to get a good telling-off.

In November, Joni travelled to London to perform a solo showcase for the media and record company staff, and do some TV appearances. Before singing 'Yvette in English', she told the showcase audience that David Crosby 'is fading away in a Los Angeles hospital waiting for a liver transplant. Spare a thought for our David. It will take somebody else's catastrophe to save him.' Crosby underwent surgery that day and made a good recovery. A couple of months later, Joni did a similar showcase at the Gene Autry Western Hermitage Museum in Los Angeles; she decorated the tiny stage area with some of her paintings. The hour-long solo acoustic performance was broadcast live on national radio and ranged over twenty years of songs from 'Just Like This Train' (*Court and Spark*) to the new 'Facelift'. The *Rolling Stone* writer David Wild, in a review of the show, said 'Mitchell demonstrated why we're lucky she's still among us, artistically speaking: She's a songwriter *and* a singer of subtlety and expressiveness.' In conclusion, he wrote, 'Maybe next year the Rock and Roll Hall of Fame will finally get the message.'

The Rock and Roll Hall of Fame and Museum was set up in Cleveland, Ohio, to honour the great and the good of the genre – the catch-all categories of performers, non-performers and 'sidemen' ensure that everyone from the legends to the record company executives to the rock writers to the radio jocks to the managers to the studio technicians are in with a chance. The Hall of Fame foundation declared, 'Criteria considered includes the influence and significance of the artist's contribution to the development and perpetuation of rock and roll.' In October 1993 Mitchell was nominated for inclusion in the Rock Pantheon – under Hall of Fame rules an artist is eligible for nomination 25 years after their first record is released. It was the first year she had qualified, but her name was dropped after her nomination failed to get sufficient backing from the voting panel. There was considerable surprise that Mitchell's work and influence had not been deemed to be important enough – Joni herself suspected the hand of her one-time foe, *Rolling Stone* publisher Jann Wenner, a senior figure in the foundation. She'd been deeply hurt by the magazine's 'Old Lady of The Year' jibes in the early 70s and subsequently believed that it had adopted an anti-Joni policy. She has appeared in the magazine's annual 'worst of' polls, but to be fair to *Rolling Stone*, many of its writers have treated her respectfully and championed her work over the years.

The snub delivered by the Hall of Fame selectors was softened somewhat by the announcement by *Billboard* in March 1995 that it was honouring Joni Mitchell with its annual Century Award. Paying tribute to her, the editor-in-chief of the magazine, Timothy White, said:

> The sole aim of the award is to acknowledge the uncommon excellence of one artist's still-unfolding body of work ... the award focuses on those singular musicians who have not been accorded the degree of serious homage their achievements deserve.

Highlighting Mitchell's influence beyond the singer-songwriter genre, White said:

> We can think of no artist more deserving than Joni Mitchell ... in folk and blues, in jazz, in world music, and in every alternative that one must find to arrive at rock and roll, she has taken humanity's most noble strivings and made them intimate for each of us.

White had unintentionally highlighted a great irony of timing – Joni had already decided that her forthcoming appearance at the New Orleans Jazz and Heritage Festival would be her swansong. Wearied by the prospect of further diminishing emotional and financial returns the longer she stayed in the industry, she'd decided that now was the time to do what she'd been promising herself for so long – leave it all behind and devote herself to her painting. To use the imagery from 'For The Roses', the music business got out the hammer and the nails and the board one too many times. She'd even approached the producers of one of her favourite television shows, the brilliant and gently anarchic *Northern Exposure*, to suggest a storyline idea: she would appear in a cameo role, as herself, stopping in Cicely, Alaska – the fictional town where the series was set – having abandoned the music business and Los Angeles.

For all her frustrations with the industry, there were technical reasons too for it all to have become so wearing: her huge range of tunings always complicated live performances, given that it's impractical to change tunings for every song or two, and too expensive always to have several guitars and guitar technicians waiting in the wings for each change. But when her good friend Graham Nash introduced her to his new guitar, a custom-made prototype – 'Look, luv, I have this computer guitar and I've got 200 tunings in it' – she was smitten. Nash said, 'When they make it for acoustic guitars, luv, I'm going to get you one.'

Mitchell decided not to wait; she went to Fred Walecki, of Westwood Music in Los Angeles, who had been making guitars for her since she'd first arrived in the city. She told him what she needed. A week before the New Orleans festival in May, he phoned to say he'd built a prototype electric guitar, a modified Stratocaster hooked up to a Roland VG-8 computer processor that would store all of her tunings and provide an encyclopaedic range of guitar sounds. The new guitar was put to the test for the first time on the stage in New Orleans and by the time she'd got through ten songs without a single tuning problem – an unprecedented feat compared to the way conventional guitars struggled with her tunings – Joni was converted and has used it ever since. The experience helped to persuade her that giving music another chance may just be worth the gamble.

Come summertime, the radio airwaves were dominated by born-again Christian pop singer Amy Grant's cover version of 'Big Yellow Taxi'; by autumn, Reprise had released a soundtrack album from the TV series *Friends* that included a radical reworking of BYT, with Mitchell's original vocal set to a hip-hop beat. She produced the new version. Joni's growing relevance for a much younger generation of musicians and fans was also underscored when she was interviewed by Tool vocalist Maynard Keenan, for *Hypno* magazine. They compared chord changes, discussed the writing process and Keenan's affection for her song 'Black Crow'. Another young musician, drummer Brian Blade – who was soon to work with Mitchell – had discovered her music in 1986. Then 16, he'd been wooed by *Hejira* then *Mingus* and started to collect all of her albums:

It's a tribute to her. Anything that's so emotionally and intellectually strong and so strong in terms of conveying

experiences is going to stand the test of time for any generation. Her experiences, or what she writes about, will
strike across your life, no matter who [you are] or when
you receive it; it's going to get you.

Blade and Mitchell got to know each other through their mutual
friend, Daniel Lanois, who had played Joni some of the tracks that
he'd recorded with Blade. Impressed with the drummer's work,
she phoned him and told him so. They built up a friendship during several more phone calls and when Mitchell's thoughts turned
to another album, she asked Blade to come out to Los Angeles to
work with her in her home studio. He returned several times over
the next year or so, as the album took shape. Their first public gig
together was in New York in early November, where they performed a brief set at a dinner in honour of the cartoonist Garry
Trudeau. The following day, Joni decided that she, Blade and the
VG-8 still had plenty of musical energy left over – so she called a
small downtown club, the Fez, and asked to play there that night.
With no advertising beyond a brief plug on a local radio station,
the impromptu show attracted a sell-out crowd of almost two hundred people, among them Chrissie Hynde, Carly Simon, Victoria
Williams and Natalie Merchant. As Mitchell – who was about to
celebrate her 52nd birthday – made her way to the small stage,
Hynde bellowed encouragement, 'Let it out, Joni!'

Mitchell introduced one song by saying that the caretaker at
her house in Canada had said to her, 'Joni, I know you're not sad
like you are in your songs all the time. Write me something different.' She'd sat on a rock and tried to tune her guitar to the
sound of squawking birds near the sea – it didn't work; no happy
songs came. The song that did come was anything but cheerful:
'The Magdalene Laundries'. The mood at the Fez was buoyant, as
Blade recalls:

> We were just winging it, it was great! She'd just got the
> new guitar and she was so into the fact that she would-
> n't have to go through so many tuning changes. With
> just a cursor, you could go to another tuning. We would
> go through an index of songs, and she'd go to the next
> song and see what the tuning was and say, 'Let's try
> this.' We just played songs for I don't know how long.

The celebratory mood turned a little sour when numerous high-spirited if somewhat distracting interjections from La Hynde prompted Carly Simon to ask her to keep the noise down. Hynde took umbrage and allegedly grabbed Simon by the throat and, gesturing towards the stage, hissed 'That's a *real* singer up there!' Simon left, shaken but not stirred, and the evening ended with everyone singing 'Happy Birthday, Joni'. When the web-zine Addicted to Noise asked Hynde's record company, Warner Brothers, to comment on the incident, a publicist confirmed that there had been some sort of physical contact but said Chrissie had simply been showing her affection for Carly Simon: 'Yeah, she grabbed her around the neck but she was just hugging her.'

There were no such shenanigans in December, when Peter Gabriel presented Mitchell with the *Billboard* Century Award for outstanding artistic achievement. He told the audience:

> I'm here to honour one of the very few artists I believe has been a real pioneer . . . She has continuously and courageously experimented, putting substance before style, passion before packaging . . . She's been a major influence on my work as she has on so many other artists as diverse as Seal, Madonna, Sting, Natalie Merchant, Annie Lennox, and the Artist Formerly Known as the Artist Formerly Known As.

In her acceptance speech, Mitchell said:

> I've been thinking a lot about arrogance and humility, trying to find some genuine humility to bring to this situation. But I feel like I'm emerging from the McCarthy era in a certain way. I never thought of it as difficult being a woman in this industry, but it has been pointed out to me in the last few days how few women there really were, and there were some strikes against us from the beginning.

Her comments had particular relevance to the evening's events: a brief film, shown as part of the award ceremony, detailed high-lights of Mitchell's career and there was a tribute from Graham Nash and David Crosby in which they mused about their trip to

Woodstock – and how Joni had written her famous song after listening to their impressions. Mitchell was furious that they'd presented the episode in this way, given that she'd written the song after watching TV coverage of the festival and played it to them when they got back. For a moment once again she was 'the girl of the family' who had been told by David Geffen and Elliot Roberts to stay behind while the 'boys' went off and had all the fun and all the adventures.

The Century Award became the gunshot that set off the avalanche; a slew of accolades followed. Mitchell and Klein were at the Grammys ceremony in February 1996 to pick up their two awards; at the podium Joni said, 'Gee, Klein ... considering we made this album in a state of divorce ...' Her thankyous extended to their cats. Klein, for his part, thanked her for 'ten years of instruction in the arts'. The recognition that Mitchell felt had so often been withheld from her work became something of a growth industry. Sweden announced that she was to be the first woman to receive the Polar Music Prize for her outstanding achievements in music. The £100,000 award was presented to her on 8 May by King Carl Gustav. Brian Blade, who was touring Europe with Joshua Redman, came to Sweden to attend the ceremony. With Blade backing her on drums, Mitchell played two songs at the ceremony, 'The Magdalene Laundries' and 'Just Like This Train'.

Amid all the attention, Reprise had released two anthology CDs: *Hits*, a chronicle of classics including 'Both Sides, Now', 'Woodstock', 'Help Me', 'The Circle Game', 'Big Yellow Taxi', 'Free Man in Paris', 'You Turn Me On, I'm a Radio' – and for the first time on an official release, 'Urge for Going'. And just as Devo had done on Warner Brothers six years earlier with their *Greatest Hits* and *Greatest Misses* albums, *Misses* was released at Mitchell's insistence. There were some quirky choices among songs that came primarily from the period following the mid-70s *Court and Spark* era. Most – including 'A Case of You', 'For the Roses', 'Hejira', 'Dog Eat Dog', 'The Wolf That Lives in Lindsey' and 'Sex Kills' – had been buried under a landslide of constant comparisons to her work of the past. The release of *Misses* was delayed slightly when Joni asked for two tracks, 'Car on a Hill' and 'The Windfall', to be replaced. She described *Misses* as her 'songs of experience, as opposed to the younger songs on the

Hits'. The latter peaked at 161 on the US Top 200 chart; *Misses* didn't make the list.

Over a three-year period, she picked up awards, honours and placings in polls that are too numerous to mention – a tiny selection includes the US National Academy of Songwriters Lifetime Achievement Award; the ASCAP Founders Award; the Orville H. Gibson Guitar Award for 'best female acoustic guitar'; inducted into the Songwriters Hall of Fame; the Governor-General's Performing Arts Award, the highest honour conferred upon Canadian performers; Canada's equivalent of the US Emmy television awards, the Geminis, went to Mitchell for best performance in a performing arts programme, for the Much Music show; the Saskatchewan Recording Industry Association presented Saskatoon's favourite daughter with a Lifetime Achievement award. Of the numerous music press awards and polls of varying import, Mitchell was named by *Mojo* as one of the 100 Greatest Singers of All Time (at number 19) and among the Hot 100 Guitarists (at 77); Q declared *Clouds* to be one of the Best Blonde Albums of All Time and *The Hissing of Summer Lawns* among the Best Summer Albums of All Time.

Eventually, even the Rock and Roll Hall of Fame relented and, in 1997, Mitchell joined the ranks of inductees. She had been eligible to join for four years but had been left waiting in the wings. Being made to feel second-best had echoes of an award she'd won years earlier as a teenager in the late 1950s: she'd entered a contest to become Teenage Queen of Saskatoon, which was part of a campaign to promote Johnny Cash's new single, 'Ballad of a Teenage Queen', and his Canadian tour. To qualify, each contestant had to buy a copy of the single; the judges made their decision and Cash crowned the winner during his concert in each town. However, sadly, the Teenage Queen of Saskatoon died before receiving her crown and Cash instead bestowed the honour on the runner-up, Joan Anderson.

Forty years later, her fellow Year of 97 classmates in the Performer category were the Bee Gees, Buffalo Springfield, Crosby, Stills and Nash, the Jackson Five, Parliament/ Funkadelic and the Young Rascals. Mitchell did not attend the televised induction ceremony, citing work and family reasons, but she was also angry at the Hall of Fame for excluding her in the past – and for the exorbitant cost of the ticket prices charged by the ceremony organisers, for her family and close friends to attend the event with her. Her feelings were shared by Neil Young, who was being inducted as part of Buffalo Springfield. He'd been involved in past ceremonies, inducting Woody Guthrie, the Everly Brothers and the Jimi Hendrix Experience, but on this occasion he too was affronted that the organisers were charging $1,500 a ticket. At those prices, Young apparently calculated that it would cost him $25,000 to attend and, outraged at the commercialism of the event, he sent a fax to the Rock and Roll Hall of Fame declining to attend. He acknowledged that he was proud that Buffalo Springfield was being inducted and proud to be associated with the early days of the Hall of Fame:

> During those days the Hall was for musicians and record people, producers and writers of music that changed my life ... we all knew why we were there. We came to celebrate and be celebrated, free to mingle with our own and say what we pleased. That was the real Rock and Roll Hall of Fame. It could not be contained by any building. Today it is a VH1 show, edited for television and the adult contemporary market served by VH1. Cheapened forever ... The VH1 Hall of Fame presentation has nothing to with the spirit of rock and roll. It has everything to do with making money ... At over a thousand dollars a seat, many of the inductees cannot even afford to bring the family members they would like to accompany them ... I decline to take part in this presentation and be trotted out like some cheap awards show ...

Young's other former bandmates from CSN&Y did appear; Stephen Stills, a double-inductee that night, performed with David Crosby and Graham Nash. It was Nash who accepted Mitchell's award on her behalf and presented it to her in Los Angeles almost a year later. He made the presentation during a small invitation-only concert that was being filmed for a television special and the video release, *Joni Mitchell – Painting with Words and Music*. Just as Joni was introducing the song 'Woodstock', Nash came down from his seat and interrupted her. He told the audience:

I've had the privilege and pleasure of knowing Joan for
over thirty years. The night I first met her I knew then
when she played me twelve of the greatest songs I've
ever heard in my life, I knew that this woman was an
incredible talent, and she had an incredible talent to
touch people's hearts with her art, her poetry and her
music. She did not get into music, I assure you, to win
awards – millions of men's hearts, maybe – but not
awards . . .

Nash spoke about the Rock and Roll Hall of Fame induction ceremony, at which point Mitchell commented, to laughter from
the audience, 'I was a no-show!' Nash continued diplomatically,
'But you had your reasons and I'm sure they were all fine,' and
handed her the award, partially wrapped in a plastic bag – it was
in two pieces after being dropped accidentally, by someone
who'd picked it up to admire it earlier. He apologised for the bag,
to which Joni replied laughing, 'It's perfect in a garbage bag!'
The exchange was a warm and good-natured one and, thanks to
their long friendship, still managed to seem spontaneous and fun
even though, as Nash says:

She did know that I was going to present her with the
Hall of Fame award and wanted me to give it to her
during the show and also wanted me to leave it in the
plastic bag that I had it in. She is a strange and wonderful woman!

Given the renewed glare of media attention, it was perhaps
inevitable that stories would start appearing about Mitchell's
daughter. There had been a scattering over the years – from
the *Sunday Times* in the early 80s, which did not sensationalise
the issue, to the US tabloids which did, under headlines like
'Songbird Joni Searches For Love Child She Had At 19'. A
room-mate from her Toronto art school days had sold the
story. Even Joni's ex-husband, Chuck, was asked for his views
on her search for the child she'd had a few months before
they'd met. Although their marriage had ended more than
thirty years earlier, there was a trace of bitterness in Chuck
Mitchell's reply:

It's good for her to pay attention to the loose ends in her life, because she left a lot behind. But I don't think she regrets what she did – a baby would have got in her way. That's because she's very ambitious, very calculating and very self-centred – so was I. I became excess baggage for her . . . it was really hard for me. I'd waited a long time to get married. This was it. I felt, 'What's wrong with me?' and had phases of resentment and anger. But gradually this faded.

Joni herself began to talk openly in the media about her longing to find out what had happened to the child she'd had to give up:

Having a baby that nobody knew about has been playing on my mind for more than thirty years and it's been sheer hell. I'm just glad I've spoken about it at last because it means I have no skeletons in the closet any more – I'm clean. But I still can't help wondering what my daughter looks like. There's so much I need to tell her.

For so many years, Joni had been asked in interviews why she'd never had a baby or whether she ever planned to have children and her responses had always been protectively evasive, unless faced with blunt questioning from reporters who'd picked up the trail from her songs. As the news of her search became public, the local paper in Saskatoon ran a cartoon of Mitchell, strumming her acoustic guitar and singing, 'You don't know what you've got til it's gone . . . pick up a phone and give your old lady a call!' A newspaper in Calgary – where Mitchell had become pregnant – ran the story under a parochial headline that declared, 'Alberta native gave up daughter'.

At the same time as Joni Mitchell was looking for her daughter, Kilauren Gibb was looking for her mother. Strict confidentiality laws regarding adoption initially thwarted them both. The child Joni had named Kelly was adopted at the age of six months by a Toronto couple, David and Ida Gibb. They had renamed her Kilauren Andrea Christy. Gifted and accomplished as a child, she was educated at private schools, and as a teenager became a successful model. At the age of 27, pregnant with her son Marlin, she began the five-year search for the woman who'd given birth

to her. Adoption records gave just enough details to be intriguing
but not enough to be truly informative: birthdates and physical
characteristics; the bout of childhood polio; the woman's father
had run a grocery business, her mother had once been a teacher;
the woman herself had been a folk-singer from Saskatchewan
who had moved to the United States.

Synchronicity moves in mysterious ways: in one part of town,
Kilauren had too little information; in another, a woman she was
soon to meet had just enough. Annie Mandlsohn's boyfriend
introduced her to Kilauren Gibb; getting to know each other,
Kilauren had told her about her search for her birth-mother and
showed her the scant information from the adoption paperwork.
Years earlier, Mandlsohn had been told by a friend that Joni
Mitchell had had a baby when she was a young woman but that
it was a well-kept secret. When she heard about Kilauren's
efforts, she said, 'Your mother is Joni Mitchell!'

Searching the Internet, Gibb found the official Joni Mitchell
website, and going through the biographical information, discovered more than a dozen similarities with the details from the adoption agency's paperwork. She contacted the creator of the site,
Wally Breese, who encouraged her to get in touch with Mitchell's
management company. Initially sceptical, Joni's managers – who
had been inundated with queries from prospective 'daughters' –
became convinced of Kilauren's credibility after seeing copies of
the agency paperwork, and hearing her voice. It was almost identical to Joni Mitchell's. Soon after, Gibb arrived home one day to
find a message on her telephone answering-machine. It said, 'Hi,
it's Joni. Please call me. I'm here. I'm overwhelmed.'

Mitchell asked her to fax some photographs of herself as a baby;
when she received them, it was clear that Kilauren was the same
child as in photographs that she had been given years earlier by
a woman who had briefly fostered the baby. She sent first-class
air tickets for Kilauren and her young son to come out and visit
her; they spent almost three weeks together, getting to know each
other. Mitchell admitted, 'I've had joy and pain in my life but nothing like this. It's an unparalleled emotional feeling.' Kilauren
described their reunion as 'a great relief to me in every way. It
made me feel whole. It made me feel complete. I don't have any
expectations. I didn't come into this thing with expectations, I just
wanted to find my Mom.' Just as chance and coincidence had

contributed to the mother and daughter reunion, so Gibb later met her birth-father, Brad MacMath, through the same combination. She had been told that he was a photographer. Her boyfriend, Ted Barrington, contacted a photographer acquaintance and asked whether she'd ever heard of MacMath. She had – she was married to him and they ran a Toronto photographic studio together.

The reunion story had tabloid gossip sheets and serious publications alike clamouring for details. It got international coverage and was credited with opening a wider debate about Canada's laws on protecting adoption files. Mitchell's parents, although used to having a famous daughter, were not used to having a reporter stake out their house, or being repeatedly asked to talk about what they felt was a private family matter. Nothing could have prepared the unsuspecting David and Ida Gibb for the media onslaught and there was the initial anxiety of not knowing how their own relationship with Kilauren would be affected. A reporter for the *Toronto Sun*, Liz Braun, wrote:

> For Kilauren Gibb, who spent five years looking for her mother and then had to fax in her adoption papers and wait to get the nod from Mitchell's people, how can this be anything but a lose/lose situation? The worst-case scenario is that it won't work out. The best-case scenario is that everything will work out fine, which leaves Gibb and her three-year-old son free to do nothing but avoid star-seekers and advantage-takers for the rest of their lives.

The enormous media attention only highlighted the pitfalls in living out such a private drama in full view of the public. The respected Canadian weekly news magazine *Macleans* made the reunion a cover story – but when it requested an interview with Kilauren Gibb, Ted Barrington said that he would arrange it for a fee of $10,000. When told that the publication had a policy of not paying for interviews, he said, 'The money's for Kilauren . . . she doesn't have a pot to piss in . . . She's a student right now and she should really be able to profit from this, at least, monetarily.' Later, after speaking with Mitchell's manager, Barrington phoned the magazine and apologised, saying, 'I was out of line. All the good stuff is at the back end with book deals and all that. I'm just worried about Kilauren being exploited.'

After the initial intensity of the reunion and the glare of media attention subsided, the reality of creating new relationships and dealing with the changes to existing ones became clear – only fairy-tales have fairy-tale endings. Real life is much more complicated. Kilauren described the year that followed the reunion as 'very tough'. When asked whether she had reconciled herself to Joni's original decision to give her up, she said, 'That's an issue, a tough issue. It's hard to tread there. I think she really has a guilty feeling about that.' For her part, Joni has said:

> It's been wonderful and . . . oh, it's been everything . . .
> But my daughter is a difficult girl, you know?
> Mother–daughter – it's a very hard relationship, and she's
> going to have to forgive me. There's going to have to be
> a lot of forgiveness before we can really get along. But I
> expected that. I didn't think it would be all roses. Kilauren
> is holding a grudge. It's something she's going to have to
> work through. I can't really help her with it. She's going
> to have to help herself. We'll see what happens.

For all the media feeding frenzy surrounding Mitchell's reunion with her daughter, the publicity did have one positive effect – it highlighted the agonising experience of countless numbers of women and many felt encouraged to bring what had been a source of secret suffering out into the open. Women sent her flowers or wrote to her to say that hearing about her experience had changed their lives. Mitchell's mother found herself listening to intimate stories of guilt and loss, as women confided in her that they had been helped by knowing that her daughter had gone through the same thing.

In the early months following the reunion, spending time with her new family became a priority and kept Mitchell out of her studio and the limelight for weeks at a time. She ventured out, at Larry Klein's urging, to join the Walden Woods benefit concert in Los Angeles, in April 1998. Klein was the musical director of the show which was organised annually by Don Henley. It was a fund-raiser to pay for conservation of the land near Concord, Massachusetts, where the nineteenth-century Transcendentalist poet and author Henry David Thoreau had made his home. Klein and Henley had invited almost a dozen women – including

Mitchell, Bjork, Sheryl Crow, Gwen Stefani, Stevie Nicks and Shawn Colvin – to sing classic songs of the 1930s, 40s and 50s, backed by a full orchestra. On stage at the Wiltern Theater, Bjork introduced Joni by saying, 'These people who organised this are spoiling me. I have the great pleasure of introducing the most "gorgeousest" woman . . . ' Bjork and Mitchell formed an unlikely but engaging duo to sing Cole Porter's 'What Is This Thing Called Love'. Joni sang the Lena Horne classic 'Stormy Weather' and Marvin Gaye's 'Trouble Man' in her solo spot at the end of the evening. She enjoyed the experience so much that she longed to repeat it, to do her own album of standards, working with an orchestra. Two years later, she would.

But for now, the work uppermost in Mitchell's mind was the one she'd started two years earlier. The album *Taming the Tiger* was released in September and, again, it merged veiled autobiography with rage against the machine. Many of Mitchell's fans were eager to see how her fledgling relationship with her daughter would be reflected in her lyrics. In essence, it wasn't; the experience was almost too new to articulate in that way yet and most of the album had been written by the time they were reunited. But one song, 'Stay In Touch' – written after becoming involved with Donald Freed – did have strong echoes of the closeness that was evolving with Kilauren: 'This is really something People will be envious But our roles aren't clear So we mustn't rush . . . ' It was a song written during the thrilling beginnings of a new relationship when the excitement is also tempered with a measure of caution and uncertainty. Joni and Freed had both thrown the I Ching to see whether the Chinese method of predicting the future would have anything to teach them. The song was constructed from a combination of the two readings. The melody was inspired by the Rachmaninoff music she'd loved as a child.

Aspects of the relationship with Freed had inspired other songs on the album – 'Facelift' and 'The Crazy Cries of Love' which Mitchell had performed over the past couple of years. Freed is a singer-songwriter, who travels throughout Saskatchewan holding songwriting workshops for schoolchildren, mainly in isolated areas and First Nations reservations. He'd written the verses to 'The Crazy Cries of Love' after reading about a competition in the *New Yorker* magazine, to write a short

story beginning with the words 'It was a dark and a stormy night
. . . ' He hadn't entered the competition but he had started the
story which became a song. Joni wrote the choruses. When her
mother had first introduced her to Freed he had said, 'How are
you?' she replied, 'Undervalued.' She recalled later that he
looked at her, stunned. The comment was based on her feelings
about how she'd been treated by the music business. They were
addressed again in the song 'Love Puts On a New Face' in which
she despairs to Freed, 'I'm up to my neck in alligators – Jaws
gnashing at me!' The relevance to the music industry and the
hands which hold the purse-strings is emphasised even more
powerfully with the opening words of 'Lead Balloon', directed at
a corporate decision-maker: 'Kiss my ass . . . '. Joni, the non-fem-
inist, reaches an inevitable conclusion: 'An angry man is just an
angry man, But an angry woman . . . Bitch!'

Despite the awards that had rained down on her – many of which
she dismissed as 'copycat crimes', devoid of real honour – the feeling remained that she was not being taken seriously as an artist:

> At the onset [of the record], all I had to work with was a
> ferocious contempt for the record industry, for the busi-
> ness itself. That's all I had in me as a writer. Plus a tremen-
> dous desire for self-respect. [I felt] if I'm in the game but
> not of the game, it's time to get out. I'm not gonna sit
> here all suited up and not be allowed to participate. I've
> done that for twenty years and enough is enough.

The title track of the album encapsulates these feelings,
describing herself as 'a runaway from the record biz From the
hoods in the hood And the whiny white kids Boring!'
Listening to the radio at home, she hears only 'Formula music
Girlie guile Genuine junkfood For juveniles!' She borrows
from William Blake's 'The Tyger' in her tiger/music industry
correlation and again, as the stars 'chuck' down their spears,
she sees a plane in the night sky above and is reminded of
Wayne Shorter's wife, Anna Maria, who was killed in the TWA
air crash in the United States in 1996.

The film director Allison Anders asked Mitchell to write a song
for a scene in her film *Grace of My Heart* in which a character is
feeling profound grief. Joni declined, saying that she didn't write

songs to order – and the only ones on her mind at the time all had the same theme: 'I hate show biz!' Anders told her to write one of those and she'd fit it in somewhere in the film. At the same time, one of Mitchell's beloved cats, Nietzsche, went missing. The cat had taken to peeing on the furniture and one day an exasperated Joni had finally had enough. She picked him up by the stump of the tail and the nape of the neck, and put him outside. The apparently affronted cat disappeared. In the absence of a recent photograph, she spent an evening doing a painting of him, then had it printed up on leaflets which she distributed all around the neighbourhood.

Heartbroken, she wrote a song about the loss and guilt she was experiencing; Allison Anders got her 'grief' theme – 'Man From Mars', a reference to the cat's nickname – with the lines 'There is no centre to my life now, no grace in my heart'. Eighteen days after he disappeared, Mitchell got a call to say the bedraggled feline had turned up in a neighbour's garden. She included the song on *Taming the Tiger*. The album art includes paintings and a photograph of the cat, along with three paintings featuring Donald Freed, 'Edmonton', where he is seen in part-profile, 'Hyde Park' (with his hand on Mitchell's knee) and 'After the Bombing of Dresden', where he is seated at a table reading. There are Mitchell's Canadian landscapes and one of two paintings inspired by her trip to Nara, Japan, 'In the Park of the Golden Buddha'. Those works have special meaning for her because Anna Maria Shorter is one of the people pictured in the background.

Mitchell returned to her musical beginnings with 'Harlem in Havana', written in standard tuning, just as one of her first songs, 'Urge for Going', had been. The song is a memory of a friend in Saskatoon who'd scandalised her family by joining a burlesque musical revue. When the show came to town, the girl gave tickets to Joni and her young friends; they were under-age but got in anyway and were thrilled by the atmosphere of forbidden fun. Larry Klein's bass (one of only three tracks on which he played), Brian Blade's drums and Wayne Shorter's sax are crafted to convey just the right kind of carnival seediness. Mitchell's love affair with her new guitar, its orchestral effects and extraordinary versatility with her computerised tunings is obvious on every track on the album. But just occasionally, when the sound is layered and layered again, it feels almost too perfect, too much like a synthesiser and not enough like an organic instrument that can still surprise.

The social concerns of recent albums were present only on 'No Apologies', a critique that said in essence, 'It's a man's world and they can have it!' The song opens strongly with a reference to the rape of a twelve-year-old Japanese schoolgirl by three US servicemen in Okinawa in 1995, but meanders to an unsatisfactory conclusion of 'that's what little boys are made of . . . ' A world away, the last vocal track is a cover of the old Sons of the Pioneers country and western song, 'My Best to You', a loving farewell wish, with an arrangement and vintage that would be echoed in Mitchell's next album, a collection of standards. An instrumental version of 'Taming the Tiger' – 'Tiger Bones' – closes the album.

The *Washington Post* greeted *Taming the Tiger* with a reference to the Joni clones:

> While female singer-songwriters half her age and with half her talent continue to be touted as 'the new Joni Mitchell', the old Joni Mitchell, now 54, continues to make extraordinary pop music, creating albums full of poetry, passion and opinion . . . Say what you will about *Taming the Tiger*, boring it's not.

In *Q*, Stuart Maconie noted:

> she's never sung better, the clear and precise enunciations now gone nicely husky, she sounds like Elvis Costello's worldly older sister. This is tasteful and distinctive stuff but clearly a bespoke product for grown-ups. A 15-year-old is as likely to possess it as a camel-hair overcoat. Marketing men have to worry about that stuff. Joni Mitchell doesn't.

Time agreed that

> when acts like 'N Sync and Backstreet Boys cavort in the upper reaches of the charts like kids atop a treehouse . . . *Taming the Tiger* is a tough sell . . . But Joni will be Joni when the trends have trended out.

But in a review entitled 'The Dissing of Bummer Songs', *Pulse* declared:

Sticking with the passionless form of chamber pop that she's used throughout the 90s, which relies too rigidly on the brittle combination of heavily treated guitar chords and chilly-sounding synthesiser washes, Mitchell mostly writes from the point of view of a curmudgeonly cynic these days. Her self-righteousness comes across as dour and distant, especially when matched with an austere avoidance of melody.

It peaked at 75 on the US chart.

The tour to support *Taming the Tiger* took place in May, a few months before the album's release. It placed Mitchell in the unaccustomed environment of arena venues but also in good company: Bob Dylan and Van Morrison. The legendary status of all three and the rarity value of such an extraordinary line-up ensured that tickets for the seven-city North American West Coast tour sold out instantly. The tour began on 14 May in the Canadian city of Vancouver and Mitchell's 75 minute set was heavily weighted in favour of her most recent material, from the forthcoming album and *Turbulent Indigo,* with only a scattering of older songs. Each song, however, got a standing ovation, but the crowd saved most of their enthusiasm for her second encore, 'Big Yellow Taxi'. The song had undergone a renaissance since the previous year when Janet Jackson sampled it on her 'Got 'Til It's Gone' single. Mitchell's band consisted of Larry Klein on bass, Brian Blade on drums and Greg Leisz on steel and lead guitar. But immediately after the Vancouver show, she became ill. Their tour bus had been newly recarpeted and the malodorous glue, coupled with the air-conditioning, caused her to have a severe allergic reaction. As the tour moved into the US, through Washington state and northern California, she forced herself through the shows, on the brink of delirium and collapse. The final dates were in Los Angeles and Anaheim, where the closing show came on the eve of Dylan's 57th birthday.

The tour had been the powerfully eloquent response to any nay-sayers who said the Old Guard were on their way out, no longer relevant or vital. All three had long since proven that their entire careers were arguments against those criticisms. The pattern of the short tour had been that Dylan closed the show most nights, Morrison closed on the others with Mitchell's set in between. If the sell-out audiences were hoping that the dream team would share sets, that was not to be – until one night, as Joni explained:

> Bobby keeps to himself. Van came to me at one point and said, 'Have you spoken to Bobby yet?'
> And I said, 'Yeah, I saw him after the Vancouver show.'
> 'Well, he hasn't spoken to me,' he said.
> And I said, 'Well, come on, let's crash his set.'

Remembering Dylan's tricks during the 'I Shall Be Released' finale at the Great Music Experience concert in Japan, she thought that the perfect moment to surprise him would be when he launched into that song:

> Bob got a big kick out of it. It was really rough and I blew the words on it and blew the rhyme and had to make one up. And Bobby was looking at me, grinning, 'What is she going to rhyme with it?', because I got the first rhyming line wrong.

Mitchell and Dylan were reunited again briefly towards the end of the year and at their double-header show at Madison Square Garden in New York, in November, Joni left another strong hint of her next musical direction. She'd sung 'Comes Love', the song made famous by Billie Holiday and one that had become a favourite during recent shows. A *New York Times* reviewer remarked:

> Without the sudden rushes of phrasing and Ms Mitchell's signature chords wrapped around it, the song made the most of her natural voice, its bright, cutting vowels and its new depths, a gift of age. It took her into a completely new context.

The song had also featured in her set at the Day in the Garden festival, held in August on what had once been the most famous farm in the country – Max Yasgur's farm near Bethel in New York state. Mitchell had not been able to get there for Woodstock in 1969 but in the song inspired by that festival she had urged, 'We've got to get ourselves back to the garden' – and 29 years later, she did. She introduced the song by saying to the audience, 'My generation, which was given a pocket of liberty like no other generation in a century, did some of the right things for a short time.' The 60s generation was represented on the stage that weekend by Lou Reed, Pete Townshend, Don Henley, Melanie, Richie Havens, Ten Years After and Stevie Nicks; the 90s generation included Goo Goo Dolls, Joan Osborne and Third Eye Blind.

The contrast between the two festivals was marked: the hundreds of thousands of hippies who crammed into the site in 69 were replaced by a well-mannered crowd, only a fraction of that number, who showed no inclination to storm the fence that surrounded the site; the hands that would once have clasped the ubiquitous joint now held a mobile phone or bottle of designer mineral water. The miles of traffic jams that had kept the area in gridlock for days were nowhere to be seen; in 98, many people simply stayed home and watched the event on the Internet. Plans were unveiled to turn the festival site into a theme park devoted to American music.

The man who thought up the idea for Woodstock 69, Michael Lang, decided to do it all again for the thirtieth anniversary of the festival. The event at the disused Griffis air base in New York state attracted teenagers whose grandparents may well have been at the original Woodstock. This time around the weather was too hot, the food was too expensive and the kids had a low tolerance threshold: the soundtrack of their young lives was the nihilism-rock of Limp Bizkit and Insane Clown Posse, and when candles were distributed among the crowd during the finale – a Jimi Hendrix tribute – they were not about to mimic their embarrassing rock dinosaur parents and grandparents by holding lighted candles aloft in a flickering celebration of the old Woodstock spirit. Instead, fed up with the heat, the mountains of rubbish that had not been cleared, the overflowing sewers where toilets should have been, and the extortionate prices for food and water, they torched the site. One young festivalgoer later explained, 'It's the teenage mentality, "Let's break shit and burn stuff."'

In the intervening years between the original Woodstock's three days of peace, love and music and its 90s incarnation, the

folk-tinged ingenue who had articulated the spirit of 1969 had
matured into the revered elder stateswoman of rock and pop.
Her voice alone had been transformed by age and heavy smoking, from a breathy soprano to a deeper, richer timbre. As the
1990s drew to a close, she decided to take a sabbatical from writing for public consumption:

> My music is drawn from my [feelings] and I just didn't
> want to be a social commentator at this time. I feel
> these are difficult times and we all need to develop
> some sort of ... discipline or soul nourishment or
> strength to deal with all the problems facing the world,
> problems that are coming to a head in every depart-
> ment. Even I wouldn't want to hear an album of that
> stuff right now. I just feel my point of view is too real-
> istic and reality is too bleak.

For the first time in a career that had been relentless in mining
the seam of romance and relationships, she stopped trying to
articulate the pains and pleasures of love. Joni returned to the
past in order to come back reinvigorated for the future. She
turned to the songs of the 30s, 40s and 50s, to Billie Holiday
whose voice she'd loved as a child, to Frank Sinatra, Etta James,
Nat King Cole and Ella Fitzgerald. They were songs that her parents knew and her father – an avid trumpet-player – was so
enthusiastic about the project that he wanted to help choose the
tracks. But when he heard about the theme – the songs would
trace the stages of a love relationship from beginning to end – he
felt much of it would sound too sad.

Larry Klein returned as her co-producer and musical director
for the new project, *Both Sides Now* – her 21st album – and
together they listened to dozens of recordings. The selection
process was rigorous, says Klein:

> There are so many people who have done records of
> standards but I think probably the most important
> thing that made [*Both Sides Now*] transcend ninety-nine
> per cent of those records is that, being a writer herself,
> we were very careful to select songs that Joni could
> really feel [were] her own, that she sang with the same

kind of intensity as if she had written them ... If a song in one way or another didn't hold up to her standards as a songwriter, she just didn't feel that she could really immerse herself in it.

Mitchell's voice and jazz-nuanced phrasings were ideally suited to interpreting the songs she and Klein eventually chose; her younger self could not have attempted the torchy delivery with any degree of authenticity. The voice and new arrangements gave an expressive depth to the two songs of her own that had only been hinted at in the original versions. Joni, Klein and the arranger and conductor, Vince Mendoza, went to London to record with a 70-piece orchestra, which included a number of London Symphony Orchestra musicians. Over several weeks at George Martin's Air Studios, Klein says, the combination proved electric:

The orchestra we had was just so incredible. They played with such passion, and the energy between them and [Joni], especially on songs like 'A Case of You' and 'Both Sides, Now' ... the orchestra was literally weeping. We'd finish a take and half the people were getting their handkerchiefs out! I couldn't believe how great it was. [Joni] was catalysed by them. A lot of that record is live vocals, where she just nailed the vocals right away, she was so inspired by their playing and vice versa.

The orchestrations were supplemented by guest players, Herbie Hancock on piano, Peter Erskine on drums and bass-player Chuck Berghofer, who were already in London. Contributions from Wayne Shorter on sax and trumpeter Mark Isham were added back in Los Angeles.

The album began with a homage to Billie Holiday's version of 'You're My Thrill' with obsession moving into the sheer relief of 'At Last' (with a nod to the Etta James cover) and 'Comes Love' until the arc of the relationship peaks and then begins to descend with 'You've Changed' and 'Answer Me, My Love', into the glorious 'A Case of You' before the imploring 'Don't Go to Strangers', the needy 'Sometimes I'm Happy', the resigned 'Don't Worry 'Bout Me' and the classic 'Stormy Weather', revisiting the song she'd first performed with an orchestra at the Walden Woods benefit. The mood lifts with the Rodgers/Hart song 'I Wish I Were In Love Again' to end with the hindsight wisdom of 'Both Sides, Now'. In his liner notes for the album, Klein wrote:

> The results have surpassed our expectations. In singing these songs, I believe that Joni has achieved something quite extraordinary in that she has truly sung them as if, as Nietzsche would say, she had written them in her own blood.

The album came out in a special edition Valentine's Day package, which included lithographs of some of the artwork, in February 2000, and was on general release in March. The front cover was a self-portrait, painted from a photograph of Joni taken in her thirties; she'd 'aged' herself to make it look more accurate and set herself in a smoky bar, wearing a green jacket that drapes into a heart below the fold of the sleeve. The back cover was the back view of the self-portrait, showing Mitchell in a haze of smoke facing the bar and a 'no smoking' sign. The other paintings in the artwork are of Mitchell and her boyfriend, Donald Freed, and a still-life – yellow roses and a photograph of Larry Klein, clasping Joni's feet to his neck.

The *New York Times* writer Stephen Holden described the album as intermittently magnificent, and congratulated Joni on 'refusing to fight or try to camouflage the ravages of time, [she] belongs to an interpretive school that includes Billie Holiday and Frank Sinatra, whose vocal deterioration brought them greater emotional depth and realism'. The change in her vocal delivery is also highlighted in the *Toronto Globe and Mail*:

> Mitchell doesn't always sound like Mitchell in this new and transformative context; she comes across like someone who has listened a lot to Billie Holiday and at least a little to Sarah Vaughan. The strongest of her borrowings can seem studied and sometimes rather strangulated ... but, these specific points of style aside, Mitchell's singing is remarkable for its absolute pitch and phrasing.

The *NME,* however, decried the 'reek of bohemian opulence', asking

> whether the inclusions of reworkings of her own 'Both Sides, Now' (which has a reasonable case for being a modern classic) and 'A Case of You' (which doesn't) is an act of grotesque vanity or a dearth of ideas is anyone's guess . . . Nice enough, but a bit pointless.

The album reached 66 on the US chart.

Both Sides Now was the first part of a trilogy of orchestral works; an album of new arrangements of her own songs and a collection of Christmas songs will complete the trilogy. When asked why she'd decided to record an album of torch songs, Mitchell replied:

> There was no point in doing them any other time. It was the end of the century. It was time to reflect on the music that went before. It was good for the culture and music to revisit this, because we have gone so far from a melody, you know, and genuine musical ability. You've got an appalling amount of mediocrity and amateurishness in the foreground now. Because nobody cares as long as it sells.

Both Sides Now went on to win two Grammys in April 2001 – to Mitchell for Best Traditional Pop Vocal Album and to Vince Mendoza for Best Instrumental Arrangement Accompanying a Vocalist.

Preparations got under way for a tour which would take her through several cities in the US; at each stop, she performed with a local orchestra, augmented by musical director and bass-player Larry Klein, trumpeter Mark Isham, drummer Peter Erskine, and pianist Herbie Hancock. The shows were divided between songs from the *Both Sides Now* album, performed in sequence, and the second half of the show, during which she played older material. At a show in Miami, she joked about the presence of a full orchestra as well as her bandmates, saying, 'I'm just a chick with a band this time. I bought a bra and burned my guitar.'

Both Sides Now was, in part, a tribute to many of the singers and songs that Mitchell had found inspiring. Just after its release, she was the subject of a tribute concert performed by many friends and admirers who had found her work influential and inspiring. The concert, arranged as part of the American TNT network's 'Masters Series', was recorded at the Hammerstein Ballroom in New York in early April and broadcast on US television later that month. It could have turned into a schmaltzy stage show but ended up on the right side of sincerity, with video features throughout the evening highlighting aspects of her music and painting, and an eclectic bunch of artists each interpreting songs by Mitchell, as she looked on.

Although Larry Klein was appointed musical director, it was the network's show and the producers had very clear ideas about who would appear and what they would sing. Paying tribute to a legend was one thing but ignoring your audience demographic was another entirely and this was surely an element in their final choices. In general, the mix worked well. Klein says, for his part, it was a matter of 'thinking of [Joni], thinking of what she would like, what would thrill her and what she would really enjoy'.

The showbiz element was personified by the host, actress Ashley Judd, whose sister Wynonna opened the concert with Bryan Adams rocking through 'Raised on Robbery' (and she also performed 'You Turn Me On, I'm a Radio'). The artists came from jazz, folk-inspired rock, and pop: Cyndi Lauper ('Carey'), Diana Krall ('A Case of You'), k d lang ('Help Me'), Shawn Colvin and Mary-Chapin Carpenter ('Chelsea Morning', 'Big Yellow Taxi', during which James Taylor joined them, 'Amelia'), Taylor himself ('River'), Sweet Honey in the Rock ('The Circle Game'), Cassandra Wilson ('The Dry Cleaner from Des Moines'). Richard Thompson performed a confident 'Woodstock', although he'd no time to rehearse, after Stone Temple Pilots pulled out of the show at the last minute. Thompson reappeared later for his scheduled 'Black Crow', showcasing his own phenomenal guitar work. After singing 'Free Man in Paris', Sir Elton John said, 'I've played for the Queen of England and it's not as intimidating as having a great musician there,' gesturing towards Mitchell.

The musical repertoire paused briefly for Hillary Clinton to join the proceedings by video link-up, and talk about how she and her husband were inspired by Mitchell's song 'Chelsea

Morning' to name their daughter Chelsea. It seemed appropriate that the first baby-boomer President and First Lady had named their child after their favourite pop song. When Bill Clinton visited China in 1998, he was the guest of honour at a banquet hosted by President Jiang Zemin in Beijing; during the evening, the Chinese Musical Ensemble orchestra played a selection of music on traditional Chinese and western instruments – including a version of 'Chelsea Morning'.

As the tribute show neared the end, Tony Bennett came on stage to introduce Joni, who acknowledged the standing ovation and deafening applause before singing 'Both Sides, Now', accompanied by a full orchestra. The evening ended with a finale of 'The Circle Game' played out to a pre-recorded tape.

It was the second Joni tribute concert in less than a year, although the first, in Central Park, was much more informal. Vernon Reid, guitarist with Living Colour, had gathered together a range of jazz and pop musicians and crafted the show, 'Joni's Jazz', into two halves: the first presented songs from different albums and the second half was the entire sequence of *Hejira*. Again, Mitchell was in the audience. Duncan Sheik sighed, 'I am not worthy!' before launching into 'Court and Spark', Jane Siberry interspersed lines from 'People's Parties' with her own running commentary about a fantasy version of the song and later interrupted herself again on 'Strange Boy' to remark that only Joni Mitchell could have written the line 'stiff-blue-haired-house-rules'. John Kelly – the Mitchell impersonator, who has his own 'Paved Paradise' homage revue – sang 'Shadows and Light' in one of the most polished performances of the first half and Chaka Khan's was the most energetic – improvising enthusiastically on 'Don't Interrupt the Sorrow' and 'The Hissing of Summer Lawns'. At one point, she attempted an explanation of a song and looked to Joni for confirmation, only to see Mitchell put her finger to her lips in a gesture that said, 'Quiet!' In the second half, Vernon Reid's arrangements for *Hejira* were inspired: he added double-clarinet obbligatos, melodica and Hammond organ and his own guitar. After jazz veterans Annie Ross and Jon Hendricks – whom Mitchell had revered in Lambert, Hendricks and Ross – appeared for the encore, Joni came on stage as the band played 'Help Me'.

For someone who had long lamented – with justification – that she did not get the recognition she deserved, the past four years had seen a torrent of accolades and acclaim for Joni Mitchell, both from within the industry and from her peers. She had been 'rediscovered' without ever being lost; she'd never made a 'comeback' album – although some were greeted in that way – because she'd never been away. Larry Klein thinks a disavowal of her influence by other musicians, as well as Mitchell's own desire to be taken seriously, were both used against her:

> She definitely felt undervalued for quite a long time, with good cause. Then, it seemed like a sudden turnaround where people started realising in a public way the importance of the work that she had done and was still doing. It's a mystery to me why that lack of validation occurred in the first place. Part of it, I believe, had to do with the viewpoint of a lot of female singer-songwriters, who were constantly compared to her, and they all probably just got tired of having to deal with [that]. Many of them just started completely disavowing any kind of influence by her. People put together a new version of how their talent developed. In the wake of this lack of validation, her response was to be verbal in the press about what her achievements had been and that's always a dangerous thing to do because then there's a backlash against that, especially from men. A woman who articulates and refutes certain things that have been claimed by others as innovations is perceived by them as being arrogant or a bitch.

Graham Nash believes that even though Mitchell may feel that she has been neglected by the critics and sometimes misunderstood by her fans,

> she has and will always remain on her own personal course. Joan will go down in history as a great artist. She will be appreciated for her music and her painting and the way she chose to live her life in a world dominated by men.

When *Rolling Stone* invited Mitchell to contribute to its 'Party 2000' edition published in December 1999, she was asked to nominate major events. Political? 'The invention of the pill. It changed the man-and-woman relationship, for better or worse . . .' Personal? 'The return of my family . . . it just filled a hole for me, grounded me. . . . I am a matriarch now, and I enjoy the role. It's very challenging . . .' Cultural? 'I just recently won a publisher's award and I watched the writers of the winning songs take the podium . . . most of these songs are written by four to eight people. And two of them were businessmen.'

When asked for her advice for the year 2000, she said: 'Keep a good heart. That's the most important thing in life. It's not how much money or what you can acquire or anything. The art of it is to keep a good heart, because the streets are so mean now.'

12 You wanna make Van Goghs . . .

> Somewhere at the heart
> of the universe sounds the
> true mystic note: Me
> > (Peter Porter, 'Japanese Jokes', *The Last of England*, 1970)

THERE IS A BRIEF HANDWRITTEN NOTE buried in the files of the Saskatoon Public Library that reads:

Here are three prints for the Library. I hope they are suitable. Please forgive the one for its small crease and slight discoloration. I enclosed it anyway because it has a nice mood and composition. Thank you for honoring me in this way. Peace, Joni Mitchell.

The note was written in the early 1970s.

It would be almost thirty years before her artwork returned to Saskatoon and by then its arrival made national news. Although Mitchell had had several small exhibitions in England, Scotland, the US and Japan, this was the first display of her paintings in Canada. It was the brainchild of the director of the Mendel Art Gallery, Gilles Hébert, who eventually persuaded Joni that the gallery in her hometown was the ideal location for a retrospective spanning four decades of painting and photography. The event took shape over a year, as Hébert travelled to Los Angeles to confer with Mitchell on the choice of more than 80 works from her collection of several hundred pieces dating from the late 1960s to the present day. It was the biggest event in the gallery's 36-year history – an exhibition by a local artist is one thing, an exhibition by a local artist who is also a famous celebrity with a place in musical history is another. Put the two together and you have a magnet that is going to attract art lovers, music fans, the curious and the cynical, along with an impressive contingent of media people.

The Mendel approached the launch of the three-month-long retrospective – 'Voices: the work of Joni Mitchell' – on 30 June 2000, as if expecting an invasion force: roads were blocked off and extra security drafted in to cope with an expected crowd of between 5,000 and 8,000 people on opening night. In the event, around 2,000 turned out, gradually congregating at the front of the gallery, on the banks of the South Saskatchewan river. Mitchell's new album, *Both Sides Now*, was playing continuously through a sound system outside the building. Inside, Joni was giving a news conference answering questions about painting techniques, music and her inspirations. She was good-natured and the media respectful but the bonhomie faded briefly when one hapless reporter asked what influence the Saskatchewan prairies still had on her. Joni was tart: 'If you'd looked at the show, you wouldn't ask that question!' In fact, none of the journalists had been allowed to see the works before the press conference because, as one gallery official explained, Mitchell wanted to 'tweak' something in the show before letting people see it.

The mood changed again when she spoke about spirituality and her hopes for the new millennium:

> If the century unfolds as I hope it does, the four major races will begin to coerce and understand their contributions to the greater whole; that intellect – whitey's contribution – will be put in its proper perspective. And the emotionality of the black race – the end they hold up – will become an equal to it. The clarity of the yellow race, and the sensitivity and the depth of the red race will all be used by all, that we'd all borrow from one another. That's my dream.

The remarks left some of the journalists baffled, with *Vancouver Sun* reporter Adele Weber commenting that

> she didn't really mean that the races have to be coercive to get along. Still, it's tempting to smell a Freudian slip in this old-fashioned world view, where races are

pigeonholed by their in-born characteristics ... whatever she meant none of us dared to ask for an elabora-
tion. Nor did anyone report her dream in the next day's
papers. ('It was over my head', explained one reporter.)

Back on safer ground, Mitchell affirmed that her inspirations
ranged from the Canadian landscape to Vincent van Gogh. The
former is a frequent subject of her paintings and the latter inspired
one of her first serious attempts at painting, beyond her student
days. She recalled that a visit to the Van Gogh Museum in
Amsterdam in her twenties had moved her so powerfully that
she'd left the building, determined to buy some paints and start
work immediately. By the time she emerged, all of the shops were
closed. She was thwarted again, after leaving Holland for England.
She arrived in London to find that the shops were shut there for a
public holiday. Returning home to Los Angeles, the first thing she
did was stop at an arts supplies shop – just as the owner was lock-
ing up for the night. She said the man's daughter recognised her
and begged her father to leave the shop open. Grabbing the paints
she needed, Mitchell said, she returned home and painted a 'really
bad' portrait of Leonard Cohen in the style of Van Gogh: 'I gave it
to a friend and their house burned down.'

    After the news conference, Joni emerged at the front of the
gallery, along with her parents, who still live in Saskatoon, and
other official guests for the opening ceremony. Among the
speechmakers was Camille Mitchell (no relation), a sponsor of
the exhibition and the granddaughter of the founder and bene-
factor of the gallery, Fred Mendel. Joni had often visited the
Mendel family home as a teenager and it was here that she'd first
seen great art – the family's wealth, gained from owning a huge
meat-packing plant, had enabled them to buy works by Picasso
and Matisse, and the Group of Seven painters who invigorated
Canadian art in the first half of the twentieth century. It was at
the Mendel home that she first soaked up her influences, later
wearing what the art critic Robert Enright, writing in the *Toronto
Globe and Mail*, described as 'her tributary heart on her sleeve for
the critics to peck at. Picasso and Matisse are at the top of the
list.' Camille Mitchell led the crowd in a 'Welcome home, Joni!'
chant and went on to describe her as one of the world's greatest
artists, saying the exhibition had sparked the imagination of

people around the globe. Other speakers – including the premier of Saskatchewan, Roy Romanow, the mayor of Saskatoon, Henry Dayday, and the co-sponsors who were meeting the $125,000 cost of the exhibition – all paid tribute to her musical legacy and welcomed the chance to assess that of her visual art.

Mitchell herself spoke briefly, thanking the people who had helped her to develop a love of art from an early age: her parents, who had bought her first set of crayons and her seventh-grade teacher, Arthur Kratzman, who had urged her to create 'by writing in my own blood'. She said she had wanted her first major show to be in Saskatoon, to enable her parents, who were in their eighties, to attend. With the speeches over, Joni and the dignitaries left the podium and the crowd was allowed to enter the gallery. For most, this would be the first time they had seen Mitchell's artwork anywhere other than her albums. A number of the cover originals were on display including 'Wild Things Run Fast' (1981), 'Dog Eat Dog #3' (1984), 'Turbulent Indigo' (1995), 'Taming the Tiger' (1997), 'Both Sides Now 1' (front shot) and 'Both Sides Now 2' (back shot), both painted in 1999. They had a particular power, familiar yet transformed in size from the tiny dimensions of the album artwork, seeming to take on a separate life as expensively framed works of art.

The retrospective traced the evolutionary line of her development as an artist. The earliest works were the gaudy felt-tip pen sketches dating from 1967 (although these were iris print reproductions of the original drawings), including drawings of friends, 'Judy Collins in the Dressing Room' (1969) and a spectacularly glowering 'Neil Young Back-stage at the Hollywood Bowl' (1975), 'David Crosby on his Boat' (undated), 'Portrait of James Taylor' (undated), a self-portrait and domestic scenes of her cats and the home she had in Laurel Canyon. She sketched one, 'On the Road to Woodstock' (1969), while sitting in her car with her road manager, Jane Lurie, in the time it took for the petrol tank to fill up. They are uncomplicated works and most display a garish brightness and chunky composition that now looks dated.

The large abstract expressionist canvases that she painted sporadically from the 1970s show a far more adventurous approach: 'The Ice Offering' (1976), the dark and brooding Monet-inspired 'Round About Midnight' (1991) and the Vuillard-like 'The Stranger' (1991) – so named because when Hébert asked her

about it, she could not remember painting it – co-exist alongside
more familiar and accessible figurative works. A number of neo-
surrealist paintings were the result of a stay in hospital in 1977:

> Predatory doctors threatened to take out some things
> that I really needed. In protest, I ordered art supplies
> to be sent to my hospital room and I painted a series of
> works I call 'The Delirium Paintings' . . . some of
> which I don't quite understand.

The subjects in this series give few clues – they include a water
buffalo, a tuxedoed man with a huge bunch of flowers where his
head should be, a Jamaican woman pictured with graffiti that
declare 'Jah love', and given Mitchell's clash with the medical fra-
ternity it's perhaps not surprising that one work depicts a vulture
holding court on an antique-reproduction chair in an expensively
furnished doctor's office. There is also a portrait of a young Georgia
O'Keeffe looming over red New Mexican hills. For all the puzzling
imagery, delirium and illness can be a source of inspiration and
not just in the realm of the surreal. Sylvia Plath wrote to her friend,
the poet Ruth Fainlight, in the weeks after her husband Ted Hughes
left her in 1962. Unable to eat or sleep, and feverish with a high
temperature at the time, Plath wrote the majority of her Ariel
poems and told Fainlight, 'I am living like a Spartan, writing
through huge fevers and producing free stuff I had locked in me
for years. I feel astounded and very lucky.' The Mexican painter
Frida Kahlo, too, used her injuries and illnesses to provide rich
metaphors and literal scenes for her own self-portraiture.
    Much of Mitchell's 1980s work veered between the figurative
and the abstract. The use of multiple images to fragment and distort the surface of the painting was a device she often used. Two,
inspired by her native Alberta, are entitled 'The Road To Uncle
Lyle's I' and 'The Road To Uncle Lyle's II' (both 1984) and show
the unrelenting flatness of the prairie landscape while the huge
expanse of blue sky above it is broken up into segments. The
critic Robert Enright sees these works as

> attempts to frame the vast prairie space by structuring [it]
> as interlocking forms . . . She was a kind of tectonic sur-
> veyor, or a landscape gambler shuffling the components

of prairie space as if they belonged to a deck of cards. To the extent that Mitchell's hand hadn't quite caught up to her mind, they were better ideas than paintings.

Works like 'Malibu Fire' and 'Before the Avalanche' (both 1982) use the same 'tectonic surveyor' skills of a Cubist draughtswoman in employing line, angularity and geometric composition to convey three-dimensional scenes: the former is a configuration of several paintings within a painting, seen from several different angles, and including a portrait of Larry Klein and beach landscapes. The technique appears again in 'Avalanche', another autobiographical work which depicts both Mitchell and Klein in a snowstorm, but separated by a seemingly random juxtaposition of images at sharp angles across the canvas. The smiles of the couple contrast with the impending danger of the avalanche and the snowfall that smothers the landscape, the road and the vehicles on it.

The principles of abstraction that Joni had resisted as a young art student began to grow more attractive, thanks in part to her friendships with the pop artist Larry Rivers and the abstract impressionist sculptor Nathan Joseph. She rented a loft from him in Soho, New York City, between 1977 and 1987. Joseph's own studio was in the same building; his profile and the view from the roof of the building inspired her 1981 abstract work 'Up On The Roof' (also known as 'The Sun Goes Down On Jersey, Rises Over Little Italy'). At the time Joseph was experimenting with rubbing coloured pigments on to the surface of his metal sculptures, a process which produced a range of different effects on the patina of the metal, and his experiments inspired her:

Nathan's medium was galvanised metal corroded by acid and the elements and the garden hose . . . in the early 1980s, my subject matter remained figurative but eventually his work influenced me towards the abstract – mainly because of the surfaces. His surfaces seemed to be growing while my paint seemed to just be lying there – flat. I abandoned the brush and began to roll the paint onto the canvases with fruit-juice jars and rolling pins. It struck me as funny to be using such feminine tools in such a macho field.

That 'macho field' of course was dominated by artists like Mark Rothko and Jackson Pollock, and although no great fan of Pollock's work, Mitchell did find herself experiencing the same frustration he had encountered with painters' conventional tools, when he said in 1948, 'I prefer sticks, trowels, knives and dripping fluid paint or a heavy impasto with sand, broken glass and other foreign matter added.'

Two examples of Mitchell's own experiments with other utensils are the abstracts 'Black Orpheus I' and 'Black Orpheus II' (both 1985), where the layered surfaces are scraped, dripped, smoothed and coarsened. The preoccupation with the texture and surfaces of her work had become obvious in earlier pieces like 'Imperial Rags' and 'Birth Of The Earth' (both 1982) and has continued through to the present day, with a continuous revisiting of every artist's internal debate – is it *finished* yet? Renoir said the point at which he knew he had completed a work was when he had painted a woman's backside – and wanted to reach out and touch it. When Pollock was asked the same question by a wealthy woman who had come to view his work, he retorted, 'How do you know when you're finished making love?' The abstract impressionist Barnett Newman believed that the idea of a 'finished' picture is a fiction. Joni often returns to a work time and time again to add, remove or re-define – one, 'Who Killed Cock Robin?', took five years to complete for this reason. In some of her paintings, as the months and seasons have progressed, she has changed the colours accordingly. As the doors opened at the Mendel gallery, paint was still drying on some of the works after she had retouched them.

Mitchell's style became increasingly conservative and by the early 1990s she had abandoned abstraction and the works are doggedly figurative. Two landscapes seen deep in the Saskatchewan winter, '40 Below 0' and 'The Road to Waskesui' (both 1995), are among the best examples: they have a vibrant luminosity that shimmers off the canvas. Some of these accomplished landscapes are in the tradition of the Canadian artist Emily Carr, whose brooding, unsentimental depictions of the Canadian Pacific Northwest and the Indian tribes who lived there went almost completely unnoticed until the 1920s. Then Carr met Mark Tobey of the Group of Seven, and although she was never formally a member of the Group, she exhibited with it. Mitchell's Canadian landscapes, however, are recreated back in Los Angeles, working from photographs or a sketchbook. She has lived in Los Angeles far longer than she lived in Canada, but she returns often and the country is revisited again and again in her work. The prairies have been a favourite subject and only the style of depicting them has changed over the years.

Mitchell has often used photographs to provide a bridge between an event or experience and the execution of it on canvas; much of her work is done from photographs taken in the moment and then returned to later, especially the landscapes, the travelogues, the painterly versions of holiday 'snapshots' later set on canvas, and even self-portraits, including the one used to illustrate the *Both Sides Now* album which is based on a photograph of Mitchell. The work then becomes a progressive distillation of reality, re-enacted scenes copied and reconstructed from her photographs, sketchbooks, magazines, books, postcards, even a postage stamp.

One such work – 'Homage to Matisse' (earlier known as 'Spring 81') – depicts an open book displaying an illustration of one of the two decorative 'Dance' panels produced by the French painter and sculptor. The large figure compositions such as 'Dance' had heralded a new artistic style, based on simple lines, giving a rhythmic decorative pattern on a flat ground of rich colour, and Mitchell had attempted the same approach in what is essentially a still-life. Henri Matisse believed that colour, even more than drawing style, was a means of liberation, with old methods of using colour being pushed aside by the contributions of a new generation. The interest here is that while Mitchell has tried to employ the same simplicity and flat colour, the work is not a copy of the original – it is a copy of a copy of the original, a device that, although it adds nothing to his original, can still open up new artistic possibilities despite its overuse. The American artist Amy Adler, who curated an exhibition of Mitchell's work in 1999, has used a similar distillation of images, where a subject is photographed, a drawing is then done from that photograph and that drawing is, in turn, photographed.

Mitchell has often described the difference between her music and visual art as 'I sing my sorrow and I paint my joy', and much of her work underlines that, with friends, cats, favourite views, lovers and familiar landscapes dominating the subject matter. Although with those closest to her so often the theme of her painting, it is perhaps surprising that the Mendel retrospective did not include any works of her parents, her daughter or grandchildren. Her music and visual art require you to engage with her life and her world view, but the art is even more transparent than the music in this. There is no social commentary or anti-music industry treatise, there is no dispassionate third-person voice expressed, it all hinges on the Self as the centre of the universe with the satellites of people and places revolving around it.

The work is a universe away from the prevailing stylistic influences in art. The viewer does not need a knowledge of modern art to appreciate the works; there are no images designed to shock, no animal parts in formaldehyde, no installations from the detritus of building sites, bedroom floors, bathroom cupboards or children's toy boxes. There is no subtext ripped from the murky depths of the unconscious. Art critic Robert Enright:

> despite [her] early training and her persistent avocation, Mitchell emerges as a worldly version of a naïve artist, indifferent to art trends and the positioning that has so much to do with contemporary art.

The visual art is also fired by a utilitarian aspect of everydayness that would horrify the purists. She's not a hobbyist nor does she use the art as therapy, but rather as creations that usually have a job of work, either as decorative objects or informative ones or simply as memories-made-real. It's a variation on William Morris' exhortation to 'have nothing in your homes that you do not know to be useful or believe to be beautiful'. If visual art can be used to excavate the very depths of one's psyche or the harsh world outside – neither of which Mitchell chooses to do in her painting – it can also help to retrieve a beloved pet, advertise an album, share a joke among friends, keep a memory or brighten up a room. A Los Angeles radio reporter was taken aback when Mitchell said without a trace of irony, 'I don't paint for galleries, I don't paint for museums. I paint to go with my couch . . . that's as good [a reason] as any. I mean, after all, they're domestic decorations.'

Unlike the music, the visual art has usually been a private activity, a personal endeavour, immune to the commercial art world, venturing out only to adorn the albums and for the occasional exhibition. It has followed the -isms that dominate art history only as far as they influenced her influences: Cubism, impressionism, expressionism, Fauvism. This is not an artist who is asking you to look at her works with a view to buying – the only works she has sold at exhibition were in Tokyo in May 1988. She said later that she regretted selling the paintings, wishing instead that they had still been in her private collection when she came to choose works for the Mendel retrospective. Joni Mitchell, then, is clearly not an artist who needs her work to be seen in order to get a sale, a grant, a subsidy or exhibition space – she doesn't need any of it, but she does appear to need the validation for her painting that comes from those public showings. Her visual art has not given her the commercial success or artistic acclaim of her music yet she says it was her first creative passion and she remains devoted to it.

Mitchell's photography is less well-known than her painting, and the cornerstone of her photographic collection is her trademark double-exposure portraiture. The Mendel exhibition featured a twenty-part series taken in 1986. Many of these portraits had been the result of a minor mishap with the camera, during a trip to Canada. Joni had taken Larry Klein back home to show him where she'd spent the first twenty years of her life. They followed a route from Calgary where she had gone to art school, to her birthplace Fort Macleod in Alberta, then on to the places in Saskatchewan where she'd grown up: the village of Maidstone, the town of North Battleford and, finally, to the city of Saskatoon. She had taken photographs as they travelled and not realised there'd been a problem with the film, as she recalled in the catalogue for the Mendel retrospective:

> When we got back to Los Angeles and I looked at the film, I had double shot a roll and under-exposed another. Also there was Klein alone in a wheat field or me alone in a wheat field but never any shots of the two of us together. I began playing with the underexposed photos which contained two self-portraits – one shot while Klein was sleeping and I was wrestling with

my chronic insomnia, the other shot while Klein was
in a convenience store. The lamination of the self-portraits to these nostalgic images of wheat and barns and
[grain] elevators gave me great personal excitement.

The images are eye-catching: the perfectly symmetrical planes of
Mitchell's face assume an architectural importance when contrasted with the other subjects sharing the frame – her husband,
a collapsed barn, railway lines, a cloudy sky, a sleeping godchild,
a shopfront, a car window. In many, her face dominates the landscape, in others it is barely visible, little more than a ghostly presence. The self-portrait has a venerable tradition in art and for
many women artists it has been a way of inscribing their image
as their own rather than as the world sees them. The self-portrait
puts its creator at the very core of the work, as both the observer
and the observed, and this can be interpreted as self-obsession
when that eye is focused as relentlessly as in Mitchell's photo
series, as photographer and archivist Joel Bernstein explains:

> [Joni] thought that people didn't 'get' that series; she must
> have heard intimations to the effect that it was egotisti-
> cal to have included herself in the whole series . . . Some
> would say that [their] favourite painting is where the artist
> has included themself, where the artist is this little fig-
> ure over in the corner of the crowd, like Hitchcock would
> be in his films, just barely there. On the other hand some
> of the great works of art of all time are self-portraits and
> Joni's very aware of that and I'm sure she would like to
> have several of her self-portraits be considered at the top
> of her work . . . We were discussing the fact that she was
> in all of them and what the differences were between
> them and what part of the feeling of the photo comes
> from her, and what part of it comes from the part that
> isn't her and then thirdly, the relationship between them
> – all of that is happening at once in a double image like
> that . . . She said, 'To me it was just very simple, it was a
> subject/object kind of thing: I'm the observer, it's putting
> the viewer in the viewed, it's just illustrating that those
> two things are happening at once, rather than simply, as
> usual, giving you the point of view of the camera.'

Joni had been given her first camera as a child but her real interest in photography had begun when Graham Nash, himself an accomplished photographer, bought her a Leicaflex 28mm-lens camera for Christmas: 'My gift to her of the camera was deliberate. I'd always understood that she was a very visual person and I wanted to both encourage and take delight in sharing those visions.' The camera represented new possibilities in expressing her particular view of the world; Joni put down her sketchbook for a time and embraced it with a passion. In 1971, while on tour with Jackson Browne, she photographed voraciously. She took dozens of photographs of Browne – with whom she was then romantically involved – including some early double-exposure shots. The gift from Graham Nash also led to her first public exhibition: Joni, Nash and Joel Bernstein were invited to exhibit their photographs in Vancouver that year. They each had a room devoted to their own work, but helped one another choose which works to show. Bernstein recalls that Mitchell's visual sense was highly developed:

> The thing that struck me about her photographs was that they were, firstly, informed by her being a painter, [by] her painter's eye. Secondly, that they were composed to colour almost entirely; that was the overriding compositional element, more than the framing. It was a matter of colour and weight of colour, not of form so much. I think that she really could have developed her photography skills if she'd pursued it.

The double-exposure shots are taken with a conscious lack of care for any technical points like lighting, distance or manual focus, leaving some over-exposed and distorted. They are shot with an auto-focus, auto-flash, auto-exposure camera – an Instamatic or a Polaroid – that she has simply picked up and pointed back at herself. They are shot too close to be especially flattering but they are not intended to be posed and pretty. Another series of double-exposure photographs was exhibited at the Earl McGrath Gallery in West Hollywood, Los Angeles, in early 1992. The technique raised the ire of the *Los Angeles Times* critic Christopher Knight, who believed the photographs recall

the work of hobbyists and undergraduate art students
... Mitchell's multiple exposures claim a familiar
ancestry – think for instance, of Frederick Sommer's
classic photographs from the 40s, such as his famous
portrait of Max Ernst – which is why the technique is
by now standard fare among amateurs and beginning
students of photography.

At the same time, Knight also reviewed exhibitions by the
actor/director Dennis Hopper and the writer William S.
Burroughs, whose work was shown in the McGrath Gallery along
with Mitchell's. Knight expressed disquiet about the growing cult
of the celebrity artist:

This sudden burst of shows by artists whose celebrity is
linked not with his/her own work as a painter, sculptor
or photographer, but with other endeavours in other
fields, surely bespeaks the rather tough times in the art
market at the moment. Perhaps these exhibitions will
bring in temporary, tangential audiences from the
moneyed realm of show business and entertainment,
audiences who otherwise might not make the gallery
rounds and acquire art. But that's guesswork. What's
certain is that this approach cheapens the level of artistic quality in the current gallery scene, which cannot
be good for anyone.

Pushing aside elitism, at some point most artists, writers or musicians decide to unleash their work on the world. They may say
that they paint, write, sing only for themselves but few are truly
content with that audience of one. Liberated from others' expectations, from contracts, from commitments, away from the public gaze, one can write, paint, sculpt, photograph, sing whatever
one wishes. Why then even take a chance in the gladiatorial
arena when you know you will look up to see the critics and nay-
sayers gleefully turn their thumbs to the ground, when faced with
just another celebrity artist?

   In 1979 Mitchell was among six musician/artists featured in a
book, *Starart*, that examined her work along with that of
Cat Stevens, John Mayall, Klaus Voorman, Ron Wood and

Commander Cody. Since then, the much-derided phenomenon of the MTA, model-turned-actress, has morphed into the MTP, musician-turned-painter-and/or-photographer – exhibition spaces, books and album covers have been willingly given over to the works of David Bowie, John Lennon, Paul McCartney, Tony Bennett, Don van Vliet (aka Captain Beefheart), David Byrne, Ronnie Wood, Bob Dylan (famously, on *Self-Portrait*), Sinead O'Connor, Michael Stipe, Elvis Costello (masquerading for art credits purposes as Eammon Singer on *Blood and Chocolate*), Herb Alpert, Donna Summer *et al*. Only a handful have gained real respect for their visual art – certainly, Don van Vliet's reputation as a dedicated and gifted artist is richly-deserved, and Mitchell herself has enjoyed unparalleled exposure for her paintings through her album artwork.

There are limits to the 'for a guitarist, he's a great photographer' dialogue and, in Canadian art circles in 2000, the issue of celebrity artists caused a wide debate: the director of the Vancouver Art Gallery resigned rather than exhibit a series of photographs taken by the Canadian rocker Bryan Adams. The gallery's board wanted to show the photos as part of a fund-raising campaign. There was also anger expressed at the amount of public money used by the Canadian Museum of Nature in Ottawa to mount an exhibition of nature photographs taken by the astronaut Roberta Bondar. And of Mitchell's exhibition, Paul Gessell of the *Ottawa Citizen* wrote:

> Saskatoon's Mendel was probably the only significant public art gallery in Canada that would have dared risk its excellent reputation as a highly popular centre for daring, important and cutting-edge contemporary art by mounting a show of what will surely be dismissed in many quarters as 'celebrity art' better exhibited in some rock 'n' roll hall of fame ... As much as Gilles Hébert, the Mendel's director, likes to talk about the superb qualities of Joni Mitchell's art, the fact is there never would have been a show if Ms Mitchell was not a world-famous singer who just happens to be the biggest celebrity this town has ever produced. Joni Mitchell could have crocheted doilies and the Mendel would undoubtedly have had a show ...

It's hard to avoid musing about the likely reaction to the works if the painter had exhibited under a pseudonym, leaving out so many of the tell-tale portraits and focusing instead on the works that are less easily identifiable as her own. It is a bold statement of faith in one's art to lose the name but keep the work, just as Doris Lessing did when writing under a pseudonym. But it's a statement of faith that celebrities choose not to make. They can then dismiss criticisms as simply being prejudice against their celebrity yet accept any praise as being for their skill rather than their celebrity. It's undeniable that it's largely the celebrity of such painters that initially gets people through the gallery doors, but it is then only the strength or weakness of the art that determines how long they stay there.

Questions that surround this dual celebrity, whether Mitchell's music fans will also be her art fans and how the album art appears out of the context of the albums, intrigued the American artist Amy Adler sufficiently to choose Mitchell's work when she was asked to be a guest curator at the Los Angeles Contemporary Exhibitions (LACE). She knew Mitchell's music but they'd never met. They were introduced through sax-ophonist Wayne Shorter and began to talk about what would become 'Tri-Annuale Part 2, Amy Adler Curates Joni Mitchell'. The exhibition took place in December 1999. Adler visited Mitchell's home and they chose 16 works from about 50 pieces painted during the 1990s. Adler says she was confident that the work would be taken seriously:

> I thought that the question of her work could be seen in a different way than it had been in the past. I felt like a lot of people would be really interested in seeing the painting for different reasons. Because she works figu-ratively and her work is centered around some very per-sonal concerns, these are things that have – in the time that she has been a painter – typically been less valued than other ideas in art. Yet she's had this forum in which she'd exhibit this work, which has been in the context of her music, so people could know and see her paint-ing. But it was excluded from the sort of judgment and dialogue that would take place in a gallery. You can't separate [fame] from talking about the painting because

she is Joni Mitchell, and the work is vulnerable and it is fragile and it's private. It's reasonable to suspend or readjust your sense of [critical] judgment in a way.

Adler's desire to remove the musical context from the work was evidenced by her decision not to have Mitchell's music playing, even though the exhibition was held just three months before the special edition of *Both Sides Now* was released:

> [Joni] was so into the record coming out and she did want the music to be playing. I said 'I don't think so' and I was apprehensive about saying it . . . but I felt so strongly that I wanted her to be considered as a painter and I thought, if [we] play this record, then everyone's going to stop and just listen. This is the opportunity of the paintings, this is their moment, so I fought for their autonomy.

For this reason, Adler did not write an introduction to the exhibition and all of the works were labelled as 'Untitled'. Reviewing the show in *Art Issues*, Gianna Carotenuto wrote:

> Mitchell's conscious nod to Impressionism is a splash of cold water on the face of much contemporary art, providing viewers with a relatively pain-free aesthetic diversion . . . if Adler went looking for the 'girl with the guitar', as Mitchell was labelled in the 1970s, she is nowhere to be found. In her place stands a multi-dimensional woman. Far from being quaint or charming, Mitchell comes off as brave.

Benjamin Weissman, a critic writing in *Frieze*, gave the exhibition a mixed review but concluded:

> In her music, Mitchell is willing to explore the complexities of being alive. Not so in her paintings, where she seems more interested in paying tribute to the stuff she loves: solitude, male companionship, the beauty of the outdoors, boating, animals and herself. The overall tone of this work is sincerity overdrive, a mini-autobiography

without a shred of darkness . . . sentimental images that
keep you cheerful and glad to be on the planet.

Mitchell had ended the 90s with an art show, just as she had
opened the decade with one. Her first European exhibition was
held in London in 1990. The show, Diary of a Decade 1980–1990,
gathered together 28 pieces together and ran from 11 September
to 7 October at the now-defunct Rotunda Gallery in Broadgate
Circus, east London. The exhibition was part of a two-week festival of events, Canada in the City, organised by the Canadian government as a celebration of Canadian music, art and culture.
While preparations were underway for the London opening, one
of the curators flew to Los Angeles to look at the works and Joni
recalls that he was taken aback by what he encountered:

> He sees this stuff and he begins to joke: 'There are
> four different styles. The critics are going to eat you
> alive over there.' I said 'Look, don't worry about it.'
> So I'm holding his hand and thinking 'Wait a minute,
> I'm an artist; why am I holding the curator's hand
> here?' He's worried because I'm painting four styles,
> that there's something wrong with that. It's not a neg-
> ative thing, it's a positive thing. It's an appreciation of
> a wide range and the possibility of a hybrid. I may be
> on to something.

Guests at the opening night were greeted by young women
dressed in short black skirts and red Mountie-style tunics and
hats. Joni fielded questions from reporters wanting to know her
views on the environment, Canadian national identity, the fall of
the Berlin Wall, philosophical influences like Friedrich
Nietzsche, and, occasionally, the art itself. She explained that her
paintings tend to deal with smaller, more circumscribed experiences than her music: 'There are little moments,' she said, point-
ing to the artworks, 'I think there is a tenderness here that
perhaps couldn't be detailed in a song.' Painting, she told them,
was the perfect antidote when her writing faltered: 'When I get
writer's block, I don't panic – I just pick up a brush. It's like crop
rotation. It keeps the soil fertile.'
The exhibition catalogue concluded:

> The pictures produced by Joni Mitchell over the last decade lead one to the belief that she has now arrived at a point where she is able to realise an autonomous visual language capable of expressing the deepest feelings.

In December, the exhibition moved on to Scotland, where it was displayed at the Edinburgh Art Centre until mid-January 1991. Mitchell recalled:

> The Scotland hang was more orthodox. You could isolate and create a certain intimacy, whereas the hang in London was quite grand and had to be done like a string of beads. You were hanging on curved walls, so the squares actually became straight lines on three sides and then curved at the bottom. Everything had to be arranged like a mural.

Although the themes examined in her music and visual art may differ, Mitchell's experimentation in both has often happened in parallel, as styles of painting have changed in tandem with harmonic scales and compositional techniques in music, as Joel Bernstein explains:

> The art has its own arc of development, as does her songwriting or her singing or her guitar-playing; which media she chooses to use and what's on her mind. Is she working from life or photographs or is she collaging? Is she using oils? You can see that arc in parallel to her albums. Her own arc as a painter is obviously illustrated in her choice of album covers which she did over the years, from the first album, through the second album in terms of the styles, to *Ladies of the Canyon* – all three very different, *Court and Spark* [also], and then later what she was doing towards the second half of the 70s in terms of her painting and drawings, 'til you get up to *Mingus*.

That progression takes her cover art from the lush hippie fantasia of *Joni Mitchell/Song to a Seagull* to the luminous photo-realism of the bold self-portrait close-up on *Clouds* to the minimalism of the line-drawing self-portrait in an expanse of white, relieved only by a pocket of primary colours, on *Ladies of the Canyon*.

There was an interlude for *Blue* and *For the Roses* with cover photography by Tim Considine and Joel Bernstein respectively, followed by a return to the use of her own paintings on the cover, with the pastel-dominated impressionism of the *Court and Spark* cover. Its successor, *The Hissing of Summer Lawns*, used a mono-chrome precisionist New York cityscape to contrast with the green open space that separated it from the surrealism of Amazonian tribesmen bearing a huge snake through the summer lawns. These would be the only two albums out of five released between early 1974 and late 1977 to display Mitchell's own paint-ings or drawings on the front cover. The others were pho-tographs, although the cover of the live double-album *Miles of Aisles*, released in 1974, was taken by Mitchell as she sat in an empty concert hall, where part of the album was later recorded. The shot was taken from the back of the hall, from across her bejeaned knees and sandalled feet:

> Something about that [view] appealed to me as an abstract painting – the blue blobs where the knees are, the checkerboard grid at the top. I like the way it looks but more than that, it was just impulse.

The 1979 release, *Mingus*, marked a radical departure in her painting, with a series of abstract and semi-abstract works illus-trating the cover and sleeve, and a sharp turn into left-field for her music, with her collaboration with legendary jazz composer and bassist Charles Mingus – this period marked her most abstract painting, and her most heavily jazz-inspired music. The changes may have been unexpected but were hardly surprising – just as so much of pop is the music world's answer to formulaic colour-by-numbers drawing, jazz is often its abstract art.

Photographs by Joel Bernstein and Mitchell's art director, Glen Christensen, adorned the cover and sleeves of the live double-album *Shadows and Light* in 1980, but the artwork for her next release, *Wild Things Run Fast* in 1982, marked a return to the photo-realism self-portraiture of *Clouds* 13 years earlier and that style would continue, with minor variations, on several of her subsequent album covers. The exceptions included the 1988 album, *Chalk Mark in a Rainstorm,* featuring cover photography by Larry Klein, the double-exposure self-portrait on *Night Ride Home,* released in 1991, and the *Hits* and *Misses* compilations in 1996, photographed by Mitchell's long-time collaborator, Norman Seeff.

Where many artists are nurtured and stimulated by their art school environment, others rebel against it and Mitchell was one of the latter. With music initially little more than a way to pay for her tuition, she left Saskatoon for Calgary in the neighbouring province of Alberta, where she enrolled in the Alberta College of Art. Music was a hobby at art school, playing folk music in coffee houses was a way to earn money to pay for art supplies. When she arrived in Calgary, Mitchell's passion lay in the figurative and representational. But art school did little to help her realise her aims. The lecturers were enamoured of the abstract impressionism of Barnett Newman, much in vogue at the time. Classicism and tradition had been abandoned in favour of experimentation and abstraction. It was an approach that was to leave Mitchell frustrated and impatient:

> Art school was very disappointing – although I romanticised the time that Van Gogh went to art school. I thought that to go to the French Academy at that particular time – even though as a female I would have been considered an associate no matter how good I was – was the best education you could get. And yet in Van Gogh's letters to [his brother] Bernard, he's begging him to get him out of there, saying 'They're providing you with subject matter – if they have their way, they'll make a mistress of your art and you won't know your true love should you come upon it.' When I read that, I thought, 'I'm going to give myself an art education: I'm going to paint the way I want to, never mind the art world.'

Part of giving herself an art education was to want to meet her heroes, among them Pablo Picasso:

> I wanted so badly to go and visit Picasso even on the fan level that people come to me, even with the possibility that I would be turned away, I wanted desperately to go

and see him . . . I wanted to go and play him a song while he painted or something, because I had so much respect for his prolonged creativity.

Another artist with the same creative longevity was the American cultural icon and pioneering Modernist painter Georgia O'Keeffe, with whom Mitchell was to forge a friendship. O'Keeffe's comments in an exhibition catalogue in 1923 echoed Joni's own feelings:

> School, and things that painters have taught me . . . keep me from painting as I want to. I decided I was a very stupid fool not to at least paint as I wanted to and say what I wanted to say when I painted as that seemed to be the only thing I could do that didn't concern anyone but myself – that was nobody's business but my own . . . I found that I could say things with colours and shapes that I couldn't say in any other way – things that I had no words for. Some of the wise men say it is not painting, some of them say it is. Art or not art – they disagree.

Georgia O'Keeffe, too, found her time at art school – the Art Institute of Chicago – had been largely wasted. Having fled from one life-drawing class in late 1905, so discomfited was she by the sight of a nude male model, O'Keeffe would later barely acknowledge the value of her education there, saying simply 'I don't remember anything except that I finally became accustomed to the idea of the nude model.' O'Keeffe shares the duties of patron saint of women artists and avatar of creative women with Frida Kahlo – roles she would have loathed. She said once, 'The men like to put me down as the best woman painter, I think I'm one of the best painters' – a comment with deafening resonance with the way in which Joni Mitchell has so often been described: one of the great *women* singer-songwriters or musicians. The two women met and became friends in the late 1970s. They shared many similarities – the prairie upbringing that nurtured an unbreakable attachment to the land, the frustrating early art school training, the dual passion for music and painting, the experience of the seldom female in a creative world dominated by men, the classically understated distinctive personal style, the frustrations of the gender label that has been ever-present in discussions of their work, their November birthdays just a few days apart.

Interpretations of Mitchell's music and O'Keeffe's work have often laboured under similar misreadings and misunderstandings, the same over-dependence on sexuality and autobiography that have eventually removed the original meanings in part or entirely from what either woman intended. O'Keeffe's lush flower paintings are her best-known and most widely reproduced work. Their lustrous depictions of vastly magnified plant anatomy — engorged, erect stamen, and velvety petals gaping wide – were seen as explicitly sexual and never escaped the associations with female genitalia in particular, despite Georgia's protestations to the contrary:

> Well – I made you take time to look at what I saw and when you took time to really notice my flower you hung all your own associations with flowers on my flower, [she wrote in an exhibition catalogue] and you write about my flower as if I think and see what you think and see of the flower – and I don't.

Years later, in 1954, when a critic was foolish enough to doggedly pursue this point with her, Georgia snapped, 'I hate flowers . . . I paint them because they're cheaper than models and they don't move.' Even Freud – whose psychoanalytic insights into sexuality informed many of the early critiques of O'Keeffe's work – once admitted that 'sometimes a cigar is just a cigar'.

The humour in the work of both women has also often been overlooked or misread. O'Keeffe once said that a painting of a white cow's skull against a background of red and blue was partly a joke against the self-important men who were always talking about 'the Great American Novel, the Great American Play, the Great American Everything. I thought they didn't know anything about America. They never went across the Hudson!' Similarly, when Mitchell painted the self-portrait with bandaged ear – in the style of Vincent van Gogh's own work of that title – on the cover of her album *Turbulent Indigo*, it was misinterpreted as comparing her own suffering and skill to that of Van Gogh. Early in their careers, both O'Keeffe and Mitchell became so frustrated with their respective art/music worlds and the attention of the critics that they considered retiring from a public artistic life.

Both women were seen as protégées of men in the early years of their careers, portrayed as relying on the protector/mentor figure to allow them access to the wider world. Mitchell, initially with her first husband Chuck, then with her first manager, Elliot Roberts, and with David Crosby, who produced her first album; and O'Keeffe, through the man she would later marry, after he 'discovered' her, the influential Modernist photographer, gallery-owner and art dealer Alfred Stieglitz. It's part of the O'Keeffe legend that Stieglitz is said to have exclaimed upon seeing her charcoal drawings for the first time, 'Finally, a woman on paper!' He felt that the drawings broadened the boundaries of art, that at last a woman was seeing and expressing sensitively, in visual form, her own relation to the world. But his interpretations were too gender-oriented and proved an immense source of frustration to O'Keeffe, when they were picked up by (male) critics who persisted in the view that it was art by a woman, rather than art by an artist. They were unable to divide her gender from her talent, and came up with an equation that was initially enormously limiting. To O'Keeffe, her womanhood had been incidental, an accident of chromosomes that could not be allowed to impinge on or dominate her art.

Both O'Keeffe and Mitchell discovered early that music and painting were the conduits to creativity but it was to be Commerce, not Art, that determined the final decision about which would dominate in public at least. Just as it was Joni's music that brought her to mass attention, so it would be Georgia's paintings. Despite her love of music, O'Keeffe came to the realisation that it would be her artwork that would inscribe her name on the world: 'Since I couldn't sing, I decided to paint,' she said, near the end of her life. In 1915, in a letter to a friend, she had made a telling observation about the dual disciplines:

> It's a wonderful night – I've been . . . wanting to tell someone about it . . . I've laboured on the violin til all my fingers are sore . . . I imagine I could tell about the sky tonight if I could only get the noises I want to out of it . . . I'm going to try to tell you – about tonight – another way – I'm going to try to tell you about the

music of it – with charcoal – a miserable medium – for things that seem alive – and sing.

Sixty years later, she and Mitchell were to discuss whether it was possible to divide one's creativity happily between these two arts. Georgia's longing to be a violinist was subsumed to her painting; she felt it was not possible to do both. Mitchell assured her it was.

Some years before the two women met for the first time, a chance comment from a friend, visiting her at home in Laurel Canyon, intrigued Mitchell enough to want to find out more about Georgia O'Keeffe:

> One day I was hanging a blanket in a doorway when a friend dropped by. I don't know what the association was, maybe it was this blanket hanging in the doorway of a house that was very rustic – he said I reminded him of a young Georgia O'Keeffe. This was the first time I had heard her name. There were no books or anything available on her at this time. I remember asking who she was, and he told me and it didn't mean that much. I heard her name again and again and a bit of her story over and over again.

As she learned more about O'Keeffe's life, Joni came to feel a kinship with Georgia, who by now, ninety years old and almost blind, had become an institution in American cultural life. Mitchell decided to visit O'Keeffe at her home and studio in the tiny village of Abiquiu, near Santa Fe, New Mexico, during the Thanksgiving holiday in November 1977. While on a road trip from California to Texas, Mitchell took a detour to Abiquiu, intending to leave gifts for O'Keeffe: a limited edition book of her own drawings, entitled *Morning Glory on the Vine*, and a copy of her latest album, *Hejira*. She'd enclosed a handwritten note to O'Keeffe, saying:

> I want you to have this book – it is a collection of growing pains. The work it contains is not quite ripe. Nevertheless – I want you to have it out of my respect, admiration and identification with some elements of your creative spirit.

Mitchell and her boyfriend had arrived unannounced:

> The irony of this is that I had spent time by myself
> [at her home in the Canadian woods] and I was con-
> stantly besieged by people paying homage to me,
> camped on my property, waiting for me to come out.
> So having gone to such a degree and now having
> people seeking you out was something I sympathised
> with. When no one came to the door, I slipped the
> book and the record under the gate and got back into
> this van. My boyfriend said 'Go and take it to her,
> there's a break in the fence. There's a storm coming.
> It will all get wet.' So reluctantly I went through this
> gap between the gate and the wall and around to the
> side of her house. In her bedroom, which had no cur-
> tains, I saw that we had the same luggage, from a lit-
> tle store on Madison Avenue in New York. I'd never
> seen it anywhere else in the carousels of the world. I
> thought, 'That's interesting, Georgia and I have the
> same luggage.'

The couple left, still a little unsure of the fate of the gift or the
reception it would get.

O'Keeffe did find the package and when her assistant and companion, Juan Hamilton, returned from a trip to Costa Rica, O'Keeffe
asked him about Joni Mitchell. He was a fan of Mitchell's and urged
O'Keeffe to encourage her to return. Hamilton wrote on Georgia's
behalf on 13 March 1978, enclosing her private phone number:

> Dear Joni Mitchell,
> I wanted to write you and thank you for the record and
> the book you left, but I did not have an address. My
> friend, Juan Hamilton, thought I might like to meet
> you also and got your address from someone in Los
> Angeles. If you would like to come and visit for a day
> or two, please write or call Juan . . .
> Hoping you have not gotten washed away by the
> Aclifornia [sic] rains.
> Sincerely,
> Georgia O'Keeffe

The typewritten letter was despatched but would not be read for many months. It languished among sacks of fanmail at Mitchell's home in Los Angeles. When Mitchell did get around to opening the piles of letters, she described doing so with a sense of unexplained expectation, an 'omenistic' feeling about O'Keeffe:

> I got this strange feeling looking at this [sack]. And I began to sift down through this pile of mail, and oh, I would say about six months down in it I found a post-card, *Lake George With Crows*. I flipped it over and it said 'Have we offended you in some way?' And I dug down and there were odds and ends of correspondence including a formal invitation to come and visit, signed Juan Hamilton, on their behalf, with a phone number.

More time passed and, in the summer of 1978, Joni phoned O'Keeffe using the private, unlisted number that Hamilton had sent to her. She told Georgia that she was about to visit Charles Mingus in Mexico; the *Mingus* album was almost finished and Charles, already seriously ill, was in Cuernavaca receiving alternative healing treatments. Joni had told Georgia that after spending three days with Mingus, she would make her way to Abiquiu. O'Keeffe was doubtful: 'Oh, you won't get out of *there* in three days!' and she was correct.

A week after their phone conversation, Mitchell called Georgia again to say that she had been taken ill and was still across the border. O'Keeffe was eager for her to join them as soon as possible, saying that a 'young friend' – Juan Hamilton – would be leaving for New York shortly and would be disappointed if he missed Mitchell's arrival. Soon after, Mitchell left Mexico City for the short flight to Albuquerque in New Mexico; she spent the night there at a hotel near the airport and the next morning drove north for an hour to Santa Fe, the cultural centre and capital of New Mexico. The number and quality of the art galleries here have made it one of the largest art markets in the United States; many are crowded around the historic downtown area where local laws require all new construction to be in the Spanish adobe or mock-adobe style. Tourists, art patrons and artists alike flock here for the galleries, museums and the Native American crafts and jewellery. Mitchell was no exception; she spent the day in Santa Fe and bought Haida Indian rattles and ankle bells. With Georgia and Abiquiu still an hour's drive away, Mitchell was pondering what to do next:

> Just as I was debating whether to go to Georgia's the following day or that night, a crow flew across my path. Crows are talking birds – a crow is materialistic, it likes shiny things. I've thought I must have been a crow in my last life – there's something about these birds that I relate to. And this crow flew across my windshield – very tight in – with a mouse that looked like a road hit. And I looked at the numbers on my mileage gauge, and they were eights all the way across, including the fast-moving one. The bird made me see it – the auspiciousness of that number – I took that to be a signal to go on.

She drove through town and north to Española and on to Abiquiu, arriving just as the sun set in deep, rich tones above the hills. Georgia opened the door to greet her and, as she did so, she turned to Juan Hamilton and said, 'Did you see when she arrived?' Joni took this to be a sign that Georgia saw her arrival as, in some way, blessed. O'Keeffe led her guest through the large adobe house, opening the doors to several rooms, inviting her to choose a suitable bedroom; she lingered in the doorway of her studio and Mitchell felt that this was where Georgia was happiest for her to sleep. That first night the two women and Hamilton sat down to dinner and Joni later recalled the awkwardness of it:

> I only remember two points of her dinner conversation that night. The first one was, 'Well, Warhol was here, he wasn't much.' I wasn't sure why I was there. It was a bit testy. I think there is always a certain amount of testing that goes on among artists ... mettle-testing, let the wars begin ... How would you like to sit down for dinner, you're the guest, and the first thing that comes up is a discussion on how boring the last guest was? That's a bit of a trial.

The two women went to Juan Hamilton's house the following day, where Joni photographed O'Keeffe and Hamilton. All three went walking but Georgia seemed determined not to allow her guest to relax long enough to glimpse the side of her that was warm and generous, rather than acerbic, irascible or proprietary about Hamilton:

> I felt a bit like a fifth wheel and there were moments of great discomfort ... she'd say things like, 'Of course she doesn't *see* like we do, does she Juan?' And I'd say, 'Wait a minute, wait a minute – I can see perfectly fine.' Georgia was supposed to be blind at that time, and in fact her eyes were grey in the centre like an old dog's. But her peripheral vision was excellent, and she'd cock her head at the ground and say, 'Well, then do you see that bug crawling over there?' I'd have to look, and there would be this bug crawling.

They went over to Ghost Ranch about twelve miles north of Abiquiu; O'Keeffe had kept a home there for many years, where she had lived during the summer months. It's an extraordinary place, nestled below raw cliffs and the rain-eroded hills, trees and sage-brush eventually giving way to the badlands. The area, at the eastern edge of the Jemez mountain range, is immediately recognisable from O'Keeffe's landscapes: the rainbow colours of 200 million years of geological history streaked across the hills, in red, ochre, grey, purple, blue, pink, yellow, and in the distance, the Pedernal mountain.

As they walked across the arid, stony ground, Georgia spun around to a chain-smoking Mitchell and exclaimed, '*You* should stop smoking!' Juan remonstrated with her, only to have Georgia insist on the last word: 'Well, *she* should live.' This was the nearest to a declaration of affection that Mitchell was going to get for the time being and she accepted it with equanimity: 'I thought, I guess she likes me, she'd just decreed that I should live whatever the reason . . . ' O'Keeffe softened noticeably in the coming days, christening her guest with a pet name, 'Zoni', and before Joni's departure, asking her to witness a copy of her will.

It had been almost a year since Mitchell's first visit to Abiquiu and, in that time, her awareness of a spiritual bond with O'Keeffe had strengthened from a distance, heightened in part by reading a cover feature on the artist in the magazine *Artnews*. The interviewer had quizzed O'Keeffe about how she would like to return if reincarnated. The artist had responded without hesitation, 'I would come back as a blonde soprano who could sing high clear notes without fear.' Mitchell saw her own mirror image in those words in particular, and in elements of Georgia's sensibility as a whole:

> You kind of learn to trust to a certain degree in signs, especially in the arts. I think in a way, synchronistic events and auspicious things mean a great deal. And the more you trust them and the more you work with them, the more spectacular the display they seem to put up. For a long time, that's been the colour in my life and kind of my guidepost, and Georgia's too.

When she arrived home in Los Angeles, Mitchell resumed painting with renewed passion and vigour, as she explained in the Mendel catalogue:

> I had the opportunity to view [Georgia's] last painting and the leftovers from a lifetime of showing. Because much of this work was not her best it encouraged me to paint again. I did a series of paintings of Georgia and of Mingus – most of which I later destroyed and some of which I sold in Tokyo at rather inflated prices.

One that survived was 'Mingus Down in Mexico' (1978) which is featured on the *Mingus* album. The writer Geoff Dyer could almost have been describing this painting in his novelistic jazz biography, *But Beautiful,* when he wrote of Mingus:

> He travelled to Mexico, hoping the sun would thaw him, unlock the pack ice that was trapping his blood. He sat in the sun, surrounded by the still heat of the desert, his face shaded by the brim of a huge sombrero. His body had become so still he could barely feel himself breathe. Nothing moving anywhere. The sun was a copper cymbal that didn't move. It hung in the same place for three days in an unchanging sky, no wind, not a grain of sand twitching . . .

Another was 'Georgia O'Keeffe's Rainbarrel' (1978, also known as 'The Blue Barrel'), which at the Mendel retrospective became almost as well known for Mitchell's cat having peed on it than for the New Mexico home that inspired it. Among the later paintings to come out of her visit to O'Keeffe was 'The Mud Club' (1983). As Georgia's eyesight deteriorated, she turned increasingly to pot-making, encouraged by Juan Hamilton. Splattered with clay after a session at the potter's wheel, the two jokingly referred to themselves as the Mud Club.

The two women kept in touch over the years, occasionally exchanging letters or gifts. In June 1979, O'Keeffe sent Mitchell a copy of the catalogue of the Stieglitz Exhibition of Photographs in New York. She enclosed a typewritten note, saying 'I hope you enjoy it. I'm not signing these books, as the work in it is Stieglitz' and not mine.' Georgia O'Keeffe died at the age of 98 in St Vincent's Hospital, Santa Fe, on 6 March 1986. Her ashes were scattered over the land at Ghost Ranch which, along with her home and studio in Abiquiu, and the Georgia O'Keeffe Museum which opened in Santa Fe in 1997, have become places of pilgrimage.

Georgia and Joni found artistic solace and inspiration in many similar ways, in the presence and absence of romantic love, in sound and vision, in the sky and the ground. Some of their most identifiable work had come from a single source: for 17 years, O'Keeffe painted a series of sky-and-cloud works, inspired first by a view of clouds during her first aircraft journey and later, as she continued to interpret them over the years. The view inspired paintings like *Sky Above Clouds IV*, completed in 1965. Measuring 8 by 24 feet, it was O'Keeffe's largest painting and became the cornerstone of the 1970 Whitney Museum of Modern Art retrospective in New York. They were her last painted works before her eyesight failed, her final legacy. Just as Mitchell, in the mid-1960s, had taken inspiration for what may be her best-known song, 'Both Sides, Now', from her own and Saul Bellow's fictional Rain King's view of clouds, O'Keeffe had written:

> One day when I was flying back to New Mexico, the sky below was a most beautiful solid white. It looked so secure that I thought I could walk right out onto it to the horizon if the door opened. The sky beyond was a light clear blue. It was so wonderful that I couldn't wait to be home to paint it . . .

Appendix One
A Mitchell Miscellany

An open letter to Joni Mitchell:
You weren't sure, were you, Joni, that the hometown audience was really with you Friday night ... They were very quiet, weren't they? They were a little shy about joining, 'Just another hometown kid', as you put it, in the choruses of your songs. But they were with you all the way, Joni. It takes courage to face a hometown audience for the first time. They knew that. It takes even more courage to present an entire show by yourself ... A good many seasoned performers wouldn't even try to go it alone. You did, and it went fine. That was because you recognised your audience wasn't there for tinsel. You gave them substance ... But Joni, you owe your friends another favour. They've become accustomed to the sort of performer who rushes out for five curtain calls before their hands are even warmed from clapping. They thought you were coming back, but you didn't. Try to make that curtain call back here in Saskatoon, soon.
With warmest regards,
Mary L. Gilchrist
(*Saskatoon Star-Phoenix*, March 15, 1969)

When it comes to her music, Mitchell can be humourless. People describe her as 'bitter' and a 'loose cannon', and those are her friends. Over the course of three days of conversations, Mitchell will compare herself to Mozart, Blake and Picasso; she will say that the lyrics to one of her songs 'have a lot of symbolic depth, like the Bible' and describes her music as so new, it needs its own genre name. In discussing her autobiography in the works, she will explain that there is no way to fit her life into one volume, she needs to do it in four. (She already knows the first line: 'I was the only black man at the party'; colleagues say she sometimes feels like a black man in a white woman's body.)
(Neil Strauss, the *New York Times* magazine, October 4, 1998)

On May 29, 1983, Mitchell appeared as a guest on BBC Radio One's 'My Top Twelve' show, hosted by Andy Peebles. Thirteen choices were played: 'Les Trois Cloches' by Edith Piaf; an instrumental work-in-progress of her own, 'Speechless', which had been inspired by seeing a film clip of Piaf in performance; 'Lucille', Little Richard; 'Cloudburst', Lambert, Hendricks and Ross; 'Memphis Blues Again', Bob Dylan; 'Captain for a Dark Morning', Laura Nyro; 'Nefertiti', Miles Davis; Warrior Drummers of Burundi excerpt from the album, *The Music of Burundi*; 'Gaucho', Steely Dan; 'That Girl', Stevie Wonder; 'You've Changed', Billie Holiday; 'I Have the Touch', Peter Gabriel; part of the first movement of 'The Rite of Spring', Moscow Radio Symphony Orchestra.

A couple of weeks ago, on May 29, Joni Mitchell played a two-hour concert to a tiny audience on a secret soundstage in the heart of Warners Brothers' lot. The show was being filmed to promote her upcoming LP, *Taming The Tiger,* named after a saying that compares showbiz and a tiger — 'it's harder to catch and harder to tame.' Clearly nervous, the stately 55-year-old played number after number of dense and oddly tempo'ed songs, while an audience of friends and family sat raptly by, trying to absorb her peculiar vision. Near the end, the singer-songwriter currently known as Jewel quietly rose from her seat and tiptoed forward. Was she going to join Mitchell onstage for a rendition of 'Big Yellow Taxi', the song that Lilith Fair founder Sarah McLachlan often encores with? No. Jewel was rising to leave . . . the new breed hasn't gotten its clout thanks to Joni, who will be lucky if *Taming The Tiger* goes gold and can't even get Jewel to sit still for two hours . . .
(Gina Arnold, *New Times LA*, June 18–24, 1998) *Joni Mitchell was invited to appear at the phenomenally successful Lilith Fair concerts but declined.*

In the liner notes to XTC's *Homegrown* CD – a collection of demos and studio experiments for *Wasp Star,* released the previous year – Andy Partridge described an early version of the song, 'The Man Who Murdered Love', as 'Joni Mitchellin – Joni Mitchell meets Led Zeppelin'. *Homegrown* was the first release on XTC's own label, Idea.
(*Homegrown*, XTC, 2001)

In 1990, the United States clothes chain, the Gap, launched a series of advertisements featuring celebrities wearing Gap clothes. Among those featured was Joni Mitchell. In 1992, when the Gap launched a new set of celebrity ads, Joan Baez was asked to appear. She refused on principle. 'There is no contradiction,' she says, it is just about control and common sense. 'All I wear is Gap, but what would I be coming back as? A T-shirt?'
(Baez quoted in *Daily Telegraph*, March 11, 1993)

. . . many subjects did decline to be interviewed, though I suspect that in most cases these individuals do not care one way or another what [David] Geffen thinks about their decision . . . The most disappointing rejection came from Joni Mitchell, whose relationship with Geffen, I believe, boosted his career as much as it did hers . . . David Crosby warned me that an interview with Mitchell would be 'poisonous.' Geffen had said many disparaging things about her to me and worried aloud about whom I would believe in depicting their story. 'If I didn't talk to her for the rest of my life, I wouldn't miss her for a minute,' Geffen said without hesitation. I wrote several letters and placed many telephone calls to Mitchell, all of which went unanswered. Finally, in December, 1998, her manager called to say she would do a short telephone interview the next day. 'There's at least one story she wants to make sure you include in your book,' he told me. The following day, however, the manager called back and said she had reconsidered. Joni Mitchell did not want to talk about David Geffen after all. I wrote her yet another letter and – at the suggestion of a friend who had heard Mitchell mention in a National Public Radio interview that her cat Nietzsche had learned to dance – I sent a box of gourmet cat treats to her home in Bel-Air. She never responded.
(Tom King, in the introduction to his book *David Geffen: A Biography of New Hollywood*, 2000)

Edward Asner, Joni Mitchell and Kenny Loggins are among the well-known Hollywood names lending their talents to a documentary opposing development of Playa Vista, future home of Dreamworks. 'The Last Stand: The Struggle for Balona Wetlands' centres on the possibility of saving one of southern California's last wetland ecosystems and Los Angeles' largest remaining open space. Asner narrates the 56-minute film; Mitchell, Loggins and Joe Walsh provided music.
(*Reuters/Variety*, January 7, 1999). *David Geffen is a co-founder of Dreamworks.*

An assault on the American music industry by the singer and actress, Courtney Love, has prompted some of the world's biggest rock stars to challenge the companies that employ them. In a sign that their industry has come of age, they are demanding a decent pension. . . Love's efforts to overhaul the system have been boosted by fellow stars backing demands for fairer conditions. [Don] Henley, a co-founder of the Recording Artists Coalition, which represented dozens of leading artists including Eric Clapton and Joni Mitchell, said the group was building a £3.5million fund to lobby for pension and other rights.
(Tom Rhodes, *The Sunday Times*, April 1, 2001)

Things haven't quite gone according to plan for the San Francisco-based songwriter [Mark Eitzel]. His life's ambition was to be a pop star, but instead he became a cult musician, loved by a faithful few but ignored by the majority. That is strange when you consider that, with his former band American Music Club and now as a solo artist, Eitzel has always been adored by critics. His lyrics are frequently compared to Raymond Carver, and in 1991 he was named *Rolling Stone*'s songwriter of the year. Fellow musicians admire him, too. Joni Mitchell, P.J. Harvey and Elvis Costello all claim to be Eitzel's biggest fan.
(Fiona Sturges, *Independent*, April 27, 2001)

The one instance when I saw [Laura] Nyro and [Janis] Joplin on the same bill, at the Philadelphia Music Festival in 1969, Nyro took the stage in mid-afternoon, battling fierce summer heat, singing to a flagging audience in her style, which demanded full attention. She was booed off the stage. That evening, Joplin's electric kineticism ignited the crowd, her growling lightning-infused voice bringing people to their feet and keeping them there for hours. . . Both were white but assimilated the musical styles of black culture: Joplin from the blues, and Nyro from jazz. Both cleared a path for future women in rock, from Joni Mitchell and Suzanne Vega to Rickie Lee Jones, Lisa Loeb and Ani Di Franco.
(Tony Vellela, *Christian Science Monitor*, May 11, 2001)

Whatever way you choose to couch it, gender is still an issue in an industry infamous for its misogyny in packaging and dealing with women. We may have moved on from the blatant '99% Virgin' marketing ploys that were used to sell Joni Mitchell's 1968 LP but the subliminal though 99% successful revamping of an AOR chanteuse like Texas' singer Sharleen Spiteri into an Ellen von Unwerth prototype with en-suite Prada wardrobe has the same updated smack of 'sex shifts units' about it.
(Ann Donald, *The Herald*, March 30, 1998)

Joni Mitchell was the consummate 'hippy chick', Annie Hall meets urban-cowgirl, with a haunting beauty that intrigued many famous lovers from David

Crosby, Graham Nash and Stephen Stills to James Taylor, Jack Nicholson and Warren Beatty. She created her own sense of style ... she forged her own Bohemian look: long, flaxen hair peeling out from beneath a floppy cotton hat or beret; floaty, ethnic yet understated clothing, offset by bold turquoise jewellery, and a cigarette never far from her lips. ... Today, you just have to check out the spring/summer collections by Anna Sui, Nicole Farhi, Rifat Ozbek, Miu Miu and Anna Molinari to see that the Joni influence does not just stop at music.
(Laura Campbell, *Sunday Telegraph,* February 8, 1998)

Los Angeles is a town where the elite seek the elite, and flee hoi polloi as they might wildfires. It is considered vaguely demeaning to share space with anyone but one's equals. Nowhere was this more obvious than at Paramount Studios on Monday night, when California Governor Gray Davis threw an enormous party for those attending the [Democratic Party] conference ... The current A-list still spent all week obsessed with [President Clinton]. To this end a host of them were having dinner at Paramount's Studio 20 ... Guests, including Joni Mitchell, *ER* star Noah Wylie and producer Lawrence Bender, had either paid $100,000 each or raised $250,000 to have dinner with the President. ... in the end Clinton didn't eat with them – he addressed them, which is hardly considered the same thing at all.
(Grace Bradberry, *The Times,* August 18, 2000)

Name the most important lyric-writers of the past half-century. Stephen Sondheim, without question, the lyricist who single-handedly deepened the American song tradition with penetrating verbal invention and an enlivening dose of psychological complexity. But also Bob Dylan, Paul Simon and Joni Mitchell, folk balladeers who infused lyric writing with the imagery and confessional aspect of modernist poetry. Their innovations created an entirely new tradition, or perhaps, anti-tradition – that of the self-absorbed singer-songwriter for whom, in the name of personal expression, all lyric-writing rules could be broken.
(Barry Singer, *New York Times,* February 20, 2000)

... what [Bob] Dylan did for sullen, skinny boys, Joni Mitchell would do in spades for skittish, self-obsessed girls. Like all the best singer-songwriters, Mitchell moved from early simplicity into wild, exhilarating bursts of inventiveness. And like all the best, she would unwittingly inspire a legion of tedious solipsists who made up in egotism what they lacked in ability. The early '70s were clogged up with howlingly awful artistes of both sexes, each more willing than the last to plumb the very puddle of their psyche.
(David Bennun, *Guardian,* August 27, 1999)

Canadian singer/songwriter Spek first became involved in music at the age of 14 when he helped form the school hip-hop band, Blizzardz of Poetry, in Montreal. Three years later, he was invited to join the Canadian collective Dream Warriors and last year, he was featured on Nitin Sawhney's Mercury-nominated album, *Beyond Skin.* Now, at 25, he is finally releasing his first solo effort. His laconic light-hearted rapping style has been compared to Arrested Development. Spek himself cites De la Soul and Joni Mitchell as his main musical influences ...
(*Independent on Sunday,* December 10, 2000)

'Coming as I do from Canada, two very different women were naturally an early influence on me, the two of them being also Canadian,' says k.d. lang. 'One was Anne Murray, who I thought was just so cool when I first saw her on TV, barefoot on some folk show, long before she hit her peak and went MOR. Then there was Joni Mitchell. Obviously, I'm seeing things from a woman's perspective, but to me she's been one of the most major influences on pop itself, every bit as significant as Dylan and possibly more so. I wonder if she has any idea how worshipped she is?'
(k.d. lang, *The Times*, July 4, 1997)

Canadians have long suffered anonymity. The assumption being that if a person is famous, he or she is American. Now that anonymity seems to have reached into the 1,100 pages of the *Women's Who's Who*. Not that the editors assume a range of their compatriots are American: they have just not included them. Which makes for bizarre reading. Singers k.d. lang, Joni Mitchell and Anne Murray are missing, as are author Alice Munro and actress Margot Kidder. Margaret Atwood has made it, but Barbara Hall, the mayor of Toronto, hasn't.
(Claire Trevena, *The Guardian*, December 7, 1995)

Forty is where you notice you are clinging to the things of youth long past reason. I am 40, still wearing Levi's and workshirts and listening to Neil Young and James Taylor and Joni Mitchell. And yes, from time to time, I even sneak a listen to *Songs of Leonard Cohen* . . . A pitiful case.
(Fergal Keane, BBC Special Correspondent, *Independent*, January 6, 2001)

I have always said that in politics and pop, you get what you deserve – which is why I watched Channel 4's *Music of the Millennium* with both horror and a total lack of surprise. How anyone could vote Madonna above Aretha Franklin as the best female singer of the past 1,000 years is, well, heartbreaking. Joni Mitchell, another heavenly voice, was at number 20 and Barbra Streisand was nowhere near the top 10.
(Boy George, *Express on Sunday*, November 21, 1999)

The British satirical comedian, Steve Coogan, opened the first of his television comedy series based around his dysfunctional local radio DJ character Alan Partridge, with a rant at Mitchell: 'This is Radio Norwich, and that was 'Big Yellow Taxi' by Joni Mitchell, a song in which Joni complains that "they paved paradise to put up a parking lot" – a measure which actually would have alleviated traffic congestion on the outskirts of paradise – something which Joni singularly fails to point out, because it doesn't quite fit with her blinkered view of the world. It's 4.37 am and you're listening to *Up With The Partridge* . . . '

Mitchell's genius for illuminating what she feels, thinks, and sees has one stubborn flaw: She's never entirely stopped being the artsy girl, the classic middle-class, butterfly-painting adolescent, all unfettered creativity and ignorance of technique and mannered self-immersion, traces of which are to be found even in her best work. That, more than anything, may be why people are reluctant to grant her the kind of legendary status accorded to '60s-generation prophets who've had far less to say than she – though it's hard to know what to think about a culture that's put off by a little artsy-girl precious-

ness while remaining riveted by the banal self-destructiveness and baby non-sense of classic artsy boys like Jim Morrison. Go figure.
(Linda Sanders, *Entertainment Weekly*, March 1, 1991)

Jack Vettriano, 45, the son of a Leven miner, left school at 15 and went down the pit. He started painting aged 21 when a schoolteacher girlfriend bought him a box of watercolours . . . His pit-to-posh gallery story is an irresistible one, his mass-produced images are as ubiquitous and well-loved as the Scottish art establishment is openly hostile . . . But although his men wear hats and the women wear stockings, Vettriano's inspiration comes from a different, and less expected era. 'A lot of it comes from lyrics – Joni Mitchell, Leonard Cohen – before that, it was Mr Right and Miss Right are out there, they'll meet and it will be springtime all year. Fly me to the moon. All that sort of stuff.' His smile is plaintive. 'Whereas they shook it down and said, "It's not like that, we're all fucked up from start to finish." They articulate what I think. I've always been a sucker for a sad song.'
(Anna Burnside, *Sunday Herald*, December 5, 1999)

Colm Toibin, the lively Irish novelist, toasted his Booker Prize nomination by being ejected from the Groucho Club. Toibin – shortlisted for *The Blackwater Lightship* – celebrated by bawling his way through Joni Mitchell's album *Blue*. 'I was a sad nerd when I was a kid, and I just used to sit in my room listening to *Blue* over and over again,' he tells me. 'So I know it all. So I sang it all.' And was asked to leave.
(Mark Ingleford, *The Times*, September 23, 1999)

Joni Mitchell suffered a trauma while shopping in London on Thursday night. Her purse was snatched, but luckily she was only carrying £100 and a packet of chewing gum. Joni's new LP, *Dog Eat Dog*, by the way, is her best yet.
(*Mirror*, December 7, 1985)

Corey Harris has been hailed as a 'saviour of the acoustic blues tradition', a 'groundbreaking acoustic bluesman', a 'throwback to a lost era' . . . he went to Cameroon in 1991 . . . Learning the polyrhythmic drumming of indigenous Cameroonian juju music made his guitar-playing more drum-like. A Cameroonian painter and guitar-player he befriended 'was into James Brown and Joni Mitchell.' There seemed to be no limit to cultural connections.
(Mike Zwerin, *International Herald Tribune*, August 23, 2000)

It's not uncommon in the current music scene to find the cultural casserole syndrome at work. In the style cauldron are elements from various corners of the globe, sometimes with dance-happy Western touches . . . in the case of guitarist-singer Gerard Edery, the blend of varied cultural elements comes honestly, straight out of experience. . . . Born in Casablanca, Edery was exposed to Arabic music as a youth and later French musical culture when his family moved to Paris. Landing in the United States in the 1970s, he heard the folk of Bob Dylan and Joni Mitchell while studying classical and flamenco guitar and receiving classical voice training.
(Josef Woodard, *Los Angeles Times*, September 1, 2000)

As Travis plays its warm, engaging music at the Wiltern, you realise how much easier it would have been for them if they had arrived in the US a decade or so

earlier – back when such compatible acts as U2 and REM dominated the marketplace . . . Even most of Travis' musical favourites are drawn from an earlier era.' Just start with everyone at "The Last Waltz" [concert] . . . Joni Mitchell, Bob Dylan, the Band, Neil Young,' [Fran] Healy says . . . . 'Great records – just like heroic moments in sports – are like little pieces of magic that stay in your imagination like stars in the sky. Records like Joni Mitchell's *Blue* or Bob Dylan's *Blood On The Tracks* are there to inspire us. They are the stars that you use to navigate your life by, and the ones you use to find your way home when you are lost.'
(Robert Hilburn, *Los Angeles Times*, August 6, 2000)

[Karl] Wallinger says he was reminded of his dealings with major label records execs when watching 'Casablanca' on television. 'Peter Lorre says to Humphrey Bogart's character, "You don't like me very much, do you Rick?" and Bogart says "If I gave you any thought, I probably wouldn't." I think that sums up my attitude to those guys perfectly' . . . *Dumbing Up* plays to Wallinger's strengths. 'Another Thousand Years' brings to mind *White Album*-era Beatles with exquisite high harmonies. For such an authentic homage it was constructed in a surprisingly lo-fi way. 'I've got this open tuning on the acoustic guitar, which I got from Joni Mitchell's *Blue* and it really chimes.'
(Mark Edwards, *Sunday Times*, August 20, 2000)

A sadly ageing flower-child feminist tries to distract a chic young woman from her laptop with a story about the death of an infant; an HIV-infected mother instructs her mixed-race teenager on the politically correct strategies for filling out a college application; a pornographic model declares love for her homosexual photographer; a female theatre director foully stimulates a male actor in a restaurant, a profane parody of the casting couch. The vignettes that make up 'Hurricane', a sardonic breast-beating discourse – or lack of it – that sexuality confers on a woman in the post-feminist world. . . The play, by the 35-year-old Erin Cressida Wilson. . . [features] the music of – who else? – Joni Mitchell.
(Bruce Weber, *New York Times*, December 13, 1999)

It's hard to even begin to recognise 70s rock 'n' roll without acknowledging the profound influences of singer-songwriter Jackson Browne . . . The [Rock and Roll] Hall of Fame has already inducted such artists as the Eagles and Joni Mitchell. To honour them without recognising Jackson Browne is like building a home and forgetting the foundation.
(Russ Paris, *Los Angeles Times*, October 2, 2000)

Lynden David Hall. . . sings like an angel, plays almost everything on the album [*The Other Side*] himself – including wonderful bluesy guitar – and looks like the fashion-plate he already is . . . He cites Joni Mitchell's *The Hissing of Summer Lawns* and even Bob Dylan as influences, revealing as he does so, a trainspotter's eye for detail. He likes the vibes-player Victor Feldman's contribution to the Mitchell album . . .
(Phil Johnson, *Independent*, June 2, 2000)

While the underlying influences of Beth Orton's music lie in English folk, there is a wide range of other artists who have had an impact on her style. These range from the all-girl punk band The Slits to Rickie Lee Jones, through to Neil Young and Joni Mitchell. Other notable influences are from the jazz and soul

musician Terry Callier and The Chemical Brothers. It is one of the unexplainable phenomena of the music industry that Beth Orton's unique folk-influenced style found favour with mid-90s clubbers.
(*Eastern Daily Press*, March 11, 2000)

I attended a peculiar event Saturday, September 23. . . featuring, supposedly, a talk by 'the real don Juan' [subject of Carlos Castaneda's books]. . . . The location was Ron Teeguarden's Herbarium, a large home north of Sunset in Brentwood. . . Outside in the garden behind the house . . . were Rosanna Arquette and Joni Mitchell. Joni was dressed in a floor-length black leather coat and black beret. 'Grandfather Cachora' sat in Hollywood Indian splendour on a polished burlwood throne . . . Dana asked a question [and] followed up by stating that Castaneda used to say he experienced something that don Juan never experienced: the power of the mass. Joni Mitchell turned and asked disdainfully, 'You mean he drew a bigger crowd?' . . . Cachora asked for a drawing that had symbols on it – a mandala of some kind next to a much younger picture of him. He explained that he was looking for someone who could explain them. Joni said the symbols were familiar looking. She started giving a pretty credible explanation that they represented the four cardinal points, and the four different races of man. 'White at north, custodian of knowledge. Yellow Man, East. Custodian of clarity. South, black man.') Cachora cut her off and asserted that the symbol she said was west represented the three dimensions. He asked which dimension humans were in, and finally accepted the answer, 'third'.
(Corey Donovan, sustainedaction.org website, October 9, 2000) *sustainedaction.org is a website devoted to exploring and evaluating the legacy of Carlos Castaneda and investigating other possibilities for increased awareness and perception.*

Appendix Two
Source Notes

Abbreviations: **AG** Acoustic Guitar, **BB** Billboard, **BC** Border Crossings, **DB** Downbeat, **LAT** Los Angeles Times, **LAW** LA Weekly, **MC** Macleans, **MM** Melody Maker, **Mendel cat**. Mendel Art Gallery catalogue for *voices: Joni Mitchell* exhibition, **NME** New Musical Express, **NYT** New York Times, **RP** Rock Photo, **RS** Rolling Stone, **SFE** San Francisco Examiner, **SSP** Saskatoon Star Phoenix, **SST** Saskatoon Sun Times, **SR** Stereo Review, **TDS** Toronto Daily Star, **TGM** Toronto Globe and Mail, **V** Variety, **VF** Vanity Fair, **VV** Village Voice, **WP** Washington Post.

For book references, please see Bibliography.

CHAPTER ONE: The birth of rock 'n' roll days ...

18	'...the Depression'	TGM, July 1, 2000
20	'...to it'	Capital Radio, Rock Masterclass, Dec 29, 1985
20	'...European classics'	BC, Feb 2001, vol 20 no.1
21	'...my soul'	LAT, Feb 24, 1991
21	'...for me'	BC, ibid
22	'...and cooks'	LAW, Nov 25, 1994
23	'...his books'	MC, June,1974
23	'...I collapsed'	BB, Dec 9,1995
25	'...my singing'	ibid
25	'...six-year-old'	BC, ibid
26	'...a convalescent'	VF, June, 1997
26	'... so pragmatic'	Time Out, Sept 20–27, 2000
26	'...own bedroom'	Elm Street, Nov 2000
27	'... I know'	BBC Radio 2, Feb 20, 1999
28	'...out later'	ibid
28	'...very disappointing'	BC, ibid
29	The Fishbowl	Mojo, Aug, 1998
30	'...to dance'	DB, Sept 6, 1979
30	'...full power'	ibid
31	'...college mentality'	BBC Radio 2, ibid
31	'...be dancing'	SFE, Oct 30, 1998
31	'...pretty good'	BB, ibid
32	'...terrible voice'	SSP, Aug 24, 1985
33	'...in jail'	RS, July 26, 1979
34	'...the bug'	Weekend Magazine, Jan 11, 1969
34	'... can *sing*'	Elm Street, ibid
34	'...rebel against'	ibid

CHAPTER TWO: Tears and fears and feeling proud ...

36	'...about that'	Saskatoon Report 1990
38	'...the locals'	SFE, ibid
38	'...very experienced'	Jennings to author, Feb 16, 2001
39	'...her life'	Taylor to author, Feb 18, 2001
39	'...for her'	ibid
40	'...about her'	ibid
40	'...those legs'	Temple University Radio, Nov 17,1966
40	'...her well'	Taylor, ibid
41	'...me up'	BB, ibid
41	'...thrown out'	BBC Radio 2, ibid
41	'...something awful'	Temple University Radio ibid
41	Chuck Mitchell's misgivings	BBC Radio 2, ibid
42	'...the machines'	Detroit News, Feb 6, 1966
42	'...average couples'	ibid
42	'...Peyton Place'	ibid
42	'...would do'	ibid
43	'...blue eyes'	Detroit News, Mar 20, 1966
43	'...the building'	ibid
43	'...to hear'	Rush to author, Feb 19, 2000
44	'...be relevant'	ibid
45	'...sparked me'	RS, May 30, 1991
45	'...stop winter'	SSP, Feb 2, 1968
46	'...structural verses'	Heylin, *Behind the Shades*, p215
46	'...growing up'	SFE, ibid
47	'...her shoulders'	Variety, Feb 22, 1967
47	'...always evocative'	ibid
47	'...reasonably happy'	Temple University Radio, ibid
48	'...a long time'	ibid
48	'...very elegant'	Shay to author, Feb 27, 2001
49	'...use before'	Temple University Radio, ibid
50	'...that metaphorical'	Doggett, P. pp301–302
50	'...Circle Game'	Bernstein to author, 2001
51	'...the impulse!'	Rush to author, Feb 19, 2001
51	'...my writing'	Jennings, N. p92
52	'...her identity'	Rush, ibid
53	'...fairy goddess'	Shay, ibid
53	'...life is!'	Bellow, S. p46
54	'...some hope'	BBC Radio 1, Dec 20, 1970
55	'...American humour'	Musician, Jan, 1983
55	'...start afresh'	Rogan, J. p387
56	'...I moved out'	Goldmine, Feb 17, 1995
57	'...my set'	BBC Radio 2, ibid
57	'...does she'	Variety, June 28, 1967
58	'...in Flint'	WHAT-FM, Mar 12, 1967
61	'...back row'	SSP, Feb 2, 1968
62	'...own experience'	Co-Evolution Quarterly, Summer, 1976
63	'...a manager'	Goldmine, ibid
63	'...manage you!'	Much More Music, 'Speak Easy', March 2000
64	'...a manager!'	ibid
64	'...from then'	BBC Radio 2, ibid

65	'...other managers'	King, T. p69
65	'...we began'	Goldmine, ibid
66	'...as it were'	Roberts to author, May 4, 2001
66	'...to them'	ibid
67	'...audience yet'	ibid
68	'...receptive there'	ibid
69	'...selling music to'	ibid

CHAPTER THREE: Places to come from and places to go ...

71	'...to her'	Crosby to Wally Breese, jonimitchell.com, Mar 15, 1997
71	'...emotionally involved'	Crosby, D. p130
71	'...Got Away'	ibid p131
72	'...this guy'	ibid p132
73	'...we proceeded'	ibid p131
73	'...a great style'	ibid p136
73	'...been here'	rolandus.com, 1996
74	'...a night'	Crosby, D., ibid p137
74	'... know how'	Crosby/Breese, ibid
75	'...really good'	WHAT-FM, Folklore, 1968
75	'...me happy'	Breese/Crosby, ibid
77	'...about...water'	Shay to author, ibid
78	'...Neptune sits'	TDS, April 20, 1968
78	'...me too'	MM, Sept 28, 1968
79	'...her best'	Vega to author, Feb 12, 2001
79	'...of me?'	TDS, ibid
80	'...really different?'	Siberry to author, Nov 21, 2000
80	'...for them'	Crosby, D., ibid p130
80	'...frau-duties'	Sounds, June 3, 1972
81	'...lesser talent'	Current Biography, Oct 1976
82	'...like children'	RS, Dec 15, 1994
82	'...Sweet'	ibid
83	'...dental bills'	TDS, ibid
83	'...youthful talents'	Variety, April 24, 1968
84	'...that point'	Nash to author, Sept 28,2000
85	'...pair bond'	Goldmine, ibid
85	'... each other'	Crosby, D., ibid p139
86	'...of hepatitis'	Evening Bulletin, Aug 24, 1968
87	'... at all'	Heylin,C. No More Sad Refrains p77
87	'...than that'	ibid p139
87	'...about everything'	ibid p251
88	'...the enemy'	MM, ibid

CHAPTER FOUR: Songs to aging children come ...

89	'...Gemini and Virgo'	WHAT-FM, ibid
90	'...feelings myself'	Weekend Magazine, ibid
90	'...Please come'	ibid
91	'...her songs'	TGM, Feb 21, 2001; Robinson to author, Feb 25, 2001
92	'...my life'	Bernstein to author, Apr 3, 2001

92	'...can play!'	ibid
93	'...up herself'	ibid
93	'...be sheep'	RS, May 17, 1969
94	'...on it'	ibid
94	'...this year'	TDS, ibid
95	'...a teenybopper'	Weekend Magazine, ibid
95	'...felt unsafe'	Doggett, P. p6
96	'...a print-puller'	BC, ibid
98	'...you're feeling'	Taylor to author, ibid
100	'...been happier'	Nash to author, Oct 4, 2000
101	'...so moving'	Goldmine, ibid
102	'...he played'	Acoustic Guitar, Aug, 1996
102	'...top it'	Rogan, J., ibid p210
102	'...with me'	Crosby, D. ibid p163
103	'... the audience'	LAT, Aug 26, 1969
104	'...other people'	Crosby, D., ibid p175
105	'...us Watergate'	Spin, Jan. 1992, vol 7, no.10
106	'...were wrong'	BBC Radio 2, ibid

CHAPTER FIVE: Dreams have lost some grandeur coming true ...

107	'...was absurd'	Goldmine, ibid
108	'...the audience'	RS, Aug 5, 1971
108	'...human being'	Current Biography, Oct, 1976
109	'...personal relationship'	Toronto Star, Feb 9, 1974
110	'...I couldn't'	Mojo, ibid
111	'...Yellow Taxi'	BBC Radio 2, ibid
111	'...of it'	LAT, Dec 8, 1996
112	'...is twenty'	WHAT-FM, Mar 17, 1967
112	'...great singer'	VF, ibid
115	'...had changed'	AG, ibid
116	'...their stomachs'	Sounds, ibid

CHAPTER SIX: Just when you're getting a taste for worship ...

124	'...accompanies depression'	Storr, A. p143
125	'...at all'	Sounds, ibid
126	'...emotionally honest'	Grammy Magazine, Spring, 1996
126	'...absolute wreck'	Musician, ibid
126	'... whole life'	Stern, J.P. p41
127	'...1967 or 68'	Bernstein to author, Apr 11, 2001
128	'... of "meanings"'	Against Interpretation, section 4, publ. Evergreen Review, Dec 1964
128	'...their meaning'	Guardian, Apr 14, 2001
129	'...of that'	VF, ibid
131	'...popular music'	RS, ibid
132	'...my business'	Heylin, C. *No More Sad Refrains* p212
133	'...of thinking'	Sounds, ibid
134	'...walk out'	ibid
135	'... of icon'	MM, May 13, 1972
137	'...folk-style artists'	Variety, Mar 1, 1972
138	'... rewarding relationship'	NME, Feb, 1974

138   '... to resist'   Sounds, Jan, 1971
139   '...disarmingly specific'   RS, Jan 4, 1973
140   '... of thousands'   Sounds, June 10, 1972
141   '...eye lives'   RS, ibid
142   '... and better'   Bernstein to author, ibid
142   '...off for'   RS, July 26, 1979
143   ' ...nude photo'   Bernstein to author, ibid
143   '...at all'   ibid

CHAPTER SEVEN: Anima rising, queen of queens ...

144   '...us all'   Interview for KFRC RKO Radio, San Francisco,
                                   Dec 8, 1980 (published in *Imagine*, ed. Andrew
                                   Solt and Sam Egan, 1988)
144   'on it '   RS, May 30, 1991
147   '...Helen Reddy'   NME, Feb 9, 1974
148   '... of good'   MC, June 1974
148   '... be seen'   LAT, Mar. 1974
148   '...in Paris'   Mojo, Nov 1994
149   '...little deeper'   NME, ibid
151   '...play it!'   Dyer, G. p112
151   '... that again'   Musician, 1989
152   '...little different'   Doggett, Peter, unpublished interview for
                                   Record Collector, 1993
152   '...female ego'   Time, Dec 16, 1974
153   '... old boyfriends'   ibid
155   The Boho Dance   Wolfe, T. pp18-21
158   '...I'm sorry'   Musician, ibid
159   '...going on'   Heylin, C. *Behind the Shades* p427
159   Cal Deal campaign   www.graphicwitness.com;   Miami   Herald,
                                   Apr 3, 2000
160   '...your problem'   RS, Jan 15, 1976
160   '...patsy liberals'   Q, May 1988
160   '... this woman'   ibid
161   Nelson Mandela, ANC, Carter Irish Times, May 11, 2000
162   '...little awe-inspiring'   MM, April 27, 1974

CHAPTER EIGHT: Dreams and false alarms ...

163   '...of wings'   Earhart, A. 'Courage',1927; publ. in Lovell,
                                   Mary S. *The Sound of Wings*, Ch 1, 1989
164   '...like her'   Q, ibid
164   '...me nothing'   RS, Feb 24, 1977
165   '...go broke'   ibid
165   '...at once'   Grammy Magazine, ibid
166   '...key, visually'   Bernstein to author, ibid
167   '...Staten Island'   ibid
167   cocaine / 'Song for Sharon' Q, ibid
168   '...must do'   LAT, Dec 8, 1996
168   '...on *Hejira*'   ibid
169   '...that went'   Grammy Magazine, ibid
169   '...with her'   BBC Radio, Oct, 1978

170	'...his life'	Ingrid Pastorius to Wally Breese, Mar 21, 1998, jonimitchell.com
170	'...is well-taken'	High Fidelity, Mar, 1977
171	'...Joni Mitchell'	Hoskyns, B. p345
173	'...latter form'	RS, Mar 9, 1978
175	'...creative ideas'	Rock Photo, 1985
175	'...on there'	Tate to author, Jan 30, 2001
176	'...sounds, sounds'	Mingus, C. *Beneath The Underdog*
177	'...of balls'	Downbeat, Sept 6, 1979
178	'...for me?'	LAT, Nov 25, 1994
178	'...with me'	Santoro, G. p375
179	'...of this'	BBC Radio 2, ibid
179	'...do something'	TGM, July 1, 2000
179	'...very sweet'	Santoro ibid
180	'...good fun'	LAT, June 10, 1979
180	'...told Charles'	Santoro, ibid
180	Knepper injuries	Santoro, ibid p204
180	'...a writer'	Santoro, ibid p 376
182	'...very difficult'	LAT, ibid
182	'...modern jazz'	Berendt, J, p207
182	'...to be'	Downbeat, ibid
183	'...last verse'	Musician, Jan 1983
184	'...gonna miss'	BBC Radio 2, ibid
185	'...music itself'	RS, Dec 28, 1978
186	'...captured it'	Chesher, Debby, *Starart,* 1979
187	'...his perspective'	BBC Radio 2, ibid
187	'...good enough'	Downbeat, ibid
187	'...and engaging'	LAT, ibid
187	'...message carries'	Berendt. J. p386
187	'...great record'	Reder, A. and Baxter, J. p263
187	'...diminishes hers'	MM, June 16, 1979
187	'... at blackness'	Sounds, June 30, 1979
188	'... in general'	Stereo Review, Oct, 1979
188	'...with time'	Klein to author, Nov–Dec 2000
189	'...own slavery'	VV, 1992
190	'...own government'	LAT, May, 1979

CHAPTER NINE: Love's the greatest beauty ...

193	'...studio work'	Klein to author, ibid
194	'...do it!'	ibid
196	'...guitar tunings'	ibid
197	'...life solidified'	RS, Nov 25, 1982
198	'...being happy'	Klein to author, ibid
199	'...Why not?'	RS, ibid
200	'...have had'	Sunday Times, Apr 17, 1983
200	'...their breath'	RS, ibid
201	'...being alive'	NYT, Nov 7, 1982
201	'...remark on'	NME, Nov 27, 1982
202	'...on Geffen'	Goodman, F. p321
203	'...of touring'	Klein to author, ibid
204	'...before them'	Musician, 1993

204 '...compared to'   Musician, Oct, 1991
205 '...of music'   Colvin to author, Feb 9, 2001
205 '...about anything'   ibid
206 '...The guru'   ibid
206 '...until later'   Vega to author, ibid
207 '...a groove'   ibid
207 '...of cool'   Siberry to author, ibid
208 '...my world'   Reder, A. and Baxter, J. p69
208 '...and career'   LAT, Sept 20, 1998
208 '...she did'   LAT, Jan 17, 1999
209 '...the guitar'   The Times Magazine, April 24, 1999
209 '...it is'   LAW, ibid
210 '...have eternity?'   Vibe, Feb, 1997
210 '...fully appreciated'   LAW, ibid
211 '...it with'   Grammy Magazine, ibid
211 '...so forthcoming'   Tate to author, Jan 30, 2001
212 '...genderless music'   LAW, ibid

CHAPTER TEN: It's dog eat dog – I'm just waking up ...

213 '...in five minutes'   Microphone test for radio broadcast, Aug 11, 1984, quoted in New York Times, Aug 13, 1984
214 '...bombing Cuba'   Klein to author, ibid
215 '...as himself'   ibid
216 '...good to me'   ibid
217 '...isn't working'   BAM, April 22, 1983
217 '...do that?'   Canadian Musician, Feb, 1986
217 '...benign dictator'   ibid
218 '...drove me crazy'   LA Herald, March 9, 1986
219 '...ever made'   Canadian Musician, ibid
219 '...particular era'   The Express, 1988
220 '...hold hands'   Denselow, R. p263
220 '...to hell'   ibid, p267
222 '...like that'   Klein to author, ibid
223 '...rightfully expect'   High Fidelity, Jan, 1986
223 '...own sake'   Newsweek, Nov, 1986
223 '...is unnerving'   RS, Jan, 1986
224 '...*needed* a producer'   Spin, May, 1988
224 too busy with other clients Stereo Review   ibid
224 '...concerned enough'   ibid
224 '...sex and parties?'   ibid
225 '...every time'   Q ibid
226 '...*my* songs'   Klein to author, ibid
227 '...man's song'   ibid
229 '...premier talents'   MC, April 4, 1988
229 '...twenty-year career'   SSP, March 26, 1988
229 '...with time'   RS, April 21, 1988
233 '...and weep'   NYT, 1991
234 '...second stanza'   Mojo, ibid
234 '...of life'   Ellmann, R. p224
234 '...autonomous life'   Entertainment Weekly, Mar 1, 1991

235   '...an artist'   RS, Mar 21, 1991
235   '..and maturity'   LAT, 1991

CHAPTER ELEVEN: Part of this is permanent, part of this is passing ...

237   '...or ugly'   Mojo, Dec, 1994
237   '...we divorced'   BC, ibid
237   '...for months'   Klein to author, ibid
238   '...was refused'   Irish Times, Feb 26, 1999
239   '...twenty years'   Dallas Morning News, 1997
239   '...name – Yvette'   Bishop, S. *Songs In The Rough*
240   '...your wrists'   TGM, 1991
240   '...from Saskatoon'   SSP, May 24, 1991
240   '...and divisionalism'   Time, 1994
240   '...artist today?'   TGM, ibid
241   '...You did'   ibid
242   '...very sad'   RS, Dec 15, 1994
242   '...of yesteryear'   SR, Jan, 1995
242   '...was great'   Mojo, Apr, 1996
242   '...would enjoy'   Bernstein to author, ibid
243   '...million copies'   Klein to author, ibid
244   '...that tradition'   Q, Aug, 1994
244   '...up there'   Mojo, Dec, 1994
244   '...so heavy'   Mojo, Aug, 1998
245   '...of symbolic'   Regina Leader Post, Aug 6, 1994
245   '...withholding people'   Much Music, 'Intimate and Interactive', Sept
                                        23, 1994
246   '...the message'   RS, Mar 23, 1995
248   '...you one'   rolandus.com, ibid
249   '...get you'   Blade to author, Mar 22, 2001
249   '...how long'   ibid
250   '...up there'   Addicted to Noise website, Nov 9, 1995
250   '...hugging her'   ibid
253   '...awards show'   Rogan, J. p637
254   '...wonderful woman'   Nash to author, Oct 31, 2000
255   '...this faded'   Mail on Sunday, Dec 8, 1996
255   '...tell her'   ibid
257   '...their lives'   Toronto Sun, Apr 8, 1997
257   '...exploited'   MC, April 21, 1997
258   '...very tough'   TGM, Apr 11, 1998
258   '...about that'   ibid
260   '...Undervalued'   Mendel cat, p52
260   '...is enough'   Musician, 1998
261   '...hate show biz'   BB, Aug 22, 1998
262   '...it's not'   WP, Sept 30, 1998
262   '...Mitchell doesn't'   Q, Nov, 1998
263   '...of melody'   Pulse, Oct, 1998
264   '...line wrong'   Austin Chronicle, 1998
264   '...new context'   NYT, Nov 3, 1998
265   '...burn stuff'   ITV, *Blood On The Carpet*, Feb, 2001
266   '...too bleak'   LAT, Feb, 2000
267   '...in it'   Klein to author, ibid

267 '...vice versa'   ibid
268 '...and phrasing'   TGM, Mar 30, 2000
269 '...pointless'   NME, Mar 11, 2000
270 '...really enjoy'   Klein to author, ibid
272 '...a bitch'   ibid
272 '...by men'   Nash to author, ibid
273 '...mean now'   RS, Dec 30, 1999

CHAPTER TWELVE: You wanna make Van Goghs ...

275 '...my dream'   Mendel Art Gallery press conference, June
                                 30, 2000
276 '...my head'   Vancouver Sun, July 8, 2000
276 '...burned down'   Mendel presser, ibid
276 '...the list'   TGM, July 5, 2000
278 '...quite understand'   Mendel cat., p40
279 '...than paintings'   TGM, ibid
279 '...macho field'   Mendel cat., p50
280 '...matter added'   Pollock: 'Statement' in *Possibilities*, No. 1,
                                 Winter 1948–49
280 '...making love?'   Pollock: Friedman, B.H. *Jackson Pollock:
                                 Energy Made Visible,* Weidenfeld and
                                 Nicolson, 1973
280 '... a fiction'   Newman: Motherwell, Robert et al 'Artists'
                                 Session, 35 East 8th Street, New York' in
                                 Modern Artists in America, 1951
282 '...contemporary art'   TGM, ibid
282 '...domestic decorations'   KCSN Radio, Dec 21, 1999
284 '...personal excitement'   Mendel cat., p45
284 '...the camera'   Bernstein to author, ibid
285 '...those visions'   Nash to author, ibid
285 '...pursued it'   Bernstein to author, ibid
286 '...of photography'   LAT, Feb 4, 1992
286 '...for anyone'   ibid
287 '...a show'   Ottawa Citizen, July 2, 2000
289 '...a way'   Adler to author, Nov 14, 2000
289 '...their autonomy'   ibid
289 '...as brave'   Art Issues, Mar–Apr, 2000
290 '...the planet'   Frieze, Mar–Apr, 2000
290 '...to something'   RS, May 30, 1991
290 '...soil fertile'   SSP, Sept, 1990
291 '...a mural'   Guardian, Feb, 1991
291 '...to *Mingus*'   Bernstein to author, ibid
292 '...just impulse'   Rock Photo, 1985
293 '...art world'   Mojo, Aug, 1998
294 '...prolonged creativity'   Co-evolution Quarterly, 1976
295 '...the Hudson!'   Frazier, N. p27
297 '...and sing'   Robinson, R. p122
297 '...creative spirit'   Beinecke Rare Books Library/Georgia
                                 O'Keeffe Foundation
297 '...same luggage'   Hogrefe, J. p318
300 '...go on'   ibid p320

302   '...inflated prices'   Mendel cat., p49
302   '...sand twitching'   Dyer, G. p127
303   '...paint it'   Messinger, L. p186

Appendix Three
Bibliography

BOOKS

Angelou, Maya	*Wouldn't take nothing for my journey now,* Virago, 1995
Berendt, Joachim	*The Jazz Book,* Paladin, 1984
Boyd, Jenny	*Musicians in Tune,* Fireside, 1992
Chadwick, Whitney	*Women, Art and Society,* Thames and Hudson, 1996
Crosby, David and Gottlieb, Carl	*Long Time Gone: The Autobiography of David Crosby,* Mandarin Paperbacks, 1990
de Botton, Alain	*The Consolations of Philosophy,* Hamish Hamilton, 2000
Denselow, Robin	*When The Music's Over: The Story of Political Pop,* Faber and Faber, 1989
Doggett, Peter	*Are You Ready for the Country,* Viking, 2000
Dyer, Geoff	*But Beautiful: A Book about Jazz,* North Point Press, 1996
Einarson, John	*Neil Young: Don't Be Denied,* Omnibus Press, 1993
Ellmann, Richard	*Yeats: The Man and the Masks,* Penguin, 1987
Forbes, Peter (ed)	*Scanning the Century: The Penguin Book of the Twentieth Century in Poetry,* Penguin, 2000
Frazier, Nancy	*Georgia O'Keeffe,* Crescent Books, 1990
Frith, Simon and Horne, Howard	*Art into Pop,* Methuen, 1987
Gayford, Martin and Wright, Karen (eds)	*The Penguin Book of Art Writing,* Penguin, 1999
Goodman, Fred	*The Mansion on the Hill: Dylan, Young, Geffen, Springsteen and the Head-on Collision of Rock and Commerce,* Jonathan Cape, 1997
Heilbrun, Carolyn G.	*Writing a Woman's Life,* The Women's Press Ltd, 1988
Heylin, Clinton	*Bob Dylan Behind the Shades: The Biography – Take Two,* Viking, 2000
Heylin, Clinton	*No More Sad Refrains: The life and times of Sandy Denny,* Helter Skelter, 2000
Hogrefe, Jeffrey	*O'Keeffe: The Life of an American Legend,* Bantam Books, 1992

Hornby, Nick	*About a Boy*, Indigo, 1998
Hoskyns, Barney	*Across the Great Divide: The Band and America*, Hyperion, 1993
Jennings, Nicholas	*Before the Goldrush: Flashbacks to the Dawn of the Canadian Sound*, Viking, 1997
King, Tom	*David Geffen: A Biography of the New Hollywood*, Hutchinson, 2000.
Lee, Hermione	*Virginia Woolf*, Chatto and Windus, 1996
Luftig, Stacey (ed)	*The Joni Mitchell Companion: Four Decades of Commentary*, Schirmer Books, 2000
Malcolm, Janet	*The Silent Woman*, Papermac, 1995
Mendel Art Gallery	*voices: The Work of Joni Mitchell*, Mendel Art Gallery, 2000
Messinger, Lisa Mintz	*Georgia O'Keeffe*, Thames and Hudson, 2001
Mingus, Charles	*Beneath the Underdog*, Payback Press, 1995
Nilsen, Per	*DanceMusicSexRomance: Prince – The First Decade*, Firefly Publishing, 1999
Priestley, Brian	*Mingus: A Critical Biography*, Quartet, 1982
Reder, Alan and Baxter, John	*Listen To This!* Hyperion, 1999
Robinson, Roxanna	*Georgia O'Keeffe: A Life*, Bloomsbury, 1990
Rogan, Johnny	*Neil Young: Zero to Sixty*, Calidore Books, 2000
Santoro, Gene	*Myself When I Am Real: The life and music of Charles Mingus*, Oxford University Press, 2000
Stern, J.P.	*A Study of Nietzsche*, Cambridge University Press, 1979
Storr, Anthony	*Solitude*, HarperCollins, 1997
Wolfe, Tom	*The Painted Word*, Bantam, 1976

ARTICLES AND BACKGROUND

Magazines, newspapers, webzines and journals used as source material or background reading included: *Acoustic Guitar, Alberta Report, Art Issues, Austin Chronicle, Berkeley Monthly, Billboard, Border Crossings, Calgary Herald, Christian Science Monitor, Co-Evolution Quarterly, Current Biography, Daily Mail, Detroit News, Downbeat, Edmonton Journal, Edmonton Sun, Entertainment Weekly, Express, Frieze, Goldmine, Grammy Magazine, Guardian, Guitar Player, Hypno, Irish Times, Los Angeles Times, LA Weekly, Maclean's, Mail on Sunday, Melody Maker, Mendel Art Gallery catalogue for 'voices: The Work of Joni Mitchell' exhibition, Miami Herald, Mirabella, Musician, Newsweek, New York Times, NME, Observer, Ottawa Citizen, Pulse, Q, Regina Leader Post, Rock Photo, rolandus.com, Rolling Stone, San Francisco Examiner, Saskatoon Star-Phoenix, Saskatoon Sun Times, Shadows and Light, Sounds, Spin, Stereo Review, Sunday Telegraph, Sunday Times, Time, Times, Toronto Daily Star, Toronto Globe and Mail, www.usnews.com, Variety, Vanity Fair, Vibe, Village Voice, Vogue, Washington Post, Weekend Magazine, Western People.*

WEBSITES

The two best Joni Mitchell-related web sites, without doubt, are joni-mitchell.com and the joni mitchell discussion list, jmdl.com. The pride of passionate fans, both also provide excellent archives, special interest sections and links.

Larry Klein: allmusic.com;   www.worldsend.com
Crosby, Stills, Nash and Young: www.crosbystillsnash.com
Graham Nash: www.nashnet.com;   www.nasheditions.com
Tom Rush: www.tomrush.com
Suzanne Vega: www.suzannevega.com
Shawn Colvin: www.shawncolvin.com
Jane Siberry: www.sheeba.com
Shawn Phillips: www.shawnphillips.com
Rubin 'Hurricane' Carter and Dylan campaign: wwwgraphicwitness.com
Georgia O'Keeffe: www.okeeffemuseum.org
Carlos Castaneda: www.sustainedaction.com; www.fouryogas.com
Fort Macleod, Alberta: www.town.fortmacleaod.ab.ca.
Saskatoon, Saskatchewan: www.city.saskatoon.sk.ca.
Elizabeth Cotten: www.geocities.co.jp/Hollywood/1061/cotton_bio.html

Appendix Four
Art exhibitions

June–September, 2000: Mendel Art Gallery, Saskatoon, Canada
voices: Joni Mitchell.
More than 80 paintings, prints and photographs exhibited as retrospective of work from 1960s–late 1990s

December, 1999: Los Angeles Contemporary Exhibitions, Los Angeles, California, USA
Tri-Annuale (Part 2): Amy Adler curates Joni Mitchell.
Sixteen paintings from the 1990s

October, 1994: Ruth Bloom Art Gallery, Santa Monica, California, USA
More than 30 paintings to accompany launch of *Turbulent Indigo*

January, 1992: Earl McGrath Gallery, Los Angeles, California, USA
Thirty-two untitled photographs

December–January 1990–91: Scotland, UK
Diary of a Decade: Paintings 1980–1990.
Twenty-eight paintings

September–October, 1990: Rotunda Gallery, London, UK
Diary of a Decade: Paintings 1980–1990.
Twenty-eight paintings, exhibited as part of Canadian cultural festival

May 20, 1988: Parco Gallery, Tokyo, Japan
An exhibition to coincide with the release of *Chalk Mark In A Rain Storm*. This show was the first – and only exhibition – at which Mitchell has sold her paintings

October, 1985: James Corcoran Gallery, Los Angeles, California, USA
Joni Mitchell: New Paintings, New Songs
An exhibition of abstract expressionist works to accompany the launch of *Dog Eat Dog*

1984: Kamikaze Gallery, New York, USA
Two exhibitions of paintings

1979: Los Angeles, California, USA
Exhibition to launch *Starart*, a book featuring the artwork of Mitchell, Cat Stevens, John Mayall, Klaus Voormann, Ron Wood and George 'Commander Cody' Frayne

1971: Vancouver, Canada
Mitchell, Graham Nash and Joel Bernstein exhibit as a group show, each having a room devoted to their photography

Appendix Five
Discography

JONI MITCHELL/SONG TO A SEAGULL (Reprise, 1968)

I Had a King, Michael from Mountains, Night in the City, Marcie, Nathan La Franeer, Sisotowbell Lane, The Dawntreader, The Pirate of Penance, Song to a Seagull, Cactus Tree.

(UK Peak Chart Position: did not chart; US Peak Billboard Chart Position: 189)

CLOUDS (Reprise, 1969)

Tin Angel, Chelsea Morning, I Don't Know Where I Stand, That Song About the Midway, Roses Blue, The Gallery, I Think I Understand, Songs to Aging Children Come, The Fiddle and the Drum, Both Sides, Now

(UK: did not chart; US: 31)

LADIES OF THE CANYON (Reprise, 1970)

Morning Morgantown, For Free, Conversation, Ladies of the Canyon, Willy, The Arrangement, Rainy Night House, The Priest, Blue Boy, Big Yellow Taxi, Woodstock, The Circle Game

(UK: 8; US: 27)

BLUE (Reprise, 1971)

All I Want, My Old Man, Little Green, Carey, Blue, California, This Flight Tonight, River, A Case of You, The Last Time I Saw Richard

(UK: 3; US: 15)

FOR THE ROSES (Asylum, 1972)

Banquet, Cold Blue Steel and Sweet Fire, Barangrill, Lesson in Survival, Let the Wind Carry Me, For the Roses, See You Sometime, Electricity, You Turn Me On I'm a Radio, Blonde in the Bleachers, Woman of Heart and Mind, Judgment of the Moon and Stars (Ludwig's Tune)

(UK: did not chart; US: 11)

COURT AND SPARK (Asylum, 1974)

Court and Spark, Help Me, Free Man in Paris, People's Parties, Same Situation, Car on a Hill, Down to You, Just Like This Train, Raised on Robbery, Trouble Child, Twisted
(Rereleased 1992 on DCC Compact Classics)

(UK: 14; US: 2)

MILES OF AISLES (Asylum, 1974, live)

You Turn Me On I'm a Radio, Big Yellow Taxi, Rainy Night House, Woodstock, Cactus Tree, Cold Blue Steel and Sweet Fire, Woman of Heart and Mind, A Case of You, Blue, The Circle Game, People's Parties, All I Want, For Free, Both Sides Now, Carey, The Last Time I Saw Richard, Jericho, Love or Money

(UK: 34; US: 2)

THE HISSING OF SUMMER LAWNS (Asylum, 1975)

In France They Kiss on Main Street, The Jungle Line, Edith and the Kingpin, Don't Interrupt the Sorrow, Shades of Scarlet Conquering, The Hissing of Summer Lawns, The Boho Dance, Harry's House/Centrepiece, Sweet Bird, Shadows and Light

(UK: 14; US: 4)

HEJIRA (Asylum, 1976)

Coyote, Amelia, Furry Sings the Blues, A Strange Boy, Hejira, Song for Sharon, Black Crow, Blue Motel Room, Refuge of the Roads

(UK: 11; US: 13)

DON JUAN'S RECKLESS DAUGHTER (Asylum, 1977)

Overture/Cotton Avenue, Talk to Me, Jericho, Paprika Plains, Otis and Marlena, The Tenth World, Dreamland, Don Juan's Reckless Daughter, Off Night Backstreet, Silky Veils of Ardor

(UK: 20; US: 25)

MINGUS (Asylum, 1979)

Happy Birthday 1975 (Rap), God Must Be a Boogie Man, Funeral (Rap), A Chair in the Sky, The Wolf that Lives in Lindsey, I's a Muggin' (Rap), Sweet Sucker Dance, Coin in the Pocket (Rap), The Dry Cleaner from Des Moines, Lucky (Rap), Goodbye Pork Pie Hat

(UK: 24; US: 17)

SHADOWS AND LIGHT (Asylum, 1980, live)

Introduction, In France They Kiss on Main Street, Edith and the Kingpin, Coyote, Goodbye Pork Pie Hat, The Dry Cleaner from Des Moines, Amelia, Pat's Solo, Hejira, Dreamland, Band Introduction, Furry Sings the Blues, Why Do Fools Fall in Love, Shadows and Light, God Must Be a Boogie Man, Woodstock. (Additional tracks on vinyl album and 2-CD set: Black Crow, Don's Solo, Free Man in Paris.)

(UK: 63; US: 38)

WILD THINGS RUN FAST (Geffen, 1982)

Chinese Café/Unchained Melody, Wild Things Run Fast, Ladies' Man, Moon at the Window, Solid Love, Be Cool, (You're So Square) Baby, I Don't Care, You Dream Flat Tires, Man to Man, Underneath the Streetlight, Love (Re-released in 1993 on Mobile Fidelity Ultradisc II)

(UK: 32; US: 25)

DOG EAT DOG (Geffen, 1985)

Good Friends, Fiction, The Three Great Stimulants, Tax Free, Smokin' (Empty, Try Another), Dog Eat Dog, Shiny Toys, Ethiopia, Impossible Dreamer, Lucky Girl

(UK: 57; US: 63)

CHALK MARK IN A RAINSTORM (Geffen, 1988)

My Secret Place, Number One, Lakota, The Tea Leaf Prophecy (Lay Down Your Arms), Dancin' Clown, Cool Water, The Beat of Black Wings, Snakes and Ladders, The Reoccurring Dream, A Bird That Whistles

(UK: 26; US: 45)

NIGHT RIDE HOME (Geffen, 1991)

Night Ride Home, Passion Play (When All the Slaves Are Free), Cherokee Louise, The Windfall (Everything for Nothing), Slouching Towards Bethlehem, Come in from the Cold, Nothing Can Be Done, The Only Joy in Town, Ray's Dad's Cadillac, Two Grey Rooms

(UK: 25; US: 41)

TURBULENT INDIGO (Reprise, 1994)

Sunny Sunday, Sex Kills, How Do You Stop?, Turbulent Indigo, Last Chance Lost, The Magdalene Laundries, Not to Blame, Borderline, Yvette in English, The Sire of Sorrow (Job's Sad Song)
(Special edition with artwork released)

(UK: 53; US: 47)

HITS (Reprise, 1996)

Urge for Going, Chelsea Morning, Big Yellow Taxi, Woodstock, The Circle Game, Carey, California, You Turn Me On I'm a Radio, Raised on Robbery, Help Me, Free Man in Paris, River, Chinese Cafe/Unchained Melody, Come in from the Cold, Both Sides Now

(UK: did not chart; US: 161)

MISSES (Reprise, 1996)

Passion Play (When All the Slaves Are Free), Nothing Can Be Done, A Case of You, The Beat of Black Wings, Dog Eat Dog, The Wolf That Lives in Lindsey, The Magdalene Laundries, Impossible Dreamer, Sex Kills, The Reoccurring Dream, Harry's House/Centrepiece, The Arrangement, For the Roses, Hejira

(UK/US: did not chart)

TAMING THE TIGER (Reprise, 1998)

Harlem in Havana, Man from Mars, Love Puts on
a New Face, Lead Balloon, No Apologies, Taming
the Tiger, The Crazy Cries of Love, Stay in
Touch, Face Lift, My Best to You, Tiger Bones

(UK: 57; US: 75)

BOTH SIDES NOW (Reprise, 2000)

You're My Thrill, At Last, Comes Love, You've
Changed, Answer Me, My Love, A Case of You,
Don't Go to Strangers, Sometimes I'm Happy,
Don't Worry 'Bout Me, Stormy Weather, I Wish I
Were in Love Again, Both Sides Now (Special
edition released for Valentine's Day, 2000)

(UK: 50; US: 66)

SINGLES/EPs

UK:

Night in the City/I Had a King	(Reprise, July, 1968)
Chelsea Morning/Both Sides Now	(Reprise, Aug, 1969)
Big Yellow Taxi /Woodstock	(Reprise, June, 1970)
Carey/My Old Man	(Reprise, Aug, 1971)
California/A Case of You	(Reprise, April, 1972)
You Turn Me On (I'm a Radio)/Urge for Going	(Asylum, Nov, 1972)
Cold Blue Steel and Sweet Fire/ Blonde in the Bleachers	(Asylum, March, 1973)
Raised on Robbery/Court and Spark	(Asylum, Jan, 1974)
Help Me/Just Like This Train	(Asylum, March, 1974)
Free Man in Paris/Car on a Hill	(Asylum, Oct, 1974)
Big Yellow Taxi (live)/Rainy Night House (live)	(Asylum, Jan, 1975)
In France They Kiss on Main Street/Boho Dance	(Asylum, March, 1976)
You Turn Me On (I'm a Radio)/Free Man in Paris	(Asylum, July, 1976)
Coyote/Blue Motel Room	(Asylum, Feb, 1977)
Off Night Backstreet/Jericho	(Asylum, Feb, 1978)
The Dry Cleaner from Des Moines/ God Must Be a Boogie Man	(Asylum, June, 1979)
Why Do Fools Fall in Love (live)/Black Crow (live)	(Asylum, Oct, 1980)
(You're So Square) Baby I Don't Care/Love	(Geffen, Nov, 1982)
Chinese Café/Ladies Man	(Geffen, Feb, 1983)
Good Friends/Smokin' (Empty, Try Another)	(Geffen, Nov, 1985)

Shiny Toys/Three Great Stimulants	(Geffen, April, 1986)
My Secret Place/Number One	(Geffen, May, 1988)
Come in from the Cold/Ray's Dad's Cadillac	(Geffen, July, 1991)
How Do You Stop/The Sire of Sorrow (Job's Sad Song)/	(Geffen, Nov, 1994)
Moon at the Window (live)	(Geffen, Nov, 1994)

EPs:

Carey/Both Sides Now/Big Yellow Taxi/Woodstock (Reprise, May, 1974)
Big Yellow Taxi Radio Mix, Friends Album Version, Late Night Club Mix, NY
Cab to Club Mix, Double Espresso NRG Mix, Tribal Dub, Original A Cappella
with Guitar (Reprise, 1996, remixes)

12-INCHES:

Shiny Toys/Three Great Stimulants	(Geffen, April, 1986)
My Secret Place/Chinese Cafe/Good Friends	(Geffen, May, 1988)

CD SINGLES:

My Secret Place/Chinese Cafe/Good Friends	(Geffen, May, 1988)
Come in from the Cold/Ray's Dad's Cadillac	(Geffen, July,1991)
(including special edition with prints)	

BOOTLEGS:

I'm somewhat ambivalent about bootlegs, because all too often that object of
desire for a fan and the completist's treasure is appropriated by the rip-off merchants, pirates and profiteers. The very thing that could subvert the control-
freak musicians and the big record companies' power over production,
distribution and price – just as Napster and its sister enterprises tried to do – is
often used against the fans who simply love the music itself. Bootlegs are frequently poor quality recordings of unidentified provenance and laughably inaccurate song titles. There are a number of bootleg Mitchell CDs and tapes in
circulation. Many recycle the same material under different guises, e.g. the
Second Fret sets and interviews in Philadelphia in the 1960s; JM and James
Taylor in concert for the BBC; assorted radio interviews; promo CDs, etc. Unlike
artists like Neil Young, Joni Mitchell has expressed no interest in putting out a
collection of early material, out-takes, demos, etc., so her fans are unlikely to
get to hear her earliest work or her officially unrecorded material any other way.

MITCHELL AS GUEST ARTIST:

Eric Anderson: *Blue River* (Columbia, 1972): 'Blue River'; *Be True To You*
    (Arista, 1975): 'Liza, Light The Candle', 'Woman, She Was Gentle', 'Can't Get
    You Out Of My Life', 'The Blues Keep Fallin' Like the Rain', 'Love Is Just a
    Game'
David Baerwald: *Bedtime Stories* (A & M, 1990): 'Liberty Lies' (co-written with
    Larry Klein)
Joan Baez: *Gracias a la Vida* (A & M, 1973): 'Dida'; *Diamonds and Rust* (A & M,
    1975): 'Dida'
The Band: *The Last Waltz* (Warner Brothers, 1976): 'Helpless', 'Coyote', ' I Shall
    Be Released'
Brian Blade Fellowship: *Perceptual* (Blue Note, 2000): 'Steadfast'

David Blue: *Com'n Back For More* (Asylum, 1975): 'Lover, Lover, Lover'

Jackson Browne: *For Everyman* (Asylum, 1973): 'Sing My Songs To Me' (electric piano)

The Chieftains: *Tears Of Stone* (RCA, 1999): 'The Magdalene Laundries'

Shawn Colvin: *Fat City* (Columbia, 1992): 'Object Of My Affection' (percussion, handclaps)

David Crosby: *If I Could Only Remember My Name* (Atlantic, 1971): 'Laughing', 'What Are Their Names'

Crosby, Stills and Nash: *So Far* (1974) (cover art)

Kyle Eastwood: *From There To Here* (Columbia): 'Trouble Man'

Dan Fogelberg: *The Innocent Age* (Full Moon/Epic, 1981): 'Nexus'

Daryl Hall: *Three Hearts In The Happy Ending Machine* (RCA, 1986): 'Right As Rain'

Herbie Hancock: *Gershwin's World* (Verve, 1998): 'The Man I Love', 'Summertime'

Paul Horn: *Visions* (Epic, 1973): 'Blue' (vocal, piano)

Indio: *Big Harvest* (A & M, 1989): 'Big Harvest', 'Hard Sun', 'My Eyes'

Janet Jackson: *The Velvet Rope* (Virgin Records, 1997): 'Got 'Til It's Gone' (samples JM's 'Big Yellow Taxi')

Carole King: *Tapestry* (Ode, 1971): 'Will You Still Love Me Tomorrow?'(The Mitchell Taylor Boy-and-Girl Choir)

Graham Nash: *Wild Tales* (Atlantic, 1973): 'Another Sleep Song' (backcover art by JM)

Northern Lights: *We Are The World* (Polygram, 1985): 'Tears Are Not Enough'

Seal: *Seal* (ZTT/Sire/Warner Brothers, 1994): 'If I Could'

Seemon and Marijke: *Son of America* (A & M, 1971): 'Vegetable Stew'

Tom Scott and the LA Express: *Tom Cat* (Ode, 1973): 'Love Poem'; LA Express: *Shadow Play* (Caribou Records, 1975): 'Nordic Winds' (front cover painting by JM)

James Taylor: *Mud Slide Slim and the Blue Horizon* (Warner Brothers, 1971): 'Love Has Brought Me Around', 'You've Got A Friend', 'Long Ago And Far Away'; *That's Why I'm Here* (Columbia, 1985): 'Only One'

Rod Taylor: Self-titled (Asylum, 1973): 'Making A Way', 'Something Old'

Various Artists: *All-Star Release for United Nations Rainforest Charity* (Virgin, 1989): 'Spirit Of The Forest'

Various Artists: *Stormy Weather: A Concert for the Benefit of the Walden Woods Project and the Thoreau Institute* (promo CD released by AT&T, 1999): 'Stormy Weather'

Various Artists: *Friends soundtrack* (Reprise, 1995): 'Big Yellow Taxi' to self-produced hip-hop backing track

Various Artists: *Grace Of My Heart* soundtrack (MCA, 1996): 'Man From Mars' (unauthorised release, withdrawn) replaced by (MCA, 1996) with Kristen Vigard on lead vocal and JM backing track

Various Artists: *Message to Love, The Isle of Wight Festival – 1970* (Essential): 'Big Yellow Taxi', 'Woodstock'

Various Artists: *Oh What A Feeling* (Universal Music, 2001): 'Help Me'

Various Artists: *The 1969 Warner-Reprise Record Show* (Reprise, 1970): 'My American Skirt', 'Spoony's Wonderful Adventure' (Recorded live at Carnegie Hall, February 1, 1969)

Roger Waters: *The Wall – Live In Berlin 1990* (Mercury, 1990): 'Goodbye Blue Sky', 'The Tide Is Turning'

Jimmy Webb: *Letters* (Reprise, 1972): 'Simile'; *Lands End* (Asylum SD 5070, 1973): ' Feet In The Sunshine'

JONI TRIBUTES:

Various Artists: *A Case of Joni* (Reprise, 2001 tbc). Mitchell songs covered by PM Dawn ('Night in the City'), Annie Lennox ('Ladies of the Canyon'), Stevie Wonder ('Woodstock'), Janet Jackson ('Beat of Black Wings'), Duncan Sheik ('Court and Spark'), kd lang ('Help Me'), Sarah McLachlan ('Blue'), Elvis Costello ('Edith and the Kingpin'), Chaka Khan ('Hejira'), Etta James ('Amelia'), Elton John ('Free Man In Paris'), Bjork ('Boho Dance'), Lindsey Buckingham and Mick Fleetwood ('Big Yellow Taxi').
Various Artists: *Back To The Garden: A Tribute to Joni Mitchell* (Intrepid, 1992). A Canadian project featuring covers by Big Faith ('Free Man in Paris'), Sara Craig ('This Flight Tonight'), Universal Honey ('Carey'), Lorraine Scott ('Big Yellow Taxi'), Molly Johnson ('Black Crow'), Andy Stochansky ('The Beat of Black Wings'), Martha and the Muffins ('Shades of Scarlett Conquering'), Funky Bummer featuring Anne Beadle ('The Hissing of Summer Lawns'), Hugh Marsh, Jonathan Goldsmith, Rob Piltch, Martin Tielli ('River'), Kurt Swinghammer ('You Turn Me On, I'm a Radio'), Spirit of the West ('Coyote'), W.O.W ('Woodstock'), Jenny Whitely ('Night In The City'), Sloan ('A Case of You'), Squiddly featuring Maria del Mar ('Blonde In The Bleachers'), John Cody and Marti Jones ('Songs to Aging Children Come'), Rocket Science featuring Laura Hubert and Art Bergmann ('Refuge of the Roads').

COVERS:

'I don't have false modesty. I know the work is good, but I appreciate the compliment that covers are. You can never hear enough nice things.' (Joni Mitchell, *Billboard*, August 22, 1998).

There are many hundreds of cover versions of Mitchell songs. I've highlighted some of the more interesting, eccentric, accomplished and unlikely recorded and live-only versions, to show the diversity of both the songs and the artists. With thanks to Bob Muller; for a full list, see www.jonimitchell.com

Tori Amos, 'A Case of You', *Spew U* (Atlantic's CMJ Survival Kit), 1995
Chet Atkins: 'Both Sides Now', *This Is Chet Atkins*, 1970
Hoyt Axton: 'For Free', *Pistol Packin' Mama*, 1982
Lou Barlow: 'Blonde in the Bleachers', *Lou Barlow and Friends*, 1994
Harry Belafonte: 'The Circle Game', *The Warm Touch*, 1971
Bettie Serveert: 'River', *Zo, Dit Is Kerstmis*, 1998
Big Country: 'Big Yellow Taxi', *Eclectic*, 1996; 'Woodstock', *Ships* (Where Were You) CD1, 1993
Theo Bikel: 'Urge For Going', *A New Day*, 1969
Bjork: 'Boho Dance', *A Case Of Joni*, 2001
Luka Bloom: 'Urge For Going', *Keeper of the Flame*, 2000
Boomtang Boys: 'Both Sides, Now', *Greatest Hits, Volume One*, 1999
James Brown: 'How Do You Stop', *Gravity*, 1986
Lindsey Buckingham and Mick Fleetwood: 'Big Yellow Taxi', *A Case Of Joni*, 2001
Jeff Buckley: 'People's Parties', *Live at Sin-E 12/31/95*, 1995
The Byrds: 'For Free', *Byrds*, 1973
Rosanne Cash: 'River', *Spirit of '73*, 1995
Eva Cassidy: 'Woodstock', *Time After Time*, 2000
Clannad and Paul Young: 'Both Sides, Now', *Switch* soundtrack, 1991
Judy Collins: 'Both Sides, Now', *Wildflowers*, 1968; 'Chelsea Morning', *Living*, 1971

Shawn Colvin: 'Conversation' (live); 'River', Live – Christmas Radio Special, 1998; 'Urge For Going' (live).

Elvis Costello: 'Edith and the Kingpin', *A Case Of Joni*, 2001

CPR: 'For Free', 'Yvette In English' (live)

Floyd Cramer: 'Both Sides, Now', *The Big Ones*, 1970

Crosby and Nash: 'Urge For Going', *CSN Box Set*, 1971

Bing Crosby: 'Both Sides Now', *Hey Jude/Hey Bing*, 1969

David Crosby: 'Yvette In English', *Thousand Roads*, 1993

Crosby, Stills and Nash: 'For Free', *Allies*, 1983; 'Woodstock', *Deja Vu*, 1970

Tim Curry: 'All I Want', *Read My Lips*, 1978; 'Cold Blue Steel and Sweet Fire', *Fearless*, 1979

Doris Day: 'Both Sides, Now', *Que Sera Sera*, 1993

Blossom Dearie: 'Both Sides, Now', *Whisper For You*, 1997

Neil Diamond: 'Both Sides Now', *Love Songs*, 1989; 'Chelsea Morning', *Stones*, 1971; 'Free Man In Paris', *I'm Glad You're Here With Me Tonight*, 1977

Dion: 'Both Sides, Now', *Dion*, 1968

Robert Downey Jr: 'River', *A Very Ally Christmas*, 2000

Bob Dylan: 'Big Yellow Taxi', *Dylan*, 1973

Fairport Convention: 'Both Sides Now', Ashley Hutchings, The Guv'nor Vol. 4, 1996; 'Chelsea Morning', *Fairport Convention*, 1968; 'Eastern Rain', *What We Did On Our Holidays*, 1968; 'I Don't Know Where I Stand' *Heyday BBC Radio Sessions 1968-69*, 1987; 'Marcie', 'Night In The City', Ashley *Hutchings, The Guv'nor Vol. 3*, 1995; 'Woodstock' (live)

Percy Faith: 'Big Yellow Taxi', *Black Magic Woman*, 1971; 'Both Sides, Now', *Those Were The Days*, 1969

Marianne Faithfull: 'Amelia' (live)

Jason Falkner: 'Both Sides, Now', *Follow Me*, 1997

Foster and Allen: 'Both Sides Now', *100 Golden Greats*, 1997

Frente: 'Blue', *No Time*, 1993

Stan Getz: 'Both Sides, Now', *Marrakesh Express*, 1969

Dizzy Gillespie: 'Both Sides, Now', *Cornucopia*, 1969

Glenn Miller Band: 'Both Sides, Now', *Do You Wanna Dance*, 1970

Go-Betweens: 'Both Sides, Now', *16 Lovers' Lane*, 1988

Benny Goodman: 'Both Sides, Now', *Happiness Is ... Up, Up and Away With the Happy Hits Of Today*, 1970

Davey Graham: 'Both Sides, Now', *Large As Life and Twice As Natural*, 1968

Amy Grant: 'Big Yellow Taxi', *House of Love*, 1994

George Hamilton IV: 'Both Sides, Now', *Canadian Pacific*, 1969; 'The Circle Game', *The Gentle Country Sound Of ...*, 1968; 'Urge For Going', *Folksy*, 1967

Goldie Hawn: 'Carey', *Goldie*, 1972

Lee Hazlewood: 'Urge For Going', *I'll Be Your Baby Tonight*, 1973

Ian and Sylvia: 'The Circle Game', *So Much For Dreaming*, 1968

Indigo Girls: 'River', 1200 *Curfews*, 1995

Innocence Mission: 'Both Sides, Now' (live)

Janet Jackson: 'The Beat of Black Wings', *A Case of Joni*, 2001

Etta James: 'Amelia', *A Case of Joni*, 2001

Keith Jarrett: 'All I Want', *The Mourning of A Star*, 1971

Elton John: 'Free Man In Paris', *A Case of Joni*, 2001

Wynonna Judd: 'Help Me', *New Day Dawning*, 2000

Keb' Mo': 'Big Yellow Taxi', *Big Wide Grin*, 2001

Kennedy: 'Urge For Going', *Classic Kennedy*, 1999

Chaka Khan: 'Hejira', *A Case of Joni*, 2001

Kiri Te Kanawa: 'Both Sides, Now', *A Rainbow In The Sky*
Diana Krall: 'Case of You', *Bushnell's Big Bash*, 2000
Cleo Laine: 'Both Sides Now', *Woman To Woman*, 1989
k.d. lang: 'Help Me', *A Case of Joni*, 2001
Annie Lennox: 'Ladies Of The Canyon', (single) 1995
Manfred Mann's Earth Band: 'Banquet', *Criminal Tango*, 1986
Hugh Masekela: 'Both Sides, Now', *Reconstruction*, 1994
Matthews', Southern Comfort: 'Woodstock', *Later That Same Year*, 1970
David McAlmont: 'Conversation', *McAlmont*, 1994
Ian McCulloch: 'The Circle Game', *9 Tracks*
Roger McGuinn: 'Dreamland', *Cardiff Rose*, 1976
Sarah McLachlan: 'Blue', *Rarities, B-Sides and Other Stuff*, 1996
Sergio Mendes and Brasil '66: 'Chelsea Morning', *Stillness*, 1970; 'The Circle Game', *Primal Roots*, 1972
Mabel Mercer: 'Both Sides, Now', *Mabel Mercer & Bobby Short – Second Town Hall*, 1969
Natalie Merchant: 'All I Want', (single) 1996
Chuck Mitchell: 'The Circle Game', *Combinations*, 1977
Nana Mouskouri: 'Both Sides, Now', *Spotlight on Nana Mouskouri*, 1967
Graham Nash: 'A Case of You', *Graham Nash: Medium Rare*, 1992
Nazareth: 'This Flight Tonight', *Loud and Proud*, 1973
Willie Nelson: 'Both Sides, Now', *Sweet Memories*, 1979
Leonard Nimoy: 'Both Sides, Now', *The Way I Feel*, 1968
Beth Orton: 'River' (live)
John Otway: 'Woodstock', *Under the Covers and Over the Top*, 1992
P.M. Dawn: 'Night In The City', (single) 2000
Marti Pellow: 'River' (live)
Prince: 'A Case Of You', *Live at First Avenue* (video), 1983
Bonnie Raitt: 'That Song About The Midway', *Streetlights*, 1974
Joshua Redman: 'I Had A King', *Timeless Tales (For Changing Times)*, 1998
Minnie Riperton: 'Woman Of Heart And Mind', *The Best Of Minnie Riperton*, 1993
Jimmie Rodgers: 'Both Sides, Now', *Windmills Of Your Mind*, 1969
Tom Rush: 'The Circle Game', 'Tin Angel', 'Urge For Going', *The Circle Game*, 1968; 'The Circle Game' (single), 1966
Buffy Sainte-Marie: 'Song To A Seagull', 'The Circle Game', *Fire and Fleet and Candlelight*, 1967; 'For Free', *Quiet Places*, 1973
Mathilde Santing: 'I Had A King', *Mathilde 'Choosy' Santing Live*, 1996
Tom Scott: 'Woodstock', Great Scott, 1971
Earl Scruggs: 'Both Sides, Now', *Live at Kansas State 1972*, 1972
Pete Seeger: 'Both Sides, Now', *Young vs. Old*, 1969
Duncan Shiek: 'Court And Spark', *A Case of Joni*, 2001
Fred Simon: 'Both Sides, Now', 'Michael from Mountains', Songs of My Youth, Vol. 1, 2000
Frank Sinatra: 'Both Sides, Now', *Cycles*, 1968
Spin Doctors: 'Woodstock' (single), 1994
Billy Squier: 'River', *Happy Blue*, 1998
Dave Stewart and Barbara Gaskin: 'Amelia', *Spin*, 1991
Barbra Streisand: 'I Don't Know Where I Stand', *Stoney End*, 1971
Andy Summers: 'Goodbye Pork Pie Hat', *The Last Dance of Mr X*, 1997
James Taylor: 'For Free', 'Woodstock' (live)
The Supremes: 'All I Want', *The Supremes*, 1972
Three Dog Night: 'Night In The City', *Harmony*, 1971

Tir Na Nog: 'Songs To Aging Children Come', *In The Morning*, 1999
Travis: 'River', 'Urge For Going' (single), 1999 and live
United States Army Chamber Orchestra: 'Both Sides Now', *The United States Army Band presents the United States Army Chamber Orchestra*, 1973
Dave van Ronk: 'Both Sides Now', 'Chelsea Morning', *Dave van Ronk And The Hudson Dusters*, 1968; 'River', *Songs For Aging Children*, 1973; 'Song To a Seagull', *To All My Friends In Far-Flung Places*, 1994; 'That Song About The Midway', *Sunday Street*, 1976; 'Urge For Going', *Van Ronk*, 1971
Nancy Wilson: 'A Case Of You', *Live At McCabes' Guitar Shop*, 1999
Stevie Wonder: 'Woodstock', *A Case of Joni*, 2001

Index